The Adobe Illustrator

WOW!

Book for CS6 and CC

SECOND EDITION

Includes updates for Illustrator CC 2019

Sharon Steuer

AND THE ILLUSTRATOR WOW! TEAM

 PEACHPIT PRESS

The Adobe Illustrator **WOW!** Book *for CS6 and CC, Second Edition*

Sharon Steuer

Peachpit Press

www.peachpit.com

Copyright © 2019 by Sharon Steuer. All Rights Reserved.

Peachpit Press is an imprint of Pearson Education, Inc.

To report errors, please send a note to errata@peachpit.com

Executive Editor at Peachpit: Laura Norman
Senior Production Editor at Peachpit: Tracey Croom

Contributing Writers to this edition: Cristen Gillespie, Steven H. Gordon, Lisa Jackmore, Gary Ferster, Aaron McGarry, Raymond Larrett, George Coghill, Gustavo Del Vechio
Technical Editor: Jean-Claude Tremblay
WOW! Testers: Ari Weinstain, Monika Gause, Greg Geisler, Federico Platón, Chana Messer, Stéphane Nahmani, Franck Payen, Katharine Gilbert, Simona Pfreundner, Brian Stoppee, Janet Stoppee, Victor van Dijk, Kevin Stohlmeyer, Gustavo Del Vecchio, Sally Cox, and Nini Tjäder
Line Editor: Eric Schumacher-Rasmussen
Cover Designer: Mimi Heft
Cover Illustrator: Von R. Glitschka
Proofreader: Kim Wimpsett
Indexer: Rebecca Plunkett
First edition *Illustrator* WOW! *Book* designer: Barbara Sudick
WOW! Series Editor: Linnea Dayton

Notice of Rights

Notice of Liability

Trademarks

ISBN 13: 978-013-543209-9

ISBN 10: 0-13-543209-X

1 2019

The Adobe Illustrator

WOW!

Book for CS6 and CC

SECOND EDITION

Includes updates for Illustrator CC 2019

Sharon Steuer
AND THE ILLUSTRATOR WOW! TEAM

WOW!
Contents at a Glance...

vi **WOW! Contents**

xii **The Adobe Illustrator WOW! Book** *for CS6 and CC (2nd ed.)*
Team of Contributing Writers, Editors, and Testers

xiv **How to use this book...**

xviii **What's New in CC?**

xxii **Acknowledgments**

CHAPTER 1: Your Creative Workspace

2 Introduction

12 CC Introduction

17 Lessons & Galleries

30 CC Gallery

CHAPTER 2: Designing Type & Layout

32 Introduction

42 CC Introduction

44 Lessons & Galleries

60 CC Lessons & Galleries

CHAPTER 3: Rethinking Construction

64 Introduction

74 CC Introduction

82 Lessons & Galleries

101 CC Lessons & Galleries

CHAPTER 4: Expressive Strokes

110 Introduction

119 CC Introduction

122 Lessons & Galleries

152 CC Lessons & Galleries

CHAPTER 5: Color Transitions

162 Introduction
171 CC Introduction

174 Lessons & Galleries
192 CC Lessons & Galleries

CHAPTER 6: Reshaping Dimensions

195 Introduction
206 CC Introduction

208 Lessons & Galleries
228 CC Lessons & Galleries

CHAPTER 7: Mastering Complexity

232 Introduction
245 CC Introduction

246 Lessons & Galleries
271 CC Lessons & Galleries

CHAPTER 8: Creatively Combining Apps

277 Introduction
284 CC Introduction

288 Lessons & Galleries
306 CC Lessons & Galleries

307 WOW! Book Production Notes
308 Artists Appendix
312 General Index
337 Windows WOW! Glossary
338 Mac WOW! Glossary

Contents

iv **WOW! Contents at a Glance...**

xii **The Adobe Illustrator WOW! Book** *for CS6 and CC (2nd ed.)*
Team of Contributing Writers and Editors

xiv **How to use this book...**

xviii **What's New in CC?**

xxii **Acknowledgments**

Your Creative Workspace
Introduction

2 Organizing Your Workspace

5 Mastering Object Management

9 Managing Multiple Artboards

12 The Creative Cloud Workspace

12 The Home Screen

13 Workspace and Panels

17 Gallery: Mike Kimball

18 Tracing a Template: *Manually Tracing a Template Layer*

20 Basic to Complex: *Starting Simple for Creative Composition*

22 Navigating Layers: *Creating, Organizing, and Viewing Layers*

24 Basic Appearances: *Making and Applying Appearances*

26 Guides for Arcs: *Designing with Guides, Arc, and Pen Tools*

28 Auto-Scaling Art: *Apply Effects and Graphic Styles to Resize*

30 Gallery: George Coghill

Designing Type & Layout
Introduction

32 By Default New Type Is always Black

32 Three Types of Type

34 Working with Threaded Text

35 Wrapping Area Type Around Objects

35 Formatting Text

36 Using the Eyedropper with Type

37 Using the Appearance Panel with Type

38 Converting Type to Outlines

39 The Glyphs Panel

39 Advanced Features of Multiple Artboards

42 New Type Features in Illustrator CC
42 Touch Type transformations
43 Finding the Right Font

44 Graphic Novel Cover Design: *Illustrator as a Stand-Alone Layout Tool*
46 Create an Identity: *Working Efficiently with Multiple Elements*
48 Really Organized: *Streamlining File Output with Artboards*
50 Moving Your Type: *Setting Type on a Curve and Warping Type*
52 Galleries: Steven Gordon/Cartagram, LLC
54 Arcing Type: *Transforming Type with Warps & Envelopes*
56 Galleries: Yukio Miyamoto, Jean-Benoit Levy, Billie Bryan, Ryan Putnam
60 Touching Type: *Modifying Editable Letter Characters*
62 Galleries: Franck Payen, Chana Messer

3

Rethinking Construction
Introduction

64 The Eraser Tools & the Blob Brush
66 Shape Builder Tool
67 Working with Live Paint
68 Using Image Trace
69 Aligning, Joining, and Averaging
71 Draw Behind and Draw Inside
72 Compound Shapes & Compound Paths
74 New Construction Features in Illustrator CC
74 Working with Live Corners & Live Rectangles
77 Pen Tool Changes & Reshaping Paths
77 The New Pencil Settings (for other tools too)
78 The Shaper Tool
79 Global Edits vs Select Similar

82 Combining Paths: *Basic Path Construction with Pathfinders*
84 Coloring Line Art: *Using Live Paint for Fluid Productivity*
86 Blob to Live Paint: *From Sketch to Blob Brush and Live Paint*
88 Galleries: David Turton, Lance Jackson, Janet Stoppee, Danuta Markiewicz (Danka), Katharine Gilbert, Cheryl Graham, Stephen A. Klema
96 Rapid Reshaping: *Using Shape Builder to Construct Objects*

Advanced Technique:

98 Drawing Inside: *Building with Multiple Construction Modes*

100 Galleries: George Coghill, Ray Acosta

102 Rounding a Corner: *Using Live Corners to Create a Map Symbol*

104 Pencil & Pen Paths: *Using Drawing Tools to Edit Paths*

105 Galleries: Laura Coyle, George Coghill

106 Shaper Tooling

4

Expressive Strokes

Introduction

110 Width Tool and Stroke Profiles

111 The Expanded Stroke Panel

113 Brushes

116 Symbols

119 Dynamic Symbols, & New Raster Brushes in CC

122 Stroke Variance: *Creating Dynamic Variable-Width Stroke*

124 Galleries: MCKIBILLO (AKA Josh McKible), Donal Jolley, Lisa Jackmore, Ann Paidrick, Anil Ahuja/Adobe Systems

130 Brushes & Washes: *Drawing with Naturalistic Pen, Ink, Wash*

132 Galleries: Stephen Klema's Students: (Jillian Winkel, Stephanie Pernal, Amber Loukoumis, Jeffrey Martin, Nicole Dzienis, Tamara Morrison, Cinthia A. Burnett, James Cassidy, Kenneth Albert, Jamal Wynn, Suzanne Drapeau, Mahalia Johnsonl)

134 Galleries: Sharon Steuer

136 Painting Inside: *Painting with Bristle Brushes & Draw Inside*

138 Painterly Portraits: *Painting in Layers with Bristle Brushes*

Advanced Techniques:

140 Galleries: Greg Geisler, Janaína Cesar de Oliveira Baldacc

142 Pattern Brushes: *Building Characters with Pattern Brushes*

144 Galleries: Donal Jolley, Moses Tan, Nobuko Miyamoto/Yukio Miyamoto, Aaron McGarry, Lisa Jackmore, Gustavo Del Vechio

152 Brush Corners: *Pattern Brushes Made with a Raster Image*

154 Galleries: Lisa Jackmore, Sharon Steuer, Steven Gordon

5

Color Transitions

Introduction

162 Working with the Color and Swatches Panels

164 Gradients

166 Gradient Mesh

168 Edit Colors/Recolor Artwork

171 Color Features Updated in CC

174 Custom Coloring: *Creating Custom Colors & Color Groups*

176 Unified Gradient: *Creating & Editing with Pen & Pencil Modifiers*

178 Galleries: Steve King/U-Haul

180 Gradient Paths: *The Basics of Gradients on a Path*

181 Gallery: Darren

182 Bending Mesh: *Molding Transparent Mesh Layer*

Advanced Techniques:

186 Galleries: Ann Paidrick, Yukio Miyamoto

188 Recolor a Pattern: *Creating Variations on a Color Palette*

190 Galleries: Sebastian Murra (Mu!), Ann Paidrick

192 Freeform Gradients: *Contouring Gradients to Organic Objects*

193 Galleries: Shawn Sullivan, Laura Coyle,

6 Reshaping Dimensions
Introduction

196 Warps and Envelopes

198 3D Effects

203 The Perspective Grid

206 New Perspective Features & Puppet Warp in CC

208 Warp & Distort: *Bending Forms to Create Organic Variations*

210 Galleries: Dedree Drees, Von R. Glitschka

212 The Keys to 3D: *The Basics of Realistic 3D Modeling*

214 Galleries: Aaron McGarry, Anil Ahuja/Adobe Systems

216 One Perspective: *Simulating a One-Point Perspective View*

218 Amplified Angles: *Creating Details with Two-Point Perspective*

220 Modifying a Photo: *Inserting Photographs in Perspective*

222 Establishing Perspective: *Aligning Grids & Planes to an Architectural Sketch*

Advanced Techniques:

224 Galleries: Gustavo Del Vechio, Monika Gause

226 Perspective Shifts: *Locking Station Point to Auto-Update Art*

227 Gallery: Aaron McGarry

228 Puppet Warping: *Using Puppet Warp for Smooth Arcs*

230 Galleries: Ari M. Weinstein, Chana Messer

7 Mastering Complexity

Introduction
- **232** Pattern Making
- **235** Transparency
- **236** Opacity Masks
- **238** Blends
- **240** Clipping Masks
- **245** Combining Complexity with Illustrator CC

- **246** Pattern Making: *Navigating the Pattern Options Panel*
- **248** Layered Patterns: *Building Depth and Complexity in PEM*

  Advanced Techniques:
- **250** Roping in Paths: *Using Masks and Pathfinders for Shapes*
- **252** Adding Highlights: *Using Transparency to Create Highlights*
- **253** Gallery: Annie Gusman Joly
- **254** Moonlighting: *Using Transparency for Glows & Highlights*
- **256** Gallery: Chris Nielsen
- **258** Masking Images: *Simple to Complex Clipping Masks*
- **260** Galleries: MCKIBILLO (AKA Josh McKible), Monika Gause
- **262** Opacity Masking: *Smooth Transitions & Intertwining Objects*
- **264** Galleries: Dan Hubig, Pariah Burke, Jean Aubé, Richard Perez, Moses Tan, Chris Nielsen, Lance Jackson, Sharon Steuer, Von R. Glitschka, Lisa Poje, Gary Ferster

8 Creatively Combining Apps

Introduction
- **278** Linking vs. Embedding in Illustrator
- **279** Illustrator to Non-Adobe Programs
- **279** Illustrator & Adobe Photoshop
- **281** Illustrator & Adobe InDesign
- **282** Illustrator, PDF, and Adobe Acrobat
- **282** Web Graphics
- **283** Creating Animation with Layers
- **284** CC Features for Creatively Combining Apps
- **286** Exporting Graphics to Web and Mobile Devices

Illustrator & Photoshop

288 Ready to Export: *Exporting Options for Layers to Photoshop*

290 Galleries: Kevan Atteberry

Illustrator & Animation

292 Gallery: Laurie Wigham

Illustrator & After Effects

293 Gallery: LeeDanielsART

Ilustrator & iPad App Development

294 Galleries: Stikalicious™ Artists (Mark 'Atomos' Pilon, Podgy Panda, Frazer, Dacosta!, Charuca, Tokyo-go-go, Jared Nickerson, Steve Talkowski, Killamari, kaNO, MAD, Abe Lincoln Jr., Gabriel Mourelle, Shawnimals, EdWarner, Junichi Tsuneoka)

Illlustrator, After Effects, Flash, & Cinema 4D

295 Galleries: LeeDanielsART, Dave Joly & Mic Riddle

Illustrator, Painter, Go Media, & Photoshop

296 Finishing Touches: *Adding Scenic Entourage Elements & Using Photoshop for Lighting Effects*

Illustrator, CADtools, & Photoshop

298 Gallery: Rick Johnson

Illustrator & InkScribe/VectorScribe

299 Gallery: Von Glitschka

Advanced Techniques:
Illustrator & Photoshop

300 Planning Ahead: *Working Between Illustrator & Photoshop*

Illustrator & Photoshop

302 Galleries: Gustavo Del Vechio, Katharine Gilbert, Sharon Steuer

Illustrator & SVG

305 Gallery: Lance Jackson

Illustrator & Photographs

306 Gallery: Monika Gause (Vektorgarten)

307 WOW! **Book Production Notes**
308 **Artists Appendix**
312 **General Index**
337 **Windows** WOW! **Glossary**
338 **Mac** WOW! **Glossary**

The Adobe Illustrator WOW! Team
for the CS6 and CC (Second Edition)

Sharon Steuer has been teaching, exhibiting, and writing in the digital art world since 1983. Sharon is the originator and lead author of **The Adobe Illustrator WOW! Book** series (this is the fifteenth version of the book), as well as **Creative Thinking in Photoshop: A New Approach to Digital Art** (no longer in print). In between publishing projects, Sharon is a full-time artist working in traditional and digital media, often posting tutorials about her art practice in her "Digital Art Studio" column on CreativePro.com. She lives in San Francisco with the love of her life, her sound and radio professor husband Jeff Jacoby (jeffjacoby.net). She is extremely grateful to

have this opportunity to get the WOW! team back together, and she thanks the kind folks at Peachpit/Pearson, Adobe, and of course the amazingly talented WOW! artists for making this book possible. Find links to her online digital art courses at sharonsteuer.com/lynda. Keep in touch with her via **sharonsteuer.com/contact** and on social media @SharonSteuer.

Jean-Claude Tremblay is the owner of Proficiografik, a consulting and training service for the graphic and print community designed to help clients work efficiently. He is an Adobe Certified Expert Design Master and an Adobe Community Professionals member. He has been deeply involved in the Montréal Adobe Community user group. After serving as a magnificent WOW! tester, Jean-Claude returns for his sixth mandate as the WOW! technical editor, chief advisor, and resident magician. He lives in the greater Montréal area with his wonderful daughter Judith and his two cats, Gilles and Mirro.

Cristen Gillespie has contributed to other WOW! books, including coauthoring **The Photoshop WOW! Book**. She's also an Adobe Community Professional, helping folks where she can on Adobe's Feedback forum. With a decades-long enthusiasm for the digital world of art and multimedia, and a personal interest in digitally preserving family histories and art journaling, Cristen tackles step-by-step techniques, galleries, and introductions with avid interest and commitment. She most enjoys learning from wonderful artists and writers, and when we're not working on a new version of the book, she always eagerly looks forward to the next **Illustrator WOW!** family reunion.

Steven H. Gordon is a returning coauthor for step-by-step techniques and galleries. Steven has been an ace member of the team since **The Illustrator 9 WOW! Book.** He has too many boys to stay sane and pays way too much college tuition. Steven runs Cartagram (www.cartagram.com), a custom cartography company located in Madison, Alabama. He thanks Sharon and the rest of the **WOW!** team for their inspiration and professionalism.

Lisa Jackmore writes both galleries and step-by-step techniques. She is an artist both on and off the computer, creating artwork that is often inspired by her life's events and observations—whether the mundane or the extraordinary. Lisa is continually grateful for those who provide the inspiration for her illustrated thoughts. She so thoroughly enjoys being a part of the **WOW!** team that she doesn't consider it work at all.

Gary Ferster writes both step-by-step techniques and galleries and has been a featured artist in **The Illustrator WOW! Books** since the first edition (and is also a tester). He has been a freelance illustrator, animator, retoucher, trainer, and author (www.garyferster.com) for more than 20 years. When he isn't drawing, Gary can be found in the New York City area working as a SAG/AFTRA actor (and stand-in) on the CBS show *Blue Bloods.*

Eric Schumacher-Rasmussen has been writing and editing copy since long before it was his job. He's currently a freelance writer and editor, as well as editor and VP of *Streaming Media* magazine (www.streamingmedia.com), and is returning as our amazing line editor for the **WOW!** book.

Additional contributing writers: Aaron McGarry is a San Diego–based writer and illustrator who spends time in his home country of Ireland. He paints and draws to escape and relax, but finds his greatest source of joy with his wife Shannon, a glass artist, and their gorgeous daughter Fiona. Please visit www.aaronmcgarry.com. **Raymond Larrett** is a designer, illustrator, cartoonist, and most recently publisher. His Puzzled Squirrel Press (http://puzzledsquirrel.com) specializes in unique volumes on comics, history, and mind control, in exclusive eBook and print editions. **George Coghill** is a cartoon-style illustrator who specializes in cartoon logos and cartoon character design. His art can be seen at CoghillCartooning.com. **Gustavo Del Vechio** is a designer, teacher, and author of books on Adobe Illustrator published in Brazil (in Portuguese). He is an Adobe Certified Expert in Illustrator since CS2 and has been a featured artist in the **WOW!** book for a number of editions. An adapted excerpt from the automatic-corners chapter of Gustavo's book on Illustrator CC appears (translated in English) in our *Expressive Strokes* chapter.

For a thorough listing of the **WOW!** *team of testers and contributors to this CS6 and CC edition, please also see the* **Acknowledgments** *and* **Production Notes** *and (of course!) the* **Artists** *appendix.*

How to use this book...

1

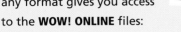

CC Brush Corners

Pattern Brushes Made with a Raster

Free Transform Touch inter

The redesigned Free

G   A

Dedicated CC content is signalled by the CC icon overlapping a purple rectangle in the upper corner on Introduction, Step-by-Step lesson pages (top and middle), or across the top on Gallery pages (bottom)

Although **The Adobe Illustrator WOW! Book** *for CS6 and CC 2nd Edition* contains much to inspire users at all levels, it has been designed and tested for intermediate through professional-level users of Adobe Illustrator. To follow along with the lessons, you'll need to know enough about the basics of Illustrator to create your own art for the techniques being demonstrated. Lessons in this book are designed to help you master techniques while you create your own art along the way. Lessons are kept deliberately short to encourage the use of this book within the confines of a supervised classroom. This icon indicates you can look for featured artwork or technical files related to that lesson within a chapter's folder from **WOW! ONLINE** (see Tip "Where are **WOW! ONLINE** files" at left for details).

Alerting you to CC content

Whether you're using Illustrator CS6 or CC, you can safely assume that unless we indicate otherwise as described below, everything you're reading is applicable to both CS6 and CC (updates to the CC creative workflow posted after the October 2018 release will be noted at wowartist.com).

   Look for this **CC** icon in the upper corner of a page to identify CC changes big and small, as follows:

1 Each universal CS6/CC section of the book is followed by a special section dedicated to **CC** content. This means that within each chapter you'll find two **CC** sections; the **CC** introduction will immediately follow the universal chapter introduction, and **CC** lessons and galleries will immediately follow that chapter's universal lessons and gallery section. You can identify **CC** introductions, lessons, and galleries by the **CC** icon overlapping a purple rectangle at the top of a page; for Introduction and lesson sections the rectangle will be in the upper corner of the page, while on Gallery pages the rectangle will be a purple banner across the entire top of the page.

2 Within the universal CS6/CC section, if a icon is the only purple in the upper corner of a page, then this signals a change between CC/CS6 functions or features. In this case, purple **CC** text and/or a purple-tinted Tip on that page will explain the change and may also direct you to find more information.

Shortcuts and keystrokes

Please start by looking at the **WOW! Glossary** in an appendix at the back of the book for a thorough list of power-user shortcuts that you'll want to become familiar with. The **WOW! Glossary** provides definitions for the terms used throughout this book, always starting with Macintosh shortcuts first and then the Windows equivalent (⌘-Z/Ctrl-Z). Conventions covered range from simple general things such as the ⌘ symbol for the Mac's Command or Apple key, and the Cut, Copy, Paste, and Undo shortcuts, to important Illustrator-specific conventions, such as ⌘-G/Ctrl-G for grouping objects, and Paste In Front (⌘-F/Ctrl-F)/Paste In Back (⌘-B/Ctrl-B) to paste items copied to the clipboard directly in front/back of the selected object, and in perfect registration. Because you can now customize keyboard shortcuts, we're restricting the keystroke references in the book to those instances when it's so standard that we assume you'll keep the default, or when there is no other way to achieve that function (such as Lock All Unselected Objects).

A critical Appearance panel setting

Illustrator initially launches with an application default that could inhibit the way Illustrator experts work. One of the most powerful features of Illustrator is that, when properly set, you can easily style your next object and choose where it will be in the stacking order by merely selecting a similar object. But in order for your currently selected object to set all the styling attributes for the next object you draw (including brush strokes, live effects, transparency, etc.), you must first disable the New Art Has Basic Appearance setting from the pop-up menu in the

Symbol Animati

Prepping & Splitting Objects for Ani

G   A

*If a **CC** icon is the only purple in the upper corner of a page, then this signals a change between CS6 and CC functions or features*

Locating CC Content

The color purple throughout this book indicates a reference to Illustrator CC. For more details and information about how this works, read the "Alerting you to **CC** content," "How This Book Is Organized," and "What's new in CC?" sections that follow.

Keyboard language differences

This book assumes English as the user language, but we realize that many of you are from other countries and use keyboards adapted to your own language. Non-English keyboards won't necessarily use the same keyboard shortcuts that we specify throughout the book, so we encourage you to check with the Adobe site for a list of keyboard shortcuts applicable to your own language.

✓ New Art Has Basic Appearance

New Art Has Basic Appearance

If you want your currently selected object to set all styling attributes for the next object, disable New Art Has Basic Appearance by choosing it from the pop-up menu in the Appearance panel

Appearance panel (✓ shows if it's enabled). Your new setting sticks even after you've quit, but it needs to be reset if you reinstall Illustrator or trash the preferences. In a few cases, we'll remind you to disable it when necessary and also, at times, when it's helpful to have it enabled.

HOW THIS BOOK IS ORGANIZED

You'll find a number of different kinds of information woven throughout this book— **Introductions, Tips, Lessons, Galleries, References, and Resources.** The book progresses in difficulty both within each chapter, and from chapter to chapter.

1 Introductions. Every chapter starts with a brief, general universal introduction that applies to CS6 and CC, followed by a dedicated **CC** section. In these introductions you'll find a quick overview of relevant creative features, as well as a robust collection of tips and tricks. In fact, there is so much info crammed in there it's likely that you'll discover new, useful information every time you take a look.

1

Every chapter begins with an Introduction section that focuses on overviews of features

2 Tips. Don't miss the useful information organized into the universal gray, **CC** purple, and **red** (important) Tip boxes throughout the book. Usually you'll find them alongside related text, but if you're in an impatient mood, you can quickly flip through, looking for interesting or relevant Tips. The red arrows, red outlines, and **red text** found in Tips (and sometimes with artwork) have been added to emphasize or further explain a concept or technique.

2

Tip boxes

Look for these gray boxes to find Tips about working with all things Adobe Illustrator for CS6 and CC.

Red Tip boxes

Red text and these red Tip boxes convey warnings or other essential information.

Purple CC Tip boxes

The purple Tip boxes contain information specific to features introduced in Illustrator **CC**.

3 Step-by-step lessons. In these detailed sections, you'll find step-by-step techniques gathered from artists and designers around the world. Most **WOW!** lessons focus on one aspect of how an image was created, though we'll often refer you to related techniques covered elsewhere in the book. In the universal lessons, we've noted those Illustrator CC features that have been updated and could alter the lesson's workflow. Feel free to start with almost any chapter, but be aware that each technique builds on those previously explained, so you should try to follow the techniques within each chapter sequentially. The later chapters include **Advanced Technique** lessons, which assume that you've assimilated the techniques found throughout the chapter. The *Mastering Complexity* chapter is packed with lessons dedicated to advanced tips, tricks, and techniques, and most will integrate techniques introduced in the earlier chapters.

4 Galleries. The Gallery pages consist of images related to techniques demonstrated nearby. Each Gallery piece is accompanied by a description of how the artist created that image, and may include steps showing the progression of a technique detailed elsewhere. Galleries that demonstrate an artist's use of a new CC feature are clearly marked with a purple banner at the top. Because these are short and descriptive, you'll want to take a look even if you're a CS6 user, in order to get a clear idea of what updating to Illustrator CC might do for your own artwork.

5 References & Resources. Within the text you'll occasionally be directed to *Illustrator Help* for more details; to access this, choose Help>Illustrator Help. Illustrator CC subscribers will also be directed to the Adobe site for more information regarding Creative Cloud services that are included with their subscription. In the back of the book you'll also find a **WOW! Glossary,** a listing of the artists featured in this book, and a **General Index**.

6 Where and what is WOW! ONLINE? The best way to learn to create with Illustrator is to examine complex art created by professionals. You're in luck! Many of the artists have allowed us to post their works for you to pick apart. Please contact the artists (find their contact info in the **Artists** appendix) to request permissions beyond personal exploration. To find these artworks and other goodies, see the Tip "Where are **WOW! ONLINE** files" at the start of this "How to use this book" section.

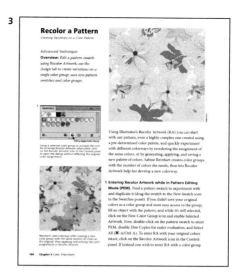

Step-by-step lessons show you how an artist or designer uses a feature to tackle a creative task

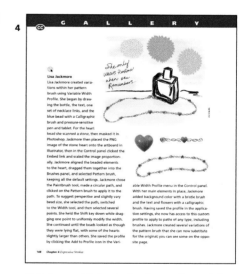

Galleries provide inspiration from artists and designers living all over the world, as well as a peek into their approach to creating artwork

Help is still available from the Window menu or by pressing the F1 key (if the OS isn't using that function), providing access to the latest list of new features and short tutorials

What's New in CC?

Illustrator CS6 marks the end to Adobe's Creative Suite. Now all software is connected to the Creative Cloud. With CC, Adobe deliberately blurs the lines between "versions" of Illustrator. Although there will still be "announce dates" for the introduction of new features, Adobe may enhance or add new Illustrator CC features at any time during the year. Because feature sets are constantly evolving, it's possible that your version of Illustrator won't exactly match our description.

If you've used Illustrator long enough, you know that the original power of this amazing program was unleashed with only a few basic tools. It's the basics that give us the power to make magic with Illustrator, though updates added in over the past few years will likely change the way you interact with Illustrator in a fundamental fashion. Many of these new features offer new approaches to creating and modifying objects with the goal of simplifying some of Illustrator's more complicated techniques. Other newer features provide you with the capacity to create things never before possible in Illustrator. Whether you're still in CS6 or you're wanting to make sure you're taking advantage of all the best of CC features, see below for some highlights about what's available as of CC 2019, and where to find more about it in the book.

Chapter 1: Your Creative Workspace

Here we focus on your workspace. A Home Screen workspace lets you start creating and opening documents as soon as you launch Illustrator. Recent documents can be viewed as thumbnails or as a list, Adobe Stock Templates might help you get started, and just in case you need to learn a new technique, the Learn tab takes you to online tutorials. An icon within your main workspace takes you back to the Home Screen anytime. You have up to 1000 artboards for your artwork and two new ways to view them: Trim and Presentation View. Trim temporarily hides all artwork that extends beyond the artboard, and

CreativePro.com

Between editions of the **WOW!** books, you'll frequently find articles by Sharon and the **WOW!** team on the Creative Pro website, teaching you how to use some of the newest **WOW!** features found in the Creative Cloud updates.

Got an internet connection?

More and more, Adobe is turning towards changes to Illustrator that are dependent on your active connection to its Cloud services. These added (and increasingly integrated) features require you to be connected to the internet.

Don't forget CS6 features!

CS6 was a major upgrade that included a Pattern Options panel for creating patterns, an enhanced Image Trace panel, gradients on Strokes, a quick access Locate Object icon in the Layers panel, and major performance upgrades.

GEORGE COGHILL

Chapter 1 *includes George Coghill making custom Tools panels and workspaces*

Presentation isolates each artboard in turn, letting you (and your client) page through one at a time with your arrow keys. A context-sensitive Properties panel contains Tool options and proxies to several different panels and common commands, with the content changing according to the tool or item selected. The main toolbar can be customized, and newer, stripped-down versions of the workspaces with a Basic toolbar are available (and may be your default). Essentials Classic workspace contains all the tools and several panels, while custom toolbars help you set up for an individual project.

Chapter 2: Designing Type & Layout

Type has a number of new features to make it easier to choose and customize type in your designs. Finding the font you want is aided by font previews, the ability to assign Favorite fonts, robust searching by classification and style, and a font's similarity to other fonts. With your Creative Cloud account you have full access to Adobe Fonts (formerly Typekit), making them accessible in your searches. By combining search features, you can narrow down a long list of fonts to just those that fit your criteria. You can substitute Alternate Glyphs, displayed when you highlight type. Additional font support includes Variable fonts that let you adjust some attributes, such as height and weight, and Open Type SVG fonts that can contain multiple colors. A Touch Type tool lets you alter the position and scale of a single letter within a word without losing the ability to edit it as live type.

Chapter 3: Rethinking Construction

Rethinking Construction includes new tools and functions to help you draw, combine, and edit objects. The Pencil and Blob brush have new Fidelity Settings to help you draw smoother curves. The Pen, Anchor Point, and Direct Selection tools have a new Reshape Segment feature, as well as several other new behaviors using modifier keys. The Curvature tool is designed to make drawing paths easier, the Join tool can speed up constructing objects,

Chapter 2 *includes many CC type features and Chana Messer's poster using the Touch Type tool*

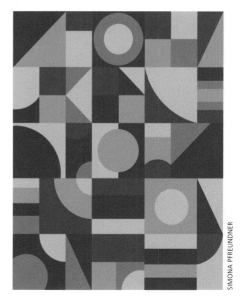

Chapter 3 *includes Simona Pfreundner gesturally drawing geometric forms, editing and combining them all using the Shaper tool, then colors her Shaper compositions using the Live Paint Bucket*

Chapter 4 *includes many examples of painterly and unexpected results including Lisa Jackmore creating a range of raster brushes (top), and Steven Gordon creating dynamic symbols that can be individually styled, but stay connected to the original (bottom)*

Chapter 5 *showcases a range of ways to transition colors, including gradients, blends, gradient mesh, and the newest Freeform Gradient tool— all used in Shawn Sullivan's illustrator above*

and the Shaper Tool is intended to make it easier to build artwork with basic, hand-drawn geometric shapes. Path corner points can be altered with Live Corners, and Rectangles, Ellipses, and Polygons can be altered using editable Shape Properties. After creating multiple objects from an original source, a Global Edit feature can help you select and edit those objects that used the same paths but weren't saved as symbols. The rules for a successful search can be complex, but this chapter covers that along with a comparison between when to choose Global Edit or the older Select Similar command.

Chapter 4: Expressive Strokes

In this chapter, new features include Dynamic Symbols, which let you edit the appearance of a symbol without needing to break the link to the original symbol. This chapter includes extensive details on how you can use raster images to create art, pattern, and scatter brushes. Pattern brushes, both vector and raster, are simpler to create now that Illustrator can to Auto-generate corner tiles.

Chapter 5: Color Transitions

The CC focus on color includes new ways of working with panels and swatches, plus a new tool for creating organic gradients. An enhanced Swatches panel includes easier searching for a specific color. The Adobe Color Themes panel lets you create color palettes locally, or you can interact with the Adobe Color website to create them or download palettes created by others. Freeform Gradients give similar results to the Gradient Mesh but can be simpler to make. You can place color points, or color points on lines, and those points will smoothly radiate color from one point to the next.

Chapter 6: Reshaping Dimensions

Reshaping Dimensions is all about bending artwork to your will. New in CC is the ability to alter a Perspective Grid's vanishing point, and at the same time alter the artwork on the grid to conform to the new perspective.

Puppet warp is designed to help you bend or distort an object or group of objects smoothly, whether you're creating a single image or a complex animation.

Chapter 7: Mastering Complexity

Here you can discover some of the myriad ways to combine all of the other features added to CC, such as incorporating the use of Live Corners and Live Shapes in a range of projects. You will explore the Pattern Editor, create storyboarding templates, and learn to rasterize complex objects to turn them into brushes.

Chapter 8: Creatively Combining Apps

This chapter demonstrates how to move files between Illustrator and other programs, teaching you the ins and outs of creating compatible files for import and export. With the rise of mobile devices, expanded SVG features help you create responsive sites and generate HTML code, and include SVG colored fonts and emojis. SVG is now an included format when using a variety of export dialogs, including Export for Screens, Export Selection, and Export As. These dialogs let you choose to export multiple objects and apply multiple options to them, such as scaling and formatting for mobile devices.

Crop Image lets you permanently delete excess pixels from a raster image, as well as reduce its resolution (useful when creating brushes), without having to make the round-trip from Illustrator to Photoshop, then back again, and saving multiple files along the way.

Creative Cloud Libraries play an increasingly important role in a seamless workflow with other Adobe applications, as well as making it easier to collaborate with others. By setting permissions, users will be able to edit the contents of the Library or only view and copy the contents to their own hard drive. And finally, when working with others, you can embed/unembed linked files and package your files so linked images travel with your files.

These and other improvements make Illustrator more productive and flexible in your workflow.

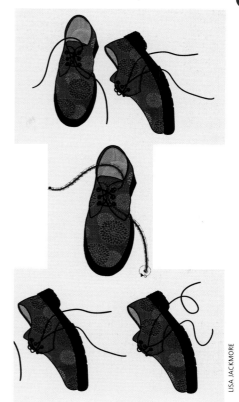

LISA JACKMORE

Chapter 6 *includes a range of applications for the Puppet Warp tool, including Lisa Jackmore's brushed-path shoelaces, as well as examples with complex groups of objects, and adjusting vector art created from Image Traced photos*

MONIKA GAUSE

To isolate details for her vector illustrations, artist Monika Gause applies Crop Image to resized duplicates of her photos (see **Chapter 8** *for details)*

Acknowledgments

As always, my most heartfelt gratitude goes to the many artists and Illustrator experts who generously allowed us to include their work and divulge their techniques. Special thanks to Jean-Claude Tremblay, our amazing technical editor. We are so lucky to have JC advising us on every technical detail of this project. Thanks to all the folks at Adobe who help answer our questions and solve our emergency issues, including Neeraj Nandkeolyar, Wayne Hoang, Anubhav Rohatgi, Ashutosh Chaturvedi, Sanjit Samanta, Gaurav Pant, and Gaurav Jain.

This fifteenth revision is, as always, the result of a major team effort by an amazing group of friends and collaborators. Thankfully, Cristen Gillespie is sticking with the team as she continues to work on so many aspects of this book. Also blessedly returning are several veteran **WOW!** cohorts: cartographer/writer Steven Gordon (who continues to create and update important lessons and galleries, join me on curatorial duties, and contribute dry wit when needed) and lyrical artist/writer Lisa Jackmore (who creates galleries, lessons, and updates the **Adobe Illustrator WOW! Course Outline**). Thanks to artist/illustrator/actor Gary Ferster for working on many of this edition's topic-critical lessons and galleries. Many more **WOW!** writers contributed to portions of the book remaining from previous editions, including wonderful artists George Coghill, Raymond Larrett, Brad Hamann, and our 3D expert, Aaron McGarry. Our astounding **WOW!** testers set this book apart by making sure that everything actually works as described. With deep gratitude I thank the multitalented group of professionals and artists who took the time to test each project for this edition, generously lending their expertise and artwork: Ari Weinstein, Monika Gause, Greg Geisler, Federico Platón, Chana Messer, Stéphane Nahmani, Franck Payen, Katharine Gilbert, and Simona Pfreundner. Thanks also to our testers from the previous edtion: Brian Stoppee, Janet Stoppee, Victor van Dijk, Kevin Stohlmeyer, Gustavo Del Vecchio, Sally Cox, and Nini Tjäder. Enthusiastic thanks to the unflappable Eric Schumacher-Rasmussen for master-juggling all the myriad edits. Thanks to fellow activist-artist Flora Davis for helping with final proofing of files, to Andy Diec for entering corrections, and Adam Z Lein for database help. Big thanks to Kim Wimpsett (proofreading) and Rebecca Plunkett (indexer) both for being so incredibly patient and flexible in our frantic dash to deadline.

Thanks to Jim Birkenseer and Peter Truskier for custom Premedia Systems scripts, and to Doug Little (Wacom) and Nick van der Walle (Astute Graphics) for keeping us up to date with great products. Shout-out to cheerleaders Teresa Roberts and Mordy Golding. Thanks to *CreativePro/InDesign Magazine's* Mike Rankin, David Blatner, and Anne-Marie Concepcion for **WOW!**-related features.

Many thanks to Laura Norman at Pearson/Peachpit for making this edition happen and Tracey Croom for continuing as my Peachpit compadre. Thanks to Ben Ferrini for contractual patience and Chuti Prasertsith for updating this edition's cover/title based on the previous lovely designs by Mimi Heft. Thanks to artist/author/educator Von Glitschka for allowing us to feature his wonderful art on the cover. Thank you Linnea Dayton for spearheading the **WOW!** series and for sharing Cristen, and thanks to **Painter WOW!** author Cher Threinan-Pendarvis for the ongoing camaraderie. And last but *not* least, tons of love and thanks to my wonderful family and friends.

1

Your Creative Workspace

Your Creative Workspace

Tabbed docs

- If more documents are open than are visible on tabs, a double-arrow at the tab bar's right will list them.
- Drag documents away from the tab to make them free-floating.
- Drag an object from one document into another by dragging over that document's tab. The tab will spring open to let you drop the object in place.

The Mac's Application Frame

On a Mac, the Application Frame (on by default) can hide most or all of your desktop. Toggle it on and off from the Window menu. **Note:** *Turn off the Application Frame with an extended monitor setup (or during video projection).*

Magically appearing panels

If you've used Tab or Shift-Tab to hide your panels, mouse carefully over the narrow strip just before the very edge of the monitor where the panels were—they'll reappear, and then they'll hide again when you move away.

This might not seem like sexy **WOW!** stuff, but to save time and stay focused on being creative, you need to work efficiently. In this chapter you'll find tons of things you might have missed or overlooked. You'll find tips for customizing your workspace along with in-depth coverage of newer organizational features.

ORGANIZING YOUR WORKSPACE

You can save time and frustration if you spend a few minutes choosing your user interface Brightness level, setting up custom workspaces, and creating your own document profiles. The panels you want handy in order to create a bristle brush painting are probably different from what you need when creating a technical illustration or the layout for a series of brochures. Not all panels are needed for every job, but by organizing all that you definitely need—eliminating all you'll rarely need or won't need at all—you'll be able to locate quickly just what you need when you need it. In addition, the Control and Appearance panels often contain the same information found in the special-purpose panels, permitting you to close some of those panels and streamline your interface even more than you might think possible (see the "Using the Appearance panel" section later in this chapter). The **CC** section at the end of this chapter intro details how the context-sensitive Properties panel can further reduce panel clutter.

In deciding which panels you want on your desktop for any given project, you'll probably first want to cluster panels that you will frequently use in sequence, such as Paragraph and Character Styles or Transform and Align. You'll also decide where each panel or group of panels should live, and whether, when you collapse them to get them out of your way, you want them to collapse to their icon and label or all the way down to their icon. When you have everything arranged to your liking, choose New Workspace either from Window> Workspace or from the pop-up menu in the Application bar. Once you've created and saved a custom workspace, its name will show up in the Window> Workspace submenu and on the Application bar (by default at the top of your working area). Switch workspaces by choosing its name. Note that any changes to a workspace, such as a panel opened or moved, are temporarily saved when you quit Illustrator so that Illustrator reopens right where you left off. To restore a workspace to its original configuration, select the workspace and choose Reset (workspace name) from the submenu. Following are tips for arranging your panels:

- **Dock panels** to the edges of your screen or, if you want them closer to your work, drag them around freely. (The Control panel docks to the top or bottom of the screen.)

- **Resize most panels** once they're open. Look for the double-arrow when hovering over an edge to see if the panel can be dragged in that direction.

- **Collapse and expand free-floating or fully expanded columns to their title bar** by double-clicking the panel name. (If the open panel is one in a column of icons that has been temporarily opened by itself, it can't be reduced to its title bar.) Double-click the top gray bar to collapse a free-floating panel to an icon. Experiment with expanding and minimizing open panels in your workspace to get used to how the panels work, and you'll save time and frustration later when you want to get a panel out of your way quickly.

- **If you need multiple panels open at once**, place each panel you want open in a separate column (drag to the side of an existing column until you see the vertical blue bar). Only one item in a column of panel icons can be open, but one from each column can be open simultaneously and will remain open until you manually close it by clicking its double-arrow in the upper-right corner. The exception is if you have enabled Auto Collapse Icon Panels in Preferences> User Interface. In that case, to close a panel that was opened from an icon, click anywhere outside the panel. Since panels are "spring-loaded," you can still drag items into them even when they're closed.

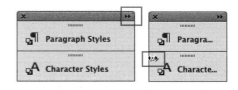

When you click the double-arrow in the upper right, open panels will cycle through contracted and expanded states, which will vary depending on how you've customized the panel; customizing the width manually when the cursor turns into a double-arrow allows you to click-drag to resize the panel

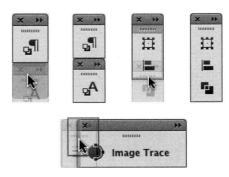

Dock and stack panels with different results by watching where the blue highlight shows up

A double-arrow in the upper left (next to the panel name) indicates that you can display more, or fewer, options in the panel; the fewest options will be shown by default

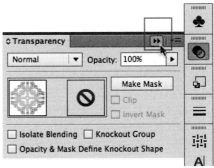

To minimize a panel opened from a column of panels that have been reduced to icons, click the double-arrow in the upper right (you can't minimize it by double-clicking the dark gray bar)

Using New Document Profiles

When you create a New Document Profile, you can establish not only the size, color mode, and resolution of your document, but also whether or not that document includes specific swatches, symbols, graphic styles, brushes, and even what font is chosen as the default. By saving this to the New Document Profiles preset folder along with your other user Library presets, the document appears in the New Document dialog. In later **CC** versions of the New Document Dialog, access New Document Profiles by clicking More Settings to open the legacy New Document dialog; then choose it from the Profile list.

Rulers, guides, Smart Guides, and grids

Since Illustrator uses multiple artboards, you can choose to display the ruler (⌘-R/Ctrl-R) as a Global ruler that extends across all your artboards or as an Artboard ruler, one for each artboard with its own x,y coordinate system. The rulers look the same, but if you Control-click/right-click a ruler or press ⌘-Option-R/Ctrl-Alt-R, the Change to (Global/Artboard ruler) command reveals which ruler is active, and you can switch rulers here. In order to be consistent with other Adobe programs, new documents by default use Artboard rulers and set the origin point at the upper-left corner, instead of the lower left. Documents created in older versions will still open with Artboard rulers active and the origin point in the upper left, but if you switch to the Global Ruler, the origin point will be at the legacy lower-left corner, as it was when the document was originally created. If you need to work with legacy positioning, switch to Global Rulers with your legacy documents to see the old X,Y coordinates. You can still change the location of the origin point by dragging from the upper-left corner of the rulers to the desired location, but you can give each artboard its own origin point when you choose Artboard Rulers.

You can apply guides globally or to individual artboards. To place a non-global guide with the Artboard tool selected (Shift-O), drag a guide from the ruler to the active artboard, being careful to drag right over the board, not between it and another. If you drag a guide in between the artboards, it will place the guide across all artboards.

If you intend to use several guides in a project, try creating separate layers for specific sets of guides. Keeping guides on named layers allows you to easily control which guides are visible and to better control locking, visibility, and clearing of guides. (If you have **CC**, see the "Better Guide Creation" section at the end of this chapter intro.)

You can also create guides by selecting an object and defining it as a guide by choosing Object> Make Guides (⌘-5/Ctrl-5, or via View> Guides). By default, guides are unlocked, but you can lock them using the Lock/Unlock toggle (in the context-sensitive or View menus); the Lock/Unlock Guides toggle is global and affects all guides in all documents. Any unlocked guide can be changed into a regular, editable path by targeting the guide and, again in the context-sensitive menu, choosing Release Guides. Guides not targeted will not be converted.

Smart Guides, which can be powerful aids for constructing and aligning objects as you draw, are helpful enough to become an essential part of your workflow. Use the toggle ⌘-U/Ctrl-U to turn them on or off. Enable or disable their options in Preferences> Smart Guides.

MASTERING OBJECT MANAGEMENT

Take control of the stacking order of objects right from the beginning and become familiar with the different ways to focus on just the necessary objects at one time.

Although probably the easiest and most important thing that you can do to keep your file organized is to name your layers as you create them, it's easy to get lazy and just click the New Layer icon. To avoid amassing a stack of ambiguously numbered layers, try to get in the habit of holding Option/Alt when you click the New Layer icon to name it in the Layer Options dialog, or double-click the layer name itself to rename it. (Of course, you can double-click to the right of the layer name at any time to access Layer Options and edit the name or other

Hide/Show Edges

The shortcut for Hide/Show Edges is ⌘-H/Ctrl-H (or choose View> Hide/Show Edges). Once you hide the selection edges (paths and anchor points), all path edges in that file will remain hidden until you show them again—and that hidden state is saved with your file! Get in the habit of toggling it off when you're done with the task at hand. And, if you open a file and can't decode the mystery of why things don't appear selected, remember to try ⌘-H/Ctrl-H.

Three grids

View Illustrator's automatic grid using View> Show Grid (⌘-"/Ctrl-"). Illustrator also offers a Perspective Grid and a Pixel Grid. For details on the Perspective Grid, see the *Reshaping Dimensions* chapter, and for information on using the Pixel Grid, see the "Web Graphics" section in the *Creatively Combining Apps* chapter.

Select buried objects

Select filled objects hidden by others by ⌘-clicking/Ctrl-clicking the top object. The first click displays the Select Behind cursor and selects the topmost object; each subsequent ⌘-click/Ctrl-click targets the next object in the stacking order. (Toggle this feature on and off in Preferences> Selection and Anchor Display.)

Layers panel and isolation

When you enter isolation mode, only the artwork in the group or layer that's isolated will be visible in the Layers panel. Once you exit isolation mode, the other layers and groups will once again appear in the Layers panel.

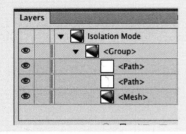

Isolation ins and outs

To enter isolation mode:

- Double-click an object or group.
- Select an object or group and click the Isolate Selected Object button on the Control panel.
- Choose Enter Isolation Mode in the Layers panel menu.

To exit isolation mode:

- Press the Esc key.
- Click any empty spot on the gray isolation bar.
- Double-click an empty spot on the artboard.
- Click the Back arrow on the isolation bar until you're out.
- Choose Exit Isolation Mode from the Layers panel menu.
- ⌘-double-click/Ctrl-double-click an empty artboard area to back up one level in Isolation.

settings.) Both the Layers and Appearance panels are designed primarily to help you locate, select, and modify your artwork objects, so you want to take full advantage of Illustrator's changing interface to know just where you are and what you'll be affecting.

Using isolation mode

Isolation mode is a quick way to isolate selected objects so you can work on them without accidentally affecting other objects. The next time you want to edit an object, group, or layer, use isolation mode instead of locking or hiding things that are in the way. In addition to *you* choosing to enter isolation mode, Illustrator will also at times automatically place you into a special form of isolation mode, such as when editing symbols, creating patterns, or working with opacity masks. Isolation mode focuses your attention as you create and edit various types of objects.

See Tip "Isolation ins and outs" at left for a summary of how to enter and exit isolation mode. Once you enter, a gray bar appears at the top of your document window, indicating that you're now in isolation mode, and the gray bar displays the hierarchy that contains the isolated object. Everything on your artboard *except* the object(s) you've just isolated will be dimmed, indicating that those other objects are temporarily locked. If you have isolated an object or group, you can expand the isolation to the sublayer or layer that the object is on by clicking the word for that layer in the gray bar. As long as isolation mode is active, anything you add to your artboard will automatically become part of the isolated group. (Disable "Double-click to Isolate" in Preferences> General to prevent a double-click from putting you in isolation mode.)

Isolation mode isn't limited to objects you've grouped yourself. Remember that other types of objects—such as blends, envelopes, or Live Paint objects—exist as groups, and isolation mode works for them, too. In addition to using isolation mode on groups, you can also use it on almost anything—layers, symbols, clipping masks, compound paths, opacity masks, images, gradient meshes, and even a single path. The next time you think you have to enter Outline mode, or lock or hide objects to avoid grabbing other objects, try isolation mode instead.

Copy and paste techniques

When you copy an object, Illustrator offers a number of power options for how the objects are pasted, including Paste in Front, Paste in Back, Paste in Place, and Paste on All Artboards. Note that none of these is affected by the ruler origin but are positioned in the same relative position to the upper-left corner of the artboard. Here are some of the distinctions:

- **If you choose Paste in Front or Paste in Back with nothing selected,** Illustrator pastes the cut or copied object at the extreme front or back of the current layer.
- **If you choose Paste in Front or Paste in Back with an object selected,** Illustrator pastes the object directly on top of or behind the selected object in the stacking order.
- **Paste in Place** is the same as Paste in Front with nothing selected, but it pastes to any selected artboard.
- **Paste on All Artboards** pastes the object in the same relative position onto each artboard.

Selecting & targeting indicators in the Layers panel

Many seasoned Illustrator artists have missed the introduction of targeting versus selecting. When you simply select objects and apply effects or adjust opacity, the effects might not be applied as you expected, and in order to remove or edit the effects you'll have to carefully reproduce this level of selection (see "Decoding appearances" on the next page). If instead you apply an effect to a targeted group, layer, or sublayer, then the effects are easy to remove (simply target that level again).

To know for sure whether you have successfully targeted a layer, look in the Layers panel, where you should see the double-circle as the target indicator for that layer, and a large square box indicating that you've selected all objects within that layer (a small square means you have only some objects on that level selected). In addition, in

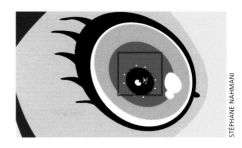

⌘-click/Ctrl-click on the topmost object to bring up the Select Behind cursor

Magical layers feature!

With Paste Remembers Layers enabled (it's off by default in the Layers panel menu), pasted objects retain their layer order, and if the layers don't exist, Paste Remembers Layers makes them for you! If you paste, and it pastes flattened (because it's disabled), Undo, reverse the toggle, and paste again.

CS6 Layers panel selection and target indicators (from left to right): 1) target indicator for any layer or subcomponent, 2) selection is also currently targeted, 3) target indicator for any targeted component with effect applied, 4) selection indicator for a container layer, 5) selection indicator when an object is selected, 6) selection indicator when all objects on a layer are selected

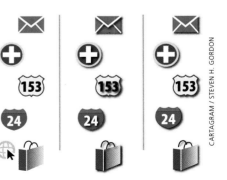

Steven Gordon at Cartagram applies drop shadows to his map icons: (left) original; (middle) after selecting ungrouped objects (or all objects on a layer) and applying an effect (it applies to each object separately); (right) after targeting the layer or selecting the group and applying the effect (it applies to the bounding paths only)

Decoding appearances

A basic appearance does not include multiple fills or strokes, transparency, effects, or brush strokes. More complex appearances are indicated by a gradient-filled circle in the Layers panel. When you need to modify artwork created by others (or open artwork you created earlier), it's essential to have both the Appearance and Layers panels visible. Unless an effect is applied at the level of a layer or a group, you might not see the filled circle icon until you expand your view of the layer to locate the object that has the effect applied.

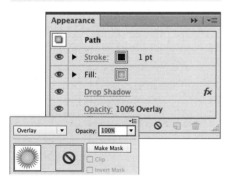

Many functions reside in the Appearance panel

Dûplicating fills/strokes/effects

To duplicate a fill or stroke: select the object and click the Add New Stroke or Add New Fill icon at the bottom of the Appearance panel, from the panel menu, or select one or more strokes, fills, and effects in the panel and drag them to the Duplicate Selected Item icon at the bottom of the panel.

the Appearance panel you should see the word "Layer" listed first as the thumbnail name (as opposed to "Group," "Path", or "Mixed Objects"). When a group, layer, or sublayer has an effect applied to it, any new objects placed into that level will immediately acquire those effects.

Using the Appearance panel

You probably know by now that many functions can be handled in the Control panel instead of individual panels. (In **CC**, you can also access the Appearance panel through the Properties panel.) The Appearance panel also can replace a number of separate panels, making it an indispensable hub for a productive and efficient workflow. Here you can view or edit a selected object's stroke, fill, or transparency; check to see if it's part of a group; or adjust an effect or named graphic style applied to it.

In the Appearance panel with a group or layer targeted, double-clicking Contents reveals object-level attributes. With a text object, double-click Characters to see the basic text attributes. You can also add additional strokes or fills to the object, apply effects and access effect dialogs, choose whether or not the next object you draw will have the same appearance, or construct a new graphic style to save for future objects. Important concepts for using the Appearance panel include the following:

- **The basic appearance** consists of a stroke and fill (even if set to None), and its transparency (0%–100% Opacity).
- **Apply an appearance** to any path, object, group, layer, or sublayer.
- **The stacking order of attributes** affects the final appearance and can be changed simply by dragging the attribute up or down in the list.
- **The visibility of attributes** can be toggled on or off by clicking the Eye icon, and multiple selected items can be unhidden with Show All Hidden Attributes from the panel menu. The visibility of thumbnails can be toggled on or off with Show/Hide Thumbnail in the panel menu.
- **Click underlined words** such as Stroke or Opacity, or on an effect such as Drop Shadow, to open their respective

panels; Shift-click a swatch icon to open the Color panel (this works in the Control panel too!).

Graphic styles and the Appearance panel

A graphic style consists of all the attributes applied to an object, group, or layer. If you have a single object selected, Control-click/right-click a style to see a large thumbnail preview of the style applied to your object (with multiple objects selected, this simply enlarges the thumbnail of the object furthest to the left). Save a current appearance by clicking the New Graphic Style button (you can also drag the thumbnail from the Appearance panel, or drag the object itself to the Graphic Styles panel). Option-drag/Alt-drag the thumbnail on top of an existing graphic style in the Graphic Styles panel to replace it.

To add a graphic style to an object that already has a graphic style without removing the existing attributes, Option-click/Alt-click the graphic style in the Graphic Styles panel. When you look at the Appearance panel, you'll see the new attributes stacked on top of the original attributes. You can also access a document's styles from another document by clicking the Graphic Styles Library Menu icon and choosing Other Library to locate and Open the document, loading the desired graphic styles.

MANAGING MULTIPLE ARTBOARDS

Having multiple artboards allows you to organize work within and across projects in a single document, whether you need to create multi-panel storyboards, set up elaborate character stagings for animations, organize many elements within a single complex project, or even keep multi-sized, collateral business material (such as cards, stationery, envelopes, postcards, and brochures) within one document. And then, of course, you can print or export to PDF any combination of the artboards that you want into one multi-page PDF, even one with multi-sized pages. In Illustrator CS6 you can have up to 100 artboards per file (in Illustrator **CC** 2019 you can have up to 1000 artboards).

Drawing with Appearances

Whether or not your new object will have the same attributes as your last-drawn object depends upon settings in the Appearance panel menu.

- **If New Art Has Basic Appearance is enabled,** you'll be drawing with only the current Stroke, Fill, and Opacity. Any other attributes from your last-drawn object are ignored.
- **If you have disabled New Art Has Basic Appearance,** your new art will have the exact same Appearance as your last object, but you can choose Reduce to Basic Appearance in the panel menu to remove all attributes except the Stroke, Fill, and Opacity.
- **To eliminate even the Basic Appearance,** click the Clear Appearance icon at the bottom of the panel, which reduces the selected object to None for Stroke and Fill, and the Default (100%) Opacity.

With a single object selected, Control-click/right-click a graphic style; an enlarged thumbnail shows the style applied to the selected object

Why use New Window?

Choose Window> New Window to display different aspects of your current image simultaneously. You can view the same art separately, and in different View modes (Preview, Outline, Overprint, or Pixel) or with different Proof Setups (including for color blindness), or Zoom levels. Use Arrange Documents on the Application bar to organize them or to make edges hidden or visible. Most choices from the View menu are saved with the file along with the new windows.

Design to the edge

By default, artwork that extends beyond an artboard won't print, making it important to watch not only for artwork left off the artboard, but also for artwork that's been manually positioned on the page in the Print dialog. If your artwork extends beyond the edge of an artboard, make sure you add a bleed setting value; if the artwork gets placed in InDesign or saved as EPS, it's all still visible.

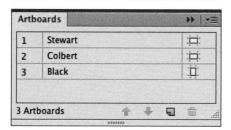

Artboards panel with reorder arrows, orientation icon (double-click to enter the Options dialog), and New Artboard and Delete Artboard icons

To help you set up, organize, and work with artboards, both the Artboards panel and the Control panel options with the Artboard tool selected provide the access and features you'll need. To manage the artboards themselves, make sure you're familiar with basic artboard functions:

- **Set up artboards** when you're configuring a new document. Adjust them later in the Artboards panel or in the Control panel when your Artboard tool is active. You can save Artboard configurations so they'll be available as a New Document Profile.

- **To add an artboard** using the same properties as the currently highlighted artboard, click the New Artboard icon. It will be added to the same row as the current artboard, but you can rearrange the artboards later.

- **Modify artboard settings by choosing Artboard Options** from the Artboards menu; double-clicking the artboard orientation icon in the Artboards panel (single-click if the artboard is already active); double-clicking the Artboard tool; or with the Artboard tool active, clicking Artboard Options in the Control or **CC** Properties panel.

- **Create and manage artboards manually** and interactively by selecting the Artboard tool (Shift-O) instead of invoking the dialog, dragging artboards to scale and position them, and using the Control panel options. Enabling Smart Guides can help with precise manual alignment.

- **Name your active artboard** by double-clicking the Artboard name and renaming it directly. Or you can select the Artboard tool and change its name either in the Control panel or in the Artboards Options dialog. The name is listed in the Artboards panel and in the list of artboard panels in the status bar (Artboard Navigation, located at the bottom right of the document window).

- **Rearrange artboards** through the Artboards panel menu or Object> Artboards> Rearrange, choose rows, columns, and spacing; whether or not to move your artwork with the artboard; and the last-used settings persist.

- **Reorder the list of artboards** in the Artboards panel using the up and down arrow icons. Reordering artboards within the Artboards panel doesn't change the way the actual artboards are arranged in your workspace. However, be aware that the order of artboards in the panel determines the order in which artboards print or are ordered when saved as a multi-page PDF.

- **Use Shift-Page Up or Shift-Page Down to navigate** the Artboard panel layers, which will fill the window with your selected artboard as you navigate.
- **Artboards have a reference point**. In the Position area of Artboard Options, choose the reference point from which artboards get resized.
- **Overlapping art across multiple artboards, or overlapping artboards onto one piece of art,** allows you to develop multiple versions of the same image without duplicating elements. Each artboard will print only those portions of the art wholly contained within its borders, allowing you to print or export duplicates, and/or portions of an art piece, from the one instance of the art (this is a useful technique for storyboarding and comic strips).
- **Convert a non-rotated rectangle** to an artboard by choosing Object> Artboards> Convert to Artboard.
- **Use Fit to Artwork Bounds and Fit to Selected Art** commands (in the Preset list on the Control panel when the Artboard tool is selected, or under Object> Artboards), for resizing artboards according to their contents.
- **To locate an artboard visually** when another artboard fills your view, choose View> Fit All in Window (⌘-Option-0/Ctrl-Alt-0). To activate it, click the artboard with the Selection tool or click its name in the Artboards panel.
- **When zooming,** the commands Fit Artboard in Window (⌘-0/Ctrl-0) and Actual Size (⌘-1/Ctrl-1) affect the active artboard. Double-clicking in the Artboards panel to the right of an inactive artboard's name or on its number on the left (single-click if it's active) also zooms that artboard to Fit Artboard in Window size.
- **Export artboards as separate TIFF, JPEG, PSD, or PNG files** when you need a rasterized version of every artboard in your document.

Copying art between artboards

Working productively and maintaining consistency within a project often means duplicating elements from one document to another. With multiple artboards you have a variety of methods to accomplish this task, depending upon your needs:

- With the "Move/Copy Artwork with Artboard" icon enabled in the Control panel (Artboard tool selected), hold down the Option/Alt key while dragging an active artboard to a new location in order to duplicate the artboard and all its contents.
- Use Edit> Paste on All Artboards (⌘-Option-Shift-V/Ctrl-Alt-Shift-V) to copy artwork from one artboard to the same position on all artboards of any size.
- Turn artwork created on one artboard into a symbol, then drag that symbol from the shared Symbols panel to any other artboard. Now just update the symbol to update all instances of it used on any artboards.
- Using the Measure tool, measure the distance between the artwork and where you want it on another artboard, and use Transform> Move to move or copy the artwork.
- Apply the Transform effect on a layer to copy "instances" of artwork to another artboard in the same relative position.

Find Help on Adobe website
Every new release brings new features, large and small. To find what's new, you can go to adobe. com/products/illustrator/features. html to see a description of the new features. Or you can choose Help> Illustrator Help. On the Learn and Support page, click User Guide. In the online guide choose "What's new in Illustrator CC" (right side of the opening page) to see the latest list of features.

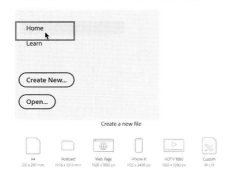

The Home Screen's opening panel where you can create new document (using either a New Document dialog or the sample presets), or open existing documents using the Open dialog or via a list or thumbnail view of your recently-opened documents

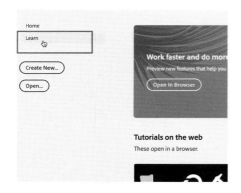

The Learn Screen (enlarged above) accessed via the Home Screen, requiring an internet connection to view tutorials online

YOUR CREATIVE CC WORKSPACE

In addition to discussing new **CC** settings and services that are integrated with Illustrator, this section will also cover updates to the way Illustrator looks and functions. With a Creative Cloud subscription, you can perform most functions without being connected to the internet or logged into your Creative Cloud account. However, some options require that you are both online and signed into Creative Cloud. For example, to receive notification of available updates, to use Adobe Fonts (formerly Typekit), or to sync Libraries, you'll need to have an active connection to your Creative Cloud account.

THE HOME SCREEN

When you first launch Illustrator, you'll see the default workspace that Adobe now calls the Home Screen. In the Home Screen workspace, you can choose from a few document presets listed at the top, launch the New Document dialog using the Create New button, or open an existing file by pressing the Open button. Using either a list or thumbnail view, select recently opened or saved files to work on again. The Home Screen is the center where you can click Learn to find links to tutorials when you have a browser connection. A browser connection is also needed for the search field in the upper right of the Home Screen, where you can search for an Illustrator term or enter a subject as a search term for Adobe Stock. To manage your account, click your avatar in the upper right when you are connected to the internet.

To skip past the Home Screen without doing anything, press the Esc key. You can press it as soon as you see the workspace open, even when it's still empty. To prevent Illustrator from automatically displaying the Home Screen, disable "Show The Home Screen When No Documents Are Open," in Preferences> General.

To access the Home Screen from your workspace, regardless of your Preference setting for showing the Home screen, click the Home icon in the upper left of the Application Bar. If it's not open, enable the Application

Bar via the Window menu. This allows you to return to use the Home Screen for visually browsing your Recent files, creating another new document, or learning about a feature you want to use.

WORKSPACE AND PANELS

Beyond the Home Screen, the Essentials workspace is the default whenever the user launches Illustrator with default settings or when the user hasn't chosen or saved another workspace. The Essentials workspace Toolbar contains only a small subset of all the tools and many fewer panels docked than you might expect.

Another "Essentials" workspace is Essentials Classic, which is the only workspace to contain a complete set of tools in the Toolbar itself (not hidden in the toolbar drawer), including any tools installed by third-party plug-ins. There are many other workspaces that you might prefer to either of these, but the real power comes with learning to customize and save your own configurations of panels and tools (read more about customizing Tools panels later in this chapter) and then saving these configurations as your own workspaces. Be aware that many of the panels are contained within, or accessible via, the robust, and ever-improving, context-sensitive Properties panel (keep reading for more about this panel).

Whatever workspace you begin with, once you make changes to the configuration of panels or tools, each of these changes temporarily saves to that workspace and should persist until you reset the workspace to default or reinstall Illustrator. At any time you can choose to save your current configuration as a new workspace or reset the current workspace to the default parameters by choosing Reset (workspace name) in the Workspace Switcher or Window> Workspace menu.

The Properties panel

The Properties panel centralizes access to the most common tool options, panel options, and commands. Like the Control panel its content changes according to

The Home button lets you return to the Home Screen even if you still have documents open or if you have disabled Show the Home Screen When No Documents Are Open in General Preferences

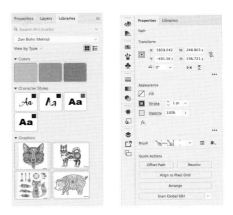

The Essentials workspace (left) with only three panels; Essentials Classic (right) with multiple panels

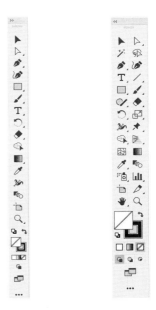

The Basic Toolbar (left), containing only a few of the tools in Illustrator; the Advanced Toolbar (right)—the only toolbar containing all tools in Illustrator, as well as automatically including tools from third party plug-ins

Another way to access tool options besides double-clicking: With no object targeted and a tool selected, a Tool Options button appears in the Properties panel that opens the dialog

Clicking ••• to display more options for the Transform panel with an object selected

Properties panel evolution

New releases of Illustrator often bring new features to the Properties panel. Because the panel is context-sensitive, review the What's New section of the User Guide in the online Help with each release to discover if anything was added that you might find useful to your own workflow or that will allow you to de-clutter your workspace even more.

what you've selected, but in a much more thorough and detailed display. To get an idea of what's possible with the Properties panel, start with a document open and nothing selected. The Properties panel displays Document properties and tools, such as units and artboards, guides and grids, and some preferences. At the bottom under Quick Actions is button access to Document Setup and Preferences. Now select an object to see that you can open the Tool Options dialog from the upper right to change tool settings. Depending upon the type of object selected, choose a fill or stroke, adjust opacity, or add an effect. You can access menu commands from the bottom of the Properties panel and apply other commands by clicking buttons in the Quick Actions section. When you see ••• in a section, that indicates there is more to the panel that opens if you click the dots. Most of the time this will open right inside the Properties panel. Some panels, such as the Appearance panel, will open separately from the Properties panel. If it's docked in your workspace, the panel opens where it's docked. Otherwise, it opens as a free-floating panel, and you can position it where you want it to open again the next time you need it.

The Toolbar and Tools panels

Illustrator allows you to customize tools in two ways: 1) you can drag subsets of tools into new custom toolbars to create floating speciality toolbars, and 2) you can customize the main Toolbar itself. Modifying your default Toolbar is a good idea if you find there are tools you rarely use on a regular basis. Most of the workspaces ship with a Basic toolbar, while Essentials Classic ships with an Advanced toolbar. If you aren't sure which default toolbar you're modifying, click ••• at the bottom of the Toolbar to open the *toolbar drawer* (All Tools) or look in Window> Toolbars.

To remove tools from a default toolbar, open the toolbar drawer and drag any top-level tool (not hidden behind another tool) into the toolbar drawer. The panel displays all the tools in their default positions in the Toolbar, with active tools ghosted and inactive tools bright. To use an inactive tool, you must first either drag it back into your default Toolbar or use its keyboard shortcut, if it has one. Clicking it in the toolbar drawer won't select it.

The toolbar drawer organizes your tools in their default order, but you can reorder or regroup the active tools within the Toolbar itself. Your third-party tools (such as Astute Graphics) can be reorganized like any other tools. If you know a tool's keyboard shortcut, you can keep it out of the toolbar (in the drawer) and still be able to access it via the shortcut. Tools selected with their keyboard shortcut will temporarily appear as the last tool in the Toolbar then disappear when you select another tool. If you don't need access to the icons at the bottom of the Toolbar—the controls from Fill/Stroke through Screen modes—you can even drag these in your toolbar drawer to hide them and further shorten your Toolbar.

Changes to a default toolbar automatically save to Preferences, which means they persist across workspaces and don't reset along with the workspace. To reset a toolbar, click • • • at the bottom of a toolbar then click the Toolbar menu icon (top/right) to access Reset, as well as to choose another toolbar or create, rename, or delete them with Manage Toolbars.

To create a separate toolbar, click • • • to access the Toolbar menu, choose New Toolbar then name it and click OK. Now click *that* new toolbar's • • • and drag desired tools from its drawer into the new toolbar. To create a stack of tools hidden beneath the top tool, select multiple tools from the toolbar drawer to drag together to your custom toolbar (hold Shift when you click a second tool to select the sequence between them or hold ⌘/Ctrl to click-select non-consecutive tools). Close the drawer and click the top tool to reveal the hidden tools. Custom toolbars are temporarily saved to whichever workspace is active when you create them. Save your custom Toolbar to reload it anytime, from any workspace. To make certain that your toolbar is saved with that workspace, then save your workspace as a New Workspace.

Displaying the Advanced toolbar and the toolbar drawer, opened by clicking • • • at the bottom of the toolbar. Tools automatically slot into place

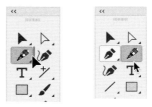

Dragging tools to reorder them in a toolbar

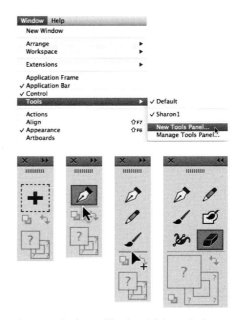

A custom Tools panel begins with just a + sign, but you can drag in as many tools as you wish, and even display it in two rows by clicking the upper-right double-arrow

Trim View & Presentation Mode

These modes help you concentrate on just the artwork by excluding everything that is extraneous to it. Trim view shows only the artwork that's on the artboard, hiding all non-printing objects and trimming anything that hangs off the artboard. Trim view doesn't change your magnification nor isolate an active artboard the way Presentation Mode does. You'll view all your artboards at once in Trim View when zoomed out, but zooming in won't "trim" artwork that overlaps another artboard. Presentation mode displays only the artwork on the artboard and nothing else, exactly as it would print or display on a screen, but also isolates your view to just one artboard. If artwork extends beyond the boundaries onto another artboard, even if one is fully encompassed by the other, any extending artwork disappears from the preview. Presentation Mode will view either the currently active artboard, or if no artboard is active, the artboard that was last active.

Keep it closed, please

When you save your file, Illustrator now remembers which of your layers were in an expanded state and which were collapsed. You'll find them as you left them when you reopen the document.

Enhanced keyboard and mouse functions

Here are a few of the added controls and functions you can now access via your keyboard or mouse (see the **CC** section of the *Rethinking Construction* chapter intro for enhancements to Pen, Pencil, and path-editing tools):

- **To draw or resize an artboard from its center,** hold down the Option/Alt key when dragging on a corner with the Artboard tool.
- **To place files without opening the File menu,** press ⌘-Shift-P/Ctrl-Shift-P.
- **To change Opacity,** click the triangle beside the numeric input field to access a slider (CS6 displays a list of presets). The slider was restored by popular request.
- **To cancel creating guides/zoom level (with the Zoom tool),** press the Esc key while still dragging and before releasing the mouse. This also cancels dragging with the Selection, Direct Selection, and Print Tiling tools, and ends drawing an open path with the Pen tool.

Better guide creation

To quickly create a guide at a specific location, double-click directly on the ruler at that location. For instance, double-click on a horizontal guide to place a vertical ruler, or press Shift and double-click to force the guide to the nearest tick mark. To create crossing horizontal and vertical guides at a specific point, hold ⌘ (Mac)/Ctrl (Windows) and then click-drag the guide from the upper-left corner of the rulers to your artboard. Pressing the Esc key before completing the drag cancels creating guides, including dragging to change the 0 location of the X,Y coordinates.

Layers panel cursors make a comeback

Feedback missing from CS6 has been restored: hold Option/Alt as you drag a layer or selection indicator to once again see a + indicating you're about to copy (instead of move).

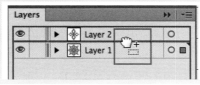

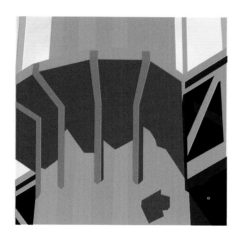

KIMBALL

Mike Kimball

Commissioned by the Golden Gate National Parks Conservancy to create a poster for the 75th anniversary of the Golden Gate Bridge, Mike Kimball produced an illustration that focused on the bridge's streamlined Art Deco design. He simplified the detail in the bridge to eliminate construction details that distracted from its design lines, and restricted the number of colors in keeping with posters of that period. Critical to achieving the strong perspective favored by the client were the hand-drawn perspective guides Kimball placed on a layer above the artwork. To make them, he drew a line along the left and right cables (the extreme right was cropped from view later), created intermediate lines with Object> Blend> Make, and then chose View> Guides> Make Guides. A second set of guides marked the cable width. He organized the illustration with separate layers for the bridge itself, the highlights, shadows, and the sky. He made extensive use of blending modes, opacity, and gradients to create highlights and shadows, while Gaussian Blur softened the clouds. When finished, Kimball's poster echoed a style from the day the famous bridge opened.

Tracing a Template

Manually Tracing a Template Layer

Overview: *Place a scan on a template layer in Illustrator; manually trace over the template using the Pencil, Pen, and Arc tools; modify paths with the Direct Selection tool; use geometric objects for ease and speed.*

Rachel Sellers used Illustrator's basic drawing tools to build this skyline for Thirty-Third Latitude Properties. Using a scanned sketch as a template, Sellers relied on Illustrator's Pencil, Pen, and basic geometric tools to draw the skyline and artwork in the logo.

1

Part of the high-contrast scan of Seller's pen sketch from photographs of Atlanta's skyline

Creating the template and a drawing layer by choosing File> Place

1 Placing a scanned image as a template. Scan your source image at a high enough resolution and contrast to see the detail you need for tracing, and save it as a PSD, TIFF, or JPG. In a new Illustrator document, choose File> Place, select your scan, enable the Template option at the lower left, and click Place. Your scan is now on a Template layer beneath the original layer. Templates have rectangle visibility icons, and italic names indicating that they're non-printing layers. Templates are also automatically locked and set to 50% opacity. To adjust settings, double-click to the right of the template name in the Layers panel.

2

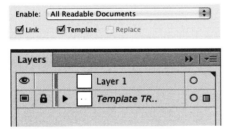

Using the Direct Selection tool and repositioning two anchor points after tracing (left) to reshape the drawing of a building (right)

2 Tracing straight lines and corners; repositioning points. With the template as a guide, select Layer 1 (the default layer in the Layers panel) and with the Pen tool, using the scan as a guide, click to place anchor points that will connect with straight lines. To draw horizontal, vertical, or diagonal lines while you trace, hold down the Shift key as you click with the Pen tool. Once you've drawn a basic path, zoom in close and use the Direct Selection tool to adjust the positioning of anchor points. Instead of being more precise, Sellers used her rough sketch as a guide for a stylized interpretation of the Atlanta skyline.

3 Tracing and adjusting curved paths. Illustrator offers several options to create and edit curved paths. The key to drawing curves with the Pen tool is to click-drag (not merely click) in the direction the curve is heading, then lift the pen and click-drag on the other side of the bump of a curve (this takes practice!). To adjust curves with the Pen tool, hold Option/Alt to click-drag to move the curve, or use the Direct Selection tool to adjust the direction handles. To toggle anchor points between corners and curves, click a Convert icon in Control or **CC** Properties panels, and to hinge a smooth curve, use the Convert Anchor Point tool to grab its direction handle.

To draw with the Pencil tool, double-click its icon to adjust the Fidelity slider. You can further control how smooth or detailed your paths are by zooming in or out before drawing or editing with the Pencil or Smooth tools. Zoom out to create smoother lines (fewer anchor points) or zoom in for more accuracy. You can also redraw any selected path by drawing close to it with the Pencil tool (you can adjust Within value in Options).

If your curve is a simple arc, consider the Arc tool (located behind the Line Segment tool). To use it, click and drag a curved path. After drawing the arc, you can reshape its path as you would any curve, by using the Direct Selection tool to adjust handles and anchor points.

4 Using basic objects to help build your image. To speed up drawing, use ready-made geometric objects like rectangles and ellipses. Create triangles using the Polygon or Star tool by clicking the desktop and changing Sides to 3 in the tool's dialog. Add paths and filled objects with the Pen or Pencil tools, or use the Pathfinder panel, Shape Builder, or **CC** Shaper tools to combine objects (more about these tools in the *Rethinking Construction* chapter).

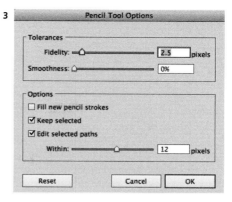

The CS6 Pencil Tool Options dialog; **CC** combines Tolerances into one Fidelity slider (see the **CC** section in the Rethinking Construction *introduction* for details on the new dialog)

(Top) The path created by the Pencil tool with zoom at 300%; (bottom) the path drawn with zoom level at 50%

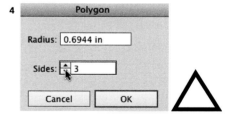

(Left) Creating a triangle with the Polygon tool by clicking the artboard and editing the Polygon menu's Sides value; (right) the resulting triangle

Stop drawing!

If you've drawn an open path and don't deselect it, your next click with the Pen tool will continue the same path. To stop the current path and start a new path, in CS6 press the P key (for the Pen tool); in **CC** you can press the Esc key.

Basic to Complex

Starting Simple for Creative Composition

Overview: *Start with simple elements to build complexity; create layers to keep elements separated for easy modifications; use a Live Paint group to organize many small details.*

1

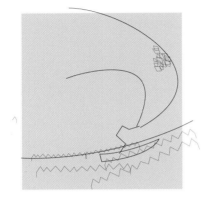

Rudmann's initial sketch to organize placement of his forms and their proportions, cropped to the artboard

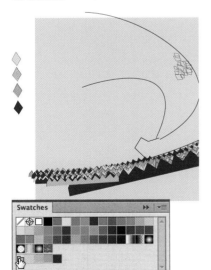

Creating diamonds and the color group

RUDMANN

When Andrew Rudmann set out to create the art piece "And Then I Swam," he began with a simple outline and a very few basic elements. He defined a color group, created clusters along with the basic elements, and then layered all of them to form more complex imagery. He also created a Live Paint group in order to draw forms without having to draw each path as a closed object. By slowly building complexity from very simple beginnings, he was able to control the results he sought to capture his vision.

1 Beginning with a simple sketch and simple objects. Rudmann began with the Pen tool (P), sketching the structure that would tell the story. Since he was going to create the water from a single diamond shape he would modify, he only needed to sketch the proportions and placement of his elements. He used the Artboard tool (Shift-O) to adjust the artboard to fit the composition.

He next auditioned his basic elements, coloring them and combining some of them into larger elements. To determine the colors for the piece, he first chose the background color: "My base color is usually very obnoxious, acidic, or uncomfortable, so I tend to dull down the other colors in the piece," he said. He selected his final choice of four colors and saved them as a color group (Boat) by clicking the New Color Group icon in the Swatches panel.

To keep the process of building up the art from basic elements as fluid as possible, he found a method that minimized working with panels and allowed him to keep his attention on the artboard. Selecting a diamond (or cluster of diamonds) that he wanted to duplicate and modify, he copied, used Paste in Front (or Back), and then used the Free Transform tool (E). He often ungrouped his clusters to freely modify and randomize a cluster by transforming some of the individual diamonds.

2 Using layers to organize complex objects. Despite working freely, Rudmann needed to be able to access portions of the image for modifications. The illusion of organic chaos and randomly placed elements requires some control, and separating sections with just a few layers, descriptively named, made all the difference as he worked. He could lock all the layers to prevent moving artwork already in place, and turn off visibility for some layers in order to concentrate on just one region without distraction. He created the illusion of depth and distance by placing small waves behind the big waves, yet kept each set of waves accessible by putting the smaller waves on a layer beneath the big waves. Rudmann sandwiched the man and his boat on a layer between the large and small diamond-shaped waves, and the big splash came last.

3 Using Live Paint to quickly fill the man with dripping water. After Rudmann drew the outlines for the boat and the man, he used the Pen tool to freely draw open paths for the dripping water on the man, and a few stripes to signify his bucket. So that he could fill the interior (white) areas where these paths overlapped, he turned them all into a Live Paint Group. He didn't have to draw fully enclosed objects before filling them, as long as the outlines overlapped and formed enclosed areas. (See the *Rethinking Construction* chapter for more on using Live Paint.)

2
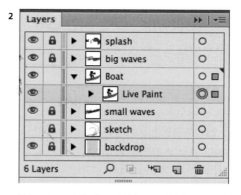
Using layers to lock and hide areas in the artwork in order to concentrate on a single area

3

A Live Paint Group allows for coloring objects without having to draw each of them as separate objects made from closed paths

Navigating Layers

Creating, Organizing, and Viewing Layers

Overview: *Customize Layers panel defaults; create layers and sublayers; move layers in the Layers panel's hierarchy; change layer colors; hide layers to view artwork.*

1

The completed layer structure showing master layers for web pages and their sublayers

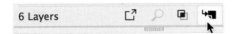

Option-clicking/Alt-clicking the Create New Sublayer icon opens the Layer Options dialog

---

Running on empty

If a layer contains any objects (or sublayers), a **>** or **V** arrow symbol will appear in front of the layer name in the Layers panel (unless you enable the Show Layers Only option in Layer Panel Options).

Layers are a great way to create and organize artwork as you work and view finished artwork when you're done. To design a mock-up of a web app for a local page on his www.cartagram.com website, Steve Gordon created the artwork for each page on its own layer. He was able to hide and show layers to see how the design of different pages looked when viewed in different sequences.

1 Changing the Layers panel defaults and creating sublayers. For his mock-up Gordon planned on creating a "master" layer for each page with separate sublayers for the artwork comprising the page header, navigation bar, content container, footer, and page background. To see more layers at once, he changed the default row height and turned off thumbnail display in the Layers panel. To set up layer options to look like Gordon's, select Layers Panel Options from the panel menu and choose Small from the Row Size list (if you prefer larger row sizes, simply disable the choices in the Thumbnails list). You can change the default layer name, "Layer 1," as Gordon did by double-clicking the layer name in the Layers panel.

To create sublayers within this first master layer, select the master layer in the panel and Option-click/Alt-click the Create New Sublayer icon at the bottom of the panel. In the Layer Options dialog, name the sublayer. Repeat this for each of the sublayers you need. Gordon completed the mock-up of the Home page by creating artwork on each of the sublayers.

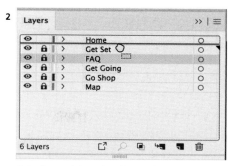

Selecting and dragging the FAQ layer above the Get Set layer

2 Duplicating and moving master layers, and changing the Layers panel display. With the first master layer completed, Gordon created master layers for other pages in his mock-up. If your design uses common artwork, like Gordon's page elements, consider duplicating a layer and then editing the artwork unique to that layer. To duplicate a layer, drag it to the panel's Create New Layer icon or select Duplicate from the Layers panel menu.

To change the order of your master layers or sublayers, select a layer (Shift-click to select contiguous layers or ⌘-click/Ctrl-click for non-contiguous layers) and drag it to the desired position in the Layers panel (watch the bar icon in the panel as you drag to make sure it's going between layers, not within another layer).

To make the Layers panel easier to navigate at a glance, give each master layer and its sublayers a unique color in the panel. For the master layer, double-click to the right of its name in the Layers panel and pick a color from the Color menu in the Layer Options dialog. For the sublayers, Shift-select them and choose Options for Selection from the panel menu.

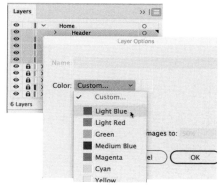

Top, selecting all sublayers; bottom, the Color menu in the Layer Options menu

3 Using the Visibility layer control to mimic user movement between pages. After Gordon completed mock-ups for each of the pages, he made all master layers visible in the Layers panel by choosing Show All Layers from the panel menu. Then Gordon clicked each layer's visibility (Eye) icon to hide its artwork, displaying the artwork of the page on the layer below it. This provided a preview of what users would see moving from one page to another, assuring that the design of the pages were compatible.

Left, all layers hidden except the Map layer; right, the Map web page artwork

Let Illustrator do the walking

Illustrator can automatically expand the Layers panel and scroll to a selected object within hidden layers; just select an object in your artwork and click the Locate Object icon.

Basic Appearances

Making and Applying Appearances

Overview: *Create appearance attributes for an object; build a two-stroke appearance, save it as a style, and then draw paths and apply the style; target a layer, create a drop shadow effect, create symbols in the layer, and then edit layer appearance if needed.*

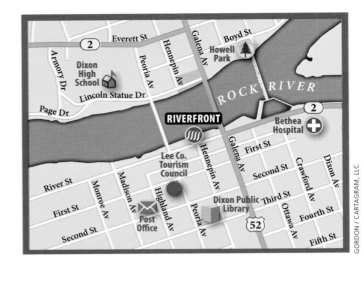

GORDON / CARTAGRAM, LLC

(Above) The river with blue fill; (below) the river with the Inner Glow effect added to the appearance attribute set

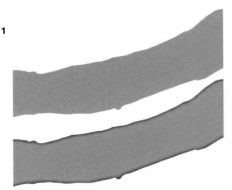

Appearance panel displaying the finished set of attributes with an Inner Glow effect applied

Complexity meets simplicity when you use Illustrator's full Appearance panel to design intricate effects, develop reusable styles, and simplify production workflow. For this map of downtown Dixon, Illinois, cartographer Steven Gordon built complex appearances and applied them to objects, groups, and layers.

1 **Building an appearance for a single object.** Gordon developed a set of appearance attributes that applied a soft vignette and blue fill to a shape representing the river. To begin building appearance attributes, open the Appearance panel and click the panel's Clear Appearance icon to clear all attributes in the shape you're about to draw (including Illustrator's default black stroke and white fill attributes). Gordon first drew the outline of the water with the Pen tool and then gave the path a medium-blue fill. To accentuate the shoreline, he applied a dark Inner Glow effect. To do this he opened the Appearance panel and clicked the Fill attribute. Then from the *fx* icon in the Appearance panel he chose Stylize> Inner Glow. In the Inner Glow dialog, he changed Mode to Multiply, set Opacity to 70%, and adjusted Blur to 0.05 inches (for the width of the vignette edge), making sure the Edge option was enabled. To finish the glow, he clicked the dialog's color swatch and chose black for the glow color.

2 Creating a style for your street paths. To create "cased" or outlined streets, make a multi-stroke style that you can apply to all streets. Gordon started by deselecting all objects and clicking the Clear Appearance icon to eliminate the attributes for the river he had created previously. To build cased streets like Gordon's, click the Stroke attribute and choose a light color swatch and a 2-pt width. Next, add a second stroke by clicking the Add New Stroke icon in the Appearance panel. Because the new stroke has the same attributes as the first stroke, select the bottom of the two strokes and change it to a darker color and a 3-pt width. To reuse this set of appearance attributes, open the Graphic Styles panel and Option-click/Alt-click the New Graphic Style icon at the bottom of the panel and then name your new style.

Appearance panel Gordon used to create the map's cased streets

3 Assigning a style to a group. If you apply a style like the cased streets to a selection of paths, the outline of a path will overlap and interrupt the outlines of paths below it. If you apply a style to a group of paths instead, the style will surround the group, merging strokes where they overlap. To do this, select the paths you wish to merge, then select and Group (⌘-G/Ctrl-G). Now make sure that Group is highlighted in the Appearance panel and apply your new cased streets style.

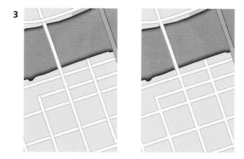

(Left) The streets with the style applied to the individual paths; (right) the style applied to street paths after they were grouped

4 Assigning appearance attributes to an entire layer. Instead of applying styles to individual objects, like the iconic "map symbols" on the map, Gordon applied a style to the layer itself and then added symbols to that layer. To do the same, create a layer for the symbols and click the layer's target indicator in the Layers panel. From the *fx* icon in the Appearance panel, select Stylize> Drop Shadow. Now each "map symbol" you draw or paste on that layer will be painted automatically with the drop shadow. You can modify the drop shadow by clicking the layer's targeting icon and then clicking the Drop Shadow attribute in the Appearance panel and changing values in the pop-up Drop Shadow dialog.

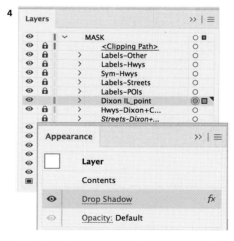

(Top) Targeting the layer in the Layers panel; (bottom) the Appearance panel showing the Drop Shadow attribute (double-click the attribute to edit Drop Shadow values)

Guides for Arcs

Designing with Guides, Arc, and Pen Tools

Overview: *Create guides on one side of the artboard; reflect and copy guides to the other side; create an arc with the Arc tool; cut and extend the arc with the Pen tool; reflect and copy the arc and join with the two arcs using the Pen tool; print templates using the Tile option.*

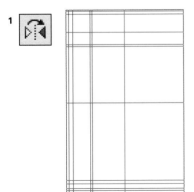

1

Reflect tool icon (top left); selected guides (colored magenta) that will be reflected and copied to the other side of the artboard

KLEMA

Tasked with building a garden gate as a functional sculpture for an outdoor exhibition on the grounds of the Norman Rockwell Museum, artist Stephen Klema sat down with Illustrator to create life-sized drawings that would serve as templates for cutting the sculpture's wood pieces.

1 Creating the document and positioning guides. To start, Klema made a new document with the same dimensions as those of the constructed gate (80" tall by 44" wide). Next, he turned on rulers (⌘-R/Ctrl-R) and dragged guides from the rulers. To position a guide more precisely, first make sure that guides are unlocked (go to View> Guides and choose Lock Guides if it has a check mark before its name), and select the guide and use the Control panel's Transform fields to enter values for the X or Y position of the guide on the artboard.

If your artwork will be symmetrical, like Klema's, you can create guides on one side of the document and then select and copy them to the other side. Start by creating a guide in the exact middle of the document. An easy way to do this is to drag a new guide from the ruler and, making sure that guides are still unlocked, click the Horizontal Align Center icon in the Control panel to center it horizontally on the artboard (be sure that you've chosen Align to Artboard in the Control panel). Next, activate Smart

Guides from the View menu (this will help position the cursor over the exact middle of the document). Finally, select all of the guides you've created, choose the Reflect tool (it's hidden under the Rotate tool icon) and Option-click/Alt-click the guide you created in the middle of the document. From the Reflect dialog, choose Vertical as the Axis and click the Copy button.

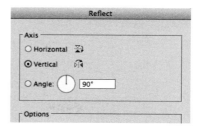

Clicking Vertical in the Reflect tool dialog

2 Drawing an arch. Klema turned to the Rectangle, Arc, Ellipse, and Pen tools to draw the different objects in his illustration. For the inner arch, Klema selected the Arc tool (hidden under the Line Segment tool) and double-clicked its icon to bring up the Arc Segment Tool Options dialog. Because he planned on drawing from the center guide outward to the left, Klema clicked the dialog's Base Along menu and selected the Y Axis option. Next, he clicked the center guide and dragged down and to the left until the arc was shaped the way he wanted. Depending on the shape of the arc you need, you may have to draw it wider or longer. If that's the case, you'll need to cut the arc with the Scissors tool as Klema did so that it fits the width of the arch shape you want. Next, extend the arc downward as a straight line by switching to the Pen tool, clicking the bottom endpoint of the arc, then Shift-clicking below to complete the straight line. Duplicate the extended arc using the Reflect tool and the center guide, just as you did in the previous step with the guides. Klema connected the bottom endpoints of the two extended arcs with the Pen tool, creating a single object.

On the left, the Arc tool icon; on the right, choosing Y Axis in Arc Segment Tool Options

The arc and the guides

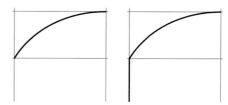

The arc after being cut with the Scissors tool on the left; on the right, the arc extended after drawing a vertical path with the Pen tool

3 Printing templates for construction. After drawing all the objects in his design, Klema printed the full illustration and separate illustrations of each of the gate parts (he used the Tile option in the Print dialog because the pieces were bigger than his printer paper). The prints served as templates that he traced on the wood so that he could precisely cut out the individual pieces of the gate. He used the full-sized illustration as a guide for assembling the gate parts into the finished sculpture.

Printed template pages assembled on wood

Auto-Scaling Art

Apply Effects and Graphic Styles to Resize

Overview: *Draw using picas and points to easily approximate feet and inches; calculate units to work with and amounts to scale by; apply a Transform effect to duplicate, scale, and move artwork in one step, and duplicate the effect to apply different settings; use a Graphic Style to save effect settings.*

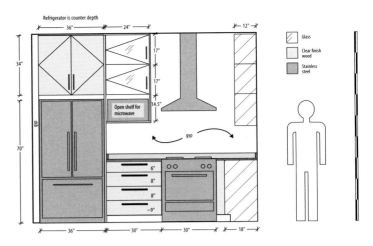

Kitchen West Elevation

WIGHAM

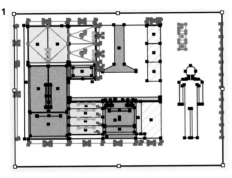

The "master" drawing nearly complete before adding the Transform effect

Getting targeted to move

To target the master layer for an effect, be sure to click directly on the layer's target (circle) and note that the square is large and the Appearance panel shows "Layer" as the selected item. If you're not really careful, you might accidentally apply an effect to an object or sublayer, instead of applying it to the master layer.

As she was designing a kitchen, Laurie Wigham learned she needed to provide others with the same model at different sizes: She worked at 1 pica to the foot, but the builders needed plans at 1/2" to a foot and the city wanted large prints. She chose the Transform effect to duplicate and scale her art so that changes made to her original plan would automatically be updated in the scaled version.

1 **Setting the scale for the architectural drawing.** To create and visualize objects in their real-world inches and feet, Wigham set Illustrator's measurement units to picas—there are 12 points per pica, so each point represented one inch and each pica one foot. She drew most of the artwork, including the keys, selected it all, and chose Object> Artboards> Fit to Artwork Bounds. When she needed to submit rough plans to her contractor, she needed to figure out how to get from this small version to the 1/2"= 1' scale. She first changed her ruler to inches and noticed that 1/2" (which would represent 1' in the larger scale) = 3 picas. Therefore if 1 pica = 1', she would need to multiply by 3 (300%) to get 3 picas to equal 1'. She then noted the width of her artboard (2.63 inches) so that plus a bit more for space gave her an approximate distance to use for moving the copy she was going to make.

2 Targeting for the Transform effect. For the Transform effect to duplicate art to other artboards as new objects are added to it, all the art has to be within a master layer, and the master layer itself must be targeted. Once an effect is properly applied to a targeted master layer, any objects added to the layers within will automatically inherit that effect (see Tip "Getting targeted to move" opposite).

3 Applying the Transform effect. With the layer targeted, Wigham clicked the *fx* icon at the bottom of the Appearance panel and chose Distort & Transform> Transform. Wigham anchored the transformation reference point to the upper-left corner (an easy reference point to work from), set the distance for the move and the amount to scale it by (300%), and entered 1 for copies. To check everything was working properly for the transform, she enabled Preview. Once Wigham saw that her artwork duplicated and scaled properly, she clicked OK. To preserve the effect to apply it any time in the future that she needed this same transformation, she created a Graphic Style (Option-click/Alt-click the New Graphic Style icon in the Graphic Styles panel to name it while adding it). Now she could freely edit, add, and subtract objects in her kitchen's West Elevation. The objects on this artboard weren't selectable or directly editable, but would print. When her plan was finished, she drew an artboard around the scaled artwork and printed it.

To make a version for the city permits, she duplicated the effect in the Appearance panel by dragging it to the Duplicate Selected Item icon. She turned off the visibility for the first instance. She next drew an 11"x17" artboard roughly 20 points to the left from the other side of her master artboard (so the master was now between the two scaled versions). She double-clicked the Transform effect to open the dialog, and this time played with the settings in the dialog until her drawing filled the page. She saved this as another Graphic Style. With both Transform effects in the Appearance panel, she toggled their visibility each time she needed one scaled version or another.

2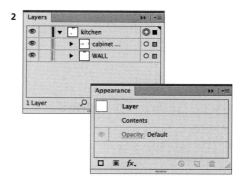

Indicators in Layers and Appearance panels showing the master layer targeted (not just objects)

3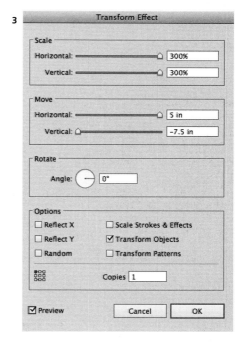

Setting up to duplicate, scale, and move artwork with the Transform effect—the Vertical setting is for viewing on the monitor only, serving no other practical purpose

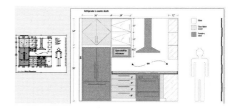

Artboards after creating the 1/2" to 1' scaled model of the elevation

George Coghill

Cartoon logo and character artist George Coghill works with two distinct sets of tools to create cartoon logos—one set for the character art, and one for the design and type elements. He's able to be even more productive now that his workspace presets include Custom Tools panels. Coghill starts cartoon logo creation with the character art, using the more organic creation tools such as the Pen tool, various Brushes, the Width tool, and the Shape Builder tool. Once the vector art for the character is complete, he then designs the full logo using the Type tool and multiple Shape tools. He includes the Pen and Selection tools in both environments. Coghill began this by creating a custom Toolbar via Window> Toolbars> New Tool (find Toolbars listed below Control). In the dialog he customized the name "Art Tools" and clicked OK. Next, he clicked ••• at the bottom of the new toolbar to open the toolbar drawer and click-dragged each desired tool from the drawer onto his new custom panel. Coghill arranged his desired layout of panels best suited for character creation (Appearance, Brushes, Swatches, Color, Layers, and Graphic Styles) and saved this new workspace configuration by choosing Window> Workspace> New Workspace, customizing the name to "Character Design" and clicking OK to save the workspace. He repeated this process for his desired custom tools and workspace panel arrangement for the logo design aspect of the creation process. Coghill can then work in a customized vector art environment suited perfectly to the task at hand and switch between the toolsets with ease.

COGHILL

2

Designing Type & Layout

Designing Type & Layout

This chapter focuses on tips and tricks related to working with the type tools, as well as design and layout. While *Chapter 1* covers the basics of working with multiple artboards, this chapter expands on some of the more advanced issues of working with multiple artboards.

The many CS6 & CC Type panels

Once you create a text object with the Type tool, before you go hunting for one of the 7 type-related panels, check to see if what you need appears in the Control panel. If you're on **CC**, you'll also have the more robust Properties panel to check. If you still want or need a more specialized type panel, access all of them from the Window> Type submenu. Here, you'll also find panels for OpenType, Tabs, and Glyphs. (For more about the Properties panel see the **CC** section in the *Chapter 1* intro.)

Character	⌘T
Character Styles	
Glyphs	
OpenType	⌥⇧⌘T
Paragraph	⌥⌘T
Paragraph Styles	
Tabs	⇧⌘T

The quick-changing Type tool

When using the regular Type tool, look at your cursor carefully in these situations:

- If you move the regular Type tool over a closed path, the cursor changes to the Area Type icon.
- If you move the Type tool over an open path, the cursor changes to the Type on a Path icon.

BY DEFAULT NEW TYPE IS ALWAYS BLACK

It doesn't matter what Fill and Stroke display as your Proxy swatches; as soon as you begin a new text object it defaults to Black Fill with a Stroke of None. With your text object or characters selected, you can restyle as you wish, or use the Eyedropper tool to pick up basic Fill and Stroke colors. If the Eyedropper doesn't work, double-click the Eyedropper tool to enable Character Style under Picks Up.

THREE TYPES OF TYPE

There are three kinds of type objects in Illustrator: *Point type*, *Area type*, and *Path type*. The Type tool lets you click to create a Point type object, click-drag to create a box for an Area type object, or click on a path to create Path type. (See the **CC** section later in this chapter intro for details on how to convert Point type to and from Area type.) Click within any existing type object to enter or edit text. To exit type editing mode, press the Esc key; to be poised to start creating or editing another type object, hold down the ⌘/Ctrl key (temporarily turning your cursor into a Selection tool) and click outside the text block, or reselect the Text tool. When manipulating type, be aware of these features:

- **Point type never wraps** to a new line. To add another line of text without also adding a new paragraph (so your paragraph style applies to all the lines), press the Shift-Return/Enter key. Use Return/Enter to add another line as a new paragraph (so you can change paragraph styles).

To scale Point type, use the Selection tool to select the type and drag on one of the handles of the bounding box. Both the type and the bounding box scale together. Use modifier keys as you would with any object to constrain proportions or scale from the center.

- **Area type automatically wraps** to the next line. Use the Return/Enter key to start a new paragraph within an Area type object.

  To scale Area type, use the Selection tool to scale just the bounding box itself; the type will reflow inside the area but remain the same size. To scale the bounding box *and* the type, press (E) for Free Transform (add Shift to constrain), then drag on the bounding box handles.

  Create a custom container for Area type by constructing a path with any tool. With a closed path, choose either of the Area Type tools and click on the path (not inside the object) to place text within the confines of the path. Hold down the Option/Alt key to create Area type with an open path when the Area Type tool is not selected.

  Use the Direct Selection tool to distort a container object for Area type by grabbing an anchor point and dragging on it, or reshape the path by adjusting direction handles. The text within your Area type object will reflow to fit the new shape of the confining object.

  Use the Area Type Options dialog (Type> Area Type Options) to gain precise control over a number of important aspects of Area type, such as numerical values for the width and height, precise values for rows and columns, offset options, the alignment of the first baseline of text, and how text flows between rows or columns (by choosing one of the Text Flow options).

- **Path type flows text** along the path of an object. Create Path type by clicking on a path with the Type tool; the path becomes unstroked and unfilled and ready for text.

  A Path type object has three brackets—the beginning bracket, which has an *in port*; a center bracket; and an end bracket, which has an *out port*. Use the ports to thread text between objects (see Tip "Ports defined" later in the chapter). Use the center bracket to control positioning the type along the path.

  To place type on a path, hold your cursor over the path until the cursor displays a curvy line through the I-beam.

Scale text frames only

By default, Illustrator's Scale tool scales both the text frame *and* its contents. To scale the text frame alone, Direct-Select it first. Then use the Scale tool, or scale it manually using the bounding box.
—*Jean-Claude Tremblay*

Turning the corner—Path type

When type on a tightly curved path is squeezed together or spread apart, choose Type> Type on a Path> Type on a Path Options and choose Center from the Align to Path menu. Set Baseline Shift to 0 in the Character panel, and move the path until the type is where you want it on the page.
—*Steven H. Gordon*

DONAL JOLLEY

Type on a Path graphic by Donal Jolley

Path type and closed paths

Although the Type tool cursor feedback seems to indicate that you can only apply Path type to open paths, you actually *can* apply Path type to both open and closed paths; hold Option/Alt to see the cursor change from the Area Type icon to the Type on a Path icon (it looks slightly different in **CC**).

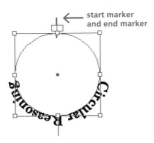

start marker
and end marker

Each Path type object has two handles (the start marker and the end marker), so be aware if you apply Path type to a circle with Align Center chosen, those start and end handles appear together at the top of the circle (see the next figure for how to fix this)

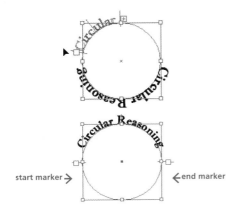

start marker → ← end marker

To center your text between the start and end markers positioned on the top portion of a circle (when it looks like the top figure on this page), grab the start marker handle and drag it to the 9 o'clock position, and then drag the end marker handle to the 3 o'clock position

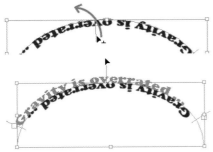

To manually flip type on a path to the other side of the path: select the type and drag the center handle (the thin blue line perpendicular to the type) across the path, as indicated by the red arrow above and the tiny T-shaped icon that appears next to the cursor as you position it near the handle; you can also flip type by choosing Type> Type on a Path> Type on a Path Options, enabling the Flip box, and clicking OK

Dragging the center bracket along the path moves the type toward the beginning or end. Dragging across the path flips the type to the other side of the path. For example, type running outside of a circle will flip to the inside.

To automatically reflow type along a path, use the Direct Selection tool to reshape the path. Set or adjust Path type attributes with the Type on a Path Options dialog (Type> Type on a Path> Type on a Path Options). Choose different Type on a Path effects (such as Rainbow or Stair Step), enable Flip to automatically flip type to the other side of the path, set the alignment of type relative to the path, and use a Spacing control to adjust the type as it moves around a curve. You can also access Type on a Path effects through the Type> Type on a Path submenu.

WORKING WITH THREADED TEXT

If an Area type or Path type object contains more text than it can display, you'll see a red plus sign indicating a loaded *out port* (see Tip "Ports defined" opposite).

To enlarge an Area type object or a Path type object on an enclosed path, allowing for more text, use the Selection tool to grab the object by a bounding side, and drag to resize it. To lengthen a path for Path type, either use the Direct Selection tool to select the last anchor and drag the path longer, or use the Pen tool to start drawing more of the path from the last anchor and then drag the end bracket to the new end of the path. Following are more techniques for dealing with threaded text:

- **To add a new text object to receive overflow text,** use the Selection tool to select the first text object. Next, click on the *out port*; your cursor changes to the "loaded text" cursor. Click on the artboard to create a new text object the same size and shape as the original (this works nicely for custom shapes), or drag to create a rectangular text object of any size. The new text object is *threaded* (linked) to the original, flowing text into the second.

- **To link existing text objects together,** click the *out port* on the first object and then click on the path of the object that will receive the overflow text. (Keep your eye on the cursor, which will change to indicate valid "drop" locations.) You can also link objects using a menu command: Select both objects and choose Type> Threaded Text> Create, and the objects become linked.

- **To disconnect one type object from another,** select the object and double-click its *in port* to break the thread to a preceding object, or double-click its *out port* to break the thread to a subsequent object. Alternatively, you can select the object and click once on either the *in port* or the *out port*. Then click on the other end of the thread to break the link.
- **To release a type object from a text thread,** select it and then choose Type> Threaded Text> Release Selection. Or, to remove the threading from an object while leaving the text in place, select it and choose Type> Threaded Text> Remove Threading.

WRAPPING AREA TYPE AROUND OBJECTS

Text wrapping is controlled as an object attribute and is set specifically for each object that will have Area type wrapped around it. These *wrap objects* affect only Area type objects that are both within the same layer and below it in the Layers panel, and do *not* affect Point type or Path type. To make a selected object into a wrap object, choose Object> Text Wrap> Make. To change options for the wrap object, keep it selected and choose Object> Text Wrap> Text Wrap Options. Here, you'll choose the amount of offset, and/or can choose Invert Wrap to reverse how the text wraps around the object.

FORMATTING TEXT

While the Character and Paragraph panels let you format text one attribute at a time, the Character Styles and Paragraph Styles panels allow you to apply multiple attributes with one click. With the Type tool or a text object selected, you can modify type options in the Character and Paragraph sections of the Control panel. In **CC** you can also access some features via the Properties panel or click • • • to access full versions of those panels.

When handling ducks you must always wear protective arm and hand covering. Many unwary duck trainers have lost fingers and even hands and suffered deep puncture wounds from careless handling methods or even brief inattention.

Some of the as the Hookbill, Orpington will and have been burns from the feathers of important that only expert close handling.

more docile breeds such Bali, Muscovy and Buff allow some minor handling even known to cuddle. Acid ducks can be serious so it is handlers attempt such

One particularly nasty Welsh Harlequin. Aptly this uncommon bird has unusual characteristic of itself behind curtains of grass only out and deliver lines in a from Shakespeare's unsuspecting animal

breed is the named, the hiding to jump melodramatic style sonnets whenever an approaches

DONAL JOLLEY

Artist Donal Jolley wrapped Area text around this duck by placing the duck above the text and choosing Object> Text Wrap> Make

Also the Touch Type Tool

In CC, in addition to being able to format text characters with the Type and Paragraph tools, you have the Touch Type tool. See the **CC** section at the end of this intro for details on using this tool.

Avoiding formatting overrides

When your project calls for several text objects using the same font, consider using a custom paragraph style. Created properly, this prevents Illustrator from applying the default, [Normal Paragraph Style], to all your new text and then adding formatting overrides to apply your specific font attributes. (Using the Control panel, you will merely be creating formatting overrides that must then be cleared in order to apply a different font with different attributes.)

- If you'll use the same font attributes in several documents, you can create a New Document Profile that will always include your preferred font attributes as part of the [Normal Paragraph Style]. (See more about profiles in the *Chapter 1* intro.)
- If you only need to change the font for a single document, double-click [Normal Paragraph Style] and modify the default for just this document, or create a new paragraph style.

—*Cristen Gillespie*

An open document always has a paragraph style applied to it even before there's any text, so if you select the Type tool and modify its attributes in the Control panel, Illustrator thinks you're intending to modify the default, [Normal Paragraph Style]. A plus sign next to the style name in the Paragraph Styles panel indicates you've applied extra formatting, or *overrides*. To avoid unneeded overrides, work with styles wherever possible, and see the Tip "Avoiding formatting overrides" at left.

- **To create a style based on existing formatting,** format the text as you want it to appear, select it, and click the New Style button (Option-click/Alt-click to name the style). The selected attributes define the new style.
- **To create a new style based on another,** highlight the style you want to copy and click the Create New Style icon. Hold Option/Alt when you click to name and/or customize the style.
- **To rename a style,** double-click the name in the panel for inline editing.
- **To apply a paragraph style to text,** just insert your cursor into the paragraph you want to format and click the name of the style in the Paragraph Styles panel. After first applying a style, to remove any overrides click again on the plus beside the Paragraph style name.
- **To apply a character style,** select characters you want to style and click a style name in the Character Styles panel.
- In **CC** you can also use the Touch Type tool (see the **CC** section later in this chapter introduction for more about the Touch Type tool).

USING THE EYEDROPPER WITH TYPE

The Eyedropper tool lets you copy styling and appearance attributes from one type object to another. Double-click the Eyedropper tool to specify in Eyedropper Options which attributes the tool will pick up or apply. Attributes you can specify include character styles and/or paragraph styles, as well as type *object* Appearance attributes (see the next section, "Using the Appearance Panel with Type" for more about Character versus Type attributes).

For a one-step method, select the type object with appearance attributes you want to change, and then move the Eyedropper tool over the unselected type object that has the attributes you want and click it.

Alternatively, the Eyedropper tool works in another mode: *sampling* and *applying*. A small **T** means it is in position to sample or apply text attributes. To copy text formatting from one object to another using the Eyedropper tool, position it over an unselected type object. When it angles downward to the left, click the type object to pick up its attributes.

Now position the Eyedropper tool over the unselected text object to which you want to apply the attributes, and hold down the Option/Alt key. In applying mode, it angles downward to the right and looks full. To apply the attributes that you just sampled, move the cursor to the text you want to change and click. (A simple click will apply the sampled attributes to the whole paragraph; you can also drag the cursor to apply the attributes only to the specific text you dragged over.)

USING THE APPEARANCE PANEL WITH TYPE

When you work with type, you work with the letter characters or with the container that holds the characters—or both. Understanding the difference between characters and their container (the "type object") will help you both access and edit the right one when you style type. To help understand the difference, you'll need to watch the Appearance panel as you work. (See the *Chapter 1* intro for details about Appearance panel basics.)

Type characters

Type characters entered with the Type tool are by default styled with a Black Fill and No Stroke. To edit a character's fill and stroke, drag across the text with the Type tool or double-click "Characters" in the Appearance panel.

You can't do the following to type *characters* (although in the section "Type objects" following you *will* be able to do these things to a type *object*): move the stroke under

DONAL JOLLEY

*Artist Donal Jolley had to convert type to outlines in order to reshape the **U** and **N** type characters*

The appearance of stroked text

To stroke type without distorting the characters, select the type using a Selection tool (*not* a Type tool), select Add New Stroke in the Appearance panel, then move this new stroke *below* the Characters.

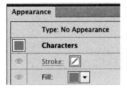

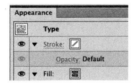

The Appearance panel showing the green fill applied to the type at the Character level

The Appearance panel showing the pattern Mezzotint Irregular (from the Decorative_Ornaments pattern library) with a Fill at the Type object level

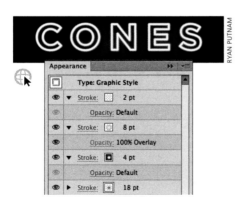

RYAN PUTNAM

A graphic style created using the Appearance panel with multiple fills and strokes applied to live type—for more details see Ryan Putnam's "Frosty" Gallery later in this chapter

the fill or fill above the stroke; apply a live effect to the fill or stroke; apply a gradient fill; add multiple fills or strokes.

Type objects

The Type object contains all the text in a Point, Area, or Path type object. You are working with the type "object" when you select the text with the Selection tool and then move the object around on your page.

With the text object you can add another fill (click the Add New Fill icon in the Appearance panel). Now there is another listing of Stroke and Fill, in the Appearance panel, but this time they are positioned above the Characters line in the panel. If you reveal the Stroke and Fill for the type by double-clicking the Characters line in the panel, you return to character editing; reselect the type object with the Selection tool to return to editing the type object rather than its characters.

When you add a new Stroke or Fill to the type object, its color and effects may mask or interact with the color of the characters. All the strokes and fills applied to type are layered on top of those listed below (including on top of the stroke and fill you see listed when you double-click Characters in the panel). So if you add a new fill to the type object and apply white to it, the type appears white (the white fill of the type object is stacked above the black default fill of the characters).

CONVERTING TYPE TO OUTLINES

You can now keep type live and editable while being able to perform many effects that once required you to outline type. Using the Appearance panel you can apply multiple strokes to characters, run type along a curve, use envelopes to distort type, and even mask with live, editable type. In the **CC** section later in this intro, see how the Touch Type tool lets you transform individual characters.

In addition, fonts at small sizes or with fine details still won't look as good on the computer screen, or print as clearly at resolutions of 600 dots per inch or less as outlines, as they would if you kept them as fonts.

However, following are some cases when you might still find the need to outline your type:

- **Convert to outlines to graphically transform or distort type.** If Warp Effects and Envelopes don't create the effect you need (see examples in this chapter and in the *Reshaping Dimensions* chapter for examples of warps and envelopes), then outlining your type will allow you to edit the individual curves and anchor points of letters or words. Your type will no longer be editable as type, but instead will be constructed of standard Illustrator Bézier curves that are editable just like any other object. Type converted to outlines may include compound paths to form the "holes" in the outlined letter forms (such as the see-through centers of an **O**, **B**, or **P**). Choose Object> Compound Path> Release to fill the "holes" with color.
- **Convert to outlines to maintain your letter and word spacing when exporting type** to another application, as many programs don't support the translation of custom kerning and word spacing.
- **Convert to outlines if you can't distribute the font to your client or service bureau,** when you don't have permission to embed the fonts, or when your service bureau doesn't have its own license for a font.

THE GLYPHS PANEL

The Glyphs panel (Window> Type> Glyphs) provides quick access to many special characters, including any ligatures, ornaments, swashes, and fractions included with a given font. Use the list box to narrow your search of a font for the type of letterform you're seeking. With the Type tool, click to place the insertion point, and then double-click the character you want in the Glyphs panel to insert it in the text (also see the "Alternate Glyphs and Stylistic Sets" in the **CC** section later in this chapter).

ADVANCED FEATURES OF MULTIPLE ARTBOARDS

This section focuses on some of the advanced features of working with artboards. To learn about the basics of artboard creation, management, and output, please start with

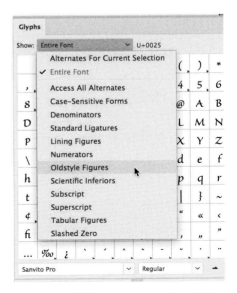

You can use the Show pop-up menu to restrict the visible character set in the Glyphs panel

SMALL CAPS
SMALL CAPS
SMALL CAPS

Illustrator's Small Caps option (in the Character panel menu) converts all selected characters to small caps (top). However, if true-drawn small caps aren't available in a font, Illustrator creates the fake, scaled-down version (middle), which is a typographic taboo. To prevent Illustrator from creating fake small caps, go to File> Document Setup> Type> Options, and change the Small Caps percentage from 70% to 100%. This option is used *only* when Illustrator is faking small caps, so when your small caps are the size of capital letters, you'll instantly recognize it (bottom). This option doesn't persist between documents, so you'll have to choose it each time. (Go to **http://www.creativepro.com/content/typetalk-small-caps-illustrator** to read the full article.)
—*Ilene Strizver, The Type Studio*

Working with artboards

To rename artboards, double-click their name in the panel. In **CC** you can resize an artboard from its center by holding Option/Alt as you drag with the Artboard tool.

the "Managing Multiple Artboards" section in the introduction to *Chapter 1*.

Duplicating elements to artboards

Among the more common functions you'll need when you're working in a multiple artboard document is the duplication of elements on multiple pages. Following are some of the ways you can simulate some of the functions of working with "master pages":

- **To duplicate elements when adding another artboard,** select the Artboard tool, enable "Move/Copy Artwork with Artboard," and hold down the Option/Alt key while dragging an active artboard to a new location.
- **Turn artwork created on one artboard into a symbol,** and then drag that symbol from the shared Symbols panel to any other artboard. Now just update the symbol to update all instances of it used on any artboards.
- **To copy "instances" of artwork to another artboard,** use the Transform effect.
- **To copy objects to all other artboards** in the same relative location, use Paste on All Artboards.
- **To move or copy the artwork a specified distance,** measure the distance between the artwork and where you want it on another artboard. Then use Transform> Move and enter the measurement in the Distance input.

Managing artboards

This section covers some of the features that help you keep your artboards organized. One trick that's sure to save you time: When you're done using the Artboard tool, press the Esc key to return to the tool you were previously using.

- **To renumber artboards using the Artboard panel,** either drag artboard names to rearrange them, or highlight one artboard and click the up or down arrow icons. Renumbering artboards can be very helpful if you're using them for presentations and storyboarding.
- **Rearrange artboard positions** using either the Artboard panel menu or Object> Artboards> Rearrange. (In **CC**, you can also access Rearrange All from the Quick Actions

section of the Properties panel.) A dialog lets you determine the order in which they repeat, whether across the monitor or down (their layout), how far apart they are placed, how many columns they're in, and whether or not the artwork is moved with them.

- **Convert any rectangle to an artboard** using Object> Artboard> Convert to Artboard. Or use Object> Path> Split Into Grid to create several rectangles from one before converting them all to artboards.
- **To save artboards as separate files,** choose Save As> Illustrator Options to select "Save each artboard to a separate file," and choose All or enter a range of artboards.

Exporting and printing multiple artboards

All artboards in a file share the same print options, including color mode, bleed settings, and scale, and you can choose to print either to a PDF file or to a printer. In the Print dialog, print artboards as separate pages (the default), or ignore artboards and tile the artwork.

- **Print to PDF** always flattens the file. But you can choose the media, such as screen or slide, ignoring the actual artboard size—this is useful for presentations. Or you can scale the artwork to fit your media, among many other features found in the Print to PDF dialog.
- **Save As PDF** preserves transparency, editing capabilities, and top-level layers, and you can set a level of security.
- **Print only some artboards** using the Range setting. Scale them to fit your print media if desired.
- **Print artboards with landscape orientation, or a mix of landscape and portrait,** with Auto-Rotate when portrait is selected for the media. If your media is landscape-oriented, Auto-Rotate is disabled.
- **When printing pages in which two or more artboards are overlapping the same artwork,** each artboard will print with whichever portions of the artwork are visible within that artboard.
- **If your artwork overlaps multiple artboards,** each artboard will print only the artwork that is visible within its artwork bounds.

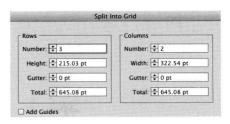

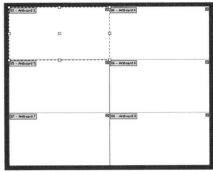

After drawing a rectangle, choosing Split into Grid (original purple stroke is preserved), and Convert to Artboard

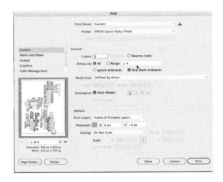

The Print dialog's opening section, allowing you to choose which artboards to print, to ignore artboards and print all on one page, whether to rotate, scale, tile, or print all layers, not just the visible layers

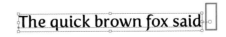

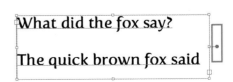

Point type (top) indicated by a hollow widget, converts to Area type (bottom), indicated by a solid widget

Boquete

THE 2013 TRAVEL GUIDE

GORDON / CARTAGRAM, LLC

Using the Touch Type tool to interactively rotate, scale, and position text characters while they remain within one editable block of text (see Steve Gordon's lesson in the CC lesson and gallery section, later in this chapter)

Limits to the Touch Type tool

The Touch Type tool works on only one character at a time, but several characters may be affected by a single transformation. You can't reposition a character past the first character to its left. You can't skew or flip a character. Characters added within a word will take on any transformation of the character preceding them, unless you first select a following character, effectively replacing it with a new glyph, then type it in again.

If Touch Type is hidden

If you don't see the Touch Type Tool in the Character panel or by clicking Character in the Control panel, toggle on Show Touch Type Tool from a Character panel menu (if it's on you can also access

the icon from ••• in the Character section of the Properties panel).

NEW TYPE FEATURES IN ILLUSTRATOR CC

Convert Point type to Area and vice versa

In **CC** if you select a Point or Area type object with the Selection tool, a circle-shaped widget appears on the right side of the bounding box. Double-click the widget to toggle that type object from Point type (hollow circle) to Area type (solid circle), or vice versa. You can also toggle between the two from Type> Convert (if no type selected, the menu item says Type Conversion). The flow of the type doesn't change; soft returns are added to Area type paragraphs to maintain the appearance, and overset text is deleted. Once you convert type, you can edit it for a different fit by removing soft returns in Point type or by adjusting Area type's bounding box to reflow text.

TOUCH TYPE TRANSFORMATIONS

Illustrator combined the on-screen interactivity of the Transform bounding box with the ability to use the Character panel to individually rotate, scale, and position characters, and came up with the Touch Type tool. To adjust a letter, choose the Touch Type tool from the Type icon in the Tools panel (Shift-T). Alternatively, click the Touch Tool icon in the Character panel or the Character section of the Control panel (if the tool isn't visible in panels, toggle on Show Touch Type tool from the Character panel menu). The tool is designed to work with any input device (including your fingers on touch-enabled devices), but there are some limitations to what you can do with it. Unlike using the Character panel to rotate and scale characters, the Touch Type tool lets you directly transform one character at a time. You can't flip or skew characters with the Touch Type tool, but without having to numerically calculate anything, simply click to select a character with the Touch Type tool, and start to transform it. To quickly return to a "neutral" position, create a character style for the base settings before you start playing with the Touch Type tool. To reset the entire text block and remove all character formatting, choose Reset Panel from the Character panel's pop-up menu.

FINDING THE RIGHT FONT

Illustrator offers a great deal of control when searching for the right font. You can start by choosing any of the search parameters, and then you can continue to add or modify parameters to further narrow the list of results. If you know the name of an installed font, or part of it, you can simply begin typing in the Search field in the Character panel or the Character section of the Control or Properties panel. You can further narrow your results using the drop-down list to restrict the search to just the first word. By default, Illustrator will search through an entire font name, so typing just a portion of a name can produce fonts that are completely unrelated to the desired font.

But perhaps you know you're looking for a Pro font, but you can't remember more of its name. However, you do know it's a serif font. With Fonts underlined in blue (active), you can use the Filter options below it to restrict your search, starting on the left with choosing a classification—in this case, Serif. Narrow your search still further by choosing a property, such as the font weight or if it's uppercase only, also in the same classification filter.

Continue to refine your search with icons that find fonts: from those you marked as Favorites (star); that you recently added (clock); and/or that are Adobe Fonts with Show Activated fonts (cloud with a checkmark).

For access to more fonts, switch your search from the Font tab to the Find More tab. For this feature, you do need an internet connection, because now Illustrator will start searching within Adobe Fonts. All the rest of the Search section is the same, although searching for favorites or those recently downloaded doesn't make sense when you're searching for new fonts on Adobe Fonts.

Once your search criteria produce a list you think is useful, you're ready to make a selection from the list if you know precisely what you're looking for, or to browse the list to see what might suit. The font list offers you a choice of text previews in the drop-down list to the right of the Filters icons. Not only can you choose what text to see, but you can choose how large the preview should be

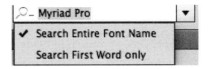

Using the disclosure triangle to reveal a choice when restricting a font search

Searching your installed fonts for the right font by filtering your list—from left to right by (font) Classification, Favorites, Recently Added, and Activated (Adobe Fonts); to the right of a font's name (not shown) are Show Similar and Add to Favorites, followed by the type of font

Highlight substituted fonts

Highlighting substituted fonts (Preferences> Type) is now global, rather than document-specific. It's enabled by default. Substituted fonts in your document will be highlighted in pink.

Illustrator's placeholder text

You can have Illustrator automatically fill in *Lorem Ipsum* placeholder text as soon as you create a new type object by enabling Fill New Type Objects With Placeholder Text in Preferences> Type (it's enabled by default). Or use Type> Fill With Placeholder Text to fill the desired space as needed.

Packaging Adobe Fonts

When you package a document to send to an outside printer, Adobe Fonts cannot be included, so if the printer doesn't have a subscription to the font service or own the fonts themselves, you may have to send it as PDF, or outline the fonts.

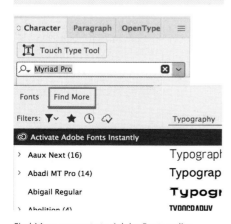

Find More connects to Adobe Fonts online

without having to leave the search results to set these. But better still is to set some type in your document that represents what you'll be placing. You also have the option to use *Lorem Ipsum* placeholder text.

Along with previewing your type live or using the preview proxy in the list, you'll notice as you hover over the right side of the list that three more icons appear. Click the first icon to have Illustrator search for fonts similar to the one you clicked. If your search field shows the full name of any font and you have filter criteria selected, you can click the star icon to mark a font as a favorite. On the far right Illustrator displays the type of font, such as True Type, Open Type, Adobe Font (the cloud icon), etc.

Using Adobe Fonts

Adobe Fonts (formerly Typekit) greatly expands your access to professional fonts by making all their fonts available with any Creative Cloud subscription, without any limit to the number of fonts you can activate. Fonts activated from the Cloud are stored on your computer in a way that allows you to use them when offline, but you don't own them. You can quickly activate missing fonts if they're from Adobe Fonts—so long as you have an active connection. You might wish to embed the fonts in a print-ready PDF or to create outlines in Illustrator. Be sure to check with the printer to know which method to use.

Missing fonts

When you open a document without having all the fonts installed, the Missing Fonts dialog will automatically open and display the names of the missing fonts. If any of the missing fonts are Adobe Fonts, you'll see the word "Available" beneath the font name and a check mark on the right under Activate Missing Fonts. To directly activate the missing fonts from Adobe Fonts, click the Activate Fonts button. If you see "Default font substituted for missing font," then the fonts are not available from Adobe Fonts. If you don't have the fonts and if the fonts aren't available from Adobe, you can either click the Find Font button to close Missing Fonts and open Find Font (to find and replace missing fonts), or you can Close the dialog.

In the Find Fonts dialog (accessible at any time from the Type menu), you can choose to replace the current font with another from the document, your recent fonts list, or your system. If the missing font is on your system, check to see if it's inactive and then activate it. If the missing font is an Adobe Font you didn't activate when you opened the document, choose Resolve Missing Fonts from the Type menu to activate that font (quick and easy), or use Find Fonts if you want to replace it with another font. To see a large thumbnail for a replacement font that you have installed, you can context-click its name in the dialog. As soon as you have either synced your missing font or replaced it with another, the font preview is updated in both the document and the Find Font or Missing Fonts dialog. Once you've replaced all your missing fonts and like the results, click Done to dismiss the dialog.

When you choose Type> Find Font with no fonts missing, the dialog still lists all the fonts in the document, and you can choose Save List to generate a .txt file with the document name already set as the default name.

Alternate Glyphs and Stylistic Sets

In **CC** you can access individual alternate glyphs directly in the document. Highlight a character in your text and Illustrator will display any alternates it can find for that character. Click one to apply it to the character

You can still use the Open Type panel to apply some types of glyphs automatically, such as ligatures, swashes, and titling alternates. However, the Open Type panel also provides access to Stylistic Sets. These are groups of alternates that have been created by the designer to use as alternates for an Open Type font. Click the "stacked 'a' block" icon in the bottom right to choose which Stylistic Set or Sets to apply to your text. More than one set can be applied at the same time, and the results can be unexpected if you don't look at the list carefully to make sure you didn't forget to disable an unwanted set.

The Missing Fonts dialog opens whenever any fonts are missing, but you can only reactivate Adobe Fonts in this dialog. Use Find Fonts for missing fonts

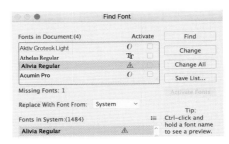

The Find Font dialog lets you access your hard drive to find and replace fonts that aren't Adobe Fonts and so can't be activated in the Missing Fonts dialog

Applying alternate glyphs

Previewing Stylistic Sets

To most easily compare available stylistic set(s), highlight a word or more, and then enable and disable one set at a time to preview the stylistic changes. Once you've found a set or combination of sets you like, save it as a character or paragraph style to be able to quickly apply those stylistic changes to additional text.

Graphic Novel Cover Design

Illustrator as a Stand-Alone Layout Tool

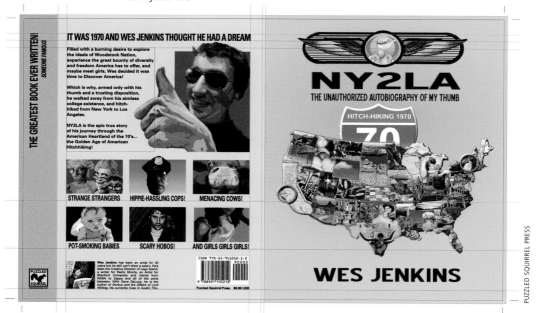

Overview: *Set your document's dimensions and bleeds; make custom guides; place vector and raster art; make Area type for columns.*

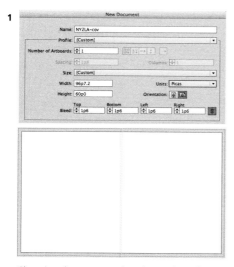

Changing the name, setting the number of Artboards to 1, changing Units to picas, setting Orientation to landscape, entering dimensions, and entering bleed measurements

Print On Demand (POD), a printing technology and business process in which new copies of a book are not printed until an order has been received, is an increasingly popular print option for independent and self-publishers, particularly those who create documents intended for both print and ePub. Raymond Larrett of Puzzled Squirrel Press finds that using Illustrator allows him to easily create cover designs that integrate vector art with raster art elements, like the ones for this graphic novel. After setting up page dimensions, bleeds, and guides for text elements, the Illustrator document can be exported as a JPEG file for ePub or web comics, and as a PDF for POD publications.

1 Setting up the page. Larrett created a new document (File> New). While in the New Document dialog, he changed the name of the file, set Number of Artboards to 1, chose Picas under Units, clicked the Landscape icon under Orientation, and entered the dimensions of his book cover (including front, back, and spine elements) in the Width and Height fields. He also entered his bleed measurement in the Top Bleed input field and clicked the "Make all settings the same" icon to populate the other Bleed fields with the same measurement. After entering all his settings, he clicked OK.

Dragging a guide out from a ruler into position; Illustrator **CC** *adds ways to make guides, including double clicking a ruler; see "Better guide creation" in the* **CC** *intro to Chapter 1 for details*

2 Customizing your guides. To make it possible to set up guides for the back cover, spine, and front cover, Larrett chose View> Show Rulers (⌘-R/Ctrl-R). To create the initial guide, he first checked to make sure that guides were unlocked (View> Guides), and then click-dragged from the left-side ruler to roughly his first position. With the guide still selected, he numerically adjusted the positions of the selected guide by relocating the X (or Y) axis positions in the Transform panel. (You can also turn selected vector objects into guides using Guides> Make Guides or ⌘-5/Ctrl-5.) With his guides in place, Larrett used the context-sensitive menu to access Lock, Hide, and Release guide functions as needed. (See this chapter's **CC** introduction for added ways to make guides in CC.)

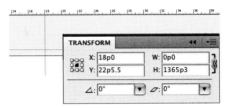

Selecting guide and numerically positioning from the Transform panel

3 Placing and refining the elements. When the page was set with the correct dimensions, bleeds, and guides, Larrett added artwork to the design. He dragged and dropped some existing vector elements, like the barcode and logo, from other Illustrator files. Larrett's design also contains raster artwork, which he imported into the document by choosing File> Place. Larrett then created rectangles with the Rectangle tool to define areas for columns of text. With the Area Type tool, he clicked on each of these rectangles, making it possible to type or paste text directly into the box. He then double-clicked on the Type tool in the Tools panel to open the Area Type Options dialog. Within the dialog, Larrett changed the Offset in the Inset Spacing field to inset the text from the edge of the text box. You can also use the Area Type Options dialog to change the Dimensions, Rows, Columns, and Text Flow options. As an alternative to using the Area Type tool, you can use the Type tool to create type for titles, headlines, and other individual type elements.

Placing artwork

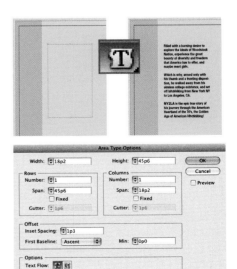

Creating rectangles with the Rectangle tool, using the Area Type tool, and setting Inset Spacing

Create an Identity

Working Efficiently with Multiple Elements

Overview: *Create artboards for each type of content; use the Artboards panel to resize the artboards and duplicate some of them; use symbols for logos; optionally, duplicate artboards with artwork for multiple variations.*

1

Setting up multiple artboards

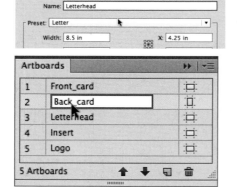

Customize, name, and reorder artboards using the Artboards panel and Artboard Options dialog

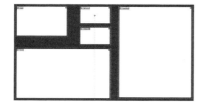

Customizing the layout using the Artboard tool and Smart Guides to help align the artboards

A company's typical identity package may contain several types and sizes of materials, such as letterhead, business cards, web pages, and ad inserts. Instead of needing to keep track of multiple files, Ryan Putnam can rely on multiple artboards and symbols to create the collateral materials in a single file, making additions or updates much simpler and less prone to errors and omissions.

1 Setting up the artboards. Putnam began by setting up four artboards using the default settings in the New dialog plus a standard bleed. Opening the Artboards panel, he double-clicked the first artboard icon, entered the dimensions of the business card, named it "Front_card," and clicked OK. He then customized the sizes and names of the other three artboards: the letterhead, an insert, and the logo design. Since he needed the same size artboard for the front and back of the business card, he used the Artboards panel to duplicate the business card by dragging "Front_card" to the New Artboard icon. In the Artboards panel he double-clicked the copy's name and typed "Back_card," and reordered the artboards (which renumbered them) by dragging "Back_card" to just below "Front_card." Because duplicate artboards automatically get added in a single row to the right of the last artboard drawn, Putnam selected the Artboard tool (Shift-O), to drag the artboards into a custom arrangement. Using

Smart Guides (⌘-U/Ctrl-U) he could easily line them up in a well-organized fashion.

2 Making symbols for replication and quick updates.
Putnam began by designing the logo. He then dragged it into the Symbols panel to save it as a symbol, named it, and clicked OK. If he modified the logo, he only had to alter the one symbol to automatically update all instances of it throughout the document. If he needed a variation of the logo, he could break the link to the original symbol to create a new symbol (see the *Expressive Strokes* chapter for more about creating and modifying symbols). Using multiple artboards with symbols adds appreciably to productivity. Artboards in one file share the same libraries, so if there were any changes in the future, Putnam wouldn't have to open separate files for each item in the identity package and then open the library containing the modified symbol. One file would always contain all the libraries and correctly-sized artboards ready for modifications.

3 Copying and duplicating artwork with artboards.
Putnam created the design for each element of the identity package, placing the logo symbol on the artboard and adding text and artwork as needed. He linked the photo to the insert, making it easy to replace for the next event. Although the letterhead and insert only required a single version, he needed to create a business card that could be duplicated and personalized later for each employee and different events. When he needed to create another business card for a different employee and/or event, he could either duplicate the front and back cards in the Artboards panel as before, or, with the Artboard tool selected and Move/Copy Artwork enabled in the Control panel, he could hold down the Option/Alt key while dragging a selected artboard. With everything in place, Putnam only had to select the text, graphic, or linked image that needed changing and quickly replace it. Now that he can include up to 100 artboards per file in CS6 (1000 artboards in **CC**), Putnam can stay organized with just one document.

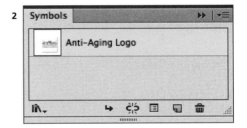

Using symbols for logos to maintain consistency, to make updates a snap, and to modify or place symbols from a shared library onto different artboards as needed

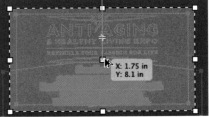

Duplicating the artboard with the artwork by enabling the Move/Copy Artwork with Artboard icon and holding down the Option/Alt key

Moving Your Type

Setting Type on a Curve and Warping Type

Overview: *Create banners that will go behind curved labels; type label text on a curved path and adjust its alignment on the path; warp text and adjust its tracking; modify the kerning of the space between words.*

Greater Bridgeport Transit hired Jack Tom to design a T-shirt supporting its new campaign to raise public awareness of the local bus system. Tom's design combined the campaign's taglines—"Go Green," "Go GBT.com," and "Go Public"—with artwork illustrating birds, butterflies, and flowery vines.

1 Creating the background art and the two banners.
After drawing the floral, bird, and butterfly figures, Tom created the banners that would serve as backgrounds for the curved "Go Green" and "Go Public" labels. You can make a symmetrical banner by first selecting the Ellipse tool and drawing an ellipse. Then cut the ellipse with the Scissors tool to make the curved path that will form the banner. Using the grid (View> Show Grid) and positioning the ellipse over a horizontal grid line will help you cut the ellipse at the same vertical position on its left and right sides, keeping the curve symmetrical. Next, make a copy of this path; you'll use it later for curving the text of the label. Now give the joined path a thick stroke (Tom used 35 pt) and then outline the path by selecting Object>

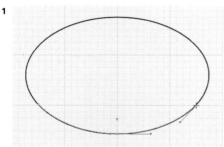

The ellipse with the left and right endpoints of the banner path cut by the Scissors tool

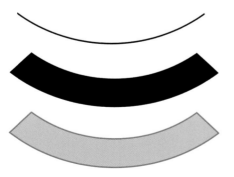

Thickening the banner path's stroke, then outlining the path and giving it stroke and fill colors

Path> Outline Stroke. You can now give the stroke a width and color the stroke and fill.

2 Curving a label. To make the curved labels for "Go Green" and "Go Public," Tom used the path he had copied in the previous step. If you use Paste in Front (⌘-F/Ctrl-F), the path will overlay the banner you created previously. After pasting the path, select the Text tool, click on the path, and type your label text. With the path still selected, click the Align center icon in the Paragraph section of the Control panel. That centers your text horizontally across the banner. Before adjusting the vertical position of the type, realign the position of the type to the path by choosing Type> Type on a Path> Type on a Path Options. From the Type on a Path Options dialog, change Align to Path from the default Baseline to Center. Also, set the baseline shift to 0 in the Character panel. This will minimize any pinching or expanding of space between the letters of the label. Now you can move the path up or down to better center the label against the banner.

3 Arcing and bending a label. Tom wanted the main label, "Go GBT.com," to bend backward in a gentle arc. To bend type, start by typing your text (you can use an Area- or a Point-type object). With the text object selected, choose Effect> Warp> Arc Lower. In the Warp Options dialog, make sure Horizontal is still active and change Bend by moving the slider or entering a number in the Bend field. A negative number will bend the type backward (Tom entered –17% for Bend).

When you warp type, the spacing between letters and words may change more than you'd like. Consider resetting or adjusting Tracking or Kerning from the Character panel. Tracking controls the distance between all letters in the selected text, while kerning requires you to adjust the distance between each pair of letters. Also, to tighten the space between words, click on the space between words and narrow the kerned space between words by holding Option/Alt and pressing the left arrow key.

2

The Align Center icon in the Control panel

The Type on a Path Options dialog with the Align to Path changed to Center

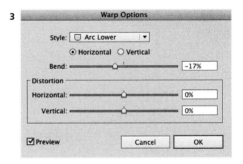

The finished label

3

Above, the Warp Options dialog; below, the type before warping (top) and after warping (below)

Above, the text with a space between words; below, negative kerning inserted between the **O** and **G** characters

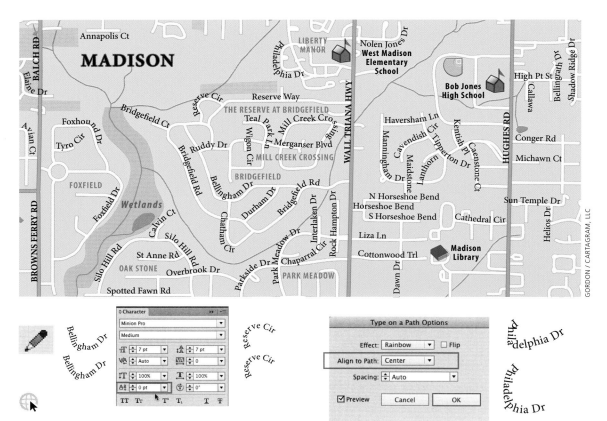

GORDON / CARTAGRAM, LLC

Steven Gordon/Cartagram, LLC

To label curving features like rivers and roads on his maps, cartographer Steve Gordon relies on type on a path. Gordon copies and pastes the river or road paths on a separate layer before applying type to them. He sets Baseline Shift to 1 pt in the Character panel in order to move the type away from the underlying road or river path. In this map of Madison, Alabama, Gordon encountered paths with sharp turns and tight curves that pinched letters together or spread them apart with unsightly gaps. He smoothed the kinks from some paths by clicking to select a path with type, selecting the Pencil tool, and then dragging it over or near the path. For paths that couldn't be smoothed solely with the Pencil, Gordon reset the path's Baseline Shift to 0 and then he dragged the type path away from the street path so that its lettering was the same distance away from the street as the labels with the 1-pt Baseline Shift. Some of the type paths required another adjustment: Gordon chose Type> Type on a Path> Type on a Path Options, and in the dialog box changed Align to Path from the default value of Baseline to Center. Gordon employed these techniques, separately or in various combinations, as he worked with hundreds of type objects in the map.

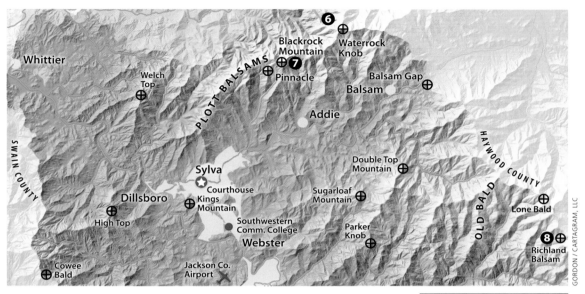

GORDON / CARTAGRAM, LLC

Steven Gordon/Cartagram, LLC

When cartographer Steven Gordon creates a map with a terrain image in the background, he has to ensure that type is not lost in the mountains of the image. For this map of North Carolina's Jackson County, Gordon received directions to create a bold, colorful terrain image by his client, *The Sylva Herald*. He began the map by creating the terrain image in Photoshop, placing it in the Illustrator file, and positioning it on the artboard. After creating the type labels, Gordon opened the Appearance panel, chose Add New Stroke from the panel menu, and dragged the Stroke attribute below Characters in the panel. Next, he set the width

of the stroke to 0.5 pt using the Stroke Weight menu and then clicked the Stroke attribute's color icon to pop up the Swatches menu and selected the white swatch. Gordon wanted to soften the contrast between the white stroke and image behind it and decided to add a white glow around the type. To do this he clicked Characters in the Appearance panel and then clicked the Add New Effect icon and chose Stylize> Outer Glow. In the Outer Glow dialog, he clicked the color picker, selected white, and changed Opacity to 100% and Blur to 0.04 inches to complete the effect.

Arcing Type

Transforming Type with Warps & Envelopes

Overview: *Create and color a title using appearances; explore the three Envelope distortions for creating an arc effect; use an Arc Warp effect to arc the type; create a graphic style and apply arc effect to other title elements.*

Putnam's 50-point Cabaret font headline

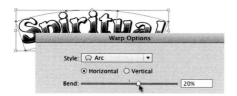

Applying Object> Envelope Distort> Make with Warp and changing the Bend to 20%

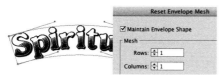

Applying Object> Envelope Distort> Make with Mesh, setting the number of Rows and Columns to 1, and editing the anchor points with the Direct Selection tool

Creating an arc-shaped object with the Pen tool over the type, selecting the arc-shaped object and type, and applying Object> Envelope Distort> Make with Top Object

Adding an arc effect to a headline turns boring type into a dynamic engaging headline that grabs the viewers' attention. With Illustrator you can explore a number of ways to create arcing text; using effects and graphic styles, you can quickly create an arcing effect easily applicable to any other titles or subtitles! (See the *Reshaping Dimensions* chapter for more about warps, blends, and graphic styles.)

1 Creating your headline text. To create headline text, choose a font with distinct, bold characteristics. For his headline text, Ryan Putnam chose 50-point Cabaret font.

Among the many ways to create an arcing effect in Illustrator, there are three different Envelope distortions that you can apply to your text: Warp, Mesh, and Make with Top Object.

First, Putnam applied Object> Envelope Distort> Make with Warp. Next, he chose Arc from the Warp options and changed Bend to 20%. For a second option, he then applied Object> Envelope Distort> Make with Mesh, set the number of Rows and Columns to 1, and edited the anchor points with the Direct Selection tool. For the final option, he used the Pen tool to draw a separate arc-shaped object over the type, selected the type and arc-shaped object, and applied Object> Envelope Distort> Make with Top Object.

2 Applying an Arc Warp effect to arc the title. Even though using Envelope distortions created the effect Putnam was looking for and provided significant control for customizing his warp, he ultimately decided that he wanted a quick way to add the same simple arc effect to other titles and subtitles on the cover. Putnam figured out that if he created the arc using Effect> Warp, he could save his effect as a graphic style that he could then apply to additional titles.

There are 15 standard Warp shapes you can choose from when creating a title. For the "Spiritual" title, Putnam applied Effect> Warp> Arc. With Preview enabled, he changed the Bend to 20% and then clicked OK.

3 Saving and applying a graphic style. With the title selected, Putnam clicked the New Graphic Style icon in the Graphic Styles panel. With the graphic style now saved, Putnam could easily apply that style to other titles and subtitles.

To create a variant of this style: he replaced the text with "Muscles"; changed the font to 28 points; set the rotation to 355°; and clicked the New Graphic Style icon in the Graphic Styles panel.

4 Applying finishing touches. To custom color the individual characters in his headline, Putnam decided to outline the type (Type> Create Outlines). He then applied a custom gradient and adjusted it for each character. (For more about working with gradients, see the *Color Transitions* chapter.)

2

In Effect> Warp> Arc, changing the bend to 20%

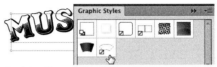

3

Selecting the title and clicking the New Graphic Style icon in the Graphic Styles panel

Applying the graphic style

Using Add New Effect from the Appearance panel, apply Distort & Transform, change the Rotation to 355°, and click the New Graphic Style icon in the Graphic Styles panel

4

Applying Type> Create Outlines to the titles

Applying a linear gradient to the titles

Applying a custom gradient

MIYAMOTO

Yukio Miyamoto

The best way to really understand how to construct complex appearances for type is to pick apart someone else's styles. Yukio Miyamoto, master of photorealism in Illustrator and author of many Japanese books on creating art with the software, has generously shared his varied collection of styles for you to you to pick apart and modify. These styles, many of which were originally created for his (Japanese) *Illustrator Appearance Book*, are downloadable in both live type and outline format, along with a PDF excerpt from his book.

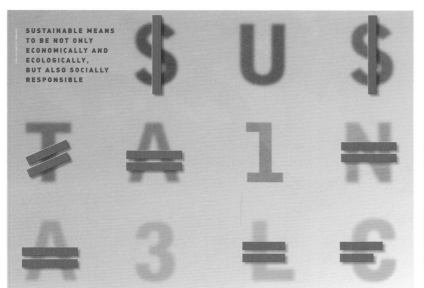

SUSTAINABLE MEANS
TO BE NOT ONLY
ECONOMICALLY AND
ECOLOGICALLY,
BUT ALSO SOCIALLY
RESPONSIBLE

LEVY

Jean-Benoit Levy

San Francisco graphic artist Jean-Benoit Levy combined letters, numbers, and red bars to create monetary symbols in this poster about societal investment in sustainability for the "Occupy: What's Next" international poster contest sponsored by the NextByDesign organization. Levy started the poster by creating the gradient-filled background. Then he selected the Type tool and created type objects for each of the characters that spell "SUSTA1NA3LC." With the Selection tool, he selected each type object and positioned it within the layout. Next, to create the blur effect for the letters, Levy selected one of the type objects and opened the Appearance panel and clicked Fill to select a dark green. Then he clicked the Add New Effect icon at the bottom of the panel, chose Blur> Gaussian Blur, and entered 32 in the Radius field. To help save time blurring the rest of the characters, he created a graphic style that he could reuse. With the type object still selected, he opened the Graphic Style panel and clicked the New Graphic Style icon to save the appearance as a style. Next, he selected all of the remaining type objects and clicked the graphic style he had created to blur them. To give each letter a unique color fill, Levy selected each type object, opened the Appearance panel, selected the Fill, and then Shift-clicked the Fill to access the Color panel. He adjusted the CMYK values until each character color looked the way he wanted. For the red bars, he drew paths with the Pen tool, converted them to outlines (Object> Path> Outline Stroke), and used the Appearance panel to add a drop shadow (Stylize> Drop Shadow).

BRYAN

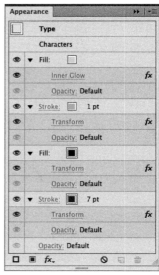

Billie Bryan

Carib Select Watersports in Grand Cayman asked Billie Bryan to design a logo to attract cruise ship passengers to their popular Stingray City excursion. Bryan began by drawing the dark blue shape of Grand Cayman island and setting the type. She duplicated the artwork layer and then hid it by clicking its visibility icon in the Layers panel. Selecting the type, Bryan opened the Appearance panel, double-clicked Characters, filled the type with light blue, clicked the Add New Effect icon, and chose Stylize> Inner Glow. She clicked the swatch next to the Stroke to change the color to a medium blue, clicked the Add New Effect icon, chose Distort & Transform> Transform, and changed the Move values to offset the stroke. She moved the stroke below the fill in the panel. Next, she selected the Add New Fill from the panel menu and dragged the new fill below the stroke. She changed its color to dark purple-blue and gave it an inner glow like the first fill. Finally, she selected Add New Stroke from the panel menu,

widened its stroke, and colored it with dark blue. She also used the Transform effect to off-set the stroke. To complete the logo, Bryan used the island shape to add a water effect to the letters. To do this, she turned on the visibility of the duplicate layer she had hidden previously. She converted the type to outlines, selected the island, moved it in front of the type outlines, and selected the island and the type. Then she opened the Pathfinder panel and chose Inter-sect. She finished the logo by recoloring the resulting shapes in a light blue.

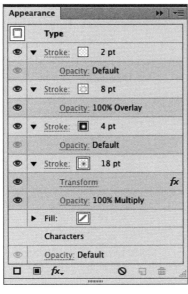

PUTNAM

Ryan Putnam

Graphic designer Ryan Putnam turned type and paths into neon tubing using Illustrator's Appearance panel and gradients on strokes in this professional portfolio piece. Putnam began by drawing a semicircle and setting the type for "CONES" on it. Then he selected the Type tool and double-clicked the type to select its characters. He opened the Appearance panel and changed the fill to None. Next, Putnam clicked the Selection tool to select the type as an object. From the Appearance panel menu, he chose Add New Stroke and set the new stroke to 2 pt. To create the gradient for the stroke, he opened the Gradient panel and then changed the Type attribute to Radial and the Stroke attribute to "Apply gradient across stroke." Putnam modified the default gradient, making the left color stop white with 10% opacity

and the right color stop white with 0% opacity. He duplicated the stroke three times and edited each duplicate, changing the colors in the gradients. For two of the duplicates, Putnam clicked the word <u>Opacity</u> (below the Stroke in the Appearance panel) and changed the blending mode to Overlay on one and Multiply on the other. He offset the bottom stroke slightly from the others by clicking the Add New Effect icon, selecting Distort & Transform> Transform, and entering 5 pt in the Move> Vertical field. When he finished, Putnam made a graphic style from the type so he could apply it to the word "Frosty." To do this, he selected the type, opened the Graphic Styles panel, and clicked the New Graphic Style icon. Then he selected the type object for "Frosty" and clicked the new graphic style he had created.

Touching Type

Modifying Editable Letter Characters

THE 2013 TRAVEL GUIDE

GORDON / CARTAGRAM, LLC

Overview: *Create a point or area text object; use the Touch Type tool to select individual letter characters; resize, rotate, and move characters in a text object; manipulate letter spacing; style the word using the Appearance panel.*

Finishing a map for a travel guide to Boquete, Panama, cartographer Steve Gordon created a title for both the map and the guide. His goal was to create a title that featured colorful, playful type and conveyed a rough, spontaneous design. The **CC** Touch Type tool in combination with the Appearance panel enabled Gordon to graphically manipulate individual letters in his title design.

1

"Boquete" typed in the default font (top); after changing font and color for each letter character (bottom)

1. Setting the type. Gordon began by selecting the Type tool, clicking on the artboard, and typing "Boquete" in Illustrator's default font. Next, he individually selected each character with the Type tool and changed its font and color from the Control panel. When he finished, each letter in the title displayed a unique font and color.

2

The Touch Type tool cursor (shown enlarged) on the left; a selected letter character (right)

Uniformly resizing a character using the upper-right control (left); using the top-center control point to rotate the character (right)

2. Distorting letters with the Touch Type tool. To give the letters a playful, disorderly look, Gordon chose to distort each character's size, dimensions, angle, and letter spacing. He also wanted to keep the type editable so he could change fonts depending on how the design developed. The Touch Type tool, hidden under the Type tool icon in the Tools panel, lets you graphically manipulate letters while preserving their editability as type. If the Character panel is open, you can also click the Touch Type tool button to enable the tool. As you move the cursor toward the type object you want to edit, notice the Touch Type cursor icon: It appears as a **T** surrounded by a box with corner points.

To change a letter, click on it with the Touch Type tool. When you select a letter, Illustrator displays a selection box with five control points around the character. You'll use these points to edit each letter.

Pushing type around

You can use the Touch Type tool on letter characters in point type, area type, and type on a path objects.

Gordon began by clicking the letter "B" with the Touch Type tool. He clicked the upper-right control point and dragged it to uniformly enlarge the character. To rotate the character, he clicked and dragged the control point above the character and dragged it to the left.

You can use the other control points to scale or reposition a character. Clicking and dragging the upper-left point will resize the character vertically while the lower-right point resizes it horizontally.

If you click the solid circle control point in the lower-left or inside the selection box, you can drag the character in any direction. If you drag to the left, the letter moves closer to the letter on its left. However, if you drag to the right, the letter won't move closer to its neighbor on the right; instead, it increases the space from its neighbor on the left. You can also change letter spacing by clicking the Type tool and adjusting the kerning or tracking.

While type remains editable when you use the Touch Type tool, be careful about selecting and replacing multiple letters if you want to reuse the Touch Type tool's graphic modifications. When you select multiple letters and retype, Illustrator applies the Touch Type's graphic modifications of the first letter you're replacing to all the letters you replace as you type. You'll need to adjust each letter separately to re-create the visual look you want.

3 Styling the title with the Appearance panel. Gordon completed his title by applying several effects from the Appearance panel to the type object. Selecting his title, he bent and distorted its characters uniformly by choosing Warp> Twist from the *fx* pop-up menu. Next, he clicked the Add New Stroke icon in the panel menu and then increased the stroke's thickness and moved the stroke underneath the Characters attribute in the panel. Gordon wanted a rough look for the stroke, so from the *fx* menu he applied the Distort & Transform> Roughen effect and then completed the title by applying the Stylize> Outer Glow effect (also from the *fx* menu) to the stroke to give the lettering a slightly blurry appearance.

Resizing a character vertically using the upper-left control (left); using the lower-right control point to resize a character horizontally (right)

Dragging the letter "U" to the left (top); dragging it to the right (bottom)

3

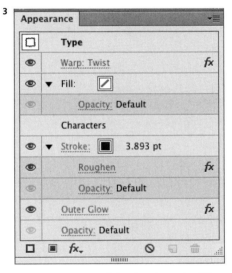

The Appearance panel showing the stroke, fill, and effects applied to the type object

Stairstepping exercise

While you can reposition letters up and down in a word using the Touch Type tool, consider doing the same with type on a path using Type> Type on a Path> Stairstep. It's easier!

Chana Messer

Artist, trainer, and Adobe Illustrator User Group host Chana Messer created this art poster to illustrate the range of techniques design-ers can use when working with type in Adobe Illustra-tor. To create the free-form cascading "TYPOGRAPHY" Messer began with a stan-dard point type text object. Using the Touch Type tool she kept the text live while graphically manipulating individual characters, shift-ing positions. After dupli-cating and then offsetting the manipulated text object, she next used the Touch Type tool to select individual letters to change fill colors. She also placed a number of colored, textured JPEG images within "TYPOGRAPHY" to make it appear as though each of the different textures was actually within only one letter. To place each texture she selected the text object (it doesn't have to be Touch Type mode), clicked the Draw Inside Mode icon, and chose a JPEG

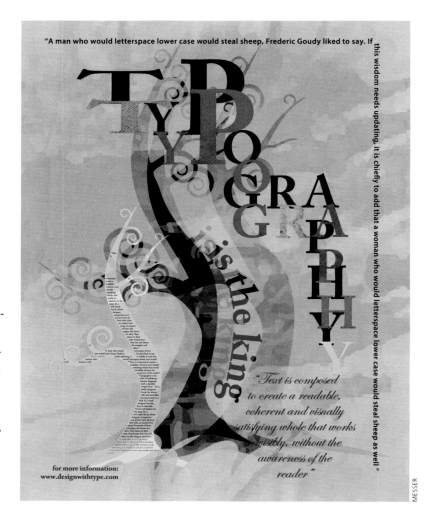

MESSER

via Edit> Place (⌘-Shift-P/Ctrl-Shift-P). With that placed image still selected, she used the Selec-tion tool to resize and position it so it appeared to be inside one specific letter. Then, switching back to the Touch Type tool, she selected that (now textured) letter, set the fill to None, and adjusted its blending mode by clicking Opacity in the Control panel (shown above left are the two of the letters with separate textures). To readjust a masked image that wasn't currently selected, she targeted it in the Layers panel.

3

Rethinking Construction

Rethinking Construction

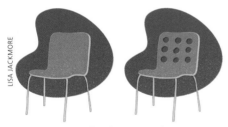

LISA JACKMORE

To put holes into this chair, Lisa Jackmore selected the chair, then clicked with the Eraser tool, automatically turning the chair into a compound path and revealing the blue underneath

The Blob Brush tool won't affect non-selected paths (left) with strokes or fill colors different from the current fill color (center), but if your current color matches the unselected path, then you can add to the original path by dragging over it with the Blob Brush tool (right)

Constructing objects is at the heart of artwork in Illustrator, and nowhere has Illustrator been more innovative than in finding new ways to construct objects from the amalgamation of simple paths and shapes. The early days of painstakingly constructing and joining every path, anchor point by anchor point, is giving way to methods of coloring shapes in ways that create new objects or more closely simulate drawing with pencil and paper. This chapter works its way from newer methods for combining and editing shapes—using the semi-automatic methods of the Blob Brush, the Shape Builder tools, Live Paint, and Image Trace, and in the **CC** section, you'll learn how to use the Shaper tool and work with Live Shapes. Here also you'll find drawing assistants—such as drawing inside or behind objects, joining paths, and aligning objects and anchor points, as well as favorite oldies such as the Pathfinder panel and working with compound paths and shapes.

THE ERASER TOOLS & THE BLOB BRUSH

One of the easiest ways to separate and combine objects is using the Eraser and the Blob Brush tools. With the Eraser tool you can cut an object into many parts, and with the Blob Brush you can combine multiple objects with the same fill attributes (and no stroke).

The Eraser tools

If nothing is selected, the Eraser tool (or the eraser end of your stylus if you're using a graphics tablet) erases objects as you drag over them. To restrict the effect of the Eraser tool, select the paths you want to edit and drag the Eraser tool through them, or enter isolation mode. If you want certain paths to be protected from the Eraser tool when nothing is selected, lock or hide those paths or their layer. To constrain the direction of the Eraser tool, Shift-drag. To erase a rectangular area Option-drag/Alt-drag a marquee to erase a rectangular area. The Eraser tool also has the calligraphic attributes of the Paintbrush tool: Double-click the Eraser tool in the Tools panel to customize it.

The Path Eraser tool (hidden beneath the Pencil in the Tools panel) erases parts of selected paths. To remove a portion of a path, you must erase along (not perpendicular to) a selected path. Erasing a midsection of a path leaves an open anchor point on either side of the erasure.

The Blob Brush tool

In case you were wondering, the Blob "brush" is in this chapter, and not with the other brushes in the *Expressive Strokes* chapter, because it functions more like the Eraser than a brush. If you paint the same brushstroke using the Blob Brush tool and the Calligraphic Paintbrush, they might at first appear similar; if you switch to Outline mode, however, the difference becomes clear. An Illustrator vector path runs down the middle of a Paintbrush stroke, and the application of the Paintbrush remains live, which means the brushstroke can be restyled or edited like any other path in Illustrator. In contrast, a mark made by the Blob Brush is expanded as soon as you complete a stroke. Where a Paintbrush brushstroke is defined by the single path down its middle, a Blob Brush brushstroke is defined by a path around its outer edge. Following are some rules and tips for painting with the Blob Brush:

- **To paint with the Blob Brush tool,** select it, set a stroke color, and drag a brushstroke. Your stroke is automatically expanded and the fill takes the current stroke color, while the stroke itself is removed. The Blob Brush merges successive brushstrokes depending upon the options you set. As long as you keep painting with the same Fill/Stroke and Opacity, overlapping brushstrokes will merge. If you change any of these, your brushstrokes will stay separate.
- **To customize the Blob Brush tool,** double-click on it in the Tools panel. If you enable Keep Selected, you can immediately alter the path with the Smooth tool or make it easy to add to an existing path in a crowded illustration by enabling the "Merge Only With Selected" option. When "Merge Only With Selected" is on, the Blob Brush

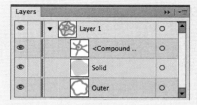

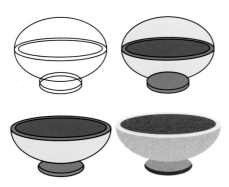

*Using Shape Builder to transform a batch of ovals into a bowl: (upper left) a series of ovals drawn with the Ellipse tool; (upper right) automatically coloring all objects using the Premedia Systems WOW! Artwork Colorizer script (**WOW! ONLINE**); (lower left) after deleting and combining objects using the Shape Builder tool; (lower right) returning to regular editing tools, shown after changing the colors and setting stroke weight to None*

Shape Builder and holes

To merge shapes and create holes in them, hold Option/Alt and click on an area or stroke to delete it. The Shape Builder tool, like the Blob Brush, can generate compound paths.

Saving Shape Builder strokes

To retain interior strokes in your drawing, click to fill the shapes separately, rather than dragging across them to join, even when you want to use the same fill on these shapes.

tool affects the selected paths only if it's selected and you drag over it using the same stroke color and opacity. Disabling this option allows the Blob Brush tool to edit paths created with the exact same appearance, regardless of whether or not the paths are selected.

- **To modify a path that was drawn using another tool,** draw the object using any Fill and a Stroke of None. Use the Blob Brush with the same Stroke color as the object's Fill, and add your brushstrokes to the object. The Blob Brush won't edit a path with a stroke, and if you edit an open path with the Blob Brush, it will create a closed path. To add to a compound shape, first expand it.
- **To modify and combine multiple objects** that share the same Fill color with no Stroke, make sure they are on the same layer and contiguous in the stacking order.
- **To create calligraphic strokes** with a pressure-sensitive stylus and tablet (such as a Wacom) use the Blob Brush Options dialog to change brush shape and drawing angle.
- **To refine the edges of a Blob Brush brushstroke,** use the Eraser tool. You can't do this with Brush tool strokes.

SHAPE BUILDER TOOL

Although it bears some similarities to Live Paint and Pathfinder commands (discussed later in this chapter), the Shape Builder tool presents a different method for constructing objects. When you initially draw, you can allow objects to overlap in the interior of the outline you want to create; e.g., drawing a three-leaf clover from three overlapping circles and an overlapping rectangle for the stem. With the Shape Builder tool, all you need to do is to first select the objects you want to combine into new shapes, then place your cursor over an area. To unite one area with others, simply click-drag across from one highlighted area to another, or Shift-drag a marquee over selected areas to unite multiple areas. Your objects don't need to reside on the same layer to start, but when they are merged with an initial shape, they will be moved to that shape's layer. To delete areas or strokes from your selected artwork using the Shape Builder tool, press the

Option/Alt key while clicking on the highlighted area or portion of a stroke.

Depending on how your options are set, you can either select swatch colors as you go (with a Swatch preview cursor), or use the colors already in the highlighted object (double-click the tool to choose which method to use). If you choose "Pick Color From Color Swatches" in the Options dialog, you can enable the Cursor Swatch Preview. Now you can use the left and right arrow keys to switch the current color to the next color in any selected color group in the Swatches panel, or the up and down arrow keys to move to another color group. If you choose "Pick Color From Artwork," the first object you click will determine the color that fills the others as you drag. Separate objects can easily become merged into a single object. The rules for filling objects can be complex, so see the Tip "Shape Builder & appearances" at right if an object's appearance isn't what you expected.

One of the most powerful aspects of Shape Builder is that you are actually reconstructing how objects are made and filled, not just how they look on the surface. When working with strokes, those you keep remain live and editable, whereas Live Paint or Pathfinder commands might result in strokes that have become unexpectedly expanded or deleted. You can continue to modify the appearance of your Shape Builder strokes. Your new objects do not become a special kind of group either, so you can freely switch between regular editing tools and the Shape Builder tool.

WORKING WITH LIVE PAINT

Hidden under the Shape Builder tool are the Live Paint Bucket and Live Paint Selection tools. Whereas the Shape Builder tool helps you to reconstruct and combine objects, Live Paint provides you with a way to recolor objects without modifying the vector paths, ignoring the normal rules about how you define a vector object. Paint lines and spaces as if you were coloring a drawing by hand. In order to use these tools, you have to first convert your objects

Shape Builder & appearances

Changing the order and direction with which you drag to apply the Shape Builder tool can alter the appearance of the resulting objects. If you aren't getting the results you want, undo and try starting the merge with a different object.

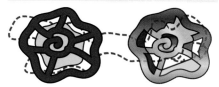

Using the Shape Builder tool to transform a duplicate of the left figure into the right figure by filling and deleting areas created by overlapping objects, and deleting strokes; once you've used Shape Builder to reconfigure objects you can simply select sections using the Direct Selection tool and continue to change the fill and stroke, adjust transparency, and more; a dashed brush beneath is shown to demonstrate transparency

Shape Builder as Paint Bucket

The Shape Builder tool can also be used like an ordinary Paint Bucket tool; click (instead of click-drag) to fill shapes without uniting them.

Adding to a Live Paint Group

Add new members to a Live Paint Group by selecting the new paths and the Live Paint Group, then clicking the Merge Live Paint button in the Control panel (or choose Object> Live Paint> Merge). Or even better, enter isolation mode with the Live Paint Group; then anything you paste or create will remain part of the Live Paint Group (see *Chapter 1: Your Creative Workspace* for more about isolation mode).

GUSTAVO DEL VECHIO

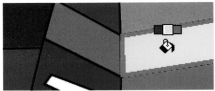

Using the Live Paint Bucket tool to both construct and color a cityscape; Intersecting open paths created enclosed areas suitable for filling with the Live Paint Bucket tool (bottom)

into a Live Paint Group; all the enclosed spaces, filled or empty, become areas you can potentially fill or clear of color. You can create a "hole" in your Live Paint object by filling with None, or you can fill an "empty" area made from adjacent vector objects with your selected color. All the lines become editable paths that you can keep, color, reshape, or delete, creating new shapes. To convert a selection to a Live Paint Group, choose the Live Paint Bucket tool and click on the object, or choose Object> Live Paint> Make (⌘-Option-X/Ctrl-Alt-X); like any other grouped object, Live Paint objects all move to the topmost layer that contained the original objects.

To change the way the Live Paint Bucket behaves, double-click it and set options, such as whether the Bucket paints fills, strokes, or both; whether you want a Cursor Swatch Preview; or the color and size of the highlight you see when you position the Bucket over an editable area. Choose how Live Paint handles gaps in the Object> Live Paint> Gap Options dialog. To edit paths and reshape areas, use normal editing tools, such as the Pen or Smooth tool. To actually alter or delete segments of paths (created from intersecting paths in Live Paint), use the Live Paint Selection tool.

USING IMAGE TRACE

Previously called Live Trace, Image Trace provides you with a variety of different ways to turn raster images into vectors. To access default presets in Image Trace (such as Photorealistic or Technical Drawing), select any raster image that you've brought into Illustrator via Open or Place, and click either the Image Trace button in the Control panel or Trace in the Image Trace panel (Window menu). Use the Image Trace panel to enable or disable preview, customize your trace settings, and save your current settings as custom presets. Image Trace leaves the traced object live and re-adjustable. If you want to edit the objects with normal vector tools, you'll need to expand the trace by clicking the Expand button on the Control panel, after which the object will no longer be live.

The Image Trace panel

In the Image Trace panel, you can specify a color mode (Color, Grayscale, or Black and White) and a palette of colors for the tracing object. The palette determines whether your trace will use a limited or unlimited number of colors, and whether to take them automatically from the object or to use a Swatch group or library (Pantone converts to global color) that is open or has been opened during the session. If you want another library or need to create a new color group, deselect the object, open the library or create the color group, and then reselect the image and choose your new library or group from the Color drop-down list. In the Image Trace panel, select the open library in the Palette drop-down list and then select a color group listed in Colors. Using sliders, you can modify how closely paths adhere to the original and set tolerances for when paths join with corner angles, or whether the trace should ignore pixels as noise. In Black and White Mode, you can choose to create Fills and/or Strokes.

Image Trace can create vector objects that abut one another (like puzzle pieces) or that overlap each other (stacking one on top of another). If you intend to edit the paths, you should probably choose the "Overlapping" option; with the "Abutting" option, the paths fit together precisely, so editing one path can create a gap between it and its neighboring (abutting) path. With Abutting as the Method, you can automatically remove a white background from your image by enabling "Ignore White."

ALIGNING, JOINING, AND AVERAGING
Align and distribute objects

Even though most Align and Distribute controls also appear in the Control panel, Distribute Spacing controls are found only in the Align panel. With an active selection, you can align objects to that selection, or the edges of the artboard, and you can Align to a Key Object (heavy outlines show you which object the others align to). To distribute the space between objects, designate one as the key; in the Align panel, enter an amount in the Distribute

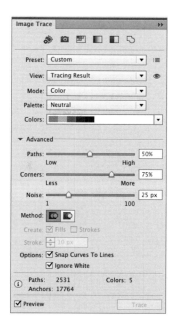

The expanded Image Trace panel showing a custom swatch library with a set selected to limit colors, default settings in Advanced, plus Ignore White enabled

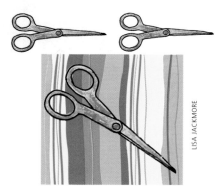

LISA JACKMORE

Lisa Jackmore scanned her scissors sketch (top left), then used Image Trace with "Ignore White" enabled (top right); the traced scissors over a striped background showing through (above)

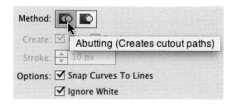

With Abutting as the Method, choosing Ignore White lets you automatically remove a white background from your tracing object

Align controls in the Align panel (top) and on the Control panel (bottom)

Path Simplify command

The Simplify command (Object> Path> Simplify) removes excess anchor points from selected paths. The higher the percentage, the more anchor points will remain, and the closer the new path will be to the original. The endpoints of an open path are never altered. The higher the Angle threshold, the more likely a corner point will remain sharp.

Resizing and stroke weight

Double-click the Scale tool to resize your selection with or without altering line weights:

- To scale a selection while also scaling line weights, enable Scale Strokes & Effects.
- To scale a selection while maintaining your line weights, disable Scale Strokes & Effects.
- To decrease line weights (50%) without scaling objects, first scale the selection (200%) with Scale Strokes & Effects disabled. Then scale (50%) with it enabled. Reverse these steps to increase line weights.

Spacing input box; then click either the Vertical or Horizontal Distribute Space icon.

Easier joins

It's now easy to join open endpoints without getting an error dialog, and you can even join multiple pairs of endpoints at the same time. To join you must first either select one pair of points with the Direct Selection tool or select one or more open paths with the Selection tool. Next, if a pair of points are *exactly* on top of each other, you can join them without a dialog by using ⌘-J/Ctrl-J or Object> Path> Join. Use the Control panel to change a join from corner to smooth, or vice versa. If points are not *exactly* on top of each other, choosing join will connect them with a line, or you can average them together first (see below for more on averaging). If you select multiple open objects and choose Join, one object will join to the next (paths won't close upon themselves). At any time you can convert points from corner to smooth, or smooth to corner, by selecting the anchor points with the Direct Selection tool and clicking the appropriate icon from the Convert section in the Control panel. Following are some rules about joining and averaging:

- **Endpoints that are precisely on top of one another join** with a corner point unless you choose "Smooth" in the Join dialog (⌘-Option-Shift-J/Ctrl-Alt-Shift-J).
- **Joining two or more open endpoints on separate paths that are not precisely on top of each other** connects the points with a straight segment using corner points. If your paths have different appearances applied, the path topmost in the stacking order determines the appearance of the paths as they are joined to it.
- **Average and join two endpoints that are not on top of each other** using ⌘-Option-Shift-J/Ctrl-Alt-Shift-J.
- **To average (without joining) endpoints,** select any number of points with the Direct Selection or Lasso tool on any number of objects; then use ⌘-Option-J/Ctrl-Alt-J to average the points along horizontal, vertical, or both axes. If you have the path selected, but not specific points,

then all points will be averaged together. If you use the Direct Selection or Lasso tool to select points, then the Align icons in the Control panel or Align panel will average the points, rather than align the objects.

DRAW BEHIND AND DRAW INSIDE

Illustrator has three drawing mode icons near the bottom of your Tools panel: Normal, Behind, and Inside. Once you click the Draw Behind icon, anything that you paste or draw will be the backmost object in your current layer, or, if you have something selected, will be placed directly behind the currently selected object. (Paste in Front and Paste in Back still work as expected and ignore the drawing mode.) If the Draw Behind mode is active when you add a new layer to your file, it will add it behind the active layer. To create an object with a different appearance from the selected object, create it first, and then change the new object's attributes. Or, if you want to be able to set an object's attributes before drawing it, enter isolation mode first. The object you're drawing behind doesn't need to be selected when you're in isolation mode. You can safely deselect it and then set the attributes for each new object before you draw it.

Draw Inside is available only when one object (or compound path or text object) is selected, and it immediately makes a *clipping mask* out of the selected object. When your originally selected object is automatically converted to this special clipping mask, it loses any attributes beyond the basic stroke and a fill, so art brushes or live effects, for instance, are removed. To set up your object for Draw Inside, first select it, then click the Drawing Mode icon in the Tools panel and choose Draw Inside. Your selected object will display the dotted corners of a bounding box. Next deselect the object (the dotted box remains); now you can choose your drawing tool or brush and its attributes. Now you only have to draw over the object to have any strokes or fills that extend outside to be clipped to the boundaries of the selected object. Your clipping mask object and whatever you have drawn inside are now

Toggle drawing modes

You can use the keyboard shortcut Shift-D to switch between available modes. Keep an eye on the changing icon to know which drawing mode you have selected.

Using Draw Inside to restrain the Bristle Brush strokes within each object as it's selected

Compound paths or shapes?

Use compound paths on simple objects for basic combining or hole-cutting. Use compound shapes on complex objects (such as those made with additional effects) and to fully control how your objects interact. Be aware that compound shapes can become too complex to print, or to be combined within some effects, and might have to be released (returning objects to their original state) or expanded (which keeps the appearance, but breaks it apart permanently). Make/release/expand compound shapes from the Pathfinder panel menu, and make/release compound paths from the Object menu.

modern
modern
modern

LISA JACKMORE

Artist Lisa Jackmore used the Draw Inside mode to add a gradient-filled rectangle to the text and then drew with a calligraphic brush, all leaving the text live and the "clipped" object separately editable

Don't forget the drawing mode

IMPORTANT: Drawing modes are persistent! If you forget what mode you're in, you'll get unexpected results. Try to get in the habit of switching to Normal mode (Shift-D) as soon as you no longer need to be in that special drawing mode.

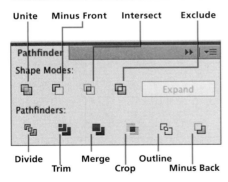

The Pathfinder panel contains two sets of icons: Shape Modes (which combine shapes), and Pathfinders (which divide paths)

Left to right: two ovals (the inner oval has no fill, but appears black because of the black fill of the larger oval behind it); as part of a compound path the inner oval knocks a hole into the outer one where they overlap; the same compound path with inner oval, which was Direct-Selected and moved to the right to show that the hole is only where the objects overlap

a group. To edit any part of this new object, use the Direct Selection tool or target it in the Layers panel and edit as a regular vector object. You can even apply effects to the entire group, if you desire. You can also copy and paste artwork in Draw Inside mode, which will clip the artwork inside text, for example. Learn more about working with clipping masks in the *Mastering Complexity* chapter.

COMPOUND SHAPES & COMPOUND PATHS

There are three additional ways to create new objects by combining and subtracting objects with and from each other: compound shapes, compound paths, and by using the commands found in the Pathfinder panel. Compound paths and compound shapes are live and can easily be released to recover the original paths. Compound paths are used primarily to create holes in objects, whereas compound shapes provide more complex ways of combining objects. The Pathfinder panel icons perform operations very much like compound shapes, except that these operations are applied permanently—Undo is the only way to reverse the effects of a pathfinder operation. If you wish to apply a live version of a Pathfinder command to a layer, type object, or a group, instead of using the Pathfinder panel, apply it from either the Effects menu or the *fx* icon from the Appearance panel.

Compound paths

A compound path consists of one or more paths that have been combined so they behave as a single unit. Compound paths can be used as a single mask, and they can create holes where the original objects overlapped (think of the letter **O**), through which you can see objects.

To create a simple compound path, draw one oval; then draw a smaller oval that will form the center hole of the **O**, and choose Object> Compound Path> Make. Apply the fill color of your choice, and the inner object remains unfilled. To adjust one of the paths within a compound path, use the Direct Selection tool; or select the compound path and enter isolation mode.

Pathfinder panel

The Pathfinder panel includes the top row of Shape Modes icons and the lower row of Pathfinder commands. The Pathfinder panel's icons alter the selected objects permanently, combining them and/or slicing them up if needed to achieve the icon's effect (see the "Compound shapes" section following about applying the top row as live effects). These permanent alterations to the objects allow you to, for example, apply the Intersect icon to selected objects so that you can pull apart and further edit the resulting pieces. Note that the Trim and Merge commands can be applied only to filled objects.

Compound shapes

Unlike pathfinders (see above), compound shapes are live functions that keep your original objects intact while they appear to be combining and/or subtracting from each other. You can make compound shapes from two or more paths or from other compound shapes, text, envelopes, blends, groups, or artwork with vector effects applied. To create compound shapes, hold the Option/Alt key as you click a Shape Mode icon in the Pathfinder panel; if you click without the Option/Alt modifier, original objects are permanently altered. You can also apply the Unite Shape mode by choosing "Make Compound Shape" from the Pathfinder panel menu. Compound shapes take on the attributes of the topmost object in the selection.

You can also continue to modify the original objects, and you can even combine multiple shape modes. Compound shapes can also be pasted into Photoshop as editable shape layers, although they won't retain their Illustrator appearance. To retain their appearance and keep them editable, paste them as vector Smart Objects (to edit a Smart Object, double-click its thumbnail in Photoshop and it will open in Illustrator; when you save, it updates in Photoshop). Release the Shape Mode to restore the original objects, or click Expand to permanently apply the effect to the objects, using Pathfinder Options from the panel's menu.

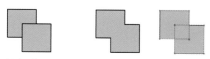

Unite (so you can see the effects more clearly: the first column shows the original shapes; the second column shows the results of the operation; and the third column shows the resulting objects selected or moved)

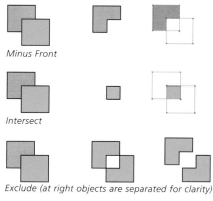

Minus Front

Intersect

Exclude (at right objects are separated for clarity)

Divide (at right objects are separated for clarity)

Trim

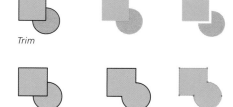

Merge (objects Merge only if both objects are the same color; otherwise Merge is the same as Trim)

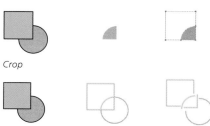

Crop

Outline (after applying Outline, Illustrator sets the stroke to 0—here, with a 2-pt stroke added)

Minus Back

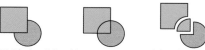

Free Transform Touch interface

The Free Transform interface has been visually redesigned for both touch devices and computers, but the tool's function hasn't changed much. Selecting the tool displays a floating strip of icons for transforming objects, and the bounding box displays new cursors to indicate the type of transformation you've selected. Using a stylus or your finger, click or tap on an icon, and if desired, drag the pivot point for rotation anywhere on the screen. Select the link icon to constrain transformations; you don't need any modifier keys. Keyboard shortcuts still perform as they used to, but now the touch interface is always displayed when you choose the Free Transform tool (E).

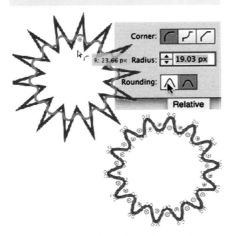

Dragging on one widget alters all selected corner anchor points—when the limit for rounding is reached as the corner anchor meets another anchor, the corner paths turn red (top). The Relative setting alters the corner shape (bottom)

NEW CONSTRUCTION FEATURES IN ILLUSTRATOR CC
WORKING WITH LIVE CORNERS AND LIVE SHAPES

Most of the geometric tools found within the Rectangle and the Line tool incorporate at least some access to Live Corners and Live Shapes. Live Corners really do make it easier to edit paths and objects—that is, once you've learned a few basic rules for dealing with them. In this section, you'll learn how to edit the corners of objects created with any tool at any time in Illustrator. In "The special properties of Live Shapes" you'll see how to use the added controls provided for working with Live Shapes.

Live Corners basics

One of the most powerful features of Live Corners is that it will recognize editable corners in any object, even if you created the object before there were Live Corners. You can create the object with geometric tools (Rectangle, Star, Polygon, etc.) or with drawing tools, such as the Pen and Pencil tools. Use the Direct Selection tool to select an entire object and display the Live Corner widgets on every corner that is editable. You can reshape selected corners interactively by dragging on one of the visible widgets.

If the entire path is selected, dragging on one widget modifies every corner equally. To restrict your edits to only some corners, select corner anchors individually with the Direct Selection tool (or select them with the Lasso tool, but then switch back to the Direct Selection tool to display widgets again). If you drag on a corner widget and a corner path turns red, your corner anchor point has run into another anchor point, and you won't be able to drag your widget any further unless you're willing to move the anchor point blocking your corner anchor.

In addition to dragging, you also have the following dialog and keyboard controls on selected widgets:

- **To cycle between corner types,** click on the widget while holding down the Option/Alt key.

- **To access the Corners dialog,** use the Direct Selection tool either to double-click on a widget or to click the Corners link in the Control panel. With the Corners dialog, you can use numeric input for the corner radius, choose from three types—Round, Inverted Round, and Chamfer (beveled)—and whether the corner should be Absolute (describing a mathematically precise arc between points, and a bit flattened), or a more natural Relative, which tends to extend the rounding in a manner you might draw by hand.

The special properties of Live Shapes

Live Shapes (currently Rectangles, Rounded Rectangles, Ellipses, Polygons, and Lines) provide some on-screen editing widgets that become active only when three conditions are met: 1) the shape is selected, 2) your active tool is the original tool itself or the regular Selection tool, and 3) you have enabled View> Show Bounding Box. With all of these conditions met, you'll then see the word <u>Shape</u> in the Control, and your geometric object will be named in the Transform and Properties panels. You can access the corner widgets on the shape or in the named-shape "Properties" section of the Transform panel (such as Rectangle Properties), or by clicking <u>Shape</u> in the Control panel or clicking ••• in the Transform section of the Properties panel.

The editing features allow you to input any relevant numeric data. For instance, Lines have fields to edit length and angles; Polygons let you modify sides and corners; Ellipses allow for rotation and a pie slice; and Rectangles and Rounded Rectangles fields include corners and separate horizontal and vertical dimensions. If your object contains corners, you can set the Corner Type here by choosing a Corner Type icon (or Option/Alt-click on a widget to cycle through them). The icon will update to display the Corner Type you selected. Enable or disable Scale Corners when you scale a rectangle or polygon with a Live Corner attribute already applied to it. When enabled, this feature will increase or decrease the corner radius to maintain the relative look of the corner as you scale the object; when disabled, it keeps the radius intact, which alters the effect of the corner as it scales.

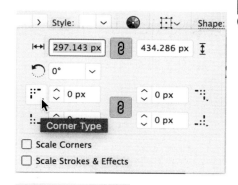

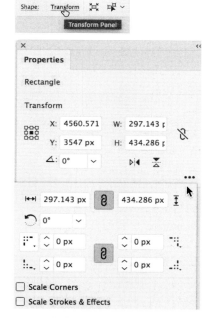

Access editable properties for Live Shapes in the Shape Properties panel (opened from the Control panel, top), as well as in the Transform drop-down from the Control panel, and also in the Properties panel

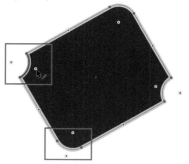

Live Shapes display not only corner widgets, but also transform control handles. Shape and Transform panels indicate dimensions, angle of rotation, corner types, and radii; the Transform panel also enables scaling corners.

Set an angle in Preferences above which no corners will be editable with the Live Corner feature

Hide Shape Widgets

With the a Live Shape tool and the object selected, toggle this icon in the Control panel to show/hide the widgets

Use Esc to end an open path

When drawing with the Pen tool, press the Esc key to end the path, allowing you to draw another path without deselecting it or switching tools.

Convert legacy rectangles

Convert static shapes in early legacy documents into Live Shapes by selecting them and choosing Object> Shape> Convert to Shape. To convert Live Shapes to ordinary paths, choose Object> Shape> Expand Shape.

Draw with a rubber band

Both the Pen tool and the Curvature tool allow you to draw using a "rubber band," which can help you preview the shape of your path. Enable/disable this feature in Preferences> Selection and Anchor Display.

If you're not sure if your object is live or if you're merely missing a condition to be able to edit it as live, find it within the Layers panel; Live Shape objects are named by their type of object (such as <Polygon>), instead of by the generic <Path>.

The conditions are tricky and if they're not all met (for instance if your active tool is the Direct Selection tool instead of the Selection tool or the tool that created it), then a Live Shape will look like, and can only be edited like, any other Live Corner object. See the previous section "Live Corners Basics" for details on editing corners.

Customizing Live Shapes Preferences

Live Corners come with a few default settings that can make your day—or ruin it. You can adjust preferences for:

- **Hide Corner Widgets by adjusting the Angle**, located in Preferences> Selection and Anchor Display. Adjusting the default angle determines the minimum angle required for the corner widgets to appear. If you're seeing too many corner widgets, decrease the angle here to hide radii for shallower corners, but be aware that if your widgets are hidden, you also won't have access to Live Corner controls.

- **Show on Shape Creation,** located in the Transform panel's pop-up menu, opens that panel into your workspace whenever you use a Shape tool if the panel isn't already in your workspace—even if the Properties panel is open. You can disable this behavior in the panel menu.

- **After drawing a live shape,** while it's still selected and the shape's tool is active, you can hide the corner widgets by toggling off the Hide Corner Widget icon in the Control panel, next to the link for Shape. It's quicker than using the View menu to show/hide corner widgets, but it works only with live shapes.

- **If you know you're not modifying corners or if your artboard is cluttered by the appearance of too many corner widgets,** choose View> Hide Corner Widget. If 100 or more widgets are selected, they're hidden by default.

PEN TOOL CHANGES & RESHAPING PATHS

Without changing your customary methods to create or edit paths, Illustrator CC adds functions, including a Reshape Segment cursor, accessible from your Pen, Direct Selection, and Anchor Point tools. When hovering over a path segment with the Pen tool, hold down the Option/Alt key to display a Reshape Segment cursor that indicates you can now drag the segment freely to reshape it. If you also hold the Shift key, your direction handles will be of equal length and perpendicular to the path. Another enhancement to the Pen tool is invoked if you press ⌘/Ctrl while dragging out Bézier handles, the In handle freezes, while you can still drag on the Out handle to make it longer or shorter without breaking the smooth pairing between them. While dragging with the Pen tool, press the spacebar to relocate the current anchor point.

The Direct Selection tool will only display the Reshape cursor if at least one of the anchor points connected to the path segment has a direction handle connected to it. You won't see the Reshape Segment cursor on straight path segments that have retracted handles on either side.

You also can use the Anchor Point tool (formerly called the Convert Anchor Point tool) to reshape path segments by dragging directly on them. Additionally, if you press Option/Alt and then click on a broken direction handle, you can convert the anchor to a smooth anchor with paired, unbroken handles.

THE NEW PENCIL SETTINGS (FOR OTHER TOOLS TOO)

The Pencil tool has undergone what appears to be a very small change, but in fact will change the way you work with it. Gone is the Smoothness slider, and instead you have one Fidelity slider. By default, the Pencil tool now smooths a hand-drawn path, which can result in fewer anchor points. However, you can double-click the Pencil tool to open Pencil Options where you can adjust the Fidelity slider from (the most) Accurate to (the most) Smooth. You'll see the same Fidelity settings for the Smooth tool, Paintbrush, and Blob Brush tools.

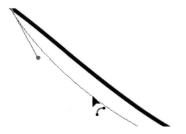

Dragging with the Reshape Segment cursor to directly adjust a segment of a path; you can access the Reshape Segment cursor from the Pen tool, the Direct Selection tool, and the Anchor Point tool (see details in "Pen Tool Changes & Reshaping Paths" section nearby)

KEVIN STOHLMEYER

Various shape Kevin Stohlmeyer drew using the Pencil tool, freeform, and with Option/Alt and click-dragging to create straight lines (top); Kevin's self-portrait making use of the new Pen, Pencil, and Smooth tool features (directly above)

Adjusting Fidelity in Pencil Tool Options

The Curvature Tool

The Curvature Tool was designed to give you a simpler way to create curves without learning to use Pen tool. Click to place points; two clicks creates a line, three points begins a curve connecting the three points. The path continues until you press Esc or deselect. As you draw, click-drag to adjust where a point is placed, or click on a previous anchor to move it. You can switch to the Direct Selection tool (if it was your last-used Selection tool, press ⌘/Ctrl key) to reveal and edit the selected path by Bézier handles and anchor points; when you release the key or re-choose the Curvature tool, you can resume drawing the path. As you draw, press Option/Alt to set a corner anchor point, or double-click an anchor point to toggle it between curve and corner. As with the Pen tool, you can enable a preview "rubberband" in Preferences> Selection & Anchor.

Intuitive Joining

Use the Join tool (in with the Pencil and Shaper tools) to connect overlapping open paths. With the Join tool, simply "scrub" the extending segments away. Paths retain their shapes, and the first object you scrub will style the joined object.

If you need to draw precisely with the Pencil, Paintbrush, or Blob Brush tools, move the Fidelity slider all the way to the far left (most Accurate). Choose the Smoother options if you want the tool to place fewer points and create more graceful curves.

If you are a seasoned Pencil user, be aware that there has been another change in its default behavior. By default when you press Option/Alt with the Pencil tool selected, it will now switch to drawing straight lines or, if within tolerances for editing the path, straighten the curve between segments. Restore the Option/Alt key access to the Smooth tool in Pencil Tool Options (double-click the Pencil tool).

The **CC** Pencil tool automatically closes a path when your end point is close to the start point. To keep the path from closing, zoom in first to increase the visual distance separating the end points (the actual distance does not change), or you can adjust the designated pixel value used to determine if the path will close (also in Pencil Tool Options).

THE SHAPER TOOL

The Shaper tool (in the toolbar with the Pencil tool) allows you to access functions that have the potential to help you to build up a complex illustration fairly quickly. The Shaper tool's first function is to guess what geometric object or line you're trying to freehand-draw and (if it understands you) will make you a perfect version of that object. You can then use a few easy gestures to combine and edit objects. Finally, you can use the Shaper tool to recolor portions of those Shaper objects, or you can work on these objects with the more powerful Live Paint tools.

The rules that constrain what you can and can't do with Shaper objects are different from, but not less confusing than, rules governing Live Color, Shape Builder, and Pathfinder objects. This section highlights some of the ways you can start to make use of the Shaper tool, so you can familiarize yourself with this tool that's clearly poised to expand in functionality.

Optimized for drawing with your finger on touch screens, the technology also can also help you to complete paths when using a mouse, stylus, or touchpad. As of this writing, the Shaper tool can help you to complete only these shapes: rectangle, ellipse, equilateral triangle, hexagon, and line. If you attempt to draw something it doesn't recognize (such as a star, or **L**-shaped path) or if you're too sloppy, then it draws nothing at all.

Shaper objects are live shapes, with on-screen widgets allowing you to convert (for instance) a six-sided polygon to a triangle, take a wedge out of an ellipse, and round sharp corners. The Shaper tool also lets you combine overlapping objects, even if they weren't created with the tool. To do this, although this feels counter-intuitive, deselect your overlapping objects. Now with the Shaper tool, draw a zigzag **Z** over the portions of overlapping objects you wish to remove. These modified objects become part of a new Shaper group; individual paths retain uniform and separate strokes, but lose any applied Width Profiles or Brushes. Each object in the group will still be editable with path editing and transformation tools, and you can drag an object away from the others without removing it from the group. For more control over coloring your Shaper group, including being able to use your saved swatches, then switch to the Live Paint Bucket (see "Working with Live Paint" earlier in this chapter). For more about the Shaper tool and examples of possible visual feedback you might encounter, see Tips and figures at right and Simona Pfreundner's lesson later in this chapter.

GLOBAL EDITS VS SELECT SIMILAR

Illustrator now provides two new distinct methods for you to be able to select (and thus be able to edit) those objects that have characteristics in common: Select Similar Objects and Global Edit. In both cases Illustrator helps you locate objects that have properties in common, searching throughout the document, whether you have one artboard or 1000, and amongst objects that might even be buried within complex layering structures; Global

Select Similar selects ALL...

Select Similar selects *all* the visible and unlocked objects in your file that meet your search parameters. This means it can be just what you need, or it can create unwanted results if the objects you're changing are out of your current view. It's not possible to limit where selects visible and unlocked objects in your file that meet your search parameters.

Select Similar is sticky

Once you choose a select similar parameter, you can actually just click the icon in the Control panel to select similar objects based on your previous selection. For maximum control, choose your target object before clicking the icon.

More powerful than Global Edit

Global Edits and Select Similar can be useful when you need to select and edit objects, but if you know in advance that you'll need to quickly select related objects, learn to use symbols. If you make an object (or even complex groups of objects) into a symbol, editing the master symbol will globally update all instances of that symbol. See the *Expressive Strokes* chapter for more on symbols, and see that chapter's **CC** intro section to learn how dynamic symbols allow you to even make local edits to instances.

edits and select similar commands will find any matching object as long as the layers containing those objects are visible and unlocked. To help you visualize the basic differences, Select Similar helps you search for objects based on their *appearance*, while Global Edit allows you to simultaneously edit objects if they've been *duplicated from the same original object*. This means you'll use Select Similar to find objects that look similar by choosing from a list of parameters that include stroke color, stroke weight, fill, and appearance. In contrast, Global Edit selects objects that were initially created by duplicating the same underlying path, but might look completely different (a rectangle search might also find an object that began as a duplicate of that rectangle but was distorted into a star with the allowable pucker and bloat live effect).

Be aware that Select Similar or Global Edit might affect objects not currently in view. When you have only a few objects on a few artboards and/or layers, it's easy to check to see that your selection and edits are being applied as intended. However, the potential to accidentally select or edit something increases significantly when you have a very large number of artboards, layers, and/or objects; a search or edit might unintentionally result in your editing something that's not currently visible.

Read more about each method for help figuring out which might work best for specific circumstances. (Also see Tip "More powerful than Global Edit" at left.)

Select Similar

Use Select Similar to find objects with these same appearance properties as your selected object or objects (see Tip "Similar Object (or Objects)?" opposite). Starting with an object selected, click the menu arrow next to the Select Similar icon to choose the parameters for your search. Those parameters will then be available when you click the icon. The chosen attributes are sticky, assuming that those attributes are applicable to the next search; if your search was for stroke color but the next selected object has no stroke, then the search parameters reset to none.

Global Edit

If you created one or more objects by duplicating another, then you can use Global Edit to select any one of them to find all the objects initially duplicated from the same path. Although there are a number of allowable transformations that let you maintain the link between duplicated paths (even if you substantially modify its appearance), there are also many ways in which you can break the relationship between these paths.

You may duplicate your original object in many ways, including Copy/Paste functions (i.e. Paste, Paste In Front, etc.), Option-drag/Alt-drag, or by duplicating the layer and/or artboard containing the object. You can then modify a number of parameters and still be able to select paths and their duplicates using Global Edit, including changing an individual object's fill, stroke weight and/or color, or adding a live effect via *fx* in the Appearance panel. Restrict a Global Edit match by artboard orientation, an artboard range to search, an object's appearance or size, or, if it's off the canvas, whether or not to include it.

Selecting grouped objects:

One key difference between Select Similar and Global Edit is only Global Edit can work with groups. If you select an object within a group, then Select Similar can find the same fill, stroke, graphic style, etc., used elsewhere. But Global Edit can find the same group used elsewhere, even if the objects within the group aren't identical in appearance. It is once again searching for the same paths that are proportionally scaled.

Another name for Global Edit

The Global Edit icon tool tip in the Control panel may say "Start editing similar shapes together."

How many were last selected?

To find out how many objects your last Global Edit selected, after running the command, click the menu arrow next to Start/Stop Global Edit; the top line displays how many matches it found. This is useful if you know there should be roughly 30 matching across 50 artboards, but it shows only 25. You'll know something is off even before you make the edit.

Select Similar with Live Shapes

You'll find Shapes in the Select Similar menu. It finds the Live Shapes—rectangles, ellipses, polygons, and lines, not other shapes. For those try Global Edit.

Similar Object (or Objects)?

Although technically you can choose multiple objects to start a Select Similar search, the only attributes that will be available from the drop-down menu for your search are the attributes the selected objects have in common.

Hiding and locking benefits and risks...

Neither Global Edit nor Select Similar will find or change objects if they're locked or hidden, and/or if they're on layers that are locked or hidden. This means locking/hiding techniques can be helpful to restrict search/change effects. However, especially if you've not created separate layers for each artboard, it's easy to accidentally "protect" objects from desired changes.

Make a shorcut for Global Edit

If you find you use Global Edit frequently, assign a keyboard shortcut for the menu toggle Select> Start/Stop Global Edit.

Combining Paths

Basic Path Construction with Pathfinders

Overview: *Create an illustration by joining and intersecting objects using the Pathfinder panel's Unite, Minus Front, and Intersect.*

1

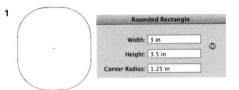

Creating a rounded rectangle by clicking on the Artboard with the Rounded Rectangle tool, setting dimensions, and increasing Corner Radius
NOTE: See the **CC** sections of this chapter for details on using Live Rectangles and Live Corners

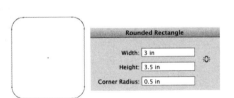

Creating a rounded rectangle by clicking on the Artboard with the Rounded Rectangle tool, setting dimensions, and decreasing Corner Radius

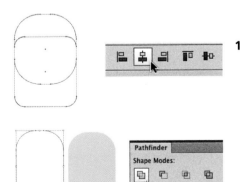

Selecting both rounded rectangles, using Horizontal Align Center, using the Unite Pathfinder command, and changing fill to cyan

PUTNAM

To create many eye-catching stock illustrations like the one above, Ryan Putnam frequently uses the Pathfinder panel. Using the Pathfinder's Unite, Minus Front, and Intersect, you too can easily create compelling character illustrations. (See the **CC** sections in this chapter for details on how to construct and modify objects created with Live Rectangles and Live Corners.)

1 Constructing the body with the Unite Pathfinder command. Ryan Putnam created the body from two rounded rectangles. To create the first object, he clicked on the Artboard with the Rounded Rectangle tool to open the Rounded Rectangle dialog. In the dialog, he set the dimensions of the rectangle to 3 in for Width, 3.5 in for Height, and increased the Corner Radius to 1.25. Putnam wanted the bottom corners of the body to be smaller, so he then created a second rectangle with the same dimensions, entered .5 for the Corner Radius, and placed the top a third of the way down from the first rectangle.

Putnam selected both rectangles, clicked the Horizontal Align Center icon in the Control panel, used the Unite command from the Pathfinder panel, and chose a Cyan swatch from the Swatches panel.

2 Constructing the mouth with the Minus Front Pathfinder command. With the Ellipse tool, Putnam drew a circle within the body object for the mouth. He then drew an encompassing rectangle halfway up from the center of the circle. He selected both, clicked the Minus Front command from the Pathfinder panel, and chose a brown swatch from the Swatches panel.

3 Constructing the teeth and tongue with Pathfinder commands. To create the tongue, Putnam created two overlapping circles within the mouth shape, selected both, and used the Unite Pathfinder command. To fit the tongue into the mouth, he first copied the mouth shape, and then chose Edit> Paste in Front. Selecting both the mouth copy and the tongue, he applied the Intersect Pathfinder command, and then chose a magenta swatch from the Swatches panel for the fill color.

To create the teeth, Putnam drew four objects with the Rounded Rectangle tool. He rotated one tooth with the Selection tool by moving the cursor along the rectangle until he saw the Rotate icon and then dragged the tooth slightly to the right. He then selected all four teeth and combined them into a single compound path using Object> Compound Path> Make (for more about compound paths, see this chapter's intro). To trim off the portions of the teeth that extend above the mouth, Putnam chose Edit> Paste in Front, selected the copied mouth and teeth, and used the Intersect Pathfinder command.

4 Creating other character features. Putnam then added a number of character features and details, such as a 15-pt stroke for the lips, a circle for the back of the mouth, another pair of circles for eyes, and a rounded rectangle for the stick.

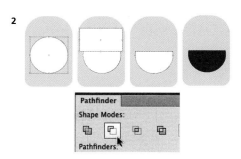

2

Drawing a circle, drawing a rectangle over the circle, selecting both, using the Minus Front Pathfinder command, and changing fill to brown

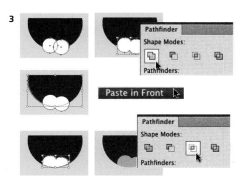

3

Drawing two ellipses, using the Unite Pathfinder command, Copying the mouth and Pasting in Front, selecting the mouth and tongue, and using the Intersect Pathfinder command

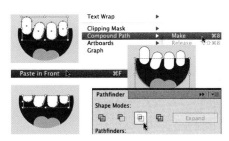

Drawing four rounded rectangles, making a compound shape, Copying the mouth and Pasting in Front, selecting the mouth and teeth, and using the Intersect Pathfinder command

4

Adding additional features with circles and rounded rectangles

Coloring Line Art

Using Live Paint for Fluid Productivity

Overview: *Draw with the Pen tool to trace the minimum paths needed to define discreet areas; color using Live Paint tools for easy selections.*

When Gustavo Del Vechio needed an illustration for his client's urban development proposal, he used Illustrator to draw the initial concept, which he developed more fully in 3D Studio Max. He then rendered the artwork and placed it back into Illustrator as a template. Seeking to create a lively and humanistic interpretation of a crowded city environment, he used the Pen tool for tracing and Live Paint to control coloring, so he could give each building its own personality.

1

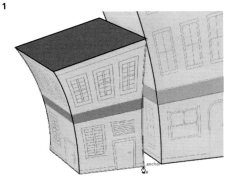

Outlining the 3D model with open paths, using the Pen tool and Smart Guides

Drawing interior details with the other layers locked and Smart Guides turned off

1 Freeform drawing with the Pen tool in preparation for Live Paint. Since he was using Live Paint, Del Vechio was able to draw open paths that would ultimately enclose the areas to be colored, instead of precisely stacking discrete objects atop one another and creating the fully closed paths that normal fills require. Paths that merely crossed over other paths created separate areas, and by drawing only enough paths to separate one area from another, he was able to draw more quickly and efficiently, using many fewer paths and layers. He kept Smart Guides turned on to help signal him as each anchor and path properly lined up with the others.

After he outlined the basic shapes of the building, Del Vechio turned Smart Guides off while he drew the doors and windows more freely on their own layer. Even though the 3D model had curved lines, in order to create the slightly off-kilter look of an illustration, he used only straight segments (except for the arched door and circular window). After tracing the artwork, he selected it all and clicked on it with the Live Paint Bucket tool (hidden under the Shape Builder tool). Once converted to a Live Paint group, the content of all the layers automatically moved into the top layer. Del Vechio next needed to select and delete a few unwanted segments. While the Selection tool selects objects and the Direct Selection tool selects paths, he was able to use the Live Paint Selection tool to select, then delete, individual faces and line segments.

Removing unwanted intersecting edges (highlighted in red) with the Live Paint Selection tool

Using Live Paint, small Swatch groups, and the left and right arrow keys to select new colors while filling faces with the Live Paint Bucket tool

2 Creating Swatch groups and using Global colors makes it easy to apply, and later edit, color. Del Vechio created a small color group for each building. Using the Live Paint Bucket tool, he colored each building, cycling through colors in a group using the left and right arrow keys, and moving between color groups using the up and down keys. He also assigned all the colors he created as Global swatches. If he later wanted to replace a color, he only had to replace the swatch itself and it would automatically update that color anywhere in the document.

To ensure he wouldn't accidentally color a stroke when he only wanted to fill a face on the buildings, Del Vechio double-clicked on the Live Paint Bucket tool and disabled Paint Strokes in the dialog. After he filled the main areas of the buildings, he created a gradient for the lights in the windows. In order to paint some of the strokes (but not all), he again opened the Live Paint dialog to enable Paint Strokes and disable Paint Fills. He then selected all the Strokes and set their weight to None. With the Stroke weight set to 0.75 pt and choosing various brown colors, he selectively filled some strokes around the windows and doors. Although the strokes were now invisible, Live Paint would highlight them when his cursor passed over them.

Finally Del Vechio reset the Live Paint Bucket Options to Paint for both Fills and Strokes, then recolored some of the areas and edges to complete his whimsical cityscape.

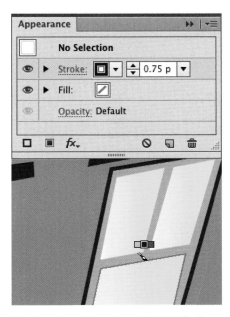

Painting a few of the edges with Paint Fills disabled, Paint Strokes enabled, and the Stroke set for color and width in the Appearance panel

Blob to Live Paint

From Sketch to Blob Brush and Live Paint

Overview: *Place sketch as a template; trace sketch with the Blob Brush tool; color with the Live Paint Bucket tool.*

PUTNAM

Ryan Putnam has a stock illustration portfolio full of hand-drawn illustrations. Putnam found that using the new Blob Brush tool and his Wacom pen tablet, he could now easily create a hand-drawn look using Illustrator. Moreover, by using Live Paint, he could quickly fill his illustration with color.

1

The original tattoo sketch

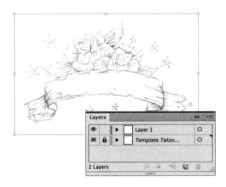

Placing sketch as a template layer

1 Creating a sketch and placing it as a template.
Putnam first created a tattoo sketch in Photoshop and placed it into Illustrator as a template. Create your own sketch, scan it, or sketch directly into a painting program (such as Painter or Photoshop). Save your sketch as PSD, JPEG, or TIF format. Next, create a new Illustrator document and choose File> Place. Locate your sketch, then enable the Template option and click Place (see the chapter *Your Creative Workspace* for more on templates).

2
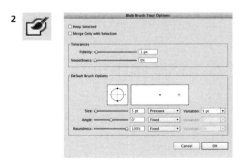

Setting up Blob Brush tool options in CS6; **CC** *combines Tolerances into one Fidelity slider (see the* **CC** *section of this intro for details)*

2 Setting Blob Brush tool options and tracing sketch.
Putnam wanted to create marks that were very true to his stylus gestures and had minimal smoothness. To create this effect with the Blob Brush tool, he first had to modify the default options. To do this, he double-clicked on the Blob Brush tool in the Tools panel. In Options, he set Fidelity to 1, Smoothness to 0, and Size to 5 pt (in **CC** set one Fidelity slider to Accurate; see "The New Pencil Settings (for other tools too)" section in this chapter's **CC** introduction for more about Fidelity changes). From the Size drop-down menu he selected Pressure, changed Size

Variation to 5 pt, and clicked OK (if you don't have a pen tablet, you can't use Pressure settings). Using these custom Blob Brush settings, Putnam began to trace the scanned sketch template into the layer above, varying his stylus pressure to re-create the hand-drawn style.

While drawing with the Blob Brush tool, Putnam used the Eraser tool, set up to work with pressure-sensitivity, to modify brush marks and correct mistakes. To do this, Putnam double-clicked the Eraser tool from the Tools panel and changed the Diameter to 5 pt. He then selected Pressure from the Diameter drop-down menu, changed the Diameter Variation to 5 pt, and clicked OK. By setting up the Eraser tool with pressure-sensitive settings, he could move easily between the two tools by simply flipping the stylus around.

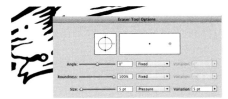

Tracing sketch with the Blob Brush tool

Setting up default Eraser tool preferences and erasing with the Eraser tool

3 Filling areas with Live Paint. If Putnam used the regular Brush tool to trace his sketch, he would have had to create additional paths defining fill areas to color the drawing. But Blob Brush objects can easily be converted into Live Paint Groups for quick and simple coloring. To convert the illustration to a Live Paint Group, Putnam selected the illustration with the Selection tool, chose the Live Paint Bucket tool from the Tools panel, and on first click, the object became a Live Paint Group. With the Live Paint Bucket tool, he hovered over the selected illustration to highlight areas to fill. With the left and right arrow keys, Putnam cycled through the swatches from the Swatch Panel until he found his desired color (see the *Color Transitions* chapter for details on creating colors). Once he found the color, he clicked in the area to fill. He repeated cycling through the swatches and filled in the other enclosed areas of the illustration.

Filling areas with the Live Paint Bucket tool

Cycling through swatches with the Live Paint Bucket tool

4 Applying finishing touches. Putnam added additional features as needed. For instance, he warped the type and added gradients to the Live Paint fills (see the "Arcing Type" lesson in the chapter *Designing Type & Layout*, and see the *Color Transitions* chapter for gradients details).

Adding a warped type treatment and gradients

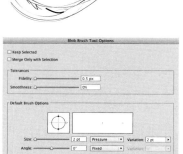

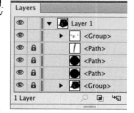

David Turton

For a powerful, yet highly detailed drawing of a tiger's head, David Turton relied upon the natural combination of the Blob Brush tool and the Wacom® Cintiq21UX tablet computer. Because Turton could draw directly on the tablet itself, and his paths would join automatically as they overlapped, he felt he had greater control over this kind of meticulous, but still freehand, pen-and-ink drawing, without having to interrupt the flow to create a new brush or adjust his stroke width. He began a rough sketch with brush settings that most closely emulated natural pen strokes. He kept Fidelity and Smoothness at their lowest settings to be as true to his hand as possible (in **CC** you adjust only one Fidelity slider, to most Accurate), and used a very fine, 2-pixel point. Gradually Turton refined the tiger's features, filling in more detail, and keeping the brush tip fine, allowing his strokes to merge naturally as he drew over them, thickening the detail in some areas for greater definition. As the file size grew, he began to lock layers he was happy with and to add more detail as the drawing progressed. This prevented strokes from merging and forcing constant re-renders of the drawing. Such extensive detail is very demanding of a computer's resources. When he had completed most of the tiger, he unlocked the layers and merged them all. Lastly, he used the Eraser tool to "draw out" the whiskers by erasing next to their lines, creating an interruption in the strokes in order to enhance the illusion of whiskers overlapping the fur.

Lance Jackson

Lance Jackson drew this fanciful animal using a combination of the Blob Brush and Eraser tools. Here is his tale of how this unusual creature came into being: "I had the opportunity to apply to a position opening for a Google doodler. Part of the preliminary interview process was to take the Google Graphics Test. The second question was 'Draw or sketch a furry animal. It can be any kind of animal, but most importantly, it should be original.' I submitted three animals. The first one was the Vegetarian Cheetah. It was initially done as a pencil sketch.

After submitting my ten drawings and digital color paintings to Google (this was a timed test) I decided to create another version in Illustrator using the Blob Brush. I first started with just the merged bodies of the running cheetah with the quizzical head of a rabbit. A week later I decided to add the background. I continued on using the Blob Brush since it helps to unify the similar colors. The Blob Brush provided the best means to merge the cheetah and rabbit together without going deep into the DNA code of both animals."

STOPPEE

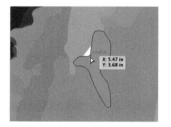

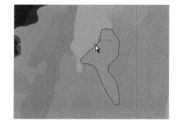

Janet Stoppee

As a graphic designer and master gardener Janet Stoppee combined her two favorite activities to create a seed packet for a Flowering Maple. She used a photo of a maple she had grown herself from seed as the basis for her illustration. Experience has shown her that prepping a photo before tracing it helps produce the desired results. In Illustrator, choosing a palette to use in Image Trace both simplifies and colorizes a photo, but Stoppee has traditionally simplified first with a favorite third-party filter (Topaz Simplify) in Photoshop. In this case, she chose the preset Painting Harsh-

Color to intensify the natural colors. In Illustrator, she opened the file, selected it, and opened the Image Trace panel. There she enabled Preview and experimented with the different presets. Stoppee chose Accurate Fidelity with the default settings. After tracing her image, she expanded it and zoomed in to 1200%. Unavoidably, even when using the Overlap method, complex tracings can still have small holes where edges don't meet. A solid background in a matching color might solve the problem, but if not, you can do as Stoppee did and manually repair the holes with the Direct Selection tool.

MARKIEWICZ

Danuta Markiewicz (Danka)

Danuta "Danka" Markiewicz is a Polish artist who lives in Italy and creates wonderful illustrated books using Illustrator and a bit of Photoshop. She scans in her sketches, then runs them through Image Trace in black and white with "Ignore White" enabled. Danka converts these traced illustrations into Live Paint objects and colors and recolors the elements. She brings in textures from Photoshop and changes the blending mode to Overlay. She brings in her texture a second time and uses Image Trace in color mode. To create the bowing she applies Effect> Warp> Arc to the image, and to both an image and a drop-shadow. Opening the images and textures in Photoshop, she combines some layers with Soft Light blending mode, while on others she runs her favorite filter: Minimum. She integrates text in either English or Polish using fonts that simulate handwriting. Though her characters are vector-based and graphic in style, her final books end up rather painterly and richly textured.

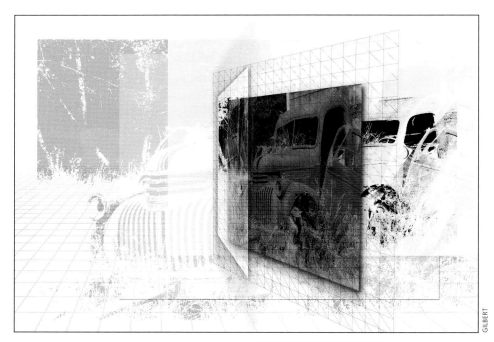

GILBERT

Katharine Gilbert

Katharine Gilbert used Illustrator and Photoshop to produce "Vintage," an image of the multiverse of a rusting truck as it appears in many dimensions. She used Image Trace to create her black and white version of the truck because Photoshop's Threshold filter doesn't retain as much detail. She reduced the Threshold setting for this dark photo in order to bring out a maximum range of contrast in the 2-color image, and she set Paths to their maximum accuracy. To keep the grungy, angular detail throughout, she also set Corners to their highest for the least amount of smoothing, and moved the Noise setting to a minimum so the finest detail would be traced. After running Image Trace, she clicked on the Expand button in the Options bar, resized the image to 6 x 4 inches, and reduced the layer's Opacity to 20%.

From there, Gilbert opened the .ai file in Photoshop (saved with PDF compatibility, it opens as a PDF), and began layering different versions of the truck. She made extensive use of Photoshop's blending modes, as well as the 3D Postcard feature, in order to reproduce the truck with varying color, tonality, and perspective.

Cheryl Graham

Cheryl Graham drew this self-portrait based on a reference photo she simplified with Image Trace. After placing the photo in Illustrator, she opened the Image Trace panel and, from Preset, chose Shades of Gray. Graham enabled Preview to see the effects as she adjusted settings until paths and corners were simple and there were just a handful of grays. With Preview selected, her setting was automatically applied when she closed the Image Trace window. Graham placed this version in a locked layer as a template to trace over; she also kept a copy of the original photo on her artboard as an additional reference. She created a dark global color so she would be able to specify various tints of the color as she drew. Graham double-clicked on the Blob Brush tool and, in the Blob Brush Options, she set Fidelity and Smoothness at their lowest settings (in **CC** she adjusts only Fidelity, to most Accurate), specified an 8-pt brush size with an 8-pt variation, and selected Pressure. In the Color panel, Graham specified a 10% tint of the global color and with the Blob Brush drew in the lightest values. She repeated the process using progressively darker tints, making a separate layer for each tint and gradually building the portrait (some of the layers shown at right). Occasionally she increased or decreased the Blob Brush size with the [ ] keys. While Graham drew, she kept an enlarged Navigator panel open (Window> Navigator). When she zoomed into an area, either drawing with the Blob Brush, or adjusting a path with the Direct Selection tool, she could refer to the Navigator panel and easily see how the changes she made in a particular area affected the entire

GRAHAM

portrait, without having to constantly zoom in and out of the drawing. Although the low fidelity Blob Brush setting in CS6 often creates too many anchor points, Graham prefers to start with this setting and later apply Object> Path> Simplify, specifying 95% for Curve Precision (if there aren't too many extra points, she skips the Simplify step and applies the Smooth tool instead). To finish the portrait, Graham made custom art brushes with tapered ends (directly above) for the details such as the eyelashes and eyebrows. She used a Round Curve Bristle Brush to create the shadows behind the head.

KLEMA

Stephen A. Klema

Stephen Klema uses Illustrator's Live Paint to assist him in the conception and construction of his sculptures. For "Wood's Revenge," he scanned his pencil sketch of the tree and saw blade, then opened it in Illustrator. To keep the outline distinct as he filled in the parts, he used the Pen tool to create a contour shape with a white fill and no stroke, and used it as a mask on the top layer. He selected the Paintbrush with a 1pt stroke to begin tracing (Live Paint converts brushstrokes to basic strokes, so the Pen or Pencil tools will also work here). After tracing some of the key lines that would become his wood shapes, Klema selected them and chose Object> Live Paint> Make. To get a clear view of the relationship between the shapes, he used the Live Paint tool (K) to fill the shapes with colors that clearly delineated

the separate pieces (above right, middle figure). Where necessary, he used the Pen tool to add and subtract anchor points, and the Direct Selection tool to adjust the paths. Klema then traced another section of his scan. To move this set of paths into the Live Paint group, he selected both the new paths and the Live Paint object, and chose Object> Live Paint> Merge. In this way, he developed all the filled shapes for his sculpture. To recolor the shapes so they more closely approximated wood and saw, he created a custom swatch group and used the Live Paint tool to refill the shapes with their final colors. Klema then removed the strokes to see how well the colors and contrast worked. With his concept finalized as a Live Paint object, he could move on to creating the template files needed to make the sculpture itself.

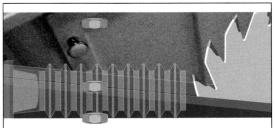 

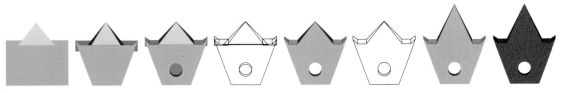

Stephen A. Klema

Stephen Klema found that the Shape Builder tool helped him to save time when creating some of the tool illustrations in his art animation and interactive design piece entitled "100 Days." To construct the drill bit, for instance, Klema began by drawing basic 4-sided objects with the Rectangle tool, and 3-sided objects using the Star tool (reducing it to three sides using the down arrow key). He then added points with the Add Anchor Point tool, and shifted the points using the Direct Selection tool (holding the Shift key to constrain movement). When the basic shapes were in the proper position, he selected them all and then used the Shape Builder tool to start combining some objects by click-dragging from one to the other (e.g., from the bottom orange object to the top triangle), and deleting others and even making holes by holding Option/Alt when clicking (or click-dragging). When the drill bit was properly combined he marquee-Direct-Selected the top anchor points and Shift-dragged the points upwards to elongate the point. Finally, he recolored the newly configured objects. See Klema's "100 Days" project at www.StephenKlema.com/100days.

Rapid Reshaping

Using Shape Builder to Construct Objects

Overview: *Create overlapping objects, color them with a Premedia Systems script, and use the Shape Builder tool to unite some parts and delete others; recolor, use drawing modes and the Bristle Brush to add a background, shading, and textures; resize artboards with another Premedia script.*

STEUER

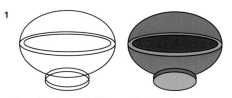

Drawing the oval objects and using the Premedia Systems Colorizer script to assign each object a different color

Dragging to unite the shapes that make up the bottom of the bowl; then deleting side pieces on foot and top shape (cursors magnified)

Sharon Steuer created this piece for a user group demo highlighting how some newer features in Illustrator—the Shape Builder tool, drawing modes, and the Bristle Brush—make constructing objects quicker and easier.

1 Constructing the bowl from overlapping objects.

Since the Shape Builder can both unite objects and delete parts of intersecting objects, using it can be much simpler and quicker than either drawing precisely with the Pen tool, or using Pathfinder commands. To follow along with the figures in this lesson, set the fill and stroke to the default (press the D key), then set the fill to None (X toggles focus between fill and stroke; the / key sets the style to None); then, with the Ellipse tool (L), draw a series of ovals that align at the center. (To help you do this quickly and efficiently, make sure that Smart Guides are on (⌘-U/Ctrl-U), use the modifier keys Option/Alt to draw from the center, and use the spacebar key to adjust the position of the oval as you draw.) It's easier to control your use of the Shape Builder tool if each object you'll be working with is a different color. A quick way to do this in **CC** is to use the Premedia Systems Colorizer script (install instructions and scripts are on **WOW! ONLINE**). With the script installed, select everything and choose File> Scripts> WOWArtworkColorizer. In the script dialog, enable "No colors" to let the script select colors and save the used colors as a swatch group (your colors may differ from the ones shown here). For the next step, you'll be using the Shape Builder tool (Shift-M) to hover over the selected shapes, looking at the highlighted areas to see how they will connect. If the areas that you wish to maintain aren't visible (for instance, the purple oval needs to be on top in order to form the foot of the bowl), then adjust the stacking order by cutting and using Paste in Front/Back. With Pick Color From Artwork enabled (double-click on the Shape Builder tool for options), drag from the red bowl through the upper half of the purple oval. To delete the side pieces of the foot and the top of the bowl, hold down Option/Alt while clicking on them.

2 Completing the composition. You can select each shape (which is now a separate object) and recolor the bowl, and you can even marquee-select all the objects and set the Stroke to None. To quickly place a background behind all objects, select the Draw Behind drawing mode, either by clicking its icon in the Tools panel, or by pressing Shift-D until you see the icon. Draw rectangles for the background objects. (Steuer drew one rectangle filled with the Plaid 2 Pattern, and another with blue.)

3 Finishing touches on the bowl. Select one bowl object (you can only select one at a time), along with the Brush tool, and choose Draw Inside mode (Shift-D), which places dotted corners around the object. Deselect the object and load the Bristle Brush library. Choose a Bristle Brush and paint on the object; Draw Inside constrains your brush strokes within the selected object. When you want to paint another object, you must first exit Draw Inside mode (Shift-D, or double-click with a selection tool). Select the next object and choose Draw Inside again (you can even draw inside a pattern, like the bowl's shadow). When Steuer was done, she wanted to crop the image for the demo she would output to PDF. The easiest way was to resize all the artboards by 72% using Premedia Systems' Artboard Resizer script. This script (also on **WOW! ONLINE)** resizes any or all artboards from the center.

2

Recoloring the bowl with the Grays swatch group; then choosing None for the objects' stroke

3

Draw Normal, Draw Behind, Draw Inside

Using Draw Inside to constrain the Mop Bristle Brush to a single, selected object, denoted by the dotted corners

Using the WOW! Artboard Resizer by Premedia Systems to resize selected artboards smaller

Easily view drawing modes

You can see (and therefore easily click) each drawing mode if your Tools panel is in double-column view; click the double-arrow in the title bar of the Tools panel to toggle the view between single and double-column. Check your drawing mode if your objects are not going where you intended.

Drawing Inside

Building with Multiple Construction Modes

Advanced Technique

Overview: *Create varying types of shading, texture, and detail within objects using Draw Inside mode; alter basic shapes and prepare them for masking using Shape Builder; add soft shading by using Blob Brush in conjunction with Draw Inside mode.*

The initial blocked-in artwork

When in Draw Inside mode, new objects added into the cliff object are clipped

Building and shading complex artwork in Illustrator can be a daunting task. Thankfully, there are clipping masks. Chris Leavens employs a combination of construction methods in his artwork, "The Gardener," including harnessing the artistic and organizational capabilities of both the Draw Inside mode (to quickly create clipping masks) and the Shape Builder tool (to combine objects).

1 Creating masks using Draw Inside, and beginning to add detail. Using the Pen tool, Leavens blocked in the composition by drawing basic, flat, colored forms. He then selected the large cliff object (which spans the width of the artwork's background) and changed the drawing mode to Draw Inside (Shift-D). Upon entering Draw Inside mode, he deselected by holding ⌘/Ctrl and clicking outside of the artboard and then added form-defining objects within the cliff object using the Pen tool. He freely plotted new anchor points outside the boundaries of the cliffs, allowing the mask created by Draw Inside mode to keep the edges clean and precise. After finishing the cliffs, Leavens repeated the same steps on the other objects, adding both shading and detail.

2 Preparing objects for Draw Inside mode with Shape Builder. To speed up the drawing process, Leavens used the Pen tool and drew the large, swooping tree in multiple pieces. In order to employ the same shading method he used for the other objects, he selected the various overlapping pieces of the tree. He then chose Shape Builder (Shift-M) and click-dragged over the overlapping objects, quickly combining them into one large object, which he shaded using the method mentioned in step one.

Leavens used Shape Builder subtractively to create the cactus. To make the cactus look broken and parched, he used the Pen tool to draw jagged forms on top of a pair of the cactus's branches. He then selected the cactus and the new, jagged shapes and switched back to the Shape Builder tool. While holding the Option/Alt key, Leavens click-dragged over the area he wanted to remove, leaving behind newly-broken branches.

3 Adding fast shading with Blob Brush and Draw Inside mode. In order to add soft, feathered shading to the puffy purple foliage on the large tree, Leavens decided to use the Blob Brush. To maintain smooth strokes, he first double-clicked the Blob Brush tool in the Tools panel, and in Options he increased the Fidelity and Smoothness settings (in **CC** there is only one Fidelity setting). He then predefined a graphic style for the shading by mixing a shade of violet using the Color panel, switching the blend mode to "Multiply" (by clicking Opacity in the Appearance panel), adding a 3-point feather effect (Effect> Stylize> Feather), and saving the style by clicking the New Graphic Style button in the Graphic Styles panel. To ensure that this style would be properly maintained once he selected and began working with it, he disabled "New Art Has Basic Appearance" from the Appearance panel menu. He selected one of the purple foliage objects, changed to Draw Inside mode (Shift-D), deselected, and chose the Blob Brush tool (Shift-B). Before adding the shading, he clicked on the newly defined Graphic Style swatch. Finally, Leavens brushed in the shading, using the Blob Brush additively to build up larger masses of darker shading, painting solitary strokes where he wanted lighter shading, and using the Eraser tool to make corrections.

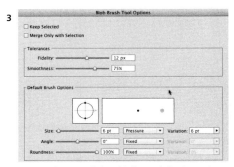

Before and after: using the Shape Builder tool to subtractively alter the cactus branch

Leavens increased the Fidelity and the Smoothness settings in the CS6 Blob Brush Tool Options panel; **CC** combines Tolerances into one Fidelity slider (see the **CC** section of this intro for details)

Final, enlarged version of the composition

COGHILL

George Coghill

Cartoon logo and character artist George Coghill uses the Shape Builder tool to quickly add interior colors to his line art illustrations. In Illustrator, Coghill places a PSD sketch as a template layer and uses the Pen tool to trace the contours of each pencil-drawn outline with black-filled objects (as opposed to stroked paths). He then selects all the objects and uses the Shape Builder tool to fill the main interior (white) areas with color. (If you create outlines using stroked or brushed paths, you'll have to first expand the paths into black-filled objects using Object> Path> Outline Path.) Coghill creates a global color group for his illustration to allow him to later edit a swatch and have it update the art instantly (for help with global colors and color groups see the *Color Transitions* chapter). Double-clicking the Shape Builder tool icon to customize options, he chooses Color Swatches from the Pick Color From drop-down menu, enables Cursor Swatch Preview, and clicks OK. Coghill then selects all objects on that layer (⌘-A/Ctrl-A) and clicks on the new custom color group's folder icon in the Swatches panel. Hovering the Shape Builder tool over the interior areas and using the left and right arrow keys, he cycles through the color swatches he created earlier in his custom color group and chooses a color for each area. The center color swatch preview under the cursor indicates which swatch is the current color. He clicks on the highlighted area to fill it with the color and continues until he has colored all the interior areas. Because he used global colors, if he double-clicks a swatch and edits the color, when he clicks OK, every object filled with that swatch will also update.

Ray Acosta

For a university-wide program developed to strengthen community, Ray Acosta created "Libertad" (Freedom) to illustrate how freedom also demands responsibility. It typifies his workflow in which he sketches his idea for the monthly message in a not during project meetings, and later scans the sketch to place it in Illustrator as a template. Next he uses the Rectangle and Pen tools to quickly and loosely approximate his sketch on a new art layer. Using Live Rectangles, Live Corners, and Reshape Segment features, Acosta starts to push and pull his paths into objects that display an organic, carefree quality. While both Live Rectangles and Live Corners have panels that let artists use precise numeric input, Acosta prefers to round his corners for

objects, such as the character's face and the bill of the hat, using the on-screen interactive widgets. With these he can directly manipulate the corners as he visually matches his sketch. He then uses the Reshape Segment feature (accessed when the Pen tool is active by holding down the Option/Alt key), to drag straight line segments into curves that closely align with his sketch. He applies color after his composition is complete, often exploring themes via the Kuler panel (now the Color Themes panel). He adds many finishing touches, such as applying charcoal art brushes to strokes to add subtle texture to the vector edges of objects and hand-drawn type (details above), and creating background textures from Image Traced photos.

Chapter 3 *Rethinking Construction*   **101**

Rounding a Corner

Using Live Corners to Create a Map Symbol

Overview: *Create text and artwork; draw a rectangle to encompass the artwork; drag corner widgets or work in the Control or Transform panels to round and invert corners.*

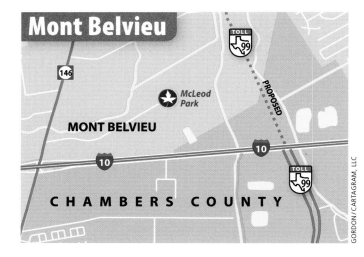

GORDON / CARTAGRAM, LLC

1

On the left, the drawn rectangle with the corner widgets; on the right, the completed Junction symbol displaying Inverted Round corners

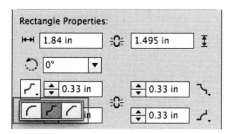

The Rectangle Properties section of the Transform panel showing the Inverted Round icon selected from the Corner Type pop-up menu

Corner on one tool

The Live Corner icons will show when you first make a rectangle with the Rectangle tool or select it with the Selection tool, but you can only convert corner points to other types using the Direct Selection tool.

Steven Gordon uses a variety of geometric shapes to build map symbols. For this location map of Mont Belvieu, Texas, Gordon designed complex road symbols using Live Rectangles and Live Corners rather than using basic geometric shapes like ellipses and rectangles.

1 Creating a scalloped map symbol by changing the corner type. Gordon needed a junction map symbol with scalloped corners. He began by typing "JCT" and then drew a rectangle around it (which automatically opened the Transform panel). To scallop corners on the selected rectangle, he first changed its corner type to Inverted Round by switching to the Direct Selection tool, holding Option/Alt and clicking once on a corner widget (the Radius must be greater than 0 to see the effect). Alternatively, you can choose Inverted Round from the Corner Type pop-up in the Transform panel, from ••• in the Transform section of the Properties panel, or via Corner or Shapes in the Control panel. Releasing Option/Alt, Gordon dragged the widget inward to scallop the corners.

2 Creating the basic artwork and text with a surrounding rectangle. For the toll road symbol, Gordon started by creating the artwork and text that would appear inside the rounded rectangle of the symbol's frame. He drew the state border of Texas with the Pen tool and created two type objects ("99" and "TOLL"). He used the Scissors tool to cut a section of the border path, deleted it, then positioned the "99" in the empty space, partially inside the state. Then he centered "TOLL" with the other objects.

After he finished creating and arranging the artwork, Gordon was ready to create the rounded rectangle that would serve as the map symbol's frame. With the Rectangle tool he clicked and dragged until the rectangle was sized appropriately for the artwork he created previously.

3 Rounding corners in the rectangular frame. After positioning the rectangle, Gordon rounded the bottom two corners to look more like an ellipse. To do this, he switched to the Direct Selection tool and selected the two anchor points at the bottom of the rectangle. With both points selected, he clicked on one of the corner widgets and dragged inward, toward the center of the rectangle. When he dragged far enough, the bottom of the rectangle collapsed into the shape of an ellipse. Gordon repeated this step for the top of the rectangle; this time he dragged inward a short distance to gently round the corners.

4 Changing individual corner radius values in the transform panel. Gordon needed another rectangle to provide a color-filled background behind "TOLL." With the rectangle still selected, he copied and pasted the copy in front (it was above the original rectangle but below the border path and type) and filled it with blue. Next, in the Transform panel, he unlinked the Link Corner Radius default setting by clicking its icon. Then he reset the corner radius of both bottom corners to 0, which squared the bottom of the rectangle while leaving the top rounded. Selecting the bottom bounding box handle, he shortened the rectangle to surround "TOLL" by dragging the handle upward.

To finalize his map symbols he added drop shadows (see the *Reshaping Dimensions* chapter for more on Live Effects), and then made each map symbol into an Illustrator symbol for easy reuse (see the *Expressive Strokes* chapter for details on creating and using symbols).

2

Creating a Live Rectangle on top of the map symbol artwork

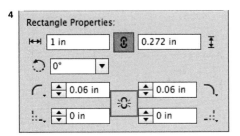

3

On the left, the bottom two Live Corner widgets moved to round the bottom of the rectangle; on the right, the top two widgets moved to round the top of the rectangle

4

The Rectangle Properties section of the Transform panel showing the unlinked Link Corner Radius Values icon and the values used for the bottom corners of the rectangle

The completed blue-filled rectangle

The final TOLL map symbol with a drop shadow

Pencil & Pen Paths

Using Drawing Tools to Edit Paths

FERSTER

Overview: *Draw freeform paths with the Pencil tool; switch to the Pen tool for straight line and Bézier curves; use modifier keys to change tools and access Reshape Segment cursor for editing paths.*

1

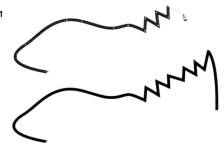

Using the Pencil tool (N) for the left lobe, then switching to the Pen tool (P) to switch from drawing a freeform path to straight lines

2

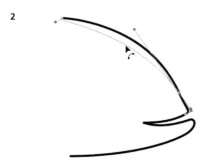

Using the Pen tool to draw the fish head using Bézier curves, holding Option/Alt to access the Reshape Segment cursor to adjust arcs while working

Pencil straight lines

Although drawing straight lines with the Pen tool is easier, now you can also draw polyline paths with the Pencil tool (see this chapter's **CC** intro for more about this).

When illustrator and designer Gary Ferster needed to create a trade show menu for Intuit Inc., he decided to use a combination of Pencil and Pen tools, along with the Reshape Segment cursor.

1 Drawing with the Pencil (N) and Pen tool (P). Ferster decided to use the Pencil tool to start the top fins of the fish. Double-clicking on the Pencil tool in the Toolbar he adjusted Fidelity and confirmed that the "Keep selected" and "Edit selected" options were enabled. With the Pencil tool he drew the left lobe of the top fin. To attach a jagged edge to his selected path, he pressed the P key to switch to the Pen tool and clicked on the last point of his pencil path. Watching his rubber-band preview, he clicked to create his first segment, continuing to click to place the next point until he'd formed the jagged edge. To draw the front edge of the fin, he pressed the N key to switch back to the Pencil tool and (starting from the last anchor point) drew the front downward section of the fin.

2 Drawing (and reshaping) curves with the Pen tool. To draw the long curved arcs of the fish's head, Ferster pressed the P key to switch to the Pen tool and drew the fish's face using Bézier curves, holding Option/Alt to access the Reshape Segment cursor to adjust the arc as he worked. To complete his graphic he continued to move back and forth between the Pen and Pencil tools.

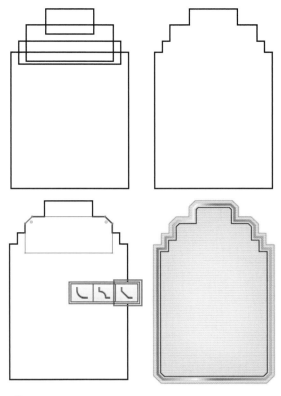

Laura Coyle

Atlanta illustrator Laura Coyle created this bottle as a design preview for a foil-stamped card filled with liquid and with a floating worm. For the background of the label, she drew four overlapping rectangles. Selecting the rectangles, she opened the Pathfinder panel. She Option/Alt-clicked the Unite icon to create a compound shape. Switching to the Direct Selection tool, Coyle selected a horizontal pair of points in the object. She pressed Option/Alt and clicked twice on one of the Live Corner widgets to cycle through the corner types until she got to the Chamfer. She dragged the Live Corner widget inward to change both corner types to Chamfer. She repeated this twice to create two

more pairs of Chamfer corners. To complete the object, Coyle opened the Appearance panel, filled the object with brown, and selected Add New Effect. She then gave the fill an Inner Glow effect. Next, she created a second fill with a line pattern and lightened its opacity. Finally, she added a thin stroke and chose an Outer Glow effect for the entire object. For the interior lines of the label, Coyle copied the object and pasted the copy in front of the original. After removing the copy's fills and effects in the Appearance panel, she added two strokes. Coyle then used the Offset Path effect to move each stroke inward. (See the *Reshaping Dimensions* chapter for more about the Appearance panel.)

Shaper Tooling
Creating & Editing with the Shaper Tool

Overview: *Draw with the Shaper tool and Smart Guides; Combine, align, and erase objects; Adjust segments with the Shaper tool, and color with the Live Paint Bucket tool.*

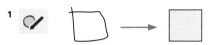

1

Using the Shaper tool, Pfreundner drew a square-shaped gesture that Illustrator converted to a perfect square

2

*With the Shaper tool (from left to right): drawing a circle; a **Z**-shaped scribble "erases"; how the resulting live shapes appear after "erasing"*

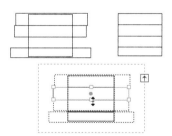

Rectangles overlapping the base square (top left); after "erasing" portions extending beyond the base (top right); clicking with the Shaper tool to access the live elements for adjustment (bottom)

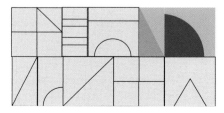

Assembling squares within the "mosaic" grid, with object sections colored using the Live Paint Bucket (see Gallery opposite for details)

PFREUNDNER

Illustrator and designer Simona Pfreundner drew perfect geometric objects, combined these objects in a variety of ways, and erased portions of objects that extended beyond her "base" square—all with the Shaper tool. After combining the squares to create a modular "mosaic" grid, she colored individual segments with the Live Paint Bucket tool.

1 Drawing with the Shaper tool and Smart Guides.
With Smart Guides on (View menu), Pfreundner began her mosaic by gesturally drawing a square with the Shaper tool; the Shaper tool replaced the gesture with a perfect square. To begin her design with this square as the base, she duplicated it (holding Option/Alt while dragging).

2 Combining, aligning, and erasing forms. Moving a base square into a work area, she gesturally drew another geometric object overlapping the base. To "erase" portions of objects that extend beyond the base, she drew a **Z**-shaped scribble over that area. With the objects joined together, she continued to use the Shaper tool to adjust object positioning, and to rotate and scale individual elements. Though Pfreundner formed all her mosaic segments with circles and rotated rectangles, the Shaper tool also draws lines, triangles, hexagons, and polygons—and it even can cut a pie shape from a circle. After dragging units together to form the mosaic, she switched to the Live Paint Bucket tool to fill segments with color (see Gallery opposite for details on the Live Paint Bucket process).

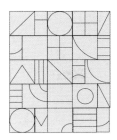

Simona Pfreundner

For a proposed line of product packaging, Simona Pfreundner created and edited geometric objects with the Shaper tool (see lesson opposite). Using her sketch as inspiration, she assembled a "mosaic" grid of these elements using the Selection tool with Smart Guides enabled. She then created a color group containing a set of custom global colors. The Shaper tool made it simple for Pfreundner to edit, combine, and erase objects and sections of objects, but she found the color controls awkward. She discovered that objects made with the Shaper and Live Paint Bucket can each be edited with the other's tools. With one of the custom colors in her group selected, she switched to the Live Paint Bucket tool so she could take advantage of its superior color controls. Her cursor now displayed three color swatches: the fill she had just selected in the center, with the color directly to the left and right of it as they appear in the Swatches panel. To fill each section, she used the left and right arrow keys to select a color, hovered until it was outlined in a red highlight, then clicked to fill it. When a section demanded adjusting, she'd switch back to the Shaper tool.

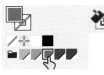

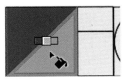

COGHILL

George Coghill

When employing a brush-and-ink style for a cartoon character illustration, artist George Coghill likes to enhance the organic look of his brush lines by using the new Path Segment Reshape feature. In order to be able to quickly access this feature while working with the Paintbrush tool, Coghill first presses the A key to activate the Direct Selection tool (so it is the last used selection tool, accessed by ⌘/Ctrl key from other tools) and then presses the B key to activate the Paintbrush tool. This way, Coghill can quickly create a brushstroke with the Paintbrush tool using a Calligraphic brush, then temporarily activate the Direct Selection tool by pressing the ⌘/Ctrl key and clicking on the segment of a path to show the anchor points. Then he can hover his cursor over the brushed path he just created and fine-tune his brush-

stroke with the Reshape Segment feature. As he works, he is able to make subtle adjustments along the way (see the *Expressive Brushstrokes* chapter for more on working with brushes).

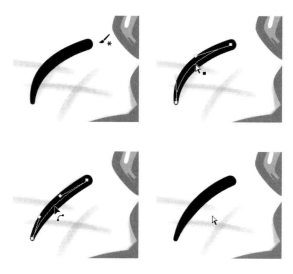

4

Expressive Strokes

Expressive Strokes

DONAL JOLLEY

Creating discontinuous curves from continuous curves with the Width tool when creating a flag

Illustrator gives you an abundance of ways to create Strokes with organic, hand-drawn lines, painterly effects, shading, and much more. You can manually adjust the contours of a path with the Width tool to emulate calligraphy and save its form (profile) in the Stroke panel to apply to another path. You can specify precisely where the middle section of an art brush will stretch along a path and where the ends (such as arrowheads) will be protected from distortion. You have control over how pattern brushes and dashed lines fit around corners. You can use "natural media" bristle brushes to make complex and painterly marks, emulating airbrush, pastel, and wet paint, and using traditional brush shapes like flat or fan. And symbols can be sprayed and manipulated using a special set of Symbolism tools.

WIDTH TOOL AND STROKE PROFILES

The Width tool (Shift-W) varies the width of strokes created with the drawing and geometric shape tools or art and pattern brushes. The path doesn't have to be selected; hover over it with the Width tool and the path will highlight, along with hollow diamonds indicating existing width points that were set automatically, such as the end points of a path or that you have set. As you move your cursor over the path, still hovering, a hollow diamond moves with your cursor, ready to become a width point at whatever location along the path you click. You can modify paths between two existing width points, and can create either a flowing, *continuous* curve or a *discontinuous* one with a sharp break between sections.

If width points are spaced apart, the path gradually gets wider or narrower from one point to the next in a continuous curve. If width points are placed on top of each other, you create a sharp break between the two widths, causing the curve to abruptly widen or narrow, much like adding an arrowhead to the path. Modify strokes on either side of the path by either adjusting the stroke weight evenly along the path or placing more weight on one side of the path than the other. Your custom stroke profile is temporarily stored in the Stroke panel, making it possible to apply the same stroke to as many paths in the document as you wish. An asterisk in the Appearance panel beside Stroke denotes a width profile. You can also save a custom profile as part of a Graphic Style and/or to the Profiles list using the Save icon at the bottom of the Stroke panel list. The Reset icon restores the default width profiles, replacing any custom profiles you've saved; see the Warning Tip (on the previous page) "Save those width profiles." You can modify width points in a variety of ways with the Width tool:

- **To numerically adjust a Width Point,** double-click on a path or existing width point to open the Width Point Edit dialog. Enter the stroke weight for each side of the path, and/or choose to have adjoining width points adjusted at the same time.
- **To interactively adjust the width point,** click-drag on a handle to symmetrically adjust the stroke width.
- **To adjust one side of a stroke,** press Option/Alt while dragging on a handle.
- **To adjust or move multiple width points,** Shift-click to select the points (not anchors) you want to alter and then drag on one point or handle to adjust the others with it.
- **To adjust or move all adjoining width points** (up to the next corner anchor point), hold Shift while dragging.
- **To copy selected points,** hold Option/Alt as you drag.
- **To delete a selected width point,** press the Delete key.
- **To deselect a width point,** click on an empty space away from the path, or press the Esc key.

THE EXPANDED STROKE PANEL

The Stroke panel controls settings for the many different types of strokes, from how they align to the path of an object to how they join at corners. Dashed lines, end caps, and arrowheads all are part of the Stroke panel, as well as stored width profiles, from a normal even width to a

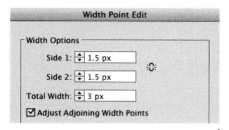

To numerically adjust one or more selected width points, double-click one to open the dialog and make adjustments; select just one point before entering the dialog if you want to enable Adjust Adjoining Width Points

(Top) The starting stroke with width points already added and adjusted; (middle) the width point at the right end adjusted again to make the end wider and Adjust Adjoining Width Points disabled; (bottom) with Adjust Adjoining Width Points enabled when adjusting the same original right-end width point—starting stroke shown for clarity in red on top of both adjusted strokes

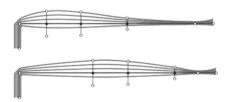

Shift-selecting just some contiguous (shown) or non-contiguous (not shown) width points on a pattern brushstroke, releasing Shift, then moving them all at once

A path shown first in Outline, then in Preview with a Miter join, Round join, and Bevel join

The Profiles list at the bottom of any Stroke panel lets you apply save, and delete custom Width Profiles, and restore the Uniform default width

SALLY COX

(Top) When Dashes with round caps are added to art by Sally Cox, the default option in the Stroke panel preserves dash size but are unevenly distributed around the frame; (bottom) changing the option to Align to corners dash size varies the size of dashes but evens spacing

fully calligraphic profile. Here you can also customize and save your carefully crafted stroke profiles after creating a variable-width stroke, and preview how your path joins to an arrowhead. Adjust the way dashes follow a path, and scale arrowheads to suit.

Making ends meet

Sometimes stroked lines seem to match up perfectly when viewed in Outline mode, but they visibly overlap in Preview mode. You can solve this problem by selecting one of the three end cap styles in the Strokes panel. The default Butt cap causes your path to stop at the end anchor point and is essential for creating exact placement of one path against another. The Round cap is especially good for softening the effect of single line segments. The Projecting cap extends lines and dashes at half the stroke weight beyond the end anchor point. Cap styles also affect the shape of dashed lines.

Corners have joins that serve a similar purpose to end caps. The Join style in the Stroke panel determines the shape of a stroke at its corner points; the inside of the corner is always angled. The default Miter join creates a pointy corner, with the length of the point determined by the width of the stroke, the angle of the corner (narrow angles create longer points), and the Miter limit setting on the Stroke panel. The default Miter join (with a miter limit of 10x) usually looks fine, but can range from 1x (which is always blunt) to 500x. The Round join creates a rounded outside corner with a radius of half the stroke width. The Bevel join creates a squared-off outside corner, equivalent to a Miter join with the miter limit set to 1x.

Dashes behave like short lines and therefore have both end caps and, potentially, corner joins. End caps work with dashes exactly as they do with the ends of paths—each dash is treated as a very short path. However, if a dashed path goes around the corner, it can make that turn in one of two ways: The spacing between the dashes can be precise and constant, so the dash won't necessarily bend around a corner, or even reach to it, or you can click the "Aligns dashes to corners and path ends, adjusting lengths to fit" icon. Dashes won't be precisely spaced, but will look tidy at the corners. The command affects dash spacing for other shapes, from circles to stars, as well.

One more "end" to a path is an arrowhead, and the Stroke panel now offers a choice of both the types of arrowheads and how they are affixed to the ends of the paths. Click the Arrowheads pop-up list to choose to attach an arrow or feather to the start or end of the path. You can then scale it proportionally or disproportionally, reverse the start and end, or align the arrowhead so that either the tip or the end of the arrow meets the end of the path. To remove an arrowhead (or feather), choose None from the list. You can add custom arrowheads to the list without removing any of the default arrowheads (you'd have to reinstall Illustrator to make them available again if you removed them). Both dash alignment options and arrowheads can be modified again at any time.

BRUSHES

Illustrator's calligraphic, art, scatter, bristle, and pattern brushes can mimic traditional art tools, create photorealistic imagery, or provide pattern and texture to your art. You can either create brushstrokes with the Paintbrush tool, or you can apply a brush to a previously drawn path.

Calligraphic brushes create strokes that mimic real-world calligraphy pens, brushes, or felt pens. You can define a degree of variation for the size, roundness, and angle of each "nib." You can also set each of these attributes to respond to a graphics tablet and stylus (like the Wacom) with a variety of different pen characteristics (with a mouse, you can only use Fixed or Random).

Art brushes consist of one or more pieces of artwork that get fitted to the path you create with them. You can use art brushes to imitate traditional painting media, such as drippy ink pens, textured charcoal, spatter brushes, dry brushes, watercolors, and more. Or an art brush can represent real-world objects, such as a petal, leaf, ribbon, a flower, decorative flourish, or train. You can modify

Creating custom arrowheads

Illustrator Help provides directions for locating the Arrowheads file on your computer. The file contains instructions for customizing and saving arrowheads without overwriting the original file.

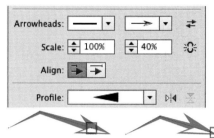

Using the Arrowheads section of the Stroke panel to align the arrowhead so the tail of the arrowhead joins the end of the path with the head extending beyond (left and as shown in the dialog), or to align the arrowhead so the tip of the arrowhead joins the end of the path (right)

Deleting arrowhead presets

To make custom arrowheads, be sure to modify only the file holding the default presets. If you delete any arrowheads in that file, you'll have to reinstall Illustrator to get them back again.

Graphics tablets & brushes

Bristle brushes, which mimic painter's brushes, respond to hand gestures when using a tablet and pen, such as the Wacom. The "Wacom 6D Art" or "Art" pens also easily retain the appearance of the individual bristles, while allowing full rotation to create unique strokes that imitate real brushes. A mouse is much more limited.

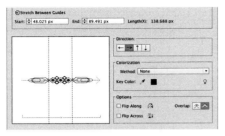

Using the Width tool to alter an art brushstroke modified by the Stretch Between Guides option

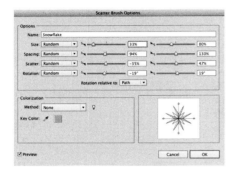

The Scatter Brush dialog varies how the artwork is scattered along a path

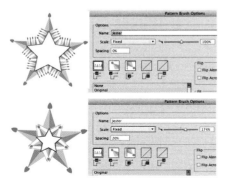

Altering Pattern Scale and Spacing to create a very different look to the brush

art brushes and their strokes using a number of different parameters, including variables affected by pressure using a Wacom tablet and stylus. Art brush marks can be made to scale proportionately to fit the length of your path or stretched to fit. You can also scale your brush non-proportionally by restricting the area of the art brush that can stretch, using two guides to create a segmented brush (choose Stretch Between Guides for the Scale option). Either or both ends of the brush are then protected from being stretched, and the middle portion is stretched to fill in the remaining length. This allows you to stretch the stem of a rose, for instance, without stretching the blossom itself. You can further modify an art brush with colorization methods, such as choosing to vary a key color by tint or hue. Modify the way the art brush follows a path by flipping its direction, and use the Overlap option to determine whether or not to allow it to overlap itself when turning a corner. You can also use the Width tool to modify an art brush.

Use scatter brushes to scatter copies of artwork along the path you create with them: bees in the air, flowers in a field, stars in the sky. The size of the objects, their spacing, how far they scatter from the path, and their rotation can be set to a Fixed or Random amount or, with a graphics tablet, can vary according to characteristics such as pressure or tilt. You can also align the rotation of the scattered objects to the direction of the path or to the edges of the page. Change the method of colorization as you would with a calligraphic or pattern brush.

Use pattern brushes to paint patterns along a path. To use a pattern brush, first define the tiles that will make up your pattern. For example, a train has several parts—engine, cars, etc. Each of these constitutes a tile where you have the start, the middle (the side tile), tiles that turn either an inside or outside corner, and the end of the path. You can either use an existing pattern swatch or Option-drag/Alt-drag art from the artboard into any tile's position in an existing brush (see the **CC** section later in this chapter for info on CC's auto-corners). In the Pattern Brush

Options dialog, select a tile and click the swatch name below the tiles that you want assigned to that tile. You can customize settings for how the tiles fit to, or flip along, the path, and to alter their color. You can also vary the appearance of the pattern brush, how it fills sharp angles (by altering the Scale in both Fixed parameters and those affected by tablet features), and the spacing between tiles.

Bristle brushes emulate traditional paint brushes, showing both the texture of the bristles and the tip shape, which can be round, flat, fan-shaped, etc. To create a bristle brush, select it as the New brush type and, in the Bristle Brush Options dialog, choose a tip shape. From there, modify the brush's bristle length, density, and thickness; whether or not the bristles are stiff or soft; and how opaquely it applies the paint. By default, these brushes use a Paint Opacity of less than 100%, so you'll see some opacity in your strokes even when you have set Opacity in the Control panel to 100% opaque. Because calculating transparency for printing often takes a long time, a dialog warns that if you have more than 30 bristle brushstrokes, you may want to select some or all of the bristle brushstrokes and choose Object> Rasterize to set raster settings for them before you attempt to print.

Working with brushes

Most brushes follow these rules (for additional CC capabilities, see the **CC** section later in this chapter):

- **To create art, scatter, and pattern brushes,** create the artwork for them from fairly basic artwork, including compound shapes, blends, groups, and some live effects such as Distort & Transform. In CS6, you *can't* create brushes from art that uses gradients, mesh objects, raster art, and advanced live effects such as Drop Shadow.
- **To modify the art that makes up a brush,** drag it out of the Brushes panel, edit the object, then drag it back into the Brushes panel. Use the Option/Alt key as you drag to replace the original art with the new art.
- **To set application-level preferences for all brushes,** double-click the Paintbrush tool. (The new preferences

Draw inside and bristle brushes

Bristle brushes are a good candidate for the Draw Inside mode (see the *Rethinking Construction* chapter). You can add the bristle texture to a vector shape while retaining some or all of the original color; Draw Inside also constrains the strokes inside the object, ensuring stray bristle marks are automatically masked.

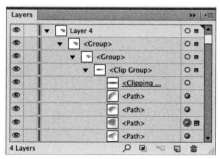

Using a bristle brush (the Footprint brush showing) to draw inside a selected path, and the Layers panel showing the Clipping Paths created by Draw Inside

Bristle brush opacity

Set bristle brush opacity:

- In bristle brush Options under Paint Opacity
- With the Paintbrush tool active, the 1–0 keys change the opacity for selected strokes, or, with no strokes selected, the setting affects the next brushstroke
- With the Opacity slider in the Appearance or Control panels

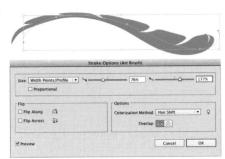

If you've modified a brushed path using the Width tool or by assigning a profile, you can make global adjustments by choosing Options of Selected Object from the Brushes panel menu

Symbols vs. scatter brushes

Scatter brushes and symbols can appear very similar on your artboard, but they're each applied and edited very, very differently. You can read about both in this introduction, but you should experiment with making the same art into a scatter brush and a symbol, and see how differently you control and edit each so you can better understand their advantages and disadvantages.

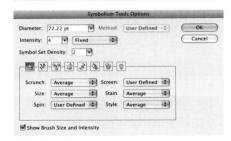

Symbolism Tools Options dialog

Quick access to Symbol features on the Control panel when a symbol object is selected in the artwork; the Reset button not grayed out indicates the symbol has been transformed and the Replace pop-up gives immediate access to the loaded Symbols library

will apply to work you do with the brushes going forward, but won't change existing work.)

- **To modify the properties of a single brushstroke,** select it and then choose Options of Selected Object in the Brush panel's menu. If you've used the Width tool to modify the stroke, your options include using the width points to calculate the profile for your next strokes.

- **To choose how to apply modifications** to existing brushstrokes, in the brush's Options dialog choose Leave Strokes to create a duplicate brush, or choose Apply to Strokes to modify every use of the brush in the document.

- **When Keep Selected and Edit Selected Paths are both enabled,** the last drawn path stays selected; drawing a new path close to the selected path will redraw that path. Disabling either of these options will allow you to draw multiple brushstrokes near each other, instead of redrawing the last drawn path.

SYMBOLS

Working with symbols in Illustrator saves file size (since objects converted to symbols aren't duplicated in the file), provides consistency whenever the same artwork needs to be used more than once, and makes it easy to update objects in your artwork simply by editing the symbol to change it wherever it has been used. Symbols can be made from almost any art you create in Illustrator; the only exceptions are a few kinds of complex groups, such as groups of graphs, and *linked* art (*embedded* art is allowed). Store and edit symbols with the Symbols and Control panels. The sections that follow cover unique ways to use and edit symbols beyond the standard editing tools.

- **To store selected artwork as a symbol,** drag it into the Symbols panel (or click the New Symbol icon in the panel). In the **CC** Symbols panel, a **+** in the lower-right of a thumbnail means it's a Dynamic Symbol, not a Static Symbol; Dynamic is now the default for new symbols (see the **CC** section later in this intro for more on Dynamic Symbols). Use the Libraries Menu icon to save the current symbols to a new library or to load other libraries.

- **To add a single instance of a symbol to your document,** drag it into your document or, with it selected, click the Place Symbol Instance icon. Drag a symbol instance into your document as often as you like, but you can use the Place Symbol Instance icon only once. It's most useful for modifying the symbol (see following).
- **To modify a symbol without modifying the original symbol** in the Symbols panel, click either the Break Link button in the Control panel or the "Break Link to Symbol" icon in the Symbols panel.
- **To modify a symbol and all instances of it** already in the document, place or drag it into your document, then click the Edit Symbol button in the Control panel and your symbol will be placed in isolation mode. After you modify the symbol and exit isolation mode, *all* instances of the symbol, including the symbol in the Symbols panel, will be updated.
- **To modify a symbol in the Symbols panel when you have already broken the link,** Option/Alt-drag the modified symbol from your artboard on top of the symbol in the Symbols panel. This will replace the original symbol with the modified artwork and update all instances of the original symbol.
- **To restore a symbol to its original size and orientation** after transforming it on the artboard, click the Reset button in the Control panel.
- **To quickly find all instances of a symbol** in your artwork, select the symbol either in the Symbols panel or in your artwork and choose Select All Instances from the Symbol panel's menu.
- **To replace one symbol with another without opening the Symbols panel,** select the symbol in the artwork and click the Replace list arrow in the Control panel. A miniature Symbols panel opens, which allows you to swap out symbols.
- **To add a sublayer to a symbol's artwork,** in isolation mode click the topmost layer with the symbol's name, and then click the New Sublayer icon. (You can't add sublayers to a <Group> or <path>.)

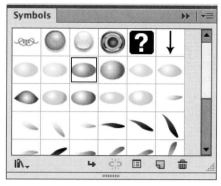

Storing symbols in the Symbols panel, with access to other symbol libraries, editing commands, and the Symbol Options dialog

Transforming symbols

When creating symbols, Illustrator has two features that are important whenever a symbol might be scaled or transformed any other way: If you use Flash, these features also affect symbols taken into Flash for animating:

- Apply 9-slice scaling to symbols in Illustrator. Doing so reduces distortion when transforming objects, especially noticeable with elements such as buttons that have custom corners. All nine areas of the symbol can be scaled independently.
- Assign a Registration point to the symbol in Illustrator. The point appears as a crosshair both in Symbol Edit Mode and when the symbol is selected in normal mode. Use the Registration point to affect any transformations applied inside Illustrator.

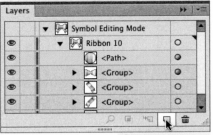

Create New Layer

Adding a new layer at the same level as a path sublayer by Option-clicking/Alt-clicking the Create New Layer icon

LISA JACKMORE

Artwork by Lisa Jackmore created with symbols

Using the Symbolism tools to modify the original set (top) for greater variety (bottom)

- **To add a new layer above a group or path sublayer at the same hierarchy level,** target the layer and then Option-click/Alt-click the New Layer icon. If the layer remains a normal layer (not a group or a path), you can continue to add new layers at that level merely by clicking the New Layer icon.

Working with the Symbolism tools

There are eight different Symbolism tools. Use the Symbol Sprayer tool to spray selected symbols onto your document, creating a symbol set. You can't select individual instances inside a set with any of the selection tools. Instead, modify them with any of the other Symbol tools. To access the symbolism tools easily, tear off the panel and float it nearby, or if working in Illustrator CC, create a custom Tools panel that reveals all of the Symbolism tools as well as any others you need for your project (see the **CC** introduction to *Your Creative Workspace* for instructions). Add symbols to a selected set by selecting a symbol in the Symbols panel—the symbol can be the same as or different from the symbols already present in the instance set—and spray. To add or modify symbols in a set, make sure you've selected both the set and the corresponding symbol(s) in the Symbols panel that you want to affect. The Symbolism tools only affect symbols in a selected set that are also selected in the Symbols panel, thus making it easy to modify just one of the symbols in a mixed set.

To adjust the properties of the Symbolism tools, double-click to open Symbolism Tools Options. Vary the diameter (the range over which the tool operates), the rate at which it applies a change, and the density with which it operates on a set. If you're using the default Average mode, your new symbol instances can inherit attributes (size, rotation, transparency, style) from nearby symbols in the same instance set. For example, if nearby symbols are 50% opaque, symbols added to the set will also be 50% opaque. You can also change the default Average mode to User Defined or Random. (See Illustrator Help for more information about choosing User Defined.)

To remove symbols from an existing instance set, you can remove one instance at a time by holding the Option/Alt key and clicking. To remove multiple instances with the Symbol Sprayer tool, click and drag your cursor over the ones you want to remove—they'll be deleted when you lift your cursor.

DYNAMIC SYMBOLS, & NEW RASTER BRUSHES IN CC
Dynamic Symbols

With the addition of Dynamic symbols, you can now edit some aspects of a symbol's appearance without using symbolism tools and without breaking the link to the original symbol. Because you can edit individual objects within a dynamic symbol instance, including Stroke, Fill, Opacity, and Live Effect, without needing to save yet new symbols for every minor variation, Dynamic symbols are more efficient than Static symbols. If you change the original symbol in some fashion, all the other instances will update to reflect the change except each instance's local over-rides: However, you can't edit the shape (path or live shape attributes) of a symbol instance. Use the Direct Selection tool to select the symbol instance, or part of it, that you want to edit. The Selection tool selects the entire symbol for transforming and the appearance can't be modified, so click away from the symbol to deselect it if necessary, then click back with the Direct Selection tool. A thick outline lets you know that the object is selected and ready for editing. Edit the appearance of the object as desired and click outside the symbol again to deselect it.

Raster image brushes

Art, pattern, and scatter brushes have been supercharged. Finally you can use embedded raster artwork in the brushes you create, and you can mix raster with vector in the same brush. You'll find several examples of raster brush art in this chapter, but keep in mind the following points when creating brushes from raster artwork:

• **Limit the size** (in pixels) for pattern and art brushes to approximately one megapixel, though scatter brushes

Back to the original symbol
If you've altered the appearance of a Dynamic symbol instance, such as its color, there's no way to restore it to the original color by "removing an override." You'll have to first swap it with another symbol, then swap *that* symbol with the original Dynamic symbol.

Dynamic symbols and Strokes
Stroke and Fill are treated like a single appearance in a Dynamic symbol, so adding a Stroke to an object in a symbol instance that didn't have a Stroke in the original symbol is considered an override to both the Stroke and the Fill. Any changes made to either the Stroke or Fill of the original (master) Dynamic Symbol won't be reflected in that symbol instance.

Convert Static to Dynamic
If you want to convert a Static symbol to a Dynamic symbol, select the symbol in the Symbols panel, click Symbol Options at the bottom of the panel, and choose Dynamic Symbol for the Symbol Type (or visa versa).

Symbols vs. Dynamic Symbols
To fully understand Dynamic symbols, you need to first understand the basics of creating and using Symbols in Illustrator. If you're new to symbols, please start with the preceding "Symbols" section.

Want more help with brushes?

See videos from Sharon Steuer's "Artistic Painting with Illustrator" courses and find links for the LinkedIn/Lynda courses at **sharonsteuer.com/lynda**.

How big is a megapixel?

A megapixel is roughly one million pixels. Multiply W x H in pixels to get the total area. A filled rectangle 1024 x 1024 px is the maximum usable size, but can sometimes be larger if the artwork boundaries contains fully transparent pixels.

Embedded images for brushes

In order to make a linked image into a raster brush, click Embed in either your Control or Properties panel.

More brushes *not* patterns...

You can access more brushes via the Brushes panel's Brush Libraries menu, but if you open Patterns from your Swatch library, your Pattern Brush Options tiles will fill with patterns that won't work as brushes! To clear excess patterns, quit and restart Illustrator.

can be any size, although performance can slow down. Because the brush's redraw performance lags with larger brushes, Illustrator will offer to "optimize" (down sample) any single raster object (the copy it uses, not the original) that exceeds that limit. Illustrator can't downsample multiple objects, and may not be able to downsample very large images either. You'll see a warning to resize the artwork before creating the brush, at which point you can choose Object> Rasterize to downsample your image. Illustrator downsamples the image to match the size of the image on the artboard at the resolution you choose in the dialog. It may be enough simply to scale the image before rasterizing, or it might also require rasterizing at a lower resolution, depending upon the size you're starting with. With some artwork, you may be able to reduce the size of your raster image by cropping the image before making the artwork into a brush using Image Crop; for more details about Image Crop, see the **CC** section of the *Creatively Combining Apps* introduction. (Also see the Tip "How big is a megapixel" at left for help figuring out if your artwork is within parameters.)

- **To maintain the quality** of your artwork, create the brush as close to the size you need as possible. Brushes from raster artwork are pixel based, not vector, even if they include vector in them, and will degrade if significantly scaled. To ensure that you can access the original artwork, or to re-rasterize it at another resolution, it's best to always rasterize a copy of your object.

- **Distortion affects rasters,** and if you bend pixels along a path, as is common with art brushes, the artwork has to be interpolated. Some distortion can be too extreme for Illustrator to fill in the gaps. There's a significant difference between choosing Stretch to Fit and Scale Proportionally with art brushes, so experiment to get the results you want when working with images in your brushes.

- **With a pattern brush**, if your art isn't oriented properly to the path, you must rotate it first on the artboard. You should note that although you can change the orientation of your artwork in the Art Brush Options dialog,

Illustrator doesn't always rotate large or complex raster art correctly. To avoid difficulty, rotate the artwork on the artboard before attempting to create the brush.

- **Raster portions of brushes** can't be colorized. Changing the Colorization settings in the Brush Options dialog won't have any effect on the raster portions of your brush, only vector elements (see Sharon Steuer's "shell" gallery later in this section for an example of this).

Corner tiles for pattern brushes

Corner tiles have been a stumbling block for many of us when we create pattern brushes. Illustrator CC has partially addressed the problem by providing auto-generated corner tiles. Whenever you create a side tile for a pattern brush, you can click the down arrow beside an inner or outer corner tile field and choose from four tiles that Illustrator generates: Auto-Centered, Auto-Between, Auto-Sliced, and Auto-Overlap.

Plus, if you like an auto-generated corner, you can reuse it as a corner for another pattern by dragging it out of one brush and into another (see the "Hearts" example at left). See Lisa Jackmore's "Castle Brush" in the **CC** gallery section later in this chapter to learn how to extract a corner for use with another brush.

When one of these auto-generated corners works for the brush, you don't have to do anything more than choose it for your corner(s), but if it isn't quite right, you still either edit the corner or create a corner from scratch. You can also simply try eliminating the corners, rounding the path instead (see Sharon Steuer's "Paper Dolls" in the **CC** gallery section later in this chapter). You can find more examples of rasters in brushes, as well as more about auto-corners, in the lessons and galleries both in the **CC** section at the end of this chapter and in the **CC** section at the end of the *Mastering Complexity* chapter.

Another small change to be aware of is that in the Pattern Brush Options dialog, the individual pattern tiles that together define the behavior of a pattern brush are ordered differently than they were in CS6.

In this example from Sharon Steuer's "Artistic Painting with Illustrator" course on lynda.com, she liked the auto-corner generated by her heart pattern (top) better than the auto-corner generated by the "fixed" heart pattern (middle); for the final she manually replaced the "fixed" auto-corner with the one generated by the original (see Lisa Jackmore's "Castle Brush" gallery later in this chapter for details on how to do this)

Edit automatic corner tiles

When you drag a brush from the Brushes panel onto the artboard, the artwork is expanded into a group of vectors, each tile within its own sub-group. Some of the expanded tiles contain an outer unfilled/unstroked bounding rectangle. In order for an edited tile to correctly replace an original, you must retain the size of the tile you're replacing, including (if it has one) its bounding rectangle.

*The **CC** Pattern Brush Options dialog displays a new order of tiles.*

Stroke Variance

Creating Dynamic Variable-Width Strokes

Overview: *Place sketch and trace with Pen tool; modify strokes with Width tool; save width profile and apply to other strokes.*

1

The original sketch

Hand-traced sketch

2

Width tool (Shift-W) adjusting middle of stroke

PUTNAM

Ryan Putnam creates many character illustrations for websites, branding projects, and more. Putnam now uses the Width tool to add depth and variance in the strokes of the illustrations. Using the Profile feature in the Stroke panel, he can save his custom stroke modifications to apply to other paths in current and future projects.

1 Placing a sketch template and tracing with Pen tool. Putnam first created a character sketch in Photoshop, chose File> Place in Illustrator, enabled Template, and clicked OK. Putnam then traced basic paths of the sketch with the Pen tool in the layer above.

2 Adjusting strokes with the Width tool. Putnam wanted his strokes to have some variance compared to the uniform strokes created by the Pen tool. He created two distinct stroke widths to use on the majority of the paths in the illustration. For the first stroke adjustment, Putnam created a stroke with a thicker middle and tapered ends. To do this, he used the Width tool to click in the middle of the desired path and drag a width point to the desired width. For the second custom width, Putnam created a stroke with a thicker end and a tapered end. Again, he used the Width tool, but this time clicked on the far right side of the desired path and dragged a width point to the desired width.

Width tool (Shift-W) adjusting end of stroke

If you like to be precise with your adjustments, you can double-click a width point to open the Width Point Edit dialog, allowing you to numerically adjust the width of the stroke in the Side 1, Side 2, and Total Width fields.

3 Saving stroke profiles and applying to other paths. Instead of adjusting every path in the illustration to match the two custom widths he created with the Width tool, Putnam saved time and ensured consistency by saving his two custom stroke profiles. To save each profile, he selected the modified stroke and clicked the Add to Profiles icon in the Stroke panel. With both of his strokes saved as custom profiles, Putnam could select a uniform stroke, click the saved Variable Width Profile at the bottom of the Stroke panel, and select the saved profile from the drop-down list. These custom profiles will then be available in other new Illustrator files.

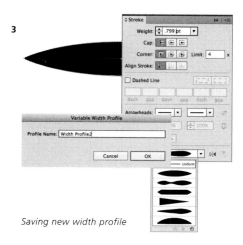

Saving new width profile

After Putnam applied the custom profile to all the desired paths, he utilized specific keyboard commands with the Width tool to further adjust individual paths. For example, holding down the Option/Alt key when dragging width points creates non-uniform widths, the Delete key deletes selected width points, and holding the Shift key while dragging adjusts multiple width points. Other keyboard modifiers with the Width tool include holding down Option/Alt while dragging a width point to copy the width point, holding down Option-Shift/Alt-Shift while dragging to copy and move all the points along a path, Shift-clicking to select multiple width points, and using the Esc key to deselect a width point.

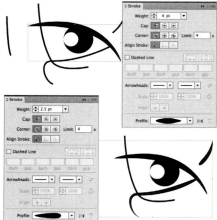

Applying a saved width profile

4 Applying finishing touches. Putnam added additional elements as needed, including creating simple shapes with the Pen tool, which he then filled with grayscale colors.

Adjusting a path with Width tool and keyboard commands

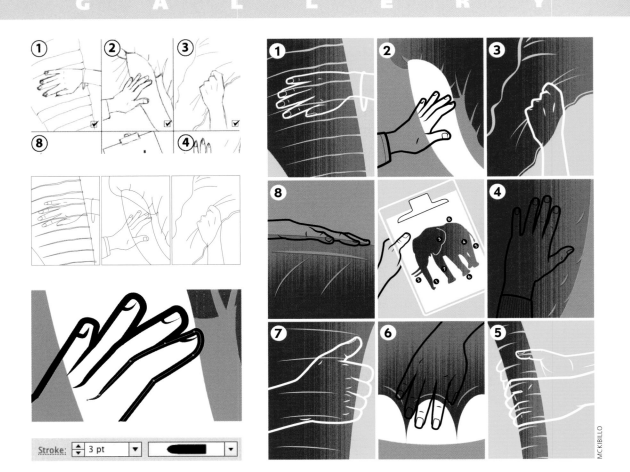

MCKIBILLO

MCKIBILLO (AKA Josh McKible)

For a commissioned piece on different management styles, MCKIBILLO used the parable of the Blind Men and the Elephant as the basis for his illustration. He began with a sketch created in Alias SketchBook Pro that he traced in Illustrator using the Pen tool. While the image was in progress, he used a fine, uniform line in bright magenta so it wouldn't visually disappear. When it came to finessing his linework, MCKIBILLO frequently applied a couple of the default width profiles from the Profile pop-up in the Stroke panel to create many of the lines. If he needed even more control over the shape of his strokes, however, he used the Width tool to modify both width and anchor placement along a curve. In this illustration, he manually delineated the hands and fingernails with the Width tool. Most of his strokes used a rounded cap, but he occasionally varied the cap according to the way the lines joined. Using the Width tool and then saving and reusing profiles (from Profile in the Stroke panel), MCKIBILLO was able to quickly develop a style that appears completely hand-drawn, yet has the advantage of remaining easily edited throughout the course of a project.

JOLLEY

Donal Jolley

To create his "Rubber Ducky," Donal Jolley began by drawing the basic lines with the Pencil tool. Then with the Width tool, he adjusted each stroke so it curved gently and came to a sharp angle at the end (his custom profiles are shown above). To finalize the line work, he used the Scissors and Eraser tools to clean up the extra anchor points that sometimes occur at the end of brushstrokes. He then locked his line work layer and created a new layer at the bottom, into which he painted the colors. He works very intuitively with the brushes, saying, "Usually I will open a brush category, choose a brush, and then make a stroke with a sharp angle and a gentle curve to see how it behaves with the color I want to use. Because many of the strokes have certain transparent qualities that do not truly mix with the underlying color (or white), I make sure of the stroke before I employ it. I check for opacity, form, and how it 'bends,' because many brushes tend to give unpredictable results at sharper angles." Then, using his chosen default bristle and calligraphic brushes, Jolley painted the ducky's colors, varying pressure and angles with his Wacom Intuos tablet and 6D Art Pen.

JACKMORE

Lisa Jackmore

For drawings as fluid as this floral design, Lisa Jackmore finds that initially drawing with the Paintbrush tool and a calligraphic brush is the most natural and intuitive way to begin. However, when she wants to create specific variations to the strokes, she then converts the brushstrokes to Basic stroked paths, so she can use the Width tool (you can't use the Width tool on calligraphic brushstrokes). To do this, she clicked the Basic Brush in the Brushes panel (the basic stroke version is shown directly above). Jackmore then selected the Width tool (Shift-W) and clicked on the stroke itself, dragging the handle outward to evenly widen the path. To make adjustments to one side, she held the Option/Alt key while dragging the handle. To make even further variations to the strokes, Jackmore clicked the stroke, added new width

points, and adjusted them. She saved several profiles by selecting each modified stroke, then from the Variable Width Profile menu in the Control panel clicking the Add to Profile button, naming it, and clicking OK. To finish the design, she selected each of the remaining paths, applied one of her saved width profiles from the Control panel, and then increased the stroke weight on all of the paths. Jackmore's background includes a gradient mesh object and a few bristle brushstrokes drawn with the Paintbrush tool.

PAIDRICK

Ann Paidrick

For Ann Paidrick, the Width tool was key to creating the hand-drawn look for this pair of spiral patterns. Starting with the Spiral tool (hidden under the Line tool), she used the up and down arrow keys to vary the wind of each spiral as she drew. To begin, she chose an orange fill and black stroke. Clicking Stroke in the Control panel, she chose the Round Cap. For each spiral she set a stroke weight between 5 and 8 pts. Next she used the Width tool on each spiral to thicken some areas while narrowing others. For final tweaks to the paths, she used the Direct Selection tool to move anchor points and direction lines just enough to create a hand-drawn feel. After assembling a cluster of spirals together, she entered Pattern Edit Mode (PEM), where she finished arranging the elements until the pattern worked as a whole. After saving the orange and black pattern, she remained in PEM, where she created and then saved the version at top by changing spiral fill and stroke colors and putting a rectangle with a purple fill beneath the spirals (for more about PEM, see the *Mastering Complexity* chapter).

JACKMORE

Lisa Jackmore

To make interesting brushstrokes, Lisa Jackmore used variations of a few calligraphic and bristle brushes, painted using a Wacom Intuos4 tablet and Art Pen. In creating the variations for the brushes, Jackmore changed the parameters for Pressure, Rotation, and Tilt. When she wanted to customize a brush, she double-clicked the brush and made changes to the options. For the tree outline, she used a 3-pt Flat calligraphic brush, set Diameter to Pressure (with a 2-pt variation), Roundness to Tilt (34°, with a variation of 15°), and Angle to Rotation (with a 125° variation). For the long sweeping lines of the tree, she found the combination of using Rotation and a chisel tip of the Art Pen worked the best to vary the brushstroke. As she drew, she slightly rotated and tilted the pen and created variations in her stroke. To create an irregular

ink-like appearance in the words, she used a 1-pt Round calligraphic brush and set Angle to 30° (fixed) and Roundness to Tilt (60°, with a 29% variation). Jackmore used several other variations of calligraphic brushes to draw the suitcases and background pattern. To make the pattern, she drew several paths with a customized calligraphic brush, grouped the brushstrokes, and dragged the pattern tile to the Swatches panel. After she drew all of the black brushstrokes, she colored the illustration with a gradient mesh object for the background, and used variations of the Fan, Round Blunt, and Round Point bristle brushes for other areas, such as the bird, suitcases, and shadows. Finally, Jackmore used the Rectangle tool to make a frame and then applied a Charcoal brush to the stroke.

AHUJA

Anil Ahuja/Adobe Systems

Adobe's Product Specialist Anil Ahuja used a range of tools and techniques to create his dragonfly and relied upon transparency methods to obtain color accuracy to closely match his reference photo. In his three levels of objects used to create the wings (shown separately at right), this is readily apparent. After drawing the wing's black-stroked vein structure with artistic calligraphic brushes of various sizes and shapes, he selected the paths and chose Object> Expand (to outline the strokes) and then Merge (to create a compound path object). In the Appearance panel he clicked Opacity and changed Blending Mode to Darken to reduce the opacity, giving the wing its realistic brown color. With the brown and blue gradient mesh objects (residing on a layer beneath the vein structure), Ahuja used the Direct Selection tool to select individual mesh points to decrease

the opacity (ranging from 0–90%). To create wings that appeared translucent instead of just transparent, Ahuja used the Pen tool to draw an outline copy of the wings that he put on a layer below the veined structure and the mesh. He filled the outline with a color similar to the background and reduced the opacity to 30%. To complete the illustration, Ahuja created a shadow on a layer between the dragonfly and the gradient mesh background. To make the shadow, he pasted a copy of the wing outline and with the Pen tool added an outline of the body. He then reduced the opacity of the shadow object to 53% and changed the blending mode to Darken.

Brushes & Washes

Drawing with Naturalistic Pen, Ink, Wash

Overview: *Start with a placed image as a template; create a custom calligraphic brush; create variations on the brush to apply to strokes; add a wash layer below the ink layer.*

STEUER

Transparent brushstrokes

By default, calligraphic brushstrokes are opaque. You can also draw with semi-transparent brushstrokes, which you can use to simulate some types of inks or watercolors; where marks overlap, they become richer or darker. Click Opacity in the Control panel to reduce opacity or choose a blending mode.

(Top) The original photo; (bottom) brushstrokes drawn over the dimmed template photo

It's easy to create spontaneous painterly and calligraphic marks in Illustrator—perhaps with more flexibility than in many pixel-based programs. Sharon Steuer drew this sketch of Honfleur, France, using a Wacom tablet, her Art Pen for the Intuos4, and two different Illustrator brushes. She customized a brush for the thin, dark strokes and used a built-in brush for the underlying gray washes.

1 Placing artwork as a template. If you want to use a sketch or photo as a reference as you draw into layers above, set it up as a non-printing template layer. For her template image, Steuer scanned a small photo of Honfleur and saved it as a JPG and then opened it in Illustrator. To place an image as a template, choose File> Place, enable the Template option, and click the Place button. If the image imports at too large a size, unlock the layer, select the image (holding down Option-Shift/Alt-Shift keys to resize proportionally from the center), and drag on a corner of the bounding box until the image is the size you want; then lock the layer again. Illustrator automatically dims images on your template layer to 50%, but you can double-click the layer icon to adjust this and other settings in Layer Options. Toggle between hiding and showing the template layer using ⌘-Shift-W/Ctrl-Shift-W, or toggle the visibility icon in the Layers panel.

2 Customizing a calligraphic brush. In order to sketch with accurate detail, you'll need to adjust the Paintbrush Tool Options by double-clicking the Paintbrush tool icon. In Options, drag Fidelity (accuracy) and Smoothness sliders all the way to the left for maximum control (in **CC** you adjust just one Fidelity slider to Accurate). Disable "Fill new brush strokes," and if you want to be able to quickly draw strokes that overlap, disable Keep Selected.

To create a custom calligraphic brush, click the New Brush icon and select Calligraphic Brush. For this piece, Steuer chose the following settings: Angle=90°/Fixed; Roundness=10%/Fixed; Diameter=4 pt/Pressure/Variation=4 pt. If you have one of the newer Wacom Art Pens, try varying the diameter with Rotation instead of Pressure and then let the pen barrel rotate between your fingers naturally as you draw. (If you don't have a pressure-sensitive tablet, only Random will have any effect on varying your stroke.) To create a variation of a brush, duplicate it by dragging it to the New Brush icon and then double-click the copy to edit it. If you create a variety of brushes—adding minor variances in Angle, Roundness, and Diameter—you can enhance the hand-drawn appearance of your ink drawing by selecting a brushed path and choosing a new brush for it.

3 Adding a wash. For this piece, Steuer added depth by introducing gray washes underneath the dark brush-strokes. To easily edit the wash strokes without affecting the dark ink strokes, create a new layer, and draw your wash strokes into this layer between the ink and template layers. To avoid altering other layers while you brush in the washes, you may want to lock all the other layers. To toggle between locking all layers except the wash layer, and unlocking all layers at once, including the wash layer, Option-click/Alt-click the wash layer's Lock icon.

For the wash, select a light color. Steuer used the Dry Ink 2 brush from the Artistic_Ink brush library (Swatch Libraries menu). In the Layers panel, click the wash layer to make it the current drawing layer, and paint away.

2

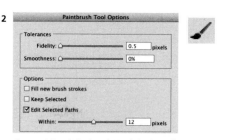

Customizing Paintbrush Tool Options (in **CC** set one Fidelity slider to Accurate)

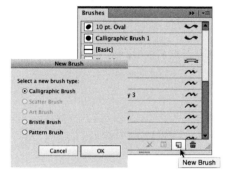

Creating a new calligraphic brush

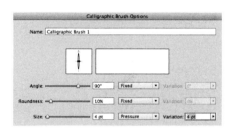

Angle, Roundness, and Size can be set to a variety of Pen characteristics (including Rotation, Tilt, Bearing), but you can only make use of these features if your tablet, and Art Pen, support them

The final ink drawing after adding a couple of people not in the original photo, and before adding the wash

WINKEL   MORRISON

PERNAL   DZIENIS

LOUKOUMIS   MARTIN

Stephen Klema's Students:
Jillian Winkel, Stephanie Pernal,
Amber Loukoumis, Jeffrey Martin,
Nicole Dzienis, Tamara Morrison

As a class assignment, Professor Stephen Klema challenged his students to create expressive graphic illustrations of organic forms. The students of Tunxis Community College used a variety of default brushes from the brushes panel. They included both calligraphic and art brushes. Before drawing, the students double-clicked the Paintbrush tool and adjusted the Paintbrush tool preferences. They dragged the Fidelity and Smoothness sliders to the desired positions (there's only the one Fidelity slider in **CC**). The Fidelity slider moved all the way to the left (Accurate) is the preferred setting for the most accurate brushstrokes, while moved toward the right yields smoother strokes. So the students would be able to draw multiple brush-strokes near each other without redrawing the previous path, they disabled the Fill New Brush Strokes and Keep Selected options. Using a pressure-sensitive tablet, the students drew varying widths and angles of brushstrokes, many either on top of or close to one another, for a spontaneous, expressive look. Extra points within the brushstrokes were deleted using the Smooth tool or the Delete Anchor Point tool.

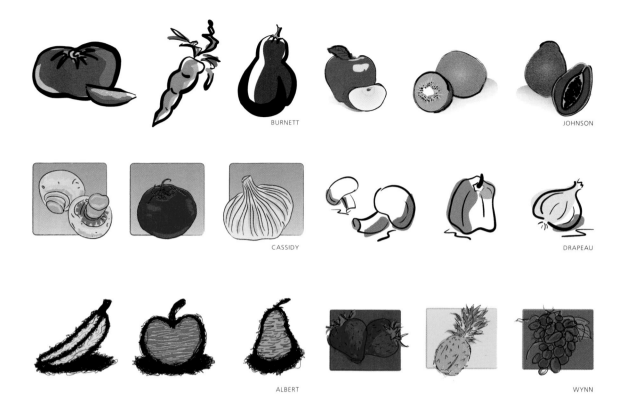

BURNETT

JOHNSON

CASSIDY

DRAPEAU

ALBERT

WYNN

Stephen Klema's Students:
Cinthia A. Burnett, James Cassidy,
Kenneth Albert, Jamal Wynn,
Suzanne Drapeau, Mahalia Johnson

Using the same techniques described on the previous page, additional student creations are shown above. In some of these illustrations, artists applied art and calligraphic brushes to paths drawn with the Pencil or Pen tools by selecting the path and then choosing a brush from the Brushes panel. You can find many additional brushes in the Brushes library. To

DRAPEAU

access more art brushes, click the Brush Libraries Menu icon found in the lower-left corner of the Brushes panel. Choose Open Brush Library> Artistic and then select the brushes you want to add to the Brushes panel. Find more artwork from Professor Klema's students on his website at www.StephenKlema.com/wow.

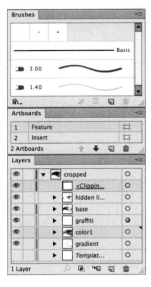

Sharon Steuer

To create this illustration for her "Good Food in the Microhood" UntappedCities.com posting, Sharon Steuer began in Photoshop, where she collaged photos she'd taken from different vantage points into one imaginary cityscape. After placing it as a JPG template in Illustrator, from another image, she copied objects styled with her custom calligraphic brushes and pasted the objects into her new file, which added the custom brushes to her current Brushes panel. She then deleted the objects and used these brushes to paint her black line drawing. In a new layer she added color using default bristle brushes and a pressure-sensitive Wacom tablet and Art Pen. To easily switch between brushes, colors, and layers, she'd first select a path styled similarly to the one she wanted to make and then deselect (⌘-Shift-A/Ctrl-Shift-A). To draw a new, blue, wide transparent bristle brush stroke on the Color layer, she selected a blue-wide stroke on the Color layer, then deselected, and drew. To draw a new calligraphic path on the lines

layer, she selected and then deselected one of those. With Edit Selected enabled in Brush Options, if she kept a brush stroke selected, she could redraw the path (instead of draw a new one). After adding a few more detail layers, she created an "unwanted lines layer" and hid it, so she could then select and move unwanted lines to that hidden layer. Lastly she created two overlapping artboards: one to frame the crop when featured on the website front page, and the other sized for insertion within the post. To see this posting, which also contains a link to an article on CreativePro.com detailing how this image was created, go to UntappedCities.com and enter "CreativePro" in the search field.

Sharon Steuer

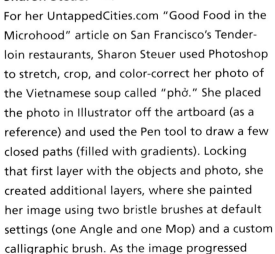

For her UntappedCities.com "Good Food in the Microhood" article on San Francisco's Tenderloin restaurants, Sharon Steuer used Photoshop to stretch, crop, and color-correct her photo of the Vietnamese soup called "phở." She placed the photo in Illustrator off the artboard (as a reference) and used the Pen tool to draw a few closed paths (filled with gradients). Locking that first layer with the objects and photo, she created additional layers, where she painted her image using two bristle brushes at default settings (one Angle and one Mop) and a custom calligraphic brush. As the image progressed

Steuer decided to modify the bowl's shape in ways that would be difficult with traditional or raster tools; she selected the bowl objects, then compressed them vertically using the bounding box. After the article posted, she reworked the image as a fine art piece titled "Vegan Phở." Resizing some elements and adding others, she printed a square variation in archival materials. Coating the print with clear acrylic medium, Steuer cut and collaged it onto a 6"x6" cradled board and then drew and painted on the surface with watercolor pencils. She applied fixative and a UV coating to the finished artwork.

Painting Inside

Painting with Bristle Brushes & Draw Inside

Advanced Technique

Overview: *Start with a placed image as a reference; create a line drawing made of closed paths; use a variety of bristle brushes and the Draw Inside mode to paint the sketch; add a rectangular background with a Charcoal art brush edge.*

1

The closed path line drawing created with the Pencil tool using a 1-pt stroke

JACKMORE

Re-enter isolation mode

When you use the Draw Inside mode (bottom of the Tools panel or Shift-D), you're actually creating a special kind of clipping mask. Once you've "drawn inside" an object, double-click it to enter into isolation mode and automatically re-enter Draw Inside mode to add to the object. To remove a "drawn inside" clipping mask from an object and return the object to its original state, choose Object> Clipping Mask> Release.

Draw Inside mode makes it easy to create a painterly illustration with bristle brushes. Lisa Jackmore drew this sketch of an artichoke using a Wacom tablet with her Art Pen and several modified brushes. After drawing a simple outline of the artichoke leaves and the stem with the Pencil tool, she utilized the Draw Inside mode and painted with a range of bristle brushes.

1 Drawing the outlines. Jackmore used a snapshot as a basic reference, but if you prefer to draw directly on top of a photo or drawing, use File> Place and enable the Template option. To create an accurate line drawing she double-clicked the Pencil tool to open Pencil Tool Options, where she chose the most Accurate Fidelity and then disabled Edit Selected Paths and Keep Selected. Into one layer she created a 1-pt line drawing using the Pencil tool, making sure that she closed each leaf and stem path so that she would later be able to add detail and color to the loosely drawn paths using the Draw Inside mode.

2 Setting up for painting using the bristle brush tool and a tablet. So she'd be able to paint freely and easily, Jackmore planned ahead and first set up her tools. She opened the Brushes panel, the Bristle Brush Library (from the Libraries menu), and the Layers panel. She also set the Wacom tablet's Touch Ring to auto scroll/zoom.

3 Painting with bristle brushes and the Draw Inside mode. To draw inside a path, she selected it, pressed Shift-D (the Draw Inside mode), then deselected the path (so the bristle brush wouldn't be applied to the outline, but would be constrained within the path). She selected the Paintbrush tool (B) and then chose a bristle brush and a stroke color. When she finished drawing inside a path, Jackmore pressed Shift-D to switch back to Normal drawing mode. She switched between the Paintbrush tool and the Selection tool by holding the ⌘/Ctrl key to temporarily switch to the Selection tool and toggled between drawing modes with Shift-D. Jackmore created a number of variations of the Round Point, Fan, Round, and Flat Blunt bristle brushes. To customize parameters for opacity, Bristle Length, Stiffness, and Thickness, she'd open Options by pressing the upper switch on the Intuos4 Pen (or double-clicking the Paintbrush tool). With the Paintbrush tool selected, she decreased/increased brush size with the [ ] keys, adjusted opacity with the number keys, and zoomed in or out by turning Wacom tablet's Touch Ring clockwise, or counter-clockwise.

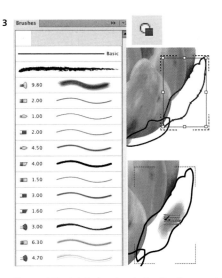

Some of the bristle brushes in the Brushes panel; selecting a leaf to Draw Inside; bristle brush icon while drawing inside the leaf

4 Organizing layers and finishing details. To reveal the correct part of the leaf as it overlapped another, as she worked, Jackmore moved each leaf into its appropriate layer. As each leaf and stem became painted enough to see the entire path, while in Normal drawing mode she set the stroke to None. To fine-tune the painted area for a particular leaf, she double-clicked that leaf to automatically enter into isolation mode while already in Draw Inside mode, allowing her to continue to paint and modify brushstrokes. For the background, on a layer below Jackmore drew a rectangle, with the same fill and stroke color and applied a 3-pt Charcoal art brush stroke. To more fully distribute the brushstroke, she slightly rotated a duplicate of the stroke by first clicking the Add New Stroke icon in the Appearance panel (to add a stroke), and from the *fx* menu she chose Distort & Transform> Transform and entered 180° for rotation.

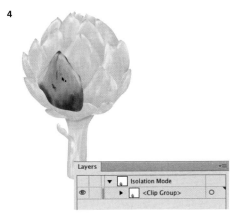

Double-clicking a leaf to enter isolation mode and automatically switch to Draw Inside mode

Detail of the lower right corner of the background before and after adding a second, rotated Charcoal art brush stroke

Painterly Portraits

Painting in Layers with Bristle Brushes

Advanced Technique

Overview: *Place a sketch as a template layer; draw with customized bristle brushes; continue to paint with custom brushes into separate layers; create frame.*

GEISLER

The template; a distorted Photoshop sketch

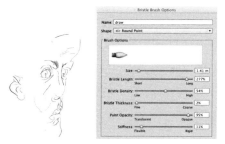

The initial bristle brush sketch made with three variations of a Round Point bristle brush; the Bristle Brush Options

Adding shadows with a wide, fairly opaque bristle brush

The myriad bristle brushes presented Greg Geisler with an infinite variety of brushes to create his expressive painterly portrait, "Blue Mirror." Commissioned by Adobe Systems, you can find this file, and a PDF ReadMe file explaining more about how he made it, on **WOW! ONLINE**.

1 Placing the initial sketch, and customizing Bristle Brush Options. Geisler placed his distorted Photoshop sketch (PSD) as a Template layer. He opened the Bristle Brush Library (from the Brush Libraries menu in the lower left of the Brushes panel) and clicked the 1-pt Round bristle brush, which automatically loaded the brush into the Brushes panel. Geisler next duplicated that brush (by dragging its icon to the New Brush icon in the Brushes panel) and then double-clicked on the New Brush icon so he could change several settings in Bristle Brush Options. He made changes to Bristle Thickness, adjusted Paint Opacity and increased the Stiffness, and then named it and clicked OK. On a layer above the template, he used this new brush to create the base sketch for the entire illustration. Geisler kept the Brushes panel and the Bristle Brush Library open throughout the drawing session, so he could continue to duplicate and customize brushes as his drawing progressed. For this layer, he created three different variations of the 1-pt Liner brush.

2 Adding highlights, midtones, and shadows. To make one of the many layers of highlights, such as the strokes in orange, Geisler customized copies of the 3-mm Flat Fan Brush in the Bristle Brushes Library, adjusting Bristle Thickness, Bristle Length, and Paint Opacity. He also drew highlights with a Round bristle brush customized with pointy variations. Geisler continued to draw in separate layers, focusing in particular on midtones, shadows, highlights, or color for each layer, using variations of the Flat Fan and Round bristle brushes.

3 Working efficiently and further modifying brush characteristics. Geisler's process is very organic in that he continually defines new brushes, and creates new layers, as he draws. He rarely deletes a stroke, preferring to layer new bristle brushstrokes upon others, choosing a more opaque brush to cover the underlying strokes. As he's drawing, he presses the [key to decrease the brush size, and the] key, to increase the bristle size. To vary the opacity, he presses the keys from 1, which is completely transparent, through 0, which is completely opaque. To add texture, as in the blue background shown at right, Geisler modifies the settings to increase the brush stiffness toward Rigid, increase the brush density toward Thick, and then decrease the bristle length.

4 Finishing touches. Geisler created an irregular-edged black frame that surrounded the portrait, on a layer between the blue texture and the face. He customized a wide Flat Fan brush to 100% Opacity (100% opaque bristle brushes lose their character within the stroke, but maintain a ragged edge) and then expanded the brushstrokes (Object> Expand) and clicked Unite in the Pathfinder panel, melding the brushstrokes into one frame object. He then used the Pencil tool to draw a few closed paths, delineating the area between the rectangular frame and the head. Marquee-selecting these paths and the frame, he filled them with black and again clicked Unite in the Pathfinder panel.

2

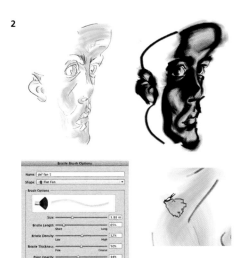

Adding highlights with a Wide Fan Brush, adding shadows; the bristle brush icon that appears when using a pressure-sensitive pen

3

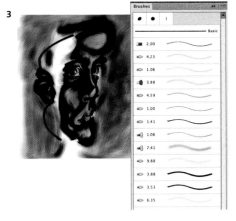

Part of the Brushes panel (right), and a later stage of the illustration with blue texture

4

Black frame made with expanded bristle brushstrokes and filled paths shown in Preview mode (detail at left), and Outline mode (right)

GEISLER

The Layers panel (right of artwork) shows layers labeled:

more BB stro...
brush lines
details
brow color
eye highlights
pupils
eye blue
eye white
right head sh...
right eye color
spikeys
lips, red
nose shadow
right face sh...
beard
chin color
chin shade
spikeys
face pinks
side shadow
purple midto...
throat highli...
ear shadows
Layer 18
ear highlights
ear fill
shirt fill
bg lines
bg fill
expanded BB...
filled frame
BB frame

32 Layers

Bristle Brush Options

Name: thick black
Shape: Flat Fan

Brush Options

Size: 10 mm
Bristle Length: 63%
Short — Long
Bristle Density: 46%
Low — High
Bristle Thickness: 84%
Fine — Coarse
Paint Opacity: 100%
Translucent — Opaque
Stiffness: 69%
Flexible — Rigid

Greg Geisler

Greg Geisler created this graphic self-portrait using a customized calligraphic brush. In the Brushes panel, Geisler double-clicked the default 3-pt round calligraphic brush, and for the Diameter settings, he changed Fixed to Pressure, and set Variation to 3 pt. Using a Wacom tablet and pressure-sensitive pen, he drew the facial outline, varying the stroke width as he changed his touch (directly above left). To block out planes of color within the face (such as the chin, beard, and cheek),

he used the Pencil tool to draw color-filled irregular paths on separate layers. Each layer contained one of the many defining areas of color (Layers panel shown above right) for highlights, shadows, or texture. To create the frame, Geisler used the same bristle brush and a technique similar to the one developed in the previous lesson (shown below the artwork). For finishing touches, Geisler drew the bright blue squiggly lines with the Pencil tool.

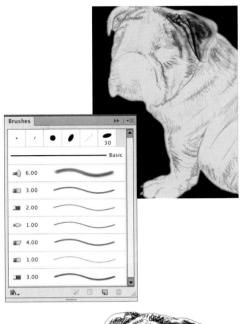

CESAR de OLIVEIRA BALDACCI

Janaína Cesar de Oliveira Baldacci

Based on a photograph taken by Tatiana Bicalho, Baldacci captured the natural undulations of the fur and folds of her pet bulldog with bristle brushes. Baldacci first drew a white outline of the dog (against the black background) with the Pen tool and applied a Gaussian Blur effect. From the Brush Libraries menu (in the bottom left of the Brushes panel), Baldacci opened the Bristle Brush Library. She then chose a few bristle brushes that had varying characteristics in Paint Opacity, Bristle Stiffness, and Bristle Density, such as Round Fan, Flat Blunt, Flat Point, and Round Curve

(a portion of her Brushes panel shown above). Baldacci then selected the Paintbrush tool (B), chose a bristle brush and a stroke color, and drew into the first of many layers (the image on the first layer is shown above in Preview and Outline modes). In layers above, she added greater definition and built the fur in stages based on color, such as white, gray, and highlights. On the uppermost layers she added the snout, eye details, and additional layers of fur until the portrait was complete.

Pattern Brushes

Building Characters with Pattern Brushes

Overview: *Create the parts that will make up a pattern brush separately; place the parts in the Swatches panel and give them distinctive names; use the Pattern Brush Options dialog to create the brushes; vary the width of the pattern brush line using the Stroke menu and the Width tool.*

Adjusting pattern brush fit

After you've applied a pattern brush to a path, you can still scale, flip, and modify its fit along the path. Modify all these settings in the Pattern Brush Options dialog, or manually reshape and scale the pattern by changing the stroke weight or using the Width tool.

1

Creating the various robot arm elements, oriented in the outward-facing position that pattern brushes use for their tiles

Dragging objects for pattern brushes into the Swatches panel and naming them

To create these stylized science-fiction robots, Raymond Larrett saved extensive tedious rendering by building the robot limbs using a custom pattern brush. Working this way allows him to quickly and easily make alterations to his art by adjusting the weight of the brush stroke, modifying or replacing the various brush elements, or even replacing the entire brush itself.

1 Creating the robot arm parts. Larrett's robot arm required four distinct elements: a "shoulder" piece where the arm joins the body, an "elbow" connecting the upper and lower arm, the "hand" (in this case a claw), and an "arm link" segment that replicates as it connects and forms the majority of the robot arm. He created these pieces individually and then turned each into a separate pattern swatch. These swatches become the "tiles," that together make up the robot arm pattern brush.

To create the shoulder piece, he first modified a shape made with the Ellipse tool. Using the Pen tool, he drew a lighter, unfilled path with a Round Cap for the highlight to complete the shoulder. He then dragged the shoulder art into the Swatches panel, naming it "shoulder" so he would recognize it as he built the pattern brush. In the same way he created the arm link, hand, and elbow swatches for the pattern brush tiles. He made sure that the various pieces were facing in the correct direction relative to the pattern tiles, which run at right angles to the path, before individually dragging each one into the Swatches panel (alternatively, you can select art and click the New Swatch icon or choose Object> Pattern> Make).

2 **Making and using the pattern brush.** To build the pattern brush for the robot arm, Larrett opened the Brushes panel, clicked New Brush in Pattern Brush Options, and then clicked OK. He clicked in the Side Tile box and selected the desired pattern swatch for the arm (CS6 and **CC** tile order and swatch selection methods differ slightly). Next he placed the other tiles in the appropriate position: the shoulder as the Start Tile, the hand as the End Tile, and the elbow as the Inner Corner Tile. He named the new pattern brush Robot Arm and clicked OK.

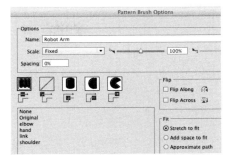

Selecting the Pattern Brush option from the New Brush dialog

To use his new pattern brush, Larrett selected the brush in the Brushes panel and then drew a path for the robot arm using the Pen tool (P). He clicked where the Start Tile (the shoulder) should go, clicked again to place a corner anchor point (necessary for the elbow tile, the Inner Side Tile, to load), and finally clicked to place the hand element (the End Tile) at the end of the path. He also sometimes drew with the Paintbrush tool or applied the brush to a drawn path.

Creating a new pattern brush by placing swatches in the appropriate tiles (CS6 and **CC** tile order and swatch selection methods differ slightly)

3 **Creating variations in the pattern brush.** Larrett then modified the art by varying the pattern brush line weight and stroke profiles. To adjust the width of a selected robot arm, he changed the line weight in the Control panel or Stroke panel by clicking in the numeric field and using the up arrow and down arrow keys to increase or decrease stroke weight as desired (adding the Shift key alters the weight by increments of 10). To manually adjust only selected portions of the robot limb, Larrett used the Width tool (Shift-W). Placing the tool over a point on a path, he moved the diamond-shaped handles to widen or narrow a portion of the path. Lastly, he combined some old and newly-made swatches to create additional brushes for other robots' limbs.

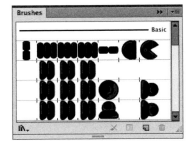

Using the Stroke panel to widen or narrow the pattern brush line weight

Using the Width tool to introduce variations in the width of your pattern brush line

Recombining and building new swatches to create new pattern brushes

WATERCOLOR STROKE 03

BRISTLE BRUSH STIPPLER

WATERCOLOR STROKE 06

BRISTLE BRUSH MOP
(NOTE STROKE POSITION TO STYLUS ANGLE)

HAND DRAWN BRUSHES 01
(OVERPRINT)

GRUNGE BRUSHES 03

SPIKEY

HAND DRAWN BRUSHES 06

ARTISTIC_CHALKCHARCOALPENCIL
_SCRIBBLE

GIVE ME JELLYBEANS

JOLLEY

Donal Jolley

This sampler by Donal Jolley, using his 6D Art Pen, demonstrates the tremendous variety you get from brushes that ship with Illustrator. When you add a Wacom pressure-sensitive pen and tablet to these out-of-the-box brushes, you can introduce even more variety into your strokes; the standard Grip Pen registers pressure, tilt, and bearing, and the optional, more sensitive Art Pens (6D Art for Intuos3, or Art Pen for Intuos4) add the ability to vary each stroke with rotation. The bristle brush responds particularly well to the Art Pens, adding a new dimension to painting. You can manually transform some of your strokes (but not those made with the calligraphic, scatter, or bristle brushes) by modifying its profile with the Width tool (such as Spikey above) and then saving that profile to apply to other strokes.

TAN

Moses Tan

Moses Tan recreated astonishing detail and captured a precise likeness of his photographic reference using mostly meticulously-drawn filled paths, but he used custom art and scatter brushes for some of the intricate details (such as the weeded area shown across, right). He preferred to use scatter brushes for the small-sized growth and art brushes for the larger foliage. To make an art or scatter brush he first drew a weed object, then dragged it into the Brushes panel and in the New Brush Options, selected Art Brush or Scatter Brush (several are shown at right). For art brushes he specified the stroke direction (either top to bottom

or left to right) so when he drew a brushstroke, the foliage was oriented correctly. He kept the other parameters at the default settings. For the scatter brushes he varied options for each weed (size, spacing, scatter, and rotation). For scatter brushes he used Page for "Rotation relative to," and to preserve the original artwork colors in all his brushes, he used a Colorization of None. To paint with a brush he would select the Paintbrush tool, a scatter or art brush, and draw paths to easily form the weeded detail in his drawing.

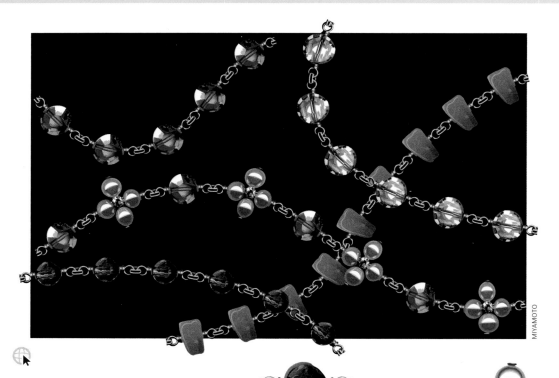

MIYAMOTO

Nobuko Miyamoto/Yukio Miyamoto

Making these intricate beaded necklaces at first glance would seem impossibly difficult, but once they carefully construct each gem, with the use of pattern brushes, the necklace virtually draws itself. Nobuko Miyamoto designed the necklace and created the bead elements (details above right) with a mixture of blended and solid filled objects. She paid careful attention to the ends of the bead to ensure that when each bead lined up with the next one there would be a seamless connection between them. Yukio Miyamoto then transformed Nobuko's designs into brushes. To make the chained ends, he selected the chain object and dragged a copy (Shift-Option/Shift-Alt) to the other side of the bead. With the chain selected, he chose the Reflect tool and clicked above and below the chain to reflect the chain

vertically. He selected and grouped each bead, and then in some cases he put the beads in pairs and then grouped a pair of beads. For each bead or pair of beads Yukio clicked the New Brush icon at the bottom of the Brushes panel, selected New Pattern Brush, and clicked OK. In the Pattern Brush Options dialog, he kept the Colorization method as None, and then under Fit he chose Stretch to Fit. To make the necklace, Nobuko drew a path with the Paintbrush tool and selected the desired bead pattern brush in the Brushes panel to apply the brush. Now with the bead as a pattern brush, the necklace can be easily adjusted to any length or path.

Aaron McGarry

For this urban portrait Aaron McGarry relied heavily upon Illustrator's Symbol Libraries and Symbols panel. He made his own panel containing only the symbols he needed using Window> Symbol Libraries> User Defined. He saved as a symbol any detail that he would need to repeat so he could easily access and apply that element. To build the roof tiles in the background building, McGarry made one tile and filled it with a solid color. He then made two duplicates and filled each with a different color. He separately dragged and dropped each into the Symbols panel, named it, and clicked OK. He was then able to quickly drag alternating tiles from the panel to lay the roof, giving it a natural look. To create the red plumbing in the foreground, he also used many duplicated parts, such as the nuts and bolts holding the assembly together, that he had saved as symbols (see detail above right). McGarry took full advantage of Illustrator's Symbol libraries to create the greenery and curb area around the pipes. He used grass, leaves, and rocks found in the libraries accessed from the Symbol Libraries icon in the Symbols panel. To create a perspective point of view he modified some of the symbols; for instance, he used Effect> Distort & Transform to turn Rock symbols into paved concrete. He also created the oil stains on the road by modifying a Dot Pattern symbol from Illustrator's library. For the dirt on the vehicle, he drew a path around its lower side and then enabled the Draw Inside drawing mode. Using the Symbol Sprayer tool he sprayed the sand symbol within the path along the vehicle's side. Lastly, he selected the path and reduced the opacity.

Chapter 4 *Expressive Strokes* **147**

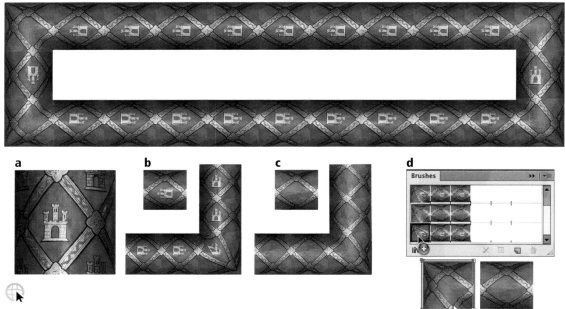

JACKMORE

a   **b**   **c**   **d**

Lisa Jackmore

Lisa Jackmore decided to use her photo of a hand-painted decoration with asymmetries as the basis for a pattern brush. It would be impossible to match all of the castle fragments perfectly (figure **a**), so in Photoshop she used the Clone Stamp tool to remove most of the castle motifs, leaving only the one complete castle. After cropping the image, Jackmore opened it in Illustrator, rotated it and then dragged it into the Brushes panel to create a pattern brush. In Pattern Brush Options she chose Auto-Centered Corner Tile, which formed the pattern well but resulted in a distorted auto-generated corner (figure **b**). To generate a smooth corner, Jackmore went back to Photoshop and used the Clone Stamp Tool—this time completely removing the castle—then used this altered version to make a new pattern (figure **c**). To replace the distorted corner in her castle brush with the new smooth corner, Jackmore first duplicated

the castle brush by dragging it to the New Brush icon in the Brushes panel. Next, setting her Brushes panel view to Thumbnail, she selected the pattern brush without the castle and then dragged it to the artboard to reveal the artwork that makes up each of the tiles. To replace the distorted corner with the smooth one, she used the Direct Selection tool to marquee the artwork that formed the smooth corner. Holding Option/Alt, she then dragged the selected art into the Brushes panel, and when the new smooth corner was directly on top of the distorted castle tile in the duplicate, she saw a **+** icon and released the cursor (figure **d**). In Pattern Brush Options she clicked OK, and the result was a new pattern brush with the smooth corner tile with subtle, small variations where some quatrefoils met at the corners. Find the link to her CreativePro article with more details about her process, at wowartist.com.

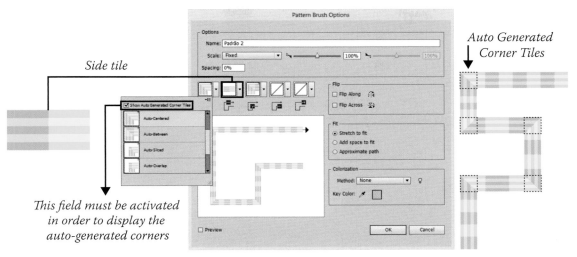

Side tile

Auto Generated Corner Tiles

This field must be activated in order to display the auto-generated corners

DEL VECHIO by permission from **Illustrator CC. O que há de novo?**

Gustavo Del Vechio

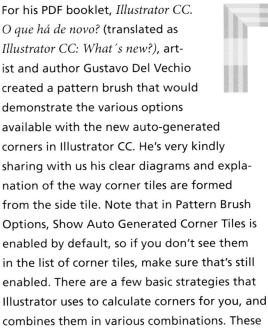

For his PDF booklet, *Illustrator CC. O que há de novo?* (translated as *Illustrator CC: What´s new?),* artist and author Gustavo Del Vechio created a pattern brush that would demonstrate the various options available with the new auto-generated corners in Illustrator CC. He's very kindly sharing with us his clear diagrams and explanation of the way corner tiles are formed from the side tile. Note that in Pattern Brush Options, Show Auto Generated Corner Tiles is enabled by default, so if you don't see them in the list of corner tiles, make sure that's still enabled. There are a few basic strategies that Illustrator uses to calculate corners for you, and combines them in various combinations. These include stretching your pattern (like an art

brush), copying and then overlaying extensions of the patterns, and finally, making cuts or "slicing" parts of the pattern in various ways, deleting the extraneous bits. These auto-generated tiles will fit with the side tile, but don't forget to look at your choices for both the Outer Corner and the Inner Corner, found on either side of your side tile in the Pattern Brush dialog, to make sure you have corners that both fit well and look good. See the following pages for a closer look at auto-corner options.

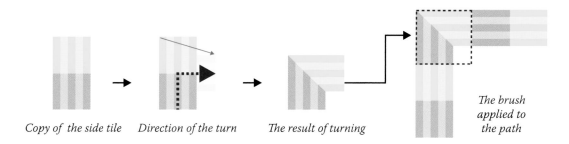

Copy of the side tile   *Direction of the turn*   *The result of turning*   *The brush applied to the path*

Gustavo Del Vechio

Auto-Centered tiles are formed by the side tile stretching along the path like an art brush and forcing it to make a 90° turn at the corner. Any extraneous portion of the pattern gets trimmed to make a smooth join, but the side tile itself isn't cut apart.

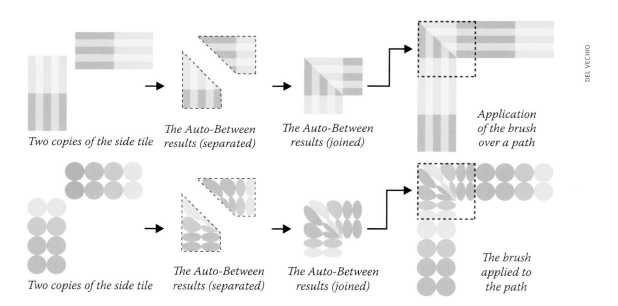

Two copies of the side tile   *The Auto-Between results (separated)*   *The Auto-Between results (joined)*   *Application of the brush over a path*

Two copies of the side tile   *The Auto-Between results (separated)*   *The Auto-Between results (joined)*   *The brush applied to the path*

DEL VECHIO

Auto-Between uses two copies of the side tile, one in a vertical orientation, the other turned horizontally by 90°, manipulated to fit the geometric shape that represents one half of the corner. Illustrator cuts each at the upper-left corner at a 45° angle and then joins them together along that cut. You'll notice distor-tions when the side tile isn't square; the more rectangular the area, the more distortion will occur. If the objects are round, the level of distortion in the tile is even more obvious. For example, a composition with straight lines (above, top) looks less distorted than one using ellipses (directly above).

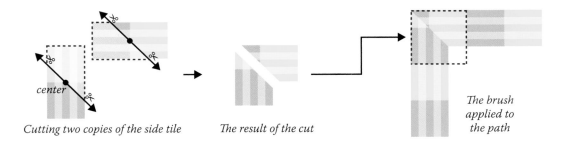

Cutting two copies of the side tile   *The result of the cut*   The brush applied to the path

Gustavo Del Vechio

Auto-Sliced also uses two copies of the side tile. Illustrator again orients one side tile vertically and one horizontally and then finds the center of the tile. It next makes a cut at a 45° angle,

top left to bottom right, through the center of each copy. After deleting the top portion of the vertical tile and the left portion of the horizontal tile, it joins the copies along the cut to form the corner tile.

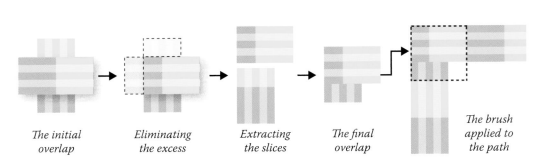

The initial overlap   *Eliminating the excess*   *Extracting the slices*   *The final overlap*   The brush applied to the path

Auto-Overlap uses two copies of the side tile, one oriented vertically and one horizontally, to align the tiles on their center points. It then removes any excess that extends above or to

the left of the tiles. The two remaining sections still overlap at their center, but the tile is cut along the overlap edge, the hidden portion is deleted, and the two parts are joined into the corner tile.

For Auto-Corners to work...

In the Pattern Brush Options field, the field Show Auto Generated Corner Tiles must be enabled in order for you to have access to the four methods of auto corners.

An inny or an outy?

You must separately set corner methods (None, Auto Generated, or from selected art) from pop-ups on either side of the main pattern (side) tile; set Outer corners on the left and Inner corners on the right.

Brush Corners

Pattern Brushes Made with a Raster Image

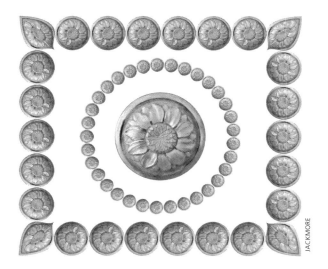

JACKMORE

Overview: *Isolate a part of a photo to use as a raster brush by creating a mask for it in Photoshop or image editor; import image into Illustrator, embed and resize image; create a Pattern Brush from the raster image; use the Pattern Brush Options to specify the attributes.*

Applying a pattern brush along a path is fairly simple, and now Illustrator can help create the corners for you. In fact, Illustrator can assist in creating corners for raster brushes!

The original image (left) and the masked image in Photoshop (right)

1 Preparing a bitmap image to use as a brush in Illustrator. In Photoshop, Lisa Jackmore selected the medallion in her photo, clicked the Layer Mask icon (to isolate it) and then with the mask selection active she chose Image> Crop to trim the file to the size of the medallion. To bring the image into Illustrator as an embedded image, she then saved it as PNG to keep the file size as small as possible. You can use either PSD or PNG to bring in a masked object with opacity. Jackmore opened the image directly in Illustrator. Alternatively if you choose Edit> Place, you can disable the Link option, or if it's already a linked image in your document you can click Embed from the Control panel. Jackmore then resized the image to the correct size for the frame she intended to make (holding Shift when she dragged the corner of the bounding box).

Making a New Pattern Brush and choosing the Pattern Brush Corner Tiles

2 Creating the Pattern Brush. Jackmore dragged the image to the Brushes panel, selected Pattern Brush, and clicked OK. For the first version of her brush, in the Pattern Brush Options, she named the brush, kept the scale Fixed (100%), Spacing 0%. She selected the Outer Corner

Tile and chose Auto-Centered and then clicked the Inner Corner Tile and chose Auto-Centered as well. Jackmore chose Approximate Path and Spacing at 0%. She made a rectangle with the Rectangle tool and selected the Medallion Pattern Brush in the Brushes panel. Because Jackmore chose the Approximate Path option and Spacing at 0%, her medallion Pattern Brush evenly distributed around the path without gaps between the medallions, and without distortion. However, depending on the size, it adjusts the path size to accommodate the pattern tile. The smaller the pattern, the less your pattern will be modified as it's applied. You can reduce the scale of your pattern by just adjusting the stroke weight in the Control panel.

By clicking Stroke in the Control panel, you can reduce the stroke weight and minimize the adjustment of your path when choosing the Approximate Path option

3 **Experimenting with brushes.** When experimenting with brushes, it's always best to work with a duplicate. To do this, drag the brush you wish to modify to the New Brush icon in the bottom right of the Brushes panel. Then to modify this brush, double-click it in the panel. In Pattern Brush Options you can then try the different spacing options as well as a different type of Auto-Corner, Fit, and Scale. Rename the brush to reflect the modifications that you chose, and click OK. You can then apply this brush to another path, or you can duplicate the original path and then apply the modified version so you can compare the brushes.

You can continue to make new brushes until you've experimented with all the different parameters, and if the brushes are meaningfully named, you'll be able to figure out if there is a different combination of Corner, Fit, and Scale you want to try. If your image is a complicated shape or has a repeating pattern, it will be more challenging to find the right Auto-Corner. If you find you do not like the Auto-Corner results, you may have to go back into your image editor and make adjustments to the image and then try the Auto-Corners again. If that doesn't completely fix your corners, you can manually edit the corners in Illustrator (see the following galleries for more about updating brush definitions).

Exacting image crops

Mask and crop your image in Photoshop to the desired tile size rather than trying to apply a clipping mask to the placed image in Illustrator, because Illustrator will use the entire placed image dimensions—and not the intended crop dimensions—as the tile size.

—*Gary Ferster*

3

Auto-Centered Corner (left), Auto-Sliced Corner (right)

Auto-Between Corner (left), Auto-Overlap Corner (right)

Lisa Jackmore

Lisa Jackmore created variations within her pattern
brush using Variable Width
Profile. She began by drawing the bottle, the text, one
set of necklace links, and the
blue bead with a Calligraphic
brush and pressure-sensitive
pen and tablet. For the heart

bead she scanned a stone and then masked it
in Photoshop. Jackmore then placed the PNG
image of the stone heart onto the artboard
in Illustrator and then in the Control panel
clicked the Embed link and scaled the image
proportionally. Jackmore aligned the beaded
elements to the heart, dragged them together
into the Brushes panel, and selected Pattern
brush, keeping all the default settings. Jackmore chose the Paintbrush tool, made a circular
path, and clicked the Pattern brush to apply it
to the path. To suggest perspective and slightly
vary bead size, she selected the path, switched
to the Width tool, and then selected several
points. She held the Shift key down while dragging one point to uniformly modify the width.
She continued until the beads looked as though
they were lying flat, with some of the hearts
slightly larger than others. She saved the profile
by clicking the Add to Profile icon in the

Variable Width Profile menu in the Control
panel. With her main elements in place,
Jackmore added background color with a bristle
brush and the text and flowers with a calligraphic brush. Having saved the profile in the
application settings, she now has access to this
custom profile to apply to paths of any type,
including brushes. Jackmore created several
variations of the pattern brush that she can
now substitute for the original; you can see
some on the opposite page.

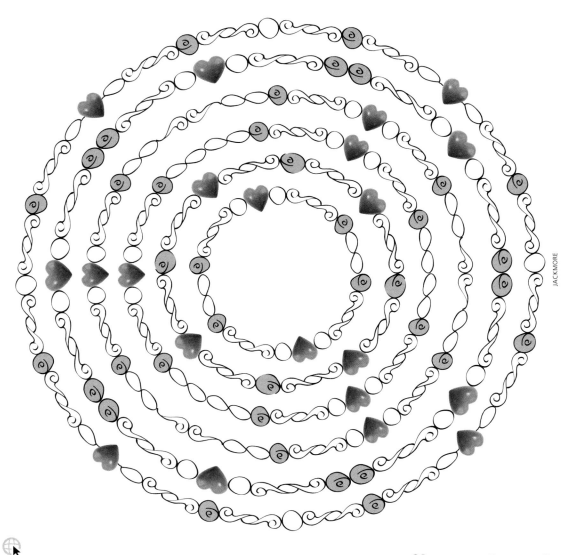

JACKMORE

Lisa Jackmore

With just a few adjustments to her designs, Lisa Jackmore was able to very quickly make variations to her pattern brushes. Shown at right are several pattern brush variations created for the opposite page, which are then applied to circle paths above.

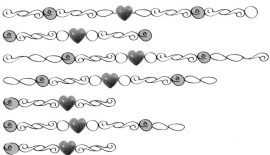

JACKMORE

Lisa Jackmore

Lisa Jackmore found inspiration for this Pattern Brush in a steel-beamed ceiling. She saved a raster image detail of the beam as a PNG image (above left) in Photoshop and then opened it in Illustrator. Jackmore dragged the embedded image to the Brushes panel and selected Pattern Brush in the New Brush dialog. In Pattern Brush Options she kept the default scale and spacing. She only needed Outer Corners for a frame, so for this pattern she chose Auto-Sliced and Approximate Path, named it, and clicked OK. She made and selected a rectangle and then clicked the pattern brush in the Brushes panel and applied the brush. Jackmore was aiming for a seamless pattern that didn't distort the image; this attempt was pretty close, but not quite perfect (directly above right). Jackmore felt she needed to tweak the pattern brush slightly so the dark seam, rivets, and bolts were better aligned and not cut off. To solve the puzzle about why her pattern repeat wasn't working perfectly, she dragged the brush from the Brushes panel onto her artboard to examine more closely how the parts fit together. An Auto-Sliced corner tile is made of two objects overlapping each other, within an unstroked, unfilled rectangle defining the corner parameters. To adjust the Corner tile, Jackmore selected one image object at a time and used the arrow keys to move it within the tile until she figured out how to solve her problem. She then went back to Photoshop and made adjustments to the original image, including deleting one of the bolts, enlarging the ends of the image to extend the bolt-free area, and adjusting the dark seam on one side to align evenly with the opposite side (directly above left). Once she thought the right changes were made, she brought the image back into Illustrator and created a new pattern brush. Because the image was complex, Jackmore had to make a few more trips to Photoshop and then back to Illustrator to make new brushes with her tiles to finally achieve the perfect image, and in the end the Auto-Corners worked perfectly (above right shown pulled apart).

STEUER

Sharon Steuer

Borrowing elements from Illustrator art she created several years earlier, Sharon Steuer reinvigorated the original calligraphic brush work with the addition of a frame made with a pattern brush, invoking the look of a craft frame made by children on a beach vacation. Steuer duplicated, scaled, and rearranged the shells and starfish. Dragging them into the Brushes panel, she chose Pattern Brush, enabled Stretch to fit (under Fit), chose Tints and Hues as the Colorization Method, and clicked OK. For the corner, she decided to use a photograph of a real shell. After masking the photo in Photoshop, she placed it as an embedded image in Illustrator. To add the photo as a corner tile to the pattern brush, she selected the masked shell and then—with the Brushes panel in Thumbnail view—held Option/Alt as she dragged the photo to the far left "tile space"of the shell pattern brush. Checking that her settings were still correct, she clicked OK. After applying the brush to a rectangle to form a frame, she didn't like the position of the photo. To figure out how to reposition the shell, she used the frame on the artboard as a reference and positioned a copy of the masked shell photo over the original corner of the frame, rotating it into the desired position. Holding down the Option/Alt key, Steuer dragged the rotated shell onto the previous corner tile in the Brushes panel, retaining the other options. To make pattern brush variations, she worked with duplicates of the original pattern brush, changing the Stroke weight in the Control panel and playing with different colorization methods in Brushes Options. To apply the color to vector objects of the pattern brush, she changed the Stroke color. To apply a shadow to the frame she selected Stroke in the Appearance panel, clicked the *fx* icon and then selected Stylize> Drop Shadow. Some of the color and scale experiments are shown above right.

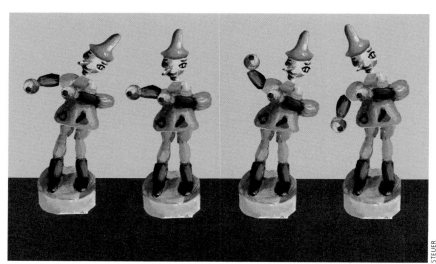

STEUER

Sharon Steuer

After discovering that she could paint with raster images in Illustrator, Sharon Steuer decided to experiment with making a pattern brush from an Italian "push puppet" in her oil paintings (one shown at right). In Photoshop she combined a number of details from different paintings in the series to form the pieces necessary to articulate three separate parts for the body (the legs and base, the torso, and the head), and three

more so she could articulate the joints of an arm (one for each end and one for the middle). Tightly masking and cropping each element, she saved them as a separate PNG files, and placed all of them as embedded objects into one Illustrator file. Rotating each of the elements so that all were oriented horizontally, she dragged the torso segment into the Brushes panel.

Choosing the Pattern Brush, she clicked OK to enter and then OK to exit Options. With the panel set to Thumbnail view, she next held Option/Alt as she dragged the legs and base into the start tile position and then applied the brush to a path to check the scale and positioning of the segment. Steuer repeated this process with the head in the end tile and then similarly created the arm brush in three stages.

Using the Pen tool, she drew with the body pattern brush and then with the arm brush. If she's careful about the path length and angles, she can position her puppet with nuance, or she can accidentally create strange effects. For links to her "Artistic Painting with Illustrator" courses (one movie shows this brush) and a 7-day free trial link, go to sharonsteuer.com/lynda.

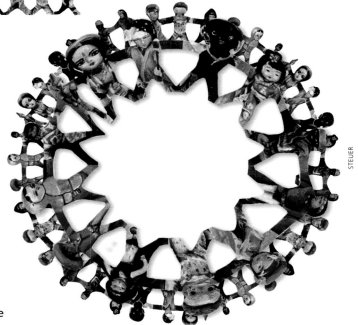

STEUER

Sharon Steuer

While preparing artwork for the pattern brush chapter in her lynda.com course "Artistic Painting with Illustrator: Object-Creation Brushes," Sharon Steuer realized that not all patterns work well with corners. She decided to revisit an art piece she created many years ago in which she digitally wrapped a line of her doll paintings around circles. Now she could achieve the same result more easily by placing the "paper doll" image in Illustrator, making it into a pattern brush, wrapping the pattern brush around a circle. After adding a drop shadow and a second smaller stroke from *fx* in the Appearance panel (see the *Reshaping Dimensions* chapter for more on the Appearance panel), she then experimented with applying this pattern to a rectangle, but none of the Auto-corners looked good, and she couldn't visualize a custom corner that would work regardless of the size of the rectangle. Steuer realized that she could eliminate corners entirely by applying her pattern to a rounded rectangle. In her "Simulating Corners" movie she demonstrated how to manually select and adjust the rectangle's anchor points to tweak how the pattern wraps around the shape. Now, with Live Rectangles, this process is much easier. Simply create a rectangle using the Rectangle tool, or if you have a previously created rectangle, choose Object> Shape> Convert to Rectangle. If your pattern isn't already applied, click Basic in the Control panel and choose your brush from the pop-up. Now, in the Control

panel (from Shape) or in the Transform panel, click the arrows to adjust the Corner Radius field. What radius value you'll prefer will vary depending on the pattern, rectangle size, and stroke weight (both versions above are 90 pt).

STEVEN H GORDON
LANDSCAPE PHOTOGRAPHY

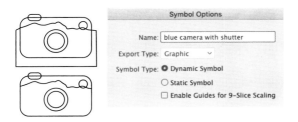

Steven Gordon

Designing a photography gallery for his Adobe Portfolio website, Steven Gordon used a dynamic symbol to prototype variations of a camera icon for his webpage banner. He started the camera icon by selecting the Rounded Rectangle tool and drawing the body of a camera. Next, he drew a mountain and filled it with black. To trim the mountain to the camera body, he duplicated the camera body, selected the mountain object, and then used Pathfinder> Intersect (see the *Rethinking Construction* chapter for more on Pathfinders). Gordon then finished the artwork by drawing the lens, flash, and shutter button objects. To complete the icon, he selected the camera body and filled it with a blue gradient to represent the sky (see the *Color Transitions* chapter for more on gradients). To preserve his artwork, Gordon turned it into a graphic symbol. To do this, he selected the icon's artwork and clicked the New Symbol icon in the Symbols panel. He made sure that

Dynamic Symbol was enabled in the Symbol Options dialog so that he'd later be able to directly edit its colors, and then clicked OK; his artwork was now replaced with his new symbol. While building the webpage, Gordon decided to prototype several color variations of the icon, to see which worked best with different webpage color schemes. To do this, he chose the Direct Selection tool and clicked on the sky area of the icon. With the gradient now selected, Gordon opened the Gradient panel and experimented with different color gradients. As he made each version, he stored it as a new symbol before reviewing all the versions and choosing the one he added to the webpage banner. By storing different versions of his camera icons as symbols, Gordon was able to create a collection of icons that he could easily use to freshen the webpage in the future, perhaps switching to a new theme color or customizing the color of a particular page.

5

Color Transitions

Color Transitions

Whether your colors are black and white, a limited palette, or a full spectrum, mastering the power of Illustrator requires a command of color transitions and groups of colors. This chapter focuses on myriad ways of coloring your objects in Illustrator, from using the various panels, to creating transitions of colors with gradients and gradient mesh; it also looks at the group of panels and functions that help you organize and adjust colors.

WORKING WITH THE COLOR AND SWATCHES PANELS

The main panels that help you work with color include Swatches, Color Guide, Gradient, Appearance, and Control panels. Click a Fill or Stroke color to reveal an arrow, which provides access to a version of the Swatches panel, or Shift-click to access the Color panel.

To save your current Stroke or Fill color as a swatch, drag it from the Toolbox or Color panel to the Swatches panel. You can also drag colors from the Color Guide to the Swatches panel. (See the **CC** section later in this chapter for info on proxy icons added in CC.) To name a single selected color as you create it (and set is as a global color if desired), click the New Swatch icon at the bottom of the Swatches panel instead. When you copy objects that contain custom swatches from one document to another, Illustrator automatically adds the swatches to the new document's panels.

You can create three kinds of solid colors in Illustrator: process colors, global process colors, and spot colors. Each is easy to distinguish visually. In **CC**, be aware that when you create a new swatch, it gets added to an active Creative Cloud Library unless you disable Add to my Library in the New Swatch dialog

- **Process colors** (solid swatch) are mixed from the CMYK colors used for printing with ink. Change the percentage of each ink to change the color, or choose a color from a swatch library, such as Pantone process uncoated.

- **Global process colors** are process colors with an added convenience: If you update the definition for a global process color, Illustrator updates that color throughout the document. Identify a global process color in the Swatches panel by the small triangle in the lower-right corner of the swatch in any view and by the Global Color icon in List view. Create a global process color by enabling the Global option if it's disabled (defaults change with versions used) in either the New Swatch or Swatch Options dialog.
- **Spot colors** are used in print jobs that require a pre-mixed ink or varnish, rather than a percentage of the four process colors. Specifying a spot color allows you to use colors that are outside of the CMYK gamut or to achieve a more precise color match to the spot color you'll be using than CMYK allows. You can specify a color as a spot color in the New Swatch dialog from the Color Type menu, or you can choose a spot color from a Swatch library, such as the various Pantone libraries (from the Swatch panel's Swatch Libraries Menu icon choose Color Books). All spot colors are global, so they update automatically if you change the definition; when the Swatches panel is in Thumbnail view, they have a small triangle in the lower-right corner, as well as a small dot or "spot." In List view, they're also marked by the Spot Color icon.

Color groups and the Color Guide

The default document profiles that ship with Illustrator include several swatches and one or two color groups to start using in your document. To create and save your own groups of colors, select multiple colors from the Swatches or the Color Guide panels, or select the objects in your artwork that contain the colors you want and click the New Color Group icon in the Swatches panel.

The Color Guide panel helps you mix and match colors according to various color schemes. At the upper left of the Color Guide panel is the "base color" swatch. You can choose a base color by clicking a color in the Color Guide, Color, or Swatches panel. To the right of the base color swatch, you can choose a harmony rule that will

Four-color-process jobs

You can print four-color-process separations from the Print dialog, even if your objects contain spot colors, by enabling the "Convert All Spot Colors to Process" (from the Output option). Be aware, however, that there might be color shifts.

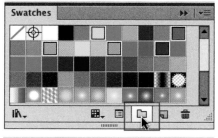

The Swatches panel, shown in list view for color swatches only; the top two user-defined swatches are process colors; the middle two are spot colors; and the last two are global colors (at left with the document in CMYK mode; at right the same colors with the document in RGB mode)

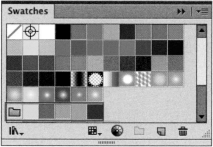

The New Color Group icon (top) makes it possible to organize your Swatches panel creating sets manually or from selected objects (shown selected at top and saved as a group at bottom); you also specify the name for the group

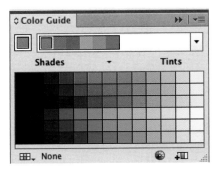

The Color Guide panel after changing the number of steps from the default 4 to 7, via Color Guide Options

Reset gradients to defaults

After you select an object that has an altered gradient angle (or highlight), new objects you draw will have the same settings. The fastest way to "re-zero" gradient settings such as angles is to press Option/Alt and then click the gradient swatch. For linear gradients, you can also type a zero in the Angle field. Or, you can use the Gradient panel to switch between Radial and Linear and then back again to reset a custom angle without removing or relocating color stops.
—*Monika Gause*

Extra big gradient panel

A special feature of the Gradient panel is that you can make it extra

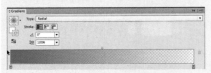

tall and wide, and the Gradient slider itself will increase in size, making it much easier to design complex gradients.

automatically select colors that go with your base color, based on scientific color theory. Or, in the Swatches panel, click the Color Group icon in a color group to load that group in the Color Guide panel. You can then preview variations of those colors by choosing to display them (using the Color Guide's panel menu) according to value, temperature, or saturation. Drag a selected swatch (or swatches) to the Swatches panel to save it, or click the "Save color group to Swatch panel" icon. Clicking the "New swatch group" icon in the Swatches panel will also save your current harmony.

To access the Harmony Rules menu, click the pop-up menu to the far right of the base color. Once a new harmony rule is selected, its colors fill the strip beside the base color. Alter how many variations of that color group you see by choosing Color Guide Options from the Color Guide panel's menu. You can change the number of steps in each color's gradient (up to 20) and the amount of variation between steps. Also in the panel's menu you will find the choice to view the colors as shades and tints, warm and cool, or vivid and muted. The Color Guide panel is one that can be resized wider and taller to accommodate the size of the grid. If you want to use your current color group as a base for even more color variations, click the Edit Colors icon at the bottom of the panel to enter the Edit Colors/Recolor Artwork dialog (for more about this icon see that section later in this chapter).

GRADIENTS

Gradients create seamless transitions from one color into another, often creating the appearance of realistic modeling. Illustrator can create either Radial or Linear gradients. You can not only apply gradients to Fills, but now in many cases, you can also apply gradients to Strokes. There are many similarities and a few distinct differences between the ways gradients can be applied to Fills versus Strokes. First, here are some of the similarities:

For both Fills and Strokes, you can choose a gradient style from the Swatches or the Gradient panels, and via

Swatch Libraries accessed with buttons in panels or from the Window menu. Click the New Swatch icon in the Swatches panel to save your current gradient or, if you've modified a gradient since it was last saved, you can save the current variation within the Gradient panel by clicking the arrow next to the main gradient icon and clicking the Add To Swatches icon.

Within the Gradient panel, you can make a variety of adjustments, including adding color points, changing the colors and opacities of stops, toggling between Radial and Linear, or reversing the direction of the gradient. See the next section for how the Gradient panel changes to display the specifics of Gradient Fills versus Strokes.

Gradient Fills and the Gradient Annotator

In addition to Linear and Radial gradient styles, you can create *elliptical* gradients by modifying the proportions of radial gradient–filled objects. To apply the current or last-used gradient style to an object, make sure Fill is active in the Gradient, Toolbar, or Color panels, then click or click-drag with the Gradient tool, placing the Annotator on your object. You can place the start and/or end point of a gradient outside the object itself with the Gradient tool and/or the Gradient Annotator. To unify the way gradients appear across multiple gradient-filled objects, select those objects at the same time and click-drag across them; this can unify even different gradients (see the "Unified Gradients" lesson later in this chapter for details). To modify the gradient fill in a selected object: use the Gradient Annotator; edit it directly in the Gradient panel; or first save the gradient as a swatch and then edit that swatch to update that fill wherever it was applied.

Probably the biggest difference between gradient fills and strokes is that only gradient fills allow you to make adjustments to the gradient on the object itself, using the Gradient tool. When the Gradient tool is active *and* Show Gradient Annotator is enabled, the Gradient Annotator appears as a bar across the gradient on the Fill of a selected object. To modify a Fill gradient using the

Shortcut for last-used gradient

The shortcut key > applies the last-used gradient and its angle (< applies the last used solid fill).

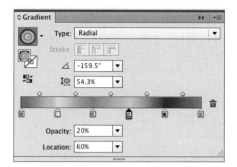

Gradient panel with Radial gradient selected

Adding color to gradients

- Drag a swatch from the Color or Swatches panel to the Gradient slider until you see a vertical line indicating where the new color stop will be added.
- Drag a solid color from the Fill or Stroke proxies in the Tools or Gradient panels.
- Hold down the Option/Alt key to drag a copy of a color stop.
- Option-drag/Alt-drag one stop over another to *swap* colors.
- For Fills, double-click the color stop on the Gradient Annotator or the slider bar in the Gradient panel, and select a color from the Swatches or Color panels.
- For Fills, hover your cursor beneath the Gradient Annotator bar or Gradient slider (where the stops are); when you see a small + next to your cursor, you can click to add a new stop.

Missing Gradient Annotator?

If you don't see the Gradient Annotator, then try using the toggle View> Show Gradient Annotator (⌘-Option-G/Ctrl-Alt-G). If you apply one unifying gradient to multiple objects, however, you'll see only one (unifying) annotator until you later reselect one or more objects, at which point you'll see one annotator per object.

Panel pop-up after double-clicking a color stop to display either the Color or Swatches panel when using the Gradient Annotator

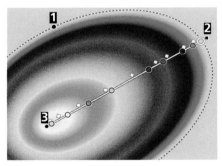

1) Dragging on the Radial Gradient circle to make it elliptical; 2) rotating or scaling the gradient (right); 3) moving the gradient start point. **CC** *Gradient Annotator pictured above*

A gradient graphic style

Aspect ratio and angle information are not saved with gradient swatches. However, if you save your gradient swatch as a graphic style, that information is saved with it.

Gradient Annotator, add and/or move the stops along the lower edge of the Annotator. Adjust the blend between the color stops by sliding the diamond shapes along the top of the Annotator, and change the color by double-clicking on a stop to open a panel you can toggle between showing the Color panel and the Swatches panel. You can set transparency for the gradient here, as well. To rotate or scale your gradient, hover over the diamond end of the Annotator until your cursor becomes a scale or rotate icon. Reposition the start point of the gradient using the hollow circle at the other end. If your object has a Radial Fill, you can also drag on the solid anchor to interactively transform the circle into an elliptical shape.

Stroke Gradients

Stroke Gradients have some unique options that aren't available to Fill gradients. In the Gradient panel you can choose from three Align options: *within* the stroke, *along* the stroke, or *across* the stroke. You can control whether a gradient applied to a stroke using the *within* option is aligned to the Inside or Outside of the path using the Stroke panel (but you can't use these options with gradients applied *along* or *across* the stroke). You can apply a gradient to a Calligraphic or Bristle Brush Stroke, but not to scatter, pattern, or art brushes. With gradients applied to brush strokes, you'll be able to Reverse the direction, but you can't apply the gradient along or across the stroke. If you Expand or Outline a Stroke gradient (Object> Expand> Expand Appearance, or Objects> Path Outline Stroke), gradients applied *within* the Stroke become gradient-filled objects and can be edited as such, but Stroke gradients applied along or across the Stroke become gradient mesh objects.

GRADIENT MESH

A *gradient mesh object* is an object on which multiple colors can flow in different directions, with smooth transitions between the *mesh points*. (For a look similar to gradient mesh, see "Freeform Gradients" in the **CC** section of this chapter.) You can transform a solid or gradient-filled object into mesh (you can't transform compound paths into mesh). Once transformed, the object will always be a mesh object, so be certain that you work with a copy of the original if it's difficult to re-create.

Transform solid filled objects into gradient mesh objects either by choosing Object> Create Gradient Mesh (so you can specify details on the mesh construction) or by clicking on the object with the Mesh tool, which manually places mesh lines. One way to get a head start in creating a mesh object is to transform a gradient-filled object into a mesh object: choose Object> Expand and enable the Gradient Mesh option.

Depending on where you click with the Mesh tool within a mesh object, you'll add points (or lines and points) to the mesh. Reshape the mesh with the Direct Selection tool, using the anchors and their handles as with any ordinary path. Select individual points, groups of points, or patches within the mesh using the Direct Selection tool, the Lasso tool, or the Mesh tool, in order to color or delete them. If the Mesh tool is selected, holding down the Option/Alt key and clicking on a mesh point deletes it. You can sample a color with the Eyedropper and either immediately have it apply to all selected areas of the mesh object, or, with the mesh object completely deselected, use the Option/Alt key to click with the Eyedropper tool on a mesh point or space between points. Adding color to a patch instead of a single point spreads the color to all surrounding points. When adding a new mesh point, the color currently selected in the Swatches panel will be applied to the new point. If you want the new mesh point to remain the color currently applied to the mesh object, hold down the Shift key while adding a new point.

To further modify the shape your gradient mesh takes, you can use any of the Distort tools, such as Warp or Pucker, to reshape it. You don't even have to select points first. Hover over the mesh to highlight it; the size of your distorting tool will determine how many mesh points and patches get distorted at the same time.

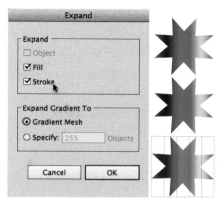

An easy way to create a gradient mesh is to begin with a linear gradient and then choose Object> Expand and enable the Gradient Mesh option under the Expand Gradient To section

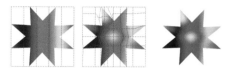

Once you've expanded a gradient-filled object to a mesh, you can edit the locations and colors of the mesh points and add mesh points and lines

PAIDRICK

Ann Paidrick builds gradient mesh objects in the "Transparent Mesh" lesson later in this chapter

Get back your (mesh) shape!

To extract an editable path from a mesh, select the mesh object, choose Object> Path> Offset Path, enter 0, and click OK. If there are too many points in your new path, try using Object> Path> Simplify.

—*Pierre Louveaux*

Where is Live Color?

Adobe introduced the term "Live Color" to describe the suite of features that included Edit Colors/ Recolor Artwork panel, and the Color Guide panel, but the term appears to be no longer in use.

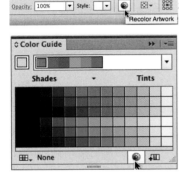

Enter the Edit Color/Recolor Artwork dialog from the Control panel (top) or from the Color Guide panel (bottom)

The Edit Color/Recolor Artwork dialog

Recoloring brushes & symbols

Using Recolor Artwork to edit brushes, patterns, or gradients automatically saves new versions of these into the appropriate panel. Using Recolor Artwork to edit symbols (without breaking links) updates the symbols themselves.

You can assign transparency to a gradient mesh object as you can to other vector objects. Simply select either the mesh points or patches you want and use either the Appearance panel (click <u>Opacity</u>) or the Transparency panel to reduce the Opacity below 100%.

Hint: Instead of applying a mesh to a complex path, try to first create the mesh from a simpler path outline, then mask the mesh with the more complex path. You also can stack simple objects with gradient mesh applied to them to construct a more complex object.

EDIT COLORS/RECOLOR ARTWORK

Housed inside a somewhat daunting dual-named dialog is Illustrator's all-in-one answer to creating new palettes and editing all of your selected artwork. The dialog changes its name depending upon what is, or is not, selected when you enter. You may still hear it referred to as "Live Color"—the phrase Adobe initially used to describe the combination of color editing features.

If you have nothing selected, you enter a mode called Edit Colors. You can access this mode by clicking the Edit Colors icon at the bottom of the Color Guide panel. Once you're in the Edit Colors dialog, you'll be in Edit mode, which means that you can mix and store colors (see the following section for specific instructions on how to do this). You'll see a tab next to the word "Edit" titled "Assign," but it will be grayed out; since you don't have any objects selected, you can't access this tab. You can only assign colors to selected objects.

If, however, you have artwork selected, this dialog will now be titled "Recolor Artwork," and you will have access to the Assign tab of the dialog, as well as Edit mode. As long as your selection contains at least two colors, you'll see the Recolor Artwork icon in the Control panel (or find Recolor in **CC** Properties panel). Another option is the icon at the bottom of the Color Guide panel mentioned earlier; be aware that when artwork is selected, this icon will now be called "Edit or Apply Colors." In the Swatches panel, with a color group selected, you can click the Edit or Apply Color Group icon. A final way into this dialog is Edit> Edit Colors> Recolor Artwork.

The Recoloring Artwork (and Editing Color) dialogs

After selecting the object(s) you want to recolor, click the Recolor Artwork button in the Control panel (or Recolor in **CC** Properties) to open the Recolor Artwork dialog; the colors from your selected art should still be all in order, and the selection edges will automatically be hidden. If you enter the Recolor Artwork dialog via Color Guide's Edit or Apply Colors icon, your image will initially appear with the color group in that panel assigned to your artwork. If that's not what you intended, click the "Get colors from selected art" icon to reload the original colors into your artwork. In fact, any time you want to quickly return to your original colors without canceling the dialog, simply click again on the "Get colors from selected art" icon.

Recolor Artwork shows a base color and active colors at the top, with a pop-up menu showing several of Adobe's Harmony Rules, just as the Color Guide panel does. Drag colors within the Active Colors field to reorder them, and your selected object(s) will be recolored according to their new positions. To change the base color, simply select another color from among the active colors.

The Color Groups section lists any color groups you saved in your Swatches panel before you entered the Recolor Artwork/Edit Colors dialog, as well as any color groups you created during this work session by clicking the New Color Groups icon. Rename a color group by double-clicking its name and entering a new one in the pop-up dialog. Clicking any color group loads those colors into your artwork. Deleting and creating new color groups in the Recolor Artwork dialog will also delete and add color groups in your Swatches panel, so don't click the Trash icon unless you're positive you want to delete that color group from your document entirely. If you create color groups you want to save during a work session, but don't want to apply the changes to your artwork, disable the Recolor Art checkbox and click OK. If you click

You can do a number of things in the upper portion of the Recolor Artwork dialog, including set the current color as the base color (on the left), choose from Harmony Rules (the arrow pop-up menu), and rename Color Groups (says "Artwork colors" above); from the upper right you can re-load the colors from your artwork

The center-right section of the Edit Colors/Recolor Artwork dialog has more powerful mini icons for "Save changes to color group," "New Color Group," and "Delete Color Group"

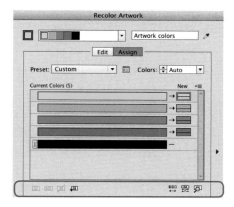

In Assign mode, these icons (circled) allow for merging, separating, excluding, and adding new color rows; you can also randomly change color order, saturation, and brightness, as well as find a particular color in your artwork

Special color sets

If your work requires that you use a very specific set of colors, such as team colors or specific "designer" hues for a season, you'll want to first create and save a Color Group (or groups) in the Swatches panel. Then, when you open Edit Colors/Recolor Artwork, your Color Groups will be in the storage area, ready to recolor your artwork.

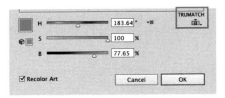

In Edit or Assign mode, clicking the miniature grid-like icon (the"Limits the color group to colors in a swatch library" icon highlighted here) will present a pop-up menu of swatch libraries

The Color Reduction Options icon (under the Assign tab in Recolor Artwork)

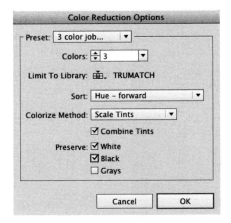

The Color Reduction Options icon opens this dialog

Cancel, all the work you did creating (or deleting) new color groups will be deleted.

The two main tabs are Edit and Assign. The Assign tab (only available with an active selection) displays horizontal color bars, with each long bar representing one of the colors in the artwork currently selected. To their right is an arrow pointing to a smaller color swatch that's initially the same color as the larger bar. This small swatch is where you can load or mix a replacement color. To protect a color from change, click the arrow to turn it into a straight bar. You can drag and drop colors within this area; you can also access context-sensitive menus.

The Edit tab contains a color wheel with markers representing the colors in the selected artwork. Depending on whether the Lock icon is enabled or disabled, you can move the markers around on the color wheel individually (unlocked) or in unison (locked) to adjust the color in your art. You can also click the display icons to select a segmented wheel or a bar view. In addition to dragging markers on the color wheel, you can use the sliders and controls just below the color wheel to adjust the various aspects of color (hue, saturation, and value). You can work in the standard color modes, or you can choose Global Adjust to affect all colors at once. As you adjust individual colors with the sliders, notice that the color marker you selected will also move on the color wheel as you move a slider.

On either the Assign or Edit tab, you can choose to limit colors to a swatch library such as a Pantone library using the "Limits the color group to colors in a swatch library" icon. On the Assign tab, you have a Preset list and a Color Reduction Options icon for restricting the colors that can be reassigned. When you restrict your colors to a swatch library, the color wheel or bar on the Edit tab displays only the library's colors, while Assign mode will replace all your original colors with those from the library that it thinks are the closest match.

The Presets on the Assign tab also help you limit the number of colors in your palette to 1, 2, or 3. This makes

Recolor Artwork a huge timesaver when you need to reduce the number of colors used in a full-color project so it can be printed with spot colors, or even need to reduce a 3-color spot color job to 1 or 2. Use the Color Reduction Options to further determine how tints, shades, and neutrals are handled when colors get reassigned.

COLOR FEATURES UPDATED IN CC

Updated Swatches panel

The **CC** Swatches panel includes new features and improved color search. The top left of the panel displays the Swatch proxy icons for Stroke and Fill, letting you quickly spot which is active or drag a swatch into the panel. At the top right of the panel you can set whether to view your swatches as a list or as thumbnails. Clicking either one sets that view to the default Small size list or thumbnail. Although you can enlarge the view from the panel menu, clicking either thumbnail resets that view back to Small.

Finding your swatches

You can now search in both the Swatches panel and the Color Swatch section of the Color Picker for named color swatches or one that has a specific percentage of an ink. Type the name of a swatch (such as Khaki) or, if the swatch is unnamed, a percentage of ink (75) or a percentage of a specific ink (c=75) in the Find field for the Swatches panel or Color Picker, and the results will display only those swatches that match your criterion. (To initially show the Find field in the Swatches panel, choose Show Find Field from the pop-up menu.) If your criterion matches a swatch contained in different groups, the Swatches panel displays the swatches with their group icons. This can help you locate a specific palette that contains a named color, an ink percentage, or a specific ink.

The Adobe Color Themes Panel

The Color Themes panel is a smaller version of Adobe Color (formerly called Adobe Kuler), the web-based

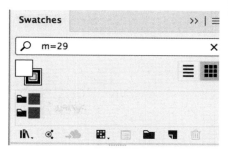

The Swatches panel displaying Swatch proxy icons and List and Thumbnail view icons, as well as the Find Field, which allows you to search for unnamed swatches that share a specified CMYK or RGB ink, a specified percentage of any ink (such as 50), or a named color

Save swatches to Cloud Library

If you want to share your swatches with other users, or simply have a swatch or swatch group always available in any document you create, click the cloud icon at the bottom of the Swatches panel to save the swatch (or set of swatches) to the current library.

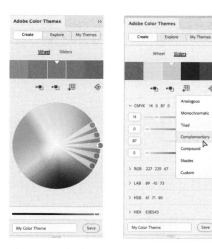

The Create tab of the Adobe Color Themes panel provides two main editing modes (Wheel and Sliders) and many pop-up options that let you modify the modifications; for the website version of Adobe Color, click ••• on the Explore tab to "View Online"

From the Explore tab in the Adobe Color Themes panel you can search by keyword such as "rainbow" (top left) or choose from a pop-up menu options (top right), but be aware the default color mode for the themes is RGB—working in CMYK color mode may affect the colors you've chosen; Setting a new base color by clicking the hollow arrow on another color to Set as Base Color (bottom)

Gary Ferster tried to create a variation of his blood cell illustration (in the Mastering Complexitiy *chapter) using Freeform Gradients, but the Point option can't make elliptical transitions (with Freeform Gradient points visible above right)*

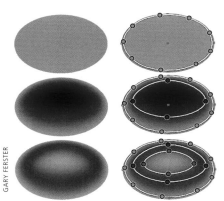

GARY FERSTER

Ferster found Freeform Gradients with the Lines option was not only superior to Points but easier to create than with the original cells he'd created with the Gradient Mesh tool (shown top to bottom in stages of progress, right side with Freeform Gradient points visible), and powerful enough to use for another of his projects (see his Freeform Gradient lesson later in this chapter)

community application for creating and sharing color palettes.

The Adobe Color Themes panel contains three tabs: Create, Explore, and My Themes. With the Create tab you can create your own new color theme from scratch. By default your current Foreground color will be the starting base color. There are a number of ways to change your base color, including clicking it, choosing a new foreground color, and then clicking the icon directly below it ("Set selected color from current color"), and directly mixing the hue you want. Click the far-right Color Rule icon to access a drop-down list of different models to generate color harmonies. You can save a color you see or make by clicking the leftmost "Click to set active color" icon (be aware that if you have any selected objects they will adopt that new active color!) and then click New Swatch to add it to the Swatches panel. To add the entire new theme, click the Add to Swatches (grid) icon.

If you have a color Library already made, clicking the Save button next to the name field lets you save the group to one of your Libraries. Swatch groups saved to a Library will also appear on the My Themes tab, where you can edit (or rename) your theme, add it to Swatches, or view it online. If you then edit your theme, you'll be taken back into Create, and when you choose to save it, you'll have the chance to replace the original theme or to save a copy.

The Explore tab requires an internet connection. This is how you access themes created and shared by the Adobe Color community. You can search for themes others have created using a variety of criteria, or search only for the ones you yourself have publicly shared. When you find a theme that interests you, click • • • to open a list where you can edit the theme, add it to your Favorites, add it to Swatches, or again, view it online, where you'll have access to the full Adobe Color online application.

Freeform Gradients

Freeform Gradients are the simpler cousin to gradients and gradient mesh, and depending on what you do, they can be easy to make or a bit harder to control. The first way to create a freeform gradient is to select the object you wish to fill with a gradient and choose the Gradient tool. Next, click the Freeform Gradient icon in the Gradient panel or in the Gradient Type section of the Control or Properties panel. By default, Illustrator automatically fills your object with a gradient generated from two or more points and colors (to change these defaults see "Secret Freeform Defaults" Tip at right). With the Gradient tool still active, click on a point to select it, and click a color swatch to change the color or double-click on the point to launch the on-screen Swatch panel proxy. Drag to relocate active points, click anywhere within the selected object to add more points, drag on the solid anchor on the dotted outline of a point to scale its circle of influence, or drag points outside the object to delete them (or click to select a point and press the delete/Backspace key). Shift-click with the Point option to select multiple points (even on Lines). If you delete all the points, you won't restore the object to its original fill; instead you'll delete all the fill. Of course, you can draw with new points, so if you want a fresh start, simply delete all the points.

Click the Lines option (next to Draw) to see how this alternate method changes the process. Points are best suited to filling an object with its basic gradient colors, but freeform lines with color stops give you more control for shading or highlighting to an object's edge, so complex curves will appear as even, continuous colors. Drawing with Lines is similar to using the Curvature tool, but without Bézier handles, and basically draws a path (open or closed) with color stops instead of anchors. With the Line option, press Esc to stop drawing a line, click an end point to continue it, or click a Point type to convert it to a Line type. To add a point to an existing line, hover over it and click when you see **+**. To toggle a point between corner and smooth, hold Option/Alt when you click. Line Freeform Gradients provide more control over contours, Point Freeform Gradients let you adjust the circle of influence, and objects can contain a mixture of the two.

Secret Freeform Defaults

Unless you change default settings, a freeform gradient will automatically begin filled with similar colors taken from surrounding areas. To control the start of your freeform gradient, make sure "Enable Context Aware Defaults" is disabled in Preferences> General; freeform gradients will instead start with your current fill color (or no fill). Be aware that both Image Crop and Puppet Warp also use Content Aware Defaults, and may not behave as expected if you change this setting.

Lines have different rules

When creating Freeform Gradient objects, there are a few differences between lines and points to keep in mind:

- To Shift-select multiple line points, switch to the Point tool
- Lines can't cross over each other
- Line anchors don't have resizable circles of influence
- Convert a Point anchor to a Line by clicking on the anchor with Line selected in the Gradient panel, then continuing to draw

Recoloring Freeform Gradients

As of this writing, in order to recolor freeform gradients, you can edit the individual color stops or a "global" color definition, but you can't use methods such as Recolor Artwork or Adjust Color Balance.

Custom Coloring

Creating Custom Colors & Color Groups

Overview: *Create an illustration; create custom swatches; create a custom color group from custom swatches; save a swatch library.*

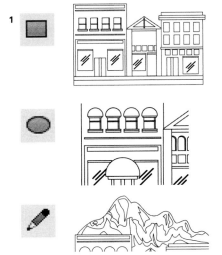

Creating an icon with the Rectangle tool, Ellipse tool, and Pencil tool

Filling icon paths with default swatches from the Swatches panel

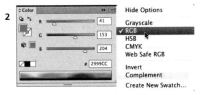

Selecting the correct color mode from the Color panel's pop-up menu

Ryan Putnam designs many illustrations he uses as icons in stock art and client projects. Creating custom swatches is an integral step in creating compelling and consistent icon illustrations. Illustrator comes with some great default color swatches, but they are not suited for most of Putnam's icon illustrations. Moreover, by creating a custom color group, Putnam can easily apply his custom swatches to other related illustrations.

1 Creating an icon illustration. To create the "Destination" icon, Putnam used the Rectangle tool, Ellipse tool, and Pencil tool. Putnam first created the buildings of the icon with varying sizes of rectangles with the Rectangle tool. He then used the Ellipse tool to create windows and awnings for the buildings. Next, he used the Pencil tool to draw the mountains. To distinguish the objects from each other, Putnam filled the building and mountain paths with default swatches from the Swatches panel by selecting each object and clicking the desired swatch.

2 Creating custom swatches. After Putnam roughed out the basic color schemes for his illustration, he then began to customize a more natural set of colors. First, he made sure the Color panel was set to the same color mode as his Document Color Mode. Since Putnam was creating his icon for his website with an RGB Document Color Mode, he chose RGB from the Color panel pop-up menu. Selecting an object, Putnam then mixed the desired color with the sliders in the Color panel. Next, he opened the Swatches panel and clicked the New Swatch icon in the bottom of the panel. In the Swatch Options dialog he then named the swatch and clicked OK. Alternatively, you can choose Create New Swatch from the Color panel pop-up menu. Yet another option is to drag the mixed color directly to the Swatches panel, though by doing so, you won't get Swatch Options and the opportunity to name the swatch. Putnam then repeated these steps for every custom color he wanted to create.

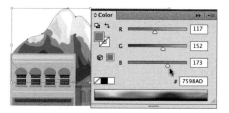

Mixing colors with the color sliders from the Color panel

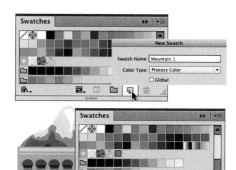

Saving custom swatches in the Swatches panel by clicking the New Swatch icon

3 **Creating a new color group.** After creating his custom swatches, Putnam wanted to organize his custom swatches so he could easily apply them to other related illustrations and icons. To do this, he created a custom color group. He selected the desired swatches in the Swatches panel by Shift-clicking to select contiguous swatches or by holding ⌘/Ctrl and clicking for non-contiguous selections. Then he clicked the New Color Group icon, where he was given the option to name his color group. The new color group was then saved for Putnam and ready for use.

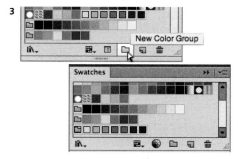

Saving custom swatches as a new color group in the Swatches panel

To use his custom color group in other documents, Putnam needed to save the color group as a custom swatch library. First, he selected all the swatches he wanted to delete from his custom color group and clicked the Delete Swatch icon in the Swatches panel. Putnam then clicked the Swatch Libraries menu icon at the lower left of the Swatches panel, chose Save Swatches, named it, and clicked OK. This saved Putnam's swatch library so it's accessible to Illustrator via the Swatch Libraries menu icon; by scrolling to the bottom of the menu, he can easily access his custom swatches library under the User Defined submenu.

From the Swatch Libraries menu icon in the Swatches panel: choosing Save Swatches to save a custom color group; and accessing it later via a User Defined library

Unified Gradients

Creating & Editing with Pen & Pencil Modifiers

Overview: *Fill objects with gradients; use the Gradient tool with the Gradient Annotator to adjust fill length and angle; unify fills across multiple objects with the Gradient tool and Gradient panel.*

1
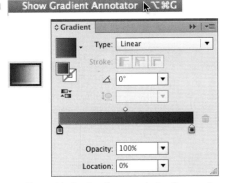

Working with the Gradient panel, Gradient tool, and Gradient Annotator

2

A single click with the Gradient tool on a selected object fills the object with either the default or last-used gradient swatch and displays the Gradient Annotator, if selected in the View menu (be sure you don't click and drag when applying for the first time—you can click-drag to adjust the gradient later)

Using the Gradient Annotator to shorten the length of the gradient and to rotate the angle when the Rotate icon appeared

Using the Gradient Annotator in conjunction with the Gradient tool, in many instances you'll be able to customize gradients without having to use the Gradient panel at all. In this illustration, Dave Joly only needed the Gradient panel to switch between Linear and Radial gradients and to work with creating unified gradients. To control the colors, length, and angle of gradients for individual objects, Joly adjusted each gradient with the Gradient Annotator. He unified gradients across multiple objects using the Gradient tool and Gradient panel.

1 Applying gradients. To apply a gradient to a single object, such as the fish's body, Joly first made sure that the toggle for the Gradient Annotator was visible (if View> Show Gradient Annotator is available, choose it). Next he selected an object and the Gradient tool and then clicked once on the object to fill it with either the document's default gradient (for the first object) or the last gradient used in the document.

2 Editing single objects with the Gradient Annotator. Joly was able to edit a gradient almost exclusively using the Gradient Annotator. With the Annotator, he could modify the gradient length, angle, and colors on the object itself. He only needed to turn to the Gradient panel to choose a different existing gradient swatch, switch the current gradient between linear and radial gradient in Type, or reverse the gradient. Joly began his edits by moving his cursor just beyond the arrow endpoint of the Gradient Annotator. When his cursor turned into the Rotate icon, he dragged to interactively set the angle he wanted the gradient to take. With his cursor directly on top of the arrow end, he click-dragged to lengthen or shorten the gradient, and he dragged the large circle at the other end to move the whole gradient to another position over the object. To adjust the colors, Joly double-clicked a color stop along the Annotator, which gave him immediate access to proxies for both the Swatches and the Color panels, and a subset of the Gradient panel, as well. After choosing a suitable color, he dragged the stops on the Annotator to position the color blends more precisely, and on the gradient sliders to adjust their blend.

3 **Unifying gradients across multiple objects.** Unifying gradients across multiple objects is a bit trickier with the Gradient Annotator involved. Joly first created the gradient swatch he would need—for the tail fins, for example. Next he selected all the objects and clicked the swatch in the Swatches panel to apply it. This automatically created a new Gradient Annotator for every object, but Joly wanted to unify the gradients under just *one* Annotator. Still using the Gradient tool with the Gradient Annotator visible, Joly dragged across all the objects. This now appeared to unify the multiple gradients under one Annotator, but it's then only possible to change the length or position of the unifying gradient. Instead, while adjusting one gradient that had been unified across multiple objects, Joly discovered the Gradient Annotator wasn't providing reliable feedback or controls. Therefore, when working with one unified gradient applied to multiple objects, instead of relying on the Gradient Annotator, he would ignore or hide the Annotator (Window> Hide Gradient Annotator). Joly simply used a combination of the Gradient tool (to make length and angle adjustments to the unified gradient) and the Gradient panel itself (for numeric precision, adjustments to color stops, and opacity).

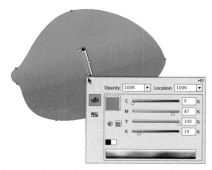

Changing the gradient colors by double-clicking the Gradient Annotator color stops to pop up both the Color and Swatches panel proxies

3

After first selecting all objects and applying a gradient tool to them, but before unifying them

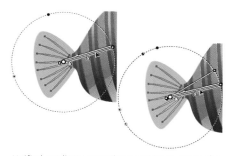

Unified gradients sometimes appear to retain the function of the Gradient Annotator, but if you attempt to edit angles or colors with the Gradient Annotator, you'll discover you aren't actually editing a single gradient

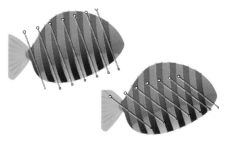

By using only the Gradient panel and/or the Gradient tool to edit unified gradients, you ensure that all changes will be made in unison

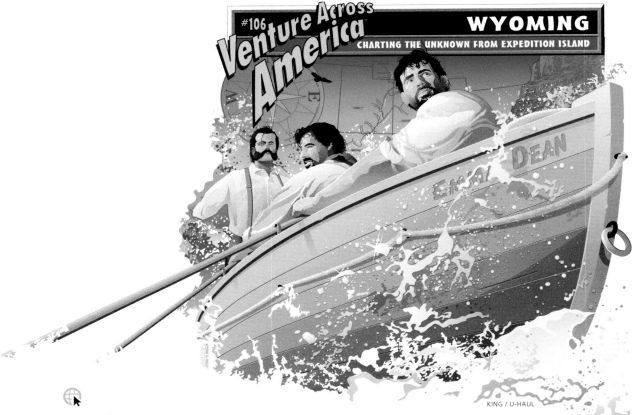

KING / U-HAUL

Steve King/U-Haul

U-Haul celebrates history and natural science with eye-catching images displayed on its trucks and vans. Steve King drew simplified shapes he filled with gradients to capture this action scene from John Wesley Powell's 1869 expedition. To create the face of each explorer, King began by drawing an object that contoured most of the neck and face, and then filled the object with a gradient. With the object still selected, King clicked the Gradient tool to display the Annotator and then click-dragged it to adjust the gradient's length and direction. He also fine-tuned the color composition by double-clicking a gradient slider (or endpoint) on the Annota-

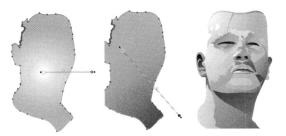

tor to edit that color in the pop-up dialog. King continued by drawing overlapping objects for the face, filling each with a gradient. He saved time by reusing some of the gradients. For each object, King fine-tuned the gradients with the Annotator to match the light and shadows falling across the scene.

#123 Venture Across America

SOUTH CAROLINA
SUBMARINE MYSTERIES AT CHARLESTON

KING

DID YOU KNOW...
Using revolutionary technology ahead of its time, the H.L. Hunley
inspired international submarine designs for decades. What
caused her to mysteriously sink in 1864?
LEARN MORE ABOUT THE "HUNLEY" PROJECT AT...
uhaul.com

Steve King/U-Haul

U-Haul celebrates history and natural science
with eye-catching images they call "Super-
Graphics" displayed on their moving vans.
Illustrator Steve King mixes intricate details
with simplified shapes in this image of the
H.L. Hunley, a Civil War submarine. King relied
on the Gradient tool to create lighting effects
and simulate the transparency of a see-through
illustration. He employed a darkening orange-
to-blue gradient fill on the submarine from the
captain's lantern backward to the propeller.
The Gradient tool gave King the economy of
creating a few gradients that he reused as fills

for different objects. To illustrate the faces of
four of the seated sailors, King drew shapes
that he filled with the same gradient. He used
the Gradient tool's Annotator to customize
the length and angle of each sailor's gradient,
which helped tie them together visually while
keeping their shapes distinct.

Gradient Paths

The Basics of Gradients on a Path

Overview: *Create paths using strokes; apply linear gradients to each path; adjust gradient sliders and Stroke options.*

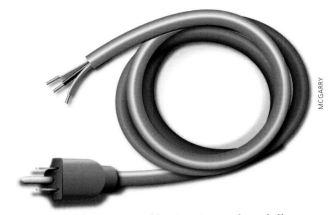

MCGARRY

1

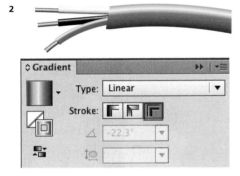

The separate parts of the power cord drawn using the Pen tool, increasing the stroke weight for each section: 7 pt for the wire, 12 pt for the insulation, and 40 pt for the jacket

2

Applying a gradient to the copper wire from the Metals library using the third Stroke option to apply it across the stroke width

The plug prong using a gradient from the Metals library using the middle Stroke option to apply it along the stroke length

This power cord was created by San Diego–based illustrator Aaron McGarry, using gradients applied to strokes.

1 Creating the cord using strokes. McGarry drew each section of the power cord separately using the Pen tool and then he increased the stroke weight for each section: the exposed copper wires, the insulation, and the cord jacket. He also used the Ellipse tool to create the coiled section of the cord and duplicated the ellipse a few times.

2 Applying gradients to strokes. McGarry applied gradients to his paths using the Gradient panel chosen from Swatch Libraries> Gradients. The copper wire, for example, used a copper gradient from the Gradients> Metals library. In the Stroke area of the Gradient panel, he chose "Apply gradient across stroke" (the third option) and then adjusted it using the slider. He also used this option for the insulation and cord jacket. Since the live and neutral plug prongs were flat straight edges, he chose "Apply gradient along stroke" (the middle Stroke option) and moved the lightest slider stop to the left to indicate where the prong turns at the tip. He duplicated these prongs and used Paste in Place to put a copy on top. He then applied a Gradient> Fades swatch to darken the end of these prongs but still expose the brass beneath, creating a more natural transition than darkening alone. For the plug body end he drew the contour with the Pen tool and applied an orange gradient to the stroke and the fill. Finally, he adjusted the stroke gradient to indicate a soft edge transition.

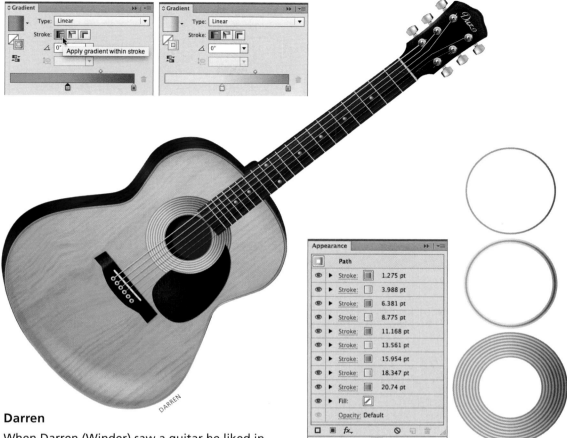

Darren

When Darren (Winder) saw a guitar he liked in a store window, he decided to reconstruct it in Illustrator with photorealistic detail. He began by constructing the basic shape and using Image Trace to add wood texture to the guitar, then created some wood-toned gradients. To mimic directional light and add an edge to the guitar progressing from dark to light, he created two paths outlining the body then applied a gradient to each stroke path. To do this, Darren selected a path and targeted its Stroke attribute in the Appearance panel, clicked the Stroke color icon, and chose his gradient. With the path still selected, he opened the Gradient panel and chose the first Stroke option (Apply gradient within stroke). This stretched the gradient the length of the path. For the guitar's sound hole, he again used gradients applied within the stroke, this time using multiple strokes on a path. Using the Appearance panel, he clicked the New Stroke icon, which created a stroke below the first in the same style as the one selected (if no attribute is selected, strokes will be added above the others). Clicking the Stroke swatch, he chose the lighter wood gradient and enlarged the stroke weight. He then continued to add alternating dark and light strokes, adjusting weights to create concentric dark and light circles from one path.

Bending Mesh

Converting Gradients to Mesh for Editing

Overview: *Draw objects and fill with linear gradients; expand gradient-filled objects into gradient meshes; use various tools to edit mesh points and colors.*

Need help with gradients?
Start with the "Unified Gradients" lesson earlier in this chapter.

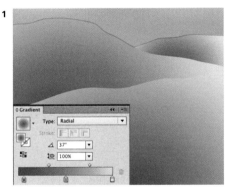

The hills shown filled with radial gradients—although there is some sense of light, it isn't possible to make the radial gradient follow the contours of the hills

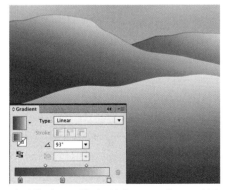

The hills shown filled with linear gradients, which when converted to gradient meshes are easier to edit than radial gradients

Lisa Jackmore created light and shadow with gradients, but she couldn't bend the transitions to fit the contours of her rolling hills. Expanding linear gradients into gradient mesh objects gave her complete control over how the colors curve and bend. Mastering mesh in simpler forms should help you to tackle the intricate mesh lessons that follow. In the **CC** section later in this chapter, see how bending colors in simple forms might be more easily accomplished with the Freeform Gradient tool.

1 Drawing objects and then filling them with linear gradients. Begin your illustration by creating closed objects with any of the drawing tools. After drawing each object, fill it with a linear gradient (although in some objects radial gradients might look better before you convert them to mesh objects, linear gradients create mesh objects that are much easier to edit). For each linear gradient, customize the colors and adjust the angle and length of the gradient transition with the Gradient tool and Gradient Annotator until you approximate the desired lighting effect. Jackmore drew three hill-shaped objects with the Pen tool, filled them with the same linear gradient, and then customized each with the Gradient tool and Annotator.

2 Expanding linear gradients into gradient meshes. To create a more natural lighting of the hills, Jackmore converted the linear gradients into mesh objects so the color transitions could follow the contours of the hills. To accomplish this, select all the gradient-filled objects that you wish to convert and choose Object> Expand. In the Expand dialog, make sure Fill is enabled and specify Expand Gradient to Gradient Mesh. Then click OK. Illustrator converts each linear gradient into a rectangle rotated to the angle matching the linear gradient's angle; each mesh rectangle is masked by the original object (see the *Mastering Complexity* chapter for help with masks).

3 Editing meshes. You can use several tools to edit gradient mesh objects (use isolation mode, or lock/hide objects on specific layers as you work). The Mesh tool combines the functionality of the Direct Selection tool with the ability to add mesh lines. With the Mesh tool, click *exactly on* a mesh anchor point to select or move that point or its direction handles. Or, click *anywhere* within a mesh, except on an anchor point, to add a new mesh point and gridline. You can also use the Add Anchor Point tool (click and hold to choose it from the Pen tool pop-up) to add a point without a gridline. To delete a selected anchor point, press the Delete key; if that point is a mesh point, the gridlines will be deleted as well.

Select points within the mesh using either the Mesh tool or the Lasso tool, using the Direct Selection tool to move multiple selected points. Move individual anchor points and adjust direction handles with the Mesh tool in order to reshape your gradient mesh gridlines. In this way, the gradient color and tonal transitions will match the contour of the mesh object. Recolor selected areas of the mesh by selecting points and then choosing a new color.

If you hold Option/Alt while you click in the area *between* mesh points with the Eyedropper tool, you'll add the Fill color to the four nearest mesh points.

By using these tools and editing techniques, Jackmore was able to create hills with color and light variations that suggest the subtlety of natural light upon the contours of organic forms.

2

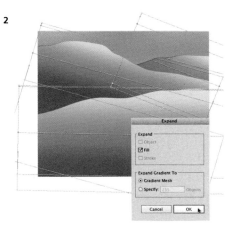

After expanding the gradients into gradient mesh objects

3

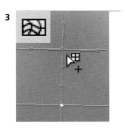

Using the Mesh tool to add a mesh line, then moving the mesh point with the Direct Selection tool

Using the Add Anchor Point tool, using the Lasso to select a point, moving selected point (or points) with the Direct Selection tool

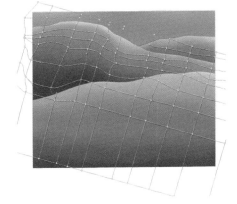

The middle hill, shown after making gradient mesh adjustments

Transparent Mesh

Molding Transparent Mesh Layers

Advanced Technique

Overview: *Draw guides and create gradient mesh objects; contour rectangles; color gradient mesh points with color sampled from reference photo; apply transparency to individual mesh points to create realism.*

1

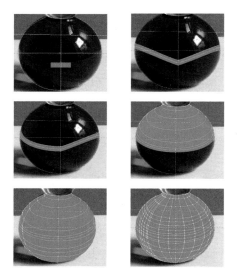

Making guides on top of the photograph in the template layer

Developing the gradient mesh object from a rectangle, adjusting points with the Direct Selection tool, adding rows and columns with the Gradient Mesh tool (left to right, top to bottom)

PAIDRICK

Ann Paidrick transformed simple rectangular objects into complex, contoured gradient mesh objects to create an exact representation of an original photograph. By incorporating actual transparency into her mesh objects, she is able to reuse the finished vase in other settings (see the gallery following this lesson).

1 Creating guides, drawing basic shapes, and then creating gradient mesh objects. Placing her JPG as a template into layers above, Paidrick drew a loose grid of paths and then turned them into guides (⌘-5/Ctrl-5) to help position her gradient mesh objects. Paidrick finds that adding a mesh to a rectangle, which she then reshapes, gives her more control over mesh points than if she added mesh to a path drawn with the Pen tool. Therefore, she always begins her gradient mesh objects by drawing one small rectangle with the Rectangle tool. To create the red globe portion of the vase, she drew a rectangle, filled it with a bright color, chose Object> Create Gradient Mesh, and specified 1 row, 1 column. With the Direct Selection tool (A), she moved points to stretch the rectangle to the edges of the vase base, and eventually the top and bottom. With the Gradient mesh tool (U), she added more rows and columns. She continued to enlarge the mesh object and contour it into the desired shape by pressing U to add mesh points and then A to adjust the points. Paidrick added individual mesh points with the Add Anchor Point tool to further define the shape of the object. She Direct-Selected points and made adjustments to refine the contour of the object and its mesh to closely follow the shading of her reference photo.

2 **Coloring the mesh objects.** To color individual mesh points, Paidrick clicked a mesh point with the Direct Selection tool (A) and then switched to the Eyedropper tool (I) and filled that point with a color sampled from the photograph. She continued to color the mesh points by pressing ⌘/Ctrl to temporarily switch to the Direct Selection tool from the Eyedropper tool, picking up color from the photo until a pixel in the photograph matched the color she wanted.

3 **Applying transparency to individual mesh points.** For effects such as reflections, she created additional mesh objects on layers above. She then selected individual points in the upper mesh objects and reduced the opacity, creating nearly invisible transitions between different mesh objects on layers above and below. She also reduced the opacity of individual mesh points to create smooth color transitions between more- and less-saturated colors (see bottom figure). To do this she first Direct-Selected a point and then reduced the Opacity in the Control, Transparency, or Appearance panels. She continued to choose mesh points and use various transparency settings throughout the illustration until she had matched the color of the reference photo as closely as possible.

2

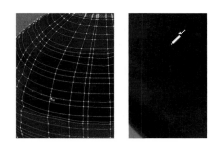

Coloring mesh points and sampling color from the reference photograph

3

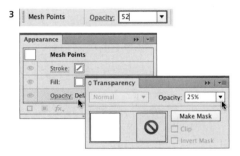

Decreasing the Opacity in Control, Appearance, and Transparency panels

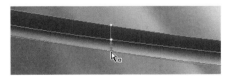

Mesh point before (top) and after (bottom) the opacity is decreased

Paidrick applied transparency to mesh points along the edges of the individual rings of color to make smooth transitions between each change of color

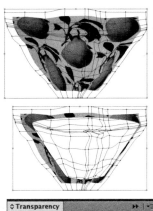

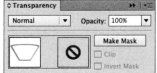

PAIDRICK

Ann Paidrick

Ann Paidrick enhanced her vase illustration from the previous lesson by adding the patterned pear wallpaper to the background. Paidrick locked all the layers of the finished vase and, on a new layer beneath these locked layers, placed a photograph of the wallpaper (saved as JPG) as the background. With the Pen tool, she drew rough outlines where the distorted pears would be and then turned these outlines into guides (⌘-5/Ctrl-5). On a separate layer above the background wallpaper, she placed another photo of the wallpaper, this time one that she had cropped in Photoshop to fit between the top and bottom of the clear glass. To use an Illustrator envelope to distort the cropped part of the photo, she had to first embed the photo by selecting the Embed icon in the Control panel. Paidrick then chose Object> Envelope Distort> Make with Mesh (6 rows, 8 columns). She used the Direct Selection tool to adjust the envelope mesh object into the shape of the interior of the glass. To add more rows and columns, Paidrick clicked with the Gradient Mesh tool and added additional mesh points with the Add Anchor Point tool. She continued to adjust the mesh points, referring to her guides until she was satisfied with the distortion results. To make the envelope mesh object fit into the vase shape, on a new layer above, she drew a closed path with the Pen tool, selected the envelope mesh object, and then chose Object> Clipping Mask> Make.

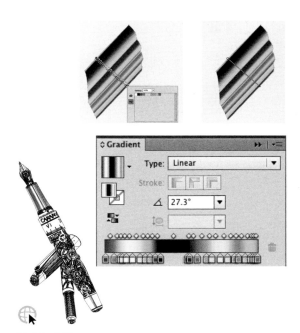

Caran d'Ache 1010 I LIMITED EDITION

MIYAMOTO

Yukio Miyamoto

Yukio Miyamoto created the numerous complex linear and radial gradients throughout this illustration with ease using the Gradient tool and the Gradient Annotator. Miyamoto drew each path with the Pen tool and filled it with either the default linear or radial gradient from the Swatches panel. He selected the Gradient tool to reveal the Gradient Annotator, which appeared on top of the object. Miyamoto double-clicked on the color stop of the Gradient Annotator to show the options. He clicked the Swatches icon and chose a custom color from the Swatches panel that he had previously created to color the stop. Miyamoto clicked along the Gradient Annotator to add more color stops. He continued to add color stops and color them until he was satisfied with the results. Miyamoto click-dragged the color stops and moved them into the exact locations to achieve the desired gradient effect. He grabbed the arrow endpoint and stretched the Gradient Annotator to change the length of the gradient. Miyamoto moved the endpoint side to side and adjusted the angle of the gradient. He made additional angular adjustments with the circular endpoint, clicked the center point, and then moved it to various positions within the gradient-filled object. The entire illustration is made of gradient-filled objects with two very small exceptions; there is one blended object (the pen tip) and one mesh object (grip area, just beneath the tip). The Gradient Annotator enabled Miyamoto to have exceptional control of the gradient fills to achieve exacting realism.

Recolor a Pattern

Creating Variations on a Color Palette

Advanced Technique

Overview: *Edit a pattern swatch using Recolor Artwork; use the Assign tab to create variations on a single color group; save new pattern swatches and color groups.*

REINHART

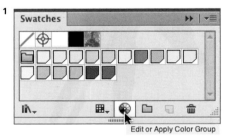

Using a selected color group to activate the icon for entering Recolor Artwork (alternately, click the Recolor Artwork icon in the Control panel to open the dialog without affecting the original color assignment)

Reinhart's new colorway after creating a new color group with the same number of colors as the original and then applying and refining the color assignments in Recolor Artwork

Using Illustrator's Recolor Artwork (RA) you can start with any pattern, even a highly complex one created using a pre-determined color palette, and quickly experiment with different colorways by reordering the assignment of the same colors or by generating, applying, and saving a new palette of colors. Sabine Reinhart creates color groups with the number of colors she needs and then lets Recolor Artwork help her develop a new colorway.

1 Entering Recolor Artwork while in Pattern Editing Mode (PEM). Find a pattern swatch to experiment with and duplicate it (drag the swatch to the New Swatch icon in the Swatches panel). If you didn't save your original colors as a color group and want easy access to the group, fill an object with the pattern, and while it's still selected, click the New Color Group icon and enable Selected Artwork. Now, double-click the pattern swatch to enter PEM, disable Dim Copies for easier evaluation, and choose Select All (⌘-A/Ctrl-A). To enter RA with your original colors intact, click the Recolor Artwork icon in the Control panel. If instead you wish to enter RA with a color group already applied to your pattern, enter via the Swatches panel—click the icon for a color group and then on the "Edit or Apply Color Group" icon at the bottom of the panel. (If the new color group doesn't contain as many colors as the original, RA reduces the number of colors, turning multiple color assignments into a single color.)

2 Creating a variation on the palette. Once in RA, to vary the color assignment for your pattern—but not allow RA to alter the actual hues, tints, or shades—click the Color Reduction icon and choose Exact for the Recolor Method. Get inspiration for different colorways by clicking the "Randomly change color order" icon at the bottom of the New column. Although your colors stay the same, they are applied to different objects in the pattern. There's no Undo in RA to recover a colorway, so when you see potential, consider saving your color group in RA, or click OK, and then save a new pattern with Save a Copy in PEM (see below). To further modify the assignment of colors, drag one new color over another to swap them. You also can drag a color from the Current Colors column into the New column to restore an original assignment. Click the "Randomly changes saturation and brightness" icon (beneath the New column) to create even greater variation between your original colorway and a new scheme that is still based on your original color group.

3 Saving color groups and pattern swatches. Applying a saved color group will only give predictable results when applied to the original pattern (not the one you just created), so as you save a group in RA, be careful to include the name of the original pattern swatch in the color group's name. To save a pattern variation, click OK in RA, and then click Save a Copy on the Pattern Isolation Mode bar. Name your pattern in the pop-up, and from this point forward, that swatch will retain both the palette and the color assignment. Remember you can still create a color group from a pattern swatch after exiting RA by following the instructions given in the first part of this lesson.

2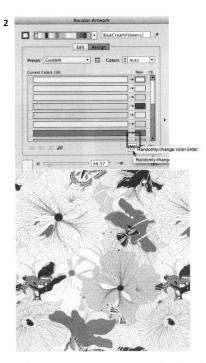

Using the Random button to reorder the color assignments for the pattern elements

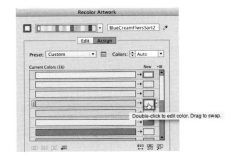

Dragging colors in the New column to swap their assignment

3

Naming color groups to keep them associated with their pattern swatch

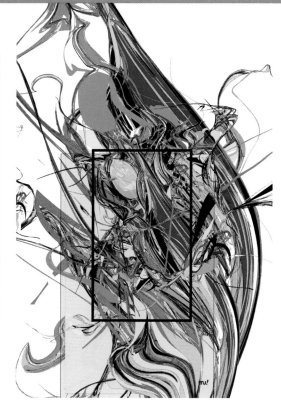

MURRA

Sebastian Murra (Mu!)

Sebastian Murra's highly abstract, organic, often edgy style seems tailor-made for smartphone cases. He used specs from the manufacturer CASE-MATE to begin with a correctly sized artboard for each device, although he only loosely observed the artboard size and orientation until the end. Without trying to restrain the art within the templates, he allowed it to flow freely beyond the boundaries. Murra began this design, "Saturday Morning Cartoons," by creating a palette inspired by the colors of fruity breakfast cereals for kids. He created several overlapping rectangles, each with a solid Fill and a very fine Stroke, and used Illustrator's Liquify tools, primarily Warp and Twirl, to push and pull the colored shapes into the swirling abstracts that are his signature style. He added

contrast and depth by transforming a few black rectangles along with the fruit-colored ones. He used blending modes, especially Hard Light and Hue, to further integrate the swirling tangle of objects. He often modified objects with the Direct Selection tool, and used Recolor Artwork to alter or introduce colors. Later he rotated everything to its final vertical orientation, and then placed overlapping white rectangles on a layer above the artwork, which allowed him to experiment with different framing options until he found the right portion of the design that fit within the required size. For the final composition, he added a yellow-filled background layer and applied a yellow tint to all the lighter colors by adding another yellow-filled rectangle, set to Darken blending mode, on the top layer.

Ann Paidrick

After hours of intricately creating gradient mesh-based artwork, Ann Paidrick can quickly and easily change colors using Recolor Artwork. Because you can't recover colors once you've changed them with Recolor Artwork, each time she wants to create a variant of her gold ribbon, she starts by duplicating the original artboard (in the Art-boards panel she drags the gold ribbon artboard to the New Artboard icon). Selecting the new ribbon objects, she clicks the Recolor Artwork/Edit Colors icon in the Control panel (or Recolor in the Properties panel). Click-ing the Edit mode tab, she enables the Lock icon and then drags the Base Color circle in the color wheel (the largest circle) until she finds a color shift she likes and clicks OK. Saving this file, she creates the next color varia-tion from another copy of the original.

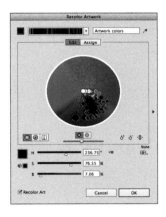

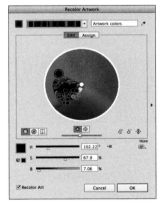

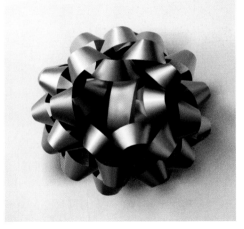

PAIDRICK

Freeform Gradients

Contouring Gradients to Organic Objects

Overview: *Turn off Context-Aware preferences; apply Freeform Gradient lines to a filled-object; adjust colors; finalize lines to form organic shapes.*

1

Enable Context Aware Defaults option in Preferences> General (top); the Freeform Gradient Icon and Lines option in the Control panel (bottom)

2

Using the Gradient Tool to plot points to create a Freeform Gradient line

3

Double-clicking a point to choose a new color

4

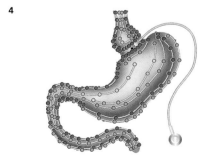

Pressing Esc to end a line and then adding additional to form the contours of an organic form

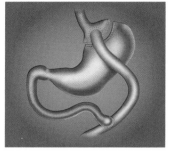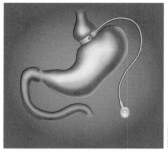

FERSTER

In this gastric bypass illustration for *Diabetes Forecast* magazine, Gary Ferster was able to easily form the organic shapes of the stomach's anatomy with Freeform Gradients.

1 Disabling the Context Aware preference. By default, Illustrator guesses starting colors and points for your freeform gradients. For complete control of his gradient colors, Ferster disabled "Enable Context Aware Defaults" in Preferences> General so freeform-gradient objects start with no gradient points and use his current fill color.

2 Applying a Freeform Gradient to a closed filled object. Ferster filled his object with one of his pre-made global colors. Fill a closed object with a "base" color, and keep it selected. In the Gradient panel, click the Freeform Gradient gradient icon and the "Draw:" Lines option. You'll automatically switch to the Gradient tool. Click in your object to begin a gradient line; then continue to click to plot additional points. Press Esc to stop drawing a line.

3 Customizing Freeform Gradient colors and adding new lines. Ferster continued to add new lines to form the contours and precisely control the color transitions within each of the differently-shaped areas. To adjust the color of a Freeform Gradient, double-click a point, and then choose a new color from the pop-up Swatches panel. Add and customize additional lines and/or points to refine your color transitions. To enhance the illusion of depth, Ferster chose darker colors for points on the lines closer to the edges of the tubular shapes and applied lighter colors to the points on the more interior lines.

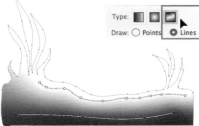

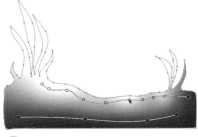

SULLIVAN

Shawn Sullivan

To create his underwater scene, Shawn Sullivan wanted to figure out when the Freeform Gradient would be the best tool for the job. Though he still used shape blends, linear gradients, and gradient mesh, this project illuminated a few places where Freeform Gradients turned out to be the perfect tool. Some of the objects on which he found the Freeform Gradient worked particularly well on the seaweed floor highlights and shadows. He first disabled Enable Context Aware Defaults in Preferences> General (see this chapter's **CC** intro for details) and then started the seaweed floor with a solid filled object (top left). With the object selected,

he double-clicked the Gradient tool to open the Gradient panel, and then clicked the Freeform Gradient icon. With the Freeform Gradient tool he first plotted a line near the bottom of the object to contain the green base color; then he clicked a white line above, near the top (middle left). The next step was to apply custom colors by double-clicking each point he wanted to adjust and selecting another of his colors from the pop-up Swatches panel (bottom left). Sullivan also used Freeform Gradient lines to form the contours of the goldfish body, creating a line of points along the left edge of the fish, and then another line on the right side.

COYLE

Laura Coyle

It takes a herculean effort to organize a group of fifth-grade students, but using keen organizational skills and the search features found in Illustrator's Swatches panel, it became an easy task. Laura Coyle opened the Swatches panel, selected Show Find Field from the Swatches panel pop-up menu, and then clicked the Show List View icon. She created global swatches for each color and named them with meaningful names, matching up a character's name with the descriptors such as line work, hair, or skin tone creating swatch names like Harriet Line work, Jason Skin tone, or Marc Hair (partial view of Swatches panel shown above). Coyle selected the color swatches by holding ⌘/Ctrl and then clicked the New Color Group icon. She kept the default name, Color Group 1, and clicked OK. Coyle repeated the process, making a separate color group for the color swatches created for the clothing.

Coyle first drew a few of the main characters. To select and apply color to a character, Coyle typed one or more of the letters of the name in the find field, and when the name appeared in the Swatches panel (below left), she chose from the list of custom colors particular to that character (such as searching teal or denim for the clothing). These central characters would appear in several different scenes throughout the project, and by using descriptive labeling, Coyle easily found the color for each figure, and kept their coloring consistent throughout the various scenes. Later, when Coyle needed to create other figures different from the central characters, she mixed and matched the custom hair and skin tone color swatches. Coyle varied their looks by searching and applying specific color swatches in the color panel, but the overall look of the project was consistent because she used the same set of colors for the entire project.

6

Reshaping Dimensions

Reshaping Dimensions

Smart people use Smart Guides

When you work with warps or envelopes, it may become difficult to edit artwork that has an appearance applied to it. With Smart Guides turned on, Illustrator highlights the art, making it easier to identify the actual artwork (and not the appearance). Use ⌘-U/Ctrl-U to toggle Smart Guides on and off. —*Mordy Golding*

The three Envelope buttons in the Control panel, from left to right: Edit Envelope, Edit Contents, and Envelope Options

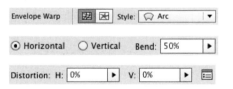

The tools that appear in the Control panel when an envelope warp is selected; you can change the shape of the warp using the pop-up menu

The controls that appear in the Control panel when an envelope mesh is selected; you can easily change the number of rows and columns, as well as restore the object to its original shape using the Reset Envelope Shape button

Isolation mode for envelopes

An easy way to edit an envelope: Double-click it to enter isolation mode. —*Jean-Claude Tremblay*

This chapter focuses on the Illustrator tools and functions that allow you to create objects that appear to move beyond two-dimensional space. With warps and envelopes you can easily use familiar vector tools to bend and bow objects (and text) in two-dimensional space, and with envelope meshes you can begin to create an illusion of depth as well. Using Illustrator's 3D effects you actually revolve, extrude, rotate, and map objects in three dimensions. Then, the Perspective Grid tool helps you to create art based on linear perspective using one, two, or three vanishing points. All of these demand a bit of a different mindset than flat Illustrator objects and the manipulating of the mesh. In their live states, 3D and the perspective grid work quite differently from other Illustrator objects. If you decide to expand the art, they become merely complex vector objects, letting you work upon them using any of Illustrator's editing tools.

WARPS AND ENVELOPES

Warps and envelopes may look similar at first, but there's an important difference between them. Warps are applied as live *effects*—meaning they can be applied to objects, groups, or layers. Warps have two advantages: They are easy to create by choosing from the predefined options in the Warp dialogs, and you can save them within a graphic style to apply them to other objects. Envelopes, on the other hand, are also live, but rather than effects, they're actual *objects* that contain artwork. You can edit or customize the envelope shape, and Illustrator will conform the contents of the envelope to the contour.

Warps

Applying a warp is actually quite simple. Target an object, group, or layer and choose Effect> Warp> Arc. (It doesn't matter which warp effect you choose, because you'll be presented with the Warp Options dialog, where you can choose from any of the 15 different warps.) While the warp effects are "canned" in the sense that you can't make adjustments to the effects directly, you can control how a warp appears by changing the Bend value, as well as the Horizontal and Vertical Distortion values.

Once you've applied a warp, you can edit it by opening the Appearance panel and clicking on the warp effect. Like all effects, a warp can be applied to just the fill or just the stroke—and if you edit the artwork, the warp updates as well. Since warps are effects, you can include them in a graphic style, which can then be applied to other artwork.

Envelopes

While warp effects do a nice job of distorting artwork (and allow you to save the effect as a graphic style), Illustrator envelopes provide a higher level of control.

There are three ways to apply envelopes. The simplest way is to create a path you want to use as your envelope. Make sure it's at the top of the stacking order—above the art you want to place inside the envelope. Then, with the artwork and your created path both selected, choose Object> Envelope Distort> Make with Top Object. Illustrator will create a special kind of object: an envelope. This object you created becomes an envelope container, which appears in the Layers panel as <Envelope>. You can edit the path of the envelope with any transformation or editing tools; the artwork inside will update to conform to the shape. To edit the contents of the envelope, click the Edit Contents button in the Control panel or choose Object> Envelope Distort> Edit Contents. If you then look at the Layers panel, you'll notice that the <Envelope> now has a disclosure triangle that reveals the contents of the envelope—the artwork you placed. You can edit the artwork directly or even drag other paths into the <Envelope> in the Layers panel. To again edit the envelope itself, choose Object> Envelope Distort> Edit Envelope.

There are two other types of envelopes, and they're closely related. Both types use meshes to provide even more distortion control. When using the first type, the

Deleting a mesh point

To delete a mesh point from a warp or mesh envelope, choose the Mesh tool and Option-click/ Alt-click the point you'd like to delete. —*Jean-Claude Tremblay*

Michael Cressy turned the building on the left into the one on the right using the drawing tools, then modified with envelopes for each of the windows, the building, and the stacks using Object> Envelope Distort> Make with Mesh

Envelope distort options

To use envelopes to distort artwork containing pattern fills or linear gradients, choose Object> Envelope Distort> Envelope Options and enable the appropriate options. —*Mordy Golding*

3D—three dialogs

There are three different 3D effects, and some features overlap. If all you need to do is change the perspective of an object, use Rotate. If you want to map a symbol to the object, use either Revolve or Extrude & Bevel (you can still rotate an object from these as well). —*Brenda Sutherland*

2D or not 2D...?

Illustrator's 3D objects are only *truly* three-dimensional while you're working with them in a 3D effect dialog. As soon as you're done tweaking your object and you click OK to close the dialog, the object's three-dimensional qualities are "frozen"—almost as if Illustrator had taken a snapshot of the object—until the next time you edit it in a 3D dialog. On the page, it's technically a 2D rendering of a 3D object that can only be worked with in two-dimensional ways. But because the effect is live, you can work with the object in 3D again any time you want. Just select the object and then double-click the 3D effect listed in the Appearance panel.

Extruding an object using the Effect> 3D> Extrude & Bevel dialog—the two-dimensional object on the left was extruded to create the three-dimensional version on the right

See the lesson explaining how Aaron McGarry created this photorealistic key and fob using Illustrator's 3D tools later in this chapter

envelope warp, you choose the overall envelope form from a pop-up list of options. When you use the *envelope mesh*, instead of starting from presets, you begin by choosing how many rows and columns your mesh will contain.

To create an envelope warp, select an object and choose Make with Warp (Object> Envelope Distort). This will open the Warp dialog. Once you choose a warp and click OK, Illustrator converts that warp to an envelope mesh. The Control panel will display the Envelope Warp controls, including a pop-up menu that lets you choose a different shape for the warp if you want to. You can edit the envelope warp's individual mesh points with the Direct Selection tool to distort not only the outer edges of the envelope shape but also the way art is distorted within the envelope itself. To provide even more control, use the Mesh tool to add, remove, and manipulate mesh points.

To create an envelope mesh, select your artwork and choose Object> Envelope Distort> Make with Mesh. After you've chosen how many mesh points you want, Illustrator will create the envelope mesh. The Envelope Mesh tools will appear in the Control panel, allowing you to easily change the number of rows and columns and restore the envelope mesh to its original shape if necessary. You can also use the Direct Selection tool to edit the points and use the Mesh tool to add mesh points. (If you use other tools, however, you'll need to switch back to the Selection tool if you want the Envelope Mesh controls to reappear in the Control panel.)

3D EFFECTS

Illustrator offers you the power to transform any two-dimensional (2D) shape, including type, into a shape that looks three-dimensional (3D). As you're working in Illustrator's 3D effect dialogs, you can change your 3D shape's perspective, rotate it, and add lighting and surface attributes. And because you're working with a live effect, you can edit the source object at any time and observe the resultant change in the 3D shape immediately. You can also rotate a 2D shape in 3D space and change its perspective. Finally, Illustrator lets you map artwork previously saved as a symbol onto any of your 3D object's surfaces. Remember that Illustrator is primarily a 2D program—its 3D capabilities are very limited when compared to the plethora of available 3D programs.

To begin, think of Illustrator's horizontal ruler as the X axis and the vertical ruler as the Y axis. Now imagine a third dimension that extends back into space, perpendicular to the flat surface of your monitor. This is the Z axis. There are two ways to create a 3D shape using 3D effects. The first method is by extruding a 2D object back into space along the Z axis, and the second is by revolving a 2D object around its Y axis, up to 360°.

To apply a 3D effect to a selected object, choose one of the 3D effects from the *fx* icon in the Appearance panel (or via the Effects menu). (To simplify the instructions throughout this chapter, we'll be using the convention "choose Effect> 3D.") Once you apply a 3D effect to an object, it will show up in the Appearance panel. As with other appearance attributes, you can edit the effect, change the position of the effect in the panel's stacking order, and duplicate or delete the effect. You can also save 3D effects as reusable graphic styles so that you can apply the same effect to a batch of objects. Once the style has been applied, you can modify any of the style parameters by clicking the underlined effect name in the Appearance panel or double-clicking the *fx* icon to the right of the effect name. Editing the 2D path will update the 3D rendering.

Following are a few of the key parameters for working in the different kinds of 3D:

- **To extrude a 2D object,** begin by creating a path; the path can be open or closed and can contain a stroke, a fill, or both (if your shape contains a fill, it's best to begin with a solid color, not a gradient or pattern). With your path selected, choose Extrude & Bevel from the Effect> 3D submenu. In the lower portion of the dialog, enter a point size for depth for your object in the Extrude Depth field, or drag the slider. Adding a cap to your object makes the

Don't worry about the ° symbol
The degree symbol automatically inserts after entering a value into 3D dialog rotation text fields.

Customized bevels!
Each of the 3D Bevel paths is actually a symbol, saved inside the "Bevels.ai" file. To add a custom bevel, open the Bevels.ai file, draw or paste a new path, drag the new paths to the Symbols panel, name the symbol, and resave the file. To find this hidden file: Control-click/ right-click the Adobe Illustrator application icon and choose "Show Package Contents," then Required> Resources; the Bevels.ai file is inside your language folder. In **CC**, the path is Application folder> Support Files> Resources>; then look inside your language folder. — *Jean-Claude Tremblay*

Left to right: Turn cap on for solid, Turn cap off for hollow, Bevel Extent In, Bevel Extent Out

Not enough steps...
In the 3D dialog click the More Options button to adjust Blend steps; find a setting between the default (25) and the maximum (256) that's smooth enough, but not too slow to draw (and print).

Revolving an object using the Effect> 3D> Revolve dialog—the open path on the left was revolved to create the 3D wine cork on the right

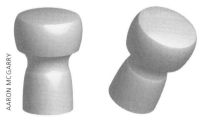

An example of rotating an object in 3D space

ends appear solid; disabling the cap option makes your object appear hollow (see the first two figures at left).

You can choose from ten different bevels to style the edges of your object; bevels can be added to the original using Bevel Extent Out or carved out of the original using Bevel Extent In (second pair of figures at left).

- **To revolve an object around its Y (vertical) axis,** begin by creating a path. The path can be open or closed and stroked, filled, or both. With your path selected, choose Effect> 3D> Revolve to open 3D Revolve Options. Drag the slider to set the number of degrees or enter a value from 1 to 360 in the Angle text field. An object that's revolved 360° will appear solid. An object revolved less than 360° appears to have a wedge carved out of it. If you offset the rotation from the object's edge, a 3D shape will appear to be carved out in the center.

- **To rotate 2D or 3D objects in 3D space,** choose Effects> 3D> Rotate. The 3D Rotate Options dialog contains a cube representing the planes that your shape can be rotated through. Choose a preset angle of rotation from the Position menu, or enter values between –180 and 180 into the X, Y, and Z text fields. To manually rotate your object around one of its three axes, simply click *on the edge* of one of the faces of the white cube and drag. The edges of each plane are highlighted in a corresponding color that tells you through which of the object's three planes you're rotating it. The object's rotation is constrained within the plane of that particular axis. If you wish to rotate your object relative to all three axes at once, click directly on a surface of the cube and drag, or click in the black area behind the cube and drag. Values in all three text fields will change. And if you simply want to rotate your object, click and drag inside the circle, but outside the cube itself.

- **To change the perspective of an object,** enter a number between 0 and 160 in the Perspective field, or drag the slider pop-up. A smaller value simulates the look of a telephoto camera lens, while a larger value simulates a wide-angle camera lens.

Applying surface shading to 3D objects

Illustrator allows you to choose different shading (ranging from dull and unshaded matte surfaces to glossy and highlighted surfaces that look like plastic), as well as customized lighting conditions. The Surface shading option appears as part of both the 3D Extrude & Bevel and the 3D Revolve Options dialogs. Choosing Wireframe as your shading option will result in a transparent object, the contours of which are overlaid with a set of outlines representing the object's geometry. Choosing No Shading results in a flat-looking shape with no discernible surfaces. Choosing the Diffused Shading option results in your object having a soft light cast on its surfaces, while choosing the Plastic Shading option will make your object look as if it's molded out of shiny, reflective plastic. For mapped surfaces, enable "Shade Artwork" in the Map Art dialog.

If you choose either the Diffused Shading or Plastic Shading option, you can further refine the look of your object by adjusting the direction and intensity of the light source illuminating it. By clicking the More Options button, the dialog will enlarge and you'll be able to make changes to the Light Intensity, Ambient Light level, Highlight Intensity, Highlight Size, and number of Blend Steps. You can also choose a custom Shading Color to add a color cast to the shaded surfaces. If you choose to maintain a spot color assigned to your Extruded object during output by enabling the Preserve Spot Colors checkbox, be aware that this removes custom shading and limits your Shading Color to Black. If you choose Preserve Spot Colors, you should enable Overprint Preview (View menu) so you can see your shading and color accurately.

When expanded, the More Options dialog includes the light source sphere (shown at right). The small white dot within this sphere indicates the position of the light source, while the black box around it highlights this light source as currently selected. There is always one light source by default. Click and drag this dot within the sphere to reposition your light. With Preview enabled the lighting will automatically update on your 3D object.

LISA JACKMORE

Rotate objects in three dimensions by using the Effect> 3D> Rotate dialog (or the upper halves of the Revolve and the Extrude & Bevel dialogs); the symbol on the left was rotated in 3D space to create the figure on the right (any 2D object can be rotated in 3D space, without making the object itself 3D)

For the smoothest 3D

When creating profile objects for 3D, draw as few anchor points as possible. Each anchor point produces an additional surface to render and might also create potential problems if you're later mapping artwork onto surfaces.

—*Jean-Claude Tremblay*

The expanded More Options dialog shows the position of your light source within the sphere; the three icons located below this appear from left to right are "Move selected light to back of object," "New Light," and "Delete Light"

- Remember to choose a surface. Select by clicking the arrow keys to view each surface.
- To identify the surface you want to map, look for the red highlight on the object itself, rather than looking at the flattened proxy in the Map Art dialog.
- If the symbol isn't mapping to a selected surface, it may be on the *inside* of the surface.
- A stroke will add more surfaces to an object than a fill because a stroke creates a hollow inside the object, which is also treated as a surface.
- A stroke can obscure mapped art on a side or inside of a surface that can't be seen.

—*Brenda Sutherland*

STAINLESS STEEL

At left are some images prepared for mapping to a 3D "washer" (shown reduced in size); middle figure shows the stroked compound path used to enter 3D Extrude & Bevel; at right is the 3D washer with art mapped to bevels and visible surfaces; at bottom the text art symbol used for mapping (shown at actual scale to the 3D object)

Mapping with gradients

Gradients saved as symbols are rasterized when they're mapped. Adjust the resolution for the rasterization in "Document Raster Effects Settings." Adjust this resolution via Effects> Document Raster Effects Settings.

Clicking the "New Light" icon (below the sphere) adds more light sources. This also selects the new light source (indicated by the black "highlight" box around it). Adjust each selected source independently using the lighting controls (to the right of the sphere). The first icon below the sphere, the "Move selected light to back of object" feature, creates back lighting for an object. When your light source is behind an object, the source indicator inverts to a black dot within a white square. When using multiple light sources, this difference helps you see which light sources are behind or in front of an object. Select a light source and click this icon to toggle the light to the front or back of your object, depending on its current position. To delete a light source, first select it and then click the Trash icon beneath the sphere (you can delete all but one default light source).

Mapping art onto an object

To map artwork onto an object (as with the design on the washer to the left), first define the art that you wish to map onto a surface as a symbol; select the artwork you want to map, and drag it to the Symbols panel. You may also want to define a number of symbols. For instance, the texture and text on the outside of the washer (at left) is one symbol. The other objects were also each saved as symbols and added to surfaces in the Map Art dialog.

Map the symbols onto your 3D objects from the Extrude & Bevel or Revolve Options dialogs. In either of these 3D options boxes, you simply click the Map Art button and then choose one of the available symbols from the menu. You can specify which of your object's surfaces the artwork will map onto by clicking the left and right arrow keys. The selected surface will appear in the window; then you can either scale the art by dragging the handles on the bounding box or make the art expand to cover the entire surface by clicking the Scale to Fit button. Note that as you click through the different surfaces, the selected surface will be highlighted with a red outline in your document window. Your currently visible surfaces will appear in light gray in the Map Art dialog, and surfaces that are currently hidden will appear dark.

Note: *To see artwork mapped onto the side surfaces of your object, make sure the object has a stroke of None.*

THE PERSPECTIVE GRID

The perspective grid allows you to create art on a ground plane representing real-world space as viewed by the human eye. Distances between edges converge as you approach the horizon, the terminal point of our vision. This tool is useful for creating scenes such as cityscapes where buildings or roads narrow in view as they recede from our vision, eventually vanishing on the horizon.

With this Perspective Grid toolset you can draw dynamically within the perspective environment itself so that shapes or objects automatically conform to the perspective grid as you create them, or you can attach existing flat vector art to the perspective grid by dragging selected art into the perspective grid using the Perspective Selection tool (see warning tip at right!). You can even position the grid on top of a reference photograph to add vector content. Symbols, text, and objects created with Illustrator's 3D effect are also supported within the perspective environment.

To begin working in perspective you must first define your perspective environment. Click the Perspective Grid tool in the Tools panel to display the perspective grid on your Artboard, or click View> Perspective Grid> Show Grid. The default is Two Point Perspective consisting of two vanishing points. For one point perspective choose View> Perspective Grid> One Point Perspective> 1P Normal View, which has a single vanishing point. For three-point perspective, choose Three Point Perspective> 3P Normal View, which has three vanishing points (if a perspective grid is customized and saved, it will appear in the respective submenu for 1P, 2P, or 3P Normal View as an additional choice).

When you select the Perspective Grid tool, your grid is displayed with grid plane control points on its extremities

The Plane Switching Widget shown left with the left side highlighted in blue indicates that the left plane (grid) is active; click a side of the cube with one of the perspective tools (or press 1, 2, or 3 on your keyboard) to activate a different plane (second and third widget); click the area outside the cube within the widget (or press 4) to deactivate perspective mode, which allows you to draw normally (widget at far right)

Grid control points can be manually adjusted on the grid itself or more precisely using the Define Perspective Grid dialog box (View> Perspective Grid> Define Grid). Presets can then be saved for reuse. View> Perspective Grid> Show Rulers displays a ruler on the visible grid

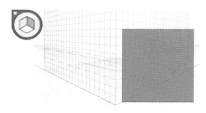

In this example, clicking within the Plane Switching Widget but outside the cube deactivated the perspective grid (note the cyan colored area surrounding the cube), so the rectangle was drawn in normal mode; to later apply perspective to the rectangle, select the Grid Selection tool, click on a widget side to activate a plane, and drag the rectangle to the desired location

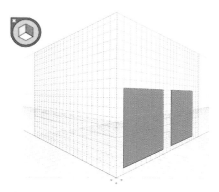

The above image shows a square drawn with the Rectangle tool. Notice the Plane Switching Widget indicates that the right plane is active, hence the illustrated shape in perspective relative to the right vanishing point (the cursor also includes a line and an arrow, which also indicates the active plane). The same square copied and moved with the Perspective Selection tool dynamically transforms it as it moves within the perspective plane

(though some disappear when the Perspective Selection tool is used). These controls allow you to manually adjust parameters such as vanishing points, angles, repositioning of planes, grid height and width, etc. Scrolling the cursor over these controls yields an indicator below the pointer showing the directional choices available for that control.

To save a customized grid choose View> Perspective Grid> Save Grid As Preset. The new grid is saved under the respective perspective type; for example, a customized one-point perspective grid will be saved as an option to 1P Normal View when the View> Perspective Grid> Two Point Perspective fly-out menu is displayed. The Define Grid dialog (View> Perspective Grid> Define Grid) allows you to adjust the grid with greater numerical precision and save as a preset for further uses.

To begin working within your defined environment, you must first make a plane active. The cube in the upper-left corner of the work area is the Plane Switching Widget. When you click on a cube side in the widget with the Perspective Grid tool (or any drawing or editing tool), the active plane is highlighted with a color. Orange, for example, is the default color for the right plane (see figures at left). Only one plane can be active at a time, and anything drawn while an active plane is selected will conform to the perspective of that specific active plane; only the active plane determines the perspective of an object, regardless of where on the artboard you draw the artwork. The Perspective Grid tool cursor also indicates this with the shaded side of a cube below its pointer.

Once you choose an active plane, you can use any drawing or editing tool to draw it in perspective mode. To test this out, choose any object-creation tool (such as the Rectangle tool) and begin drawing on the grid. Use the Perspective Selection tool (hidden under the Perspective Grid tool in the Tools panel) to select and move art within an active plane (the cursor also has a line and an arrow, indicating the active plane). Move objects within your plane using this tool, and your objects appear to recede and advance within the perspective grid. If instead you use the normal Selection tool to move an object, the object's shape becomes frozen to the current viewpoint no matter where you move it. You can also use the Perspective Selection tool to select existing vector objects and attach them to the perspective grid. To do so, activate a plane and then select and drag the object to the perspective grid. When you use the Perspective Grid tool to select an object that's already associated with the grid, the associated side of the cube automatically becomes highlighted.

Clicking in the area outside the cube within the widget (or pressing 4) deactivates all perspective planes so you can draw in normal mode (no perspective applied)—see figures opposite. Once your object is created, press 1, 2, or 3 to activate that particular plane, or click on a Widget side, and then use the Perspective Selection tool to drag the object to position it in perspective. Marquee or Shift-select multiple objects with the Perspective Selection tool to drag them together into the active plane.

If you wish to move an object perpendicular to its current location, hold down the 5 key (top row of numbers on keyboard only, not 5 on right numeric keypad) as you drag with the Perspective Selection tool; to duplicate an object and move it perpendicular to the original's position, hold Option-5/Alt-5 as you drag.

With the Perspective Grid tool, double-click on a grid plane control (the three circles below where the planes intersect) to open a Vanishing Plane or Floor Plane dialog, allowing you to move a plane precisely.

To work on an object in normal mode after applying perspective, Control-click/Right-click to choose Perspective> Release with Perspective (or via the Object menu). This function won't return an object to a pre-perspective state; it merely detaches it from the perspective plane. To reattach a detached object to a plane, use Object> Perspective> Attach to Active Plane to reattach it. Be aware that if you skip this step and instead just use the Perspective Selection tool to move the object without first reattaching the object, you'll be adding an *additional* perspective to the object.

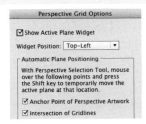

Double-click the Perspective Grid tool in the Tools panel to open the Perspective Grid Options dialog for Automatic Plane Positioning options

Stay within the grid

Lock Station Point feature is great to relocate your vanishing point within a Two or Three Point Perspective grid, but is likely to create erratic results if you try to switch between them.

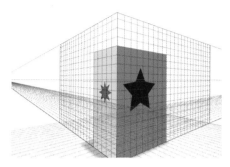

A box attached to a Two Point Perspective grid

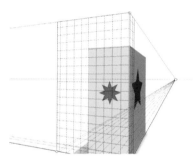

*With Lock Station Point enabled, you can adjust both the vanishing point and the perspective grid, and attached artwork will adjust automatically to match the grid (for an example of this in detail, see Aaron McGarry's lesson and gallery in the **CC** section at the end of this chapter)*

Lock Station Point limits

To avoid erratic results, choose two- or three-point perspective *before* attaching any artwork to it.

Lock Station Point is saved

When you save a file with a Perspective Grid, the state of the Lock Station Point is saved with it.

NEW PERSPECTIVE FEATURES & PUPPET WARP IN CC

Once you've developed a complex composition using a Two or Three Point Grid you can freely relocate the vanishing point by enabling Lock Station Point. Artwork that has been attached to the grid will adhere to adjustments in perspective. With Lock Station Point, moving the vanishing point for one grid plane moves the vanishing point for the other grid(s) in tandem, and your objects will realign to the new perspective.

Lock Station Point allows you to change perspective of artwork already in the grid. For instance, you can move the grid to reveal more on the right side of the grid and less of the left. To do this, choose View> Perspective Grid> Lock Station Point. Next, to change the perspective and move the attached artwork at the same time, use the Perspective Grid tool and drag the right vanishing point further to the right to see more of the right side. Your attached artwork will automatically conform to the new vanishing point. Dragging on the left vanishing point swings the perspective to reveal more of the left side of the grid; on a Three Point Perspective grid, you can also swing the vanishing point located at the bottom of the grid, which tends to skew the perspective considerably.

PUPPET WARP

Puppet Warp was first a character animation feature in After Effects and then added to Photoshop. Now we have Illustrator's vector version of Puppet Warp. With an object or objects selected, click the Puppet Warp tool to envelop your selection with a 3D-looking mesh. By default, Illustrator guesses key locations to prevent distortion, and it automatically places pins in those locations (to start without any pins, see Warning Tip "Content-Aware Defaults," opposite). Puppet Warp pins serve double-duty: Unselected pins lock mesh areas from distorting; active pins become handles and selections for distortions.

Deselecting commits puppet warp distortions, and you can only remove it using Undo during that session (see Tip "Puppet Warp isn't Live," opposite). If a pin isn't placed where you want it, click it to select it (Shift-click multiple points) and press Delete/Backspace. To place a new pin, hover with the Puppet Warp tool over a portion of the mesh without a point and click when you see a small **+** symbol. If you're close to a pin and don't see a **+**, you'll select an inactive pin instead of placing a new one. If you click on a single pin, the pin will display a dotted circle of influence that is non-adjustable, but if you hover your cursor away from the pin and within that circle, the cursor will display a rotate symbol. The pin acts as the pivot point for the rotation; click-drag clockwise or counter clockwise to rotate the pin, which will also change the curves of the attached paths. You can Shift-click to select multiple pins to move them together in any direction, but (as of Illustrator 2019), you cannot select multiple pins to then pivot or rotate any pins around another.

With an active Puppet Warp selection, the Properties panel Puppet Warp section displays a Select All Pins button and an input field for Expand Mesh (also found in the Control panel). Expand Mesh in this case refers to scaling the mesh in relation to the object. The size of the mesh is set by default to encompass 2 px (pixels) outside of the object itself. This size works for most objects, as it's both small enough you'll have control over the mesh at your object's edges, yet large enough that most objects won't distort with choppy results. Enter a new value or click the pop-up arrow to adjust a slider to expand (larger number) or contract (smaller number) the mesh. The size of the mesh affects the speed of distortion, which can impact your control over the amount of distortion as you pull on the mesh; size also affects what the mesh is able to envelop or exclude. Set a mesh that's too small, and small movements may rapidly break and distort smaller details, or even small bits of a larger object. If your mesh is too large, you may find it difficult to affect the distortion within a pin's circle of influence, or you may affect unwanted portions of objects that you thought were protected.

See "Viewing Puppet Warp mesh" at right for ways to show/hide the mesh while adjusting it.

Content Aware Defaults

Click the Puppet Warp tool with objects selected and Illustrator envelopes your objects in a mesh grid. When "Enable Content Aware Defaults" is toggled on in Preferences> General, Illustrator also attempts to automatically place pins in your mesh. Be aware that this preference also affects Freeform Gradients and Crop Image.

ARI WEINSTEIN

Ari Weinstein's "Ti the TICOON Mascot" vector illustration, before and after placing puppet warp pins and adjusting the position of a front paw (see a puppet warp lesson and a gallery in the **CC** *section at the end of this chapter)*

Viewing Puppet Warp mesh

To show or hide the Puppet Warp mesh, toggle Show Mesh in the Control or Properties panel. To briefly hide the mesh, hold down ⌘ (Mac)/Ctrl (Windows), or hover over the rulers if they're showing.

Puppet Warp isn't Live

Always duplicate objects before applying Puppet Warp. When you choose another tool, your warp may be permanently applied.

Warp & Distort

Bending Forms to Create Organic Variations

Overview: *Use Envelope Distort and Distort & Transform live effects to shape objects; use filled rectangles with blend modes to change the time of day.*

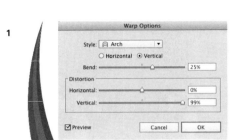

Using Warp Options to bend three rectangles into a curved and pointed arch

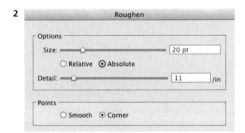

Using Roughen on a duplicate of the envelope layer to add texture to the tree trunks

When Michael Cressy needed to create scenes for an online video game, he turned to Illustrator's powerful Envelope Distort features and live effects to create a Halloween world where magic changes the shapes of things. By adding a few additional layers to colorize his images for different times of the day, his game scenes took on a consistent look with minimal fuss.

1 Using Envelope Distort to bend branches and trees.
To create the blighted trees, Cressy used the Rectangle tool to make three adjacent stripes with different fills (no stroke). He selected them and chose Object> Envelope Distort> Make with Warp. He set Style to Arch with a Vertical Bend of 25%. He then used a Distortion amount of 99% in the Vertical dimension. These settings created a slightly curved set of stripes so distorted in the vertical dimension that they came to a point. With this horn as his base element, Cressy duplicated and scaled each horn (holding Option/Alt and dragging the bounding box) to be either branches or the main tree trunks. From the context-sensitive menu, he chose Transform> Reflect, and in the dialog chose Vertical to flip half of them. And since Cressy used Envelope Distort, his settings remained live and editable throughout the development of his image.

2 Texturing the tree bark. To have some of the tree trunks stand out from the rest, Cressy decided to add texture to them. Since the Roughen effect breaks up smooth outlines with some of the outlines falling inside the original form, Cressy retained the full shape by keeping the basic shape on one layer and then duplicating it to a layer above; this layer he modified by choosing Effect> Distort & Transform> Roughen. After enabling Absolute, Cressy played with the sliders until he found the right amount of the effect to appear like rough bark on his tree trunks—modest settings prevented the Roughen effect here from creating long, sharp needles. Having again chosen a live effect to alter his basic shapes, rather than attempting to draw each of them with the Pen tool, Cressy kept his options open for future editing and was able to work quickly and interactively with the effects.

3 Using Roughen for grass and then warping it to make a broomstick. To construct the grassy hill, Cressy drew a half-oval with the Pen tool and then applied Effect> Distort & Transform> Zig Zag. He next applied Roughen with a low setting and added another instance of the Roughen effect, this time with a high setting for Details to create the tall, thin strands of grass. To create the bristles of the witch's broomstick, he used ⌘-F/Ctrl-F to paste a copy of the grassy hill in front and applied an Envelope warp using the Shell Upper preset. He then edited the envelope with the Direct Selection tool and Free Transform until he had shaped the broom end.

4 Adding layers to coordinate scenes for different times of the day. Cressy maintained consistency from one scene to the next by adding tinting layers that could be turned on or off, each representing a different time of day. For midday, he added a layer with a light brown rectangle and then clicked <u>Opacity</u> in the Control panel to lower the Opacity to 50% and chose Screen for Blending Mode. For early evening scenes, he used a white-to-dark brown radial gradient on a layer set to Multiply at reduced Opacity, and for night shots, he used a lavender-colored rectangle set to Multiply at 100% Opacity. He later reused these tinting layers with other scenes he created.

3

Creating the bristles of the broomstick from a duplicate of the grassy hill, then running Envelope Distort> Make with Warp, and choosing Shell Upper for the preset, then further transforming the envelope

4

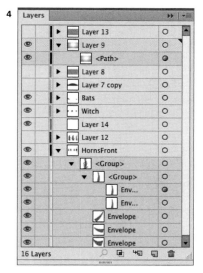

Using rectangles with different colors, blend modes, opacities, and gradients to tint the scenes

Dedree Drees

As part of her undersea illustration, "The Dory," artist and instructor Dedree Drees mimicked blades of seagrass by building an intricate blend that she then extruded as a 3D object. Drees started by drawing four overlapping, wavy lines using the Pencil tool and then giving each stroke a unique color. To begin blending, Drees selected all four lines and then double-clicked the Blend tool. In the Blend Options dialog she set Spacing> Specified Steps to 2 and then chose Object> Blend> Make. To make the lines of the blend look like flat seagrass blades, Drees extruded the blend by opening the Appearance panel and from the *fx* icon choosing 3D> Extrude & Bevel. She experimented with different Extrude Depth values to make sure that the seagrass blades would not appear thick and dense. Drees brought this object into Photoshop where she positioned it among other elements. To finish, she selected individual blades of seagrasses and created layer masks to make them transparent.

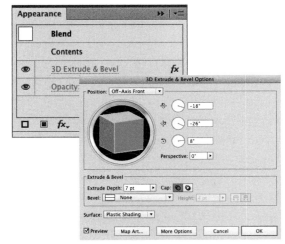

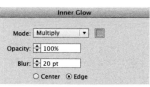

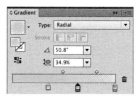

GLITSCHKA

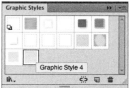

Von R. Glitschka

For "Beautiful," Von R. Glitschka placed his model and Japanese text against one of his intricate patterns (see the *Mastering Complexity* chapter for more on how to create patterns). He then used Live Effects throughout to create the interaction between his objects and their environment. To lift the Kanji characters from the background, he used Outer Glow in Multiply mode, creating an even shadow around the calligraphy. But to separate his model from the background pattern, he maintained directional lighting. He filled an object that matched her shape with the same blue as the background, moved it a bit to the right, added a 20 pixel Gaussian Blur, and set the layer to

Multiply mode with a slightly reduced opacity. He applied the Gaussian Blur effect frequently to create the shadows cast on her skin by her hair and to soften transitions when modeling the skin tones. He used the Inner Glow effect in Multiply mode to add a soft shadow within an object. Because he modeled her in a very detailed fashion, Glitschka streamlined some of his work by creating a few graphic styles to use when creating the fine shading and blending in her skin tones. Gradients—often using transparency—added to the live effects to create a soft, romantically styled illustration.

The Keys to 3D

The Basics of Realistic 3D Modeling

Overview: *Create 2D art to extrude as 3D; save graphics and images as symbols to use as maps; render and position 3D objects; map visible surfaces of the 3D object; adjust lighting; generate drop and cast shadows*

1

2D artwork before rendering as 3D objects

2

To create a realistic look for 3D surfaces, McGarry saved images and graphics as symbols to later map onto the 3D objects

Be thrifty with image maps

Size your map artwork appropriately (both in file size and dimensions) to avoid potential errors when rendering. You should also position your 3D objects first and then map only the visible surfaces.

Aaron McGarry, an illustrator working in the high-tech industry, often has to conceptualize the look and feel of a product before the physical product actually exists.

1 Creating the 2D art to be rendered in 3D. McGarry began his project by first creating the 2D art that he'd later extrude into 3D objects. Since the key blade and bow would require two different extrusion depths, he created each separately. He began creating the key blade in two parts; he drew one set of teeth and then double-clicked the Reflect tool, chose Horizontal in the dialog, and clicked Copy. After bringing both pieces together with a slight gap between, in the Pathfinder panel he clicked Unite. This joined the two parts of the key into one shape, yet allowed each of the surfaces to be separately mapped with the gap creating a center line. In total, he created eight separate pieces: two for the key, three for the key ring links, and three for the fob, all of them with a gray fill and no stroke.

2 Saving artwork as symbols to be used as maps. To create a more realistic look, McGarry gathered and created artwork and saved each one as a symbol to later map onto the visible surfaces. He used Illustrator's vector tools to create the label for the bow of the key, the security buttons on the fob, part of the key blade, and key ring links, and then saved each as a symbol (by dragging each separately to the Symbols panel). He also used File> Place to bring in two JPG photos of flat metal—one narrow strip for the fob edges and a second larger piece for the fob front—and saved each of these photos as symbols.

3 Extruding and positioning the 3D objects. He selected one object at a time and chose Effects> 3D> Extrude & Bevel. For each piece he adjusted value in the Extrude Depth field until it looked right. For objects such as the bow of the key he applied a Rounded bevel selected from the Bevel menu. He changed the fill color of the key bow to blue, but he left the other objects gray, a color similar enough to the metallic maps that some surfaces wouldn't need image maps. Next, McGarry selected objects one at a time and re-entered the Extrude & Bevel dialog, where he rotated each object to the appropriate angle using the cube widget. With all the parts now positioned, he separately applied perspective first to the fob and then the key, this time by customizing the Perspective field in the Extrude & Bevel dialog.

Unlike conventional 3D software, Illustrator's 3D objects cannot pass through other objects occupying the same space; objects can only be moved in front or behind other objects. As a result, McGarry had to create the illusion of the interconnecting links in the image as separate pieces, arranging them in front or behind each other.

4 Mapping artwork to 3D surfaces and lighting. To map a saved symbol onto a selected extruded object, he re-entered the Extrude and Bevel Options dialog and clicked the Map Art button. Since the key blade originally consisted of two joined pieces, the map dialog treated each half of this top plane as a separate surface. This enabled him to map the right half of the blade with the metal symbol and the left half with a gradient symbol, creating the dark ridge down the center to give the illusion of a worn step on the blade's left side. McGarry then entered More Options in the Extrude and Bevel dialog and adjusted lighting for each part by moving the highlight on the sphere and reducing Ambient Light to darken the side shading. Lastly, to enhance the 3D illusion he manually added shadow effects (Effects> Stylize> Drop Shadow) and then drew paths to which he applied Effect> Blur> Gaussian Blur for the blade and key ring shadows.

3

Artwork extruded and rendered as 3D objects, then positioned before applying maps

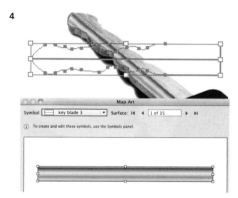

4

The Map dialog showing the selected surface outlined in red in the image, mapping a gradient map selected from the Symbol Library

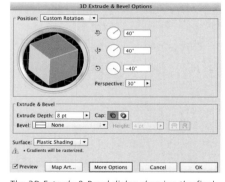

The 3D Extrude & Bevel dialog showing the final settings for the key blade; clicking the More Options button expands the dialog for lighting controls

3D shadow effects

Illustrator's 3D lighting doesn't cast shadows. Although in some situations Effects> Drop Shadows can be useful, in many cases you'll have to manually construct shadow objects with paths and blurs.

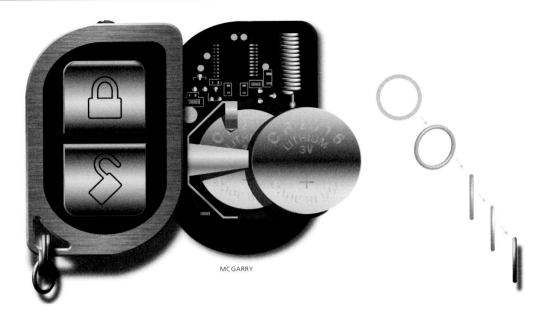

MCGARRY

Aaron McGarry

McGarry created this exploded view of a key fob using a variety of Illustrator features, including vector tools, symbols, and 3D, as well as texture and drop shadow effects. He created the PCB (printed circuit board) using basic paths and applied a variety of gradients and textures, saving some of the PCB components as symbols so he could easily duplicate them. For the batteries and buttons, he applied modified gradients from the Gradients> Metals library and placed icons on top of the buttons. For the batteries he added text on a curved path, slightly reducing the opacity of the text to blend it with the metal background. To easily apply edge bevels to the fob housing, buttons, and key ring section, McGarry separately applied Effect> 3D> Extrude & Bevel to each. While still in the Extrude & Bevel Options dialog, he also applied the image maps that he'd saved as symbols for the fob front and bevels. Clicking the Map Art

button, he navigated to the visible surfaces with the arrow keys, and for each he chose the image that he'd prepared. McGarry created the key ring using the Ellipse tool with a stroke, no fill; he extruded and applied a Rounded bevel; then rotated it in profile and applied maps and shadows (see detail above). He made three copies, shortening one to indicate the ring end. He rotated and moved the fourth ring (lowest) behind the others. Selecting each part of the fob separately, he adjusted lighting controls by clicking the More Options button in the Extrude & Bevel Options to expand the dialog. Finally, since the 3D lighting controls don't cast shadows, to create the illusion of different object depths he separately selected each part of the fob (front housing, buttons, key rings, and back) and then applied and adjusted drop shadows using Effect> Stylize> Drop Shadow.

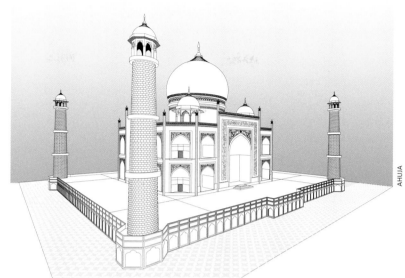

AHUJA

Anil Ahuja/Adobe Systems

Adobe Systems Product Specialist Anil Ahuja used a number of visual references to create this majestic Taj Mahal. To help him in the construction of the building in perspective, he created front- and plan-view sketches. He then referred to photos to set up the basic two-point perspective grid. As with a real structure, he built from the ground up using layers to organize his assembled pieces. The floor is a single design that he created normally (top left) and saved as a symbol. Then he dragged an instance of the symbol into the perspective grid using the Perspective Selection tool. Using a combination of Option-Shift/ Alt-Shift, he dragged to create a duplicate and then used Transform Again (⌘-D/ -D) to repeat the floor pattern. The next object was the plinth (raised base) upon which the mausoleum sits (bottom left). Drawing a rectangle in perspective on the ground plane first, he then used the Automatic Plane Positioning feature when creating the sides. Though he created symmetrical objects such as squares and rectangles in perspective, he created the more intricate designs such as the curved archways of the iwan and pishtaqs normally and then placed them into perspective. The onion dome began as outlines on the plinth. He used the perpendicular movement feature to duplicate and precisely move an outlined ring straight up off the floor plane by using the Floor Plane dialog options (click Floor Plane control point to open). Once he had positioned the rings, he drew straight lines alongside the rings to complete the cylinder and drew a simple circle without perspective behind to create the dome shape. For more info about how he created this, see his ReadMe on **WOW! ONLINE**.

One Perspective

Simulating a One-Point Perspective View

Overview: *Create a one-point perspective grid; customize the grid by moving its control points; draw tile artwork and move it onto the grid using the Perspective Selection tool; duplicate the artwork to make a row; duplicate the rows to form a floor.*

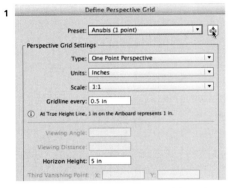

Defining and saving your custom grid from the Define Perspective Grid dialog (View menu)

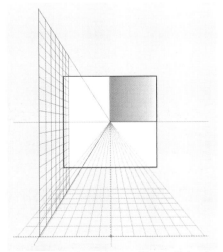

The new one-point grid created by modifying the [1P-Normal View] preset

DREW

Elaine Drew is an artist who is equally at home with traditional painting as with the latest digital drawing tools. For this Anubis image, Drew relied on Illustrator's Perspective Grid tool and presets to give the tiled floor and gradient walls the illusion of perspective.

1 Creating the one-point perspective grid. Drew designed the illustration to feature a one-point perspective view. She began by selecting the Rectangle tool and drawing the square that would form the rear wall of the room and serve as a guide for creating the perspective grid in the next step. She filled the square with a gradient.

To start the grid, Drew chose View> Perspective Grid> Define Grid. In the "Define Perspective Grid" dialog she chose the [1P-Normal View] preset and then customized it by changing Units to Inches, Gridline every to .5, and Horizon Height to 5. Drew clicked the Save icon, named and saved the preset, then clicked OK to exit the dialog.

2 Adjusting the grid to fit the illustration design. To begin customizing the grid to fit her design, Drew chose

View> Perspective Grid> One Point Perspective and selected the preset she had created previously. Selecting the Perspective Grid tool (which made the grid editable), she dragged the left Ground Level control until it met the lower-left corner of the artboard. Then she dragged the Horizontal Level control down and the Vanishing Point control to the right. Finally, to extend the bottom grid plane to the rear wall, she dragged the Extent of Grid control upward so that the grid met the bottom of the wall (to accurately see the full extent of the grid, it may be necessary to zoom in).

3 **Creating the floor tiles and moving them onto the grid.** With the grid established, Drew was ready to create the two floor tiles. She decided to create the tiles and assemble them into rows outside of the grid before moving them into the grid to form the floor. She turned off the perspective grid by clicking inside the circle of the Plane Switching Widget with the Perspective Grid tool. (The circle's background turns blue.)

Next, Drew created one circular petal and one square tile to fit within the 0.5-inch grid size she specified in the previous step. To soften the look of the artwork, she applied the Effect> SVG Filters> AI_Alpha_1 filter. She duplicated the pair of tiles several times to create a row and then duplicated the row and offset it horizontally by one tile. She continued duplicating and offsetting the rows to complete the floor. To render the tiled floor in the perspective of her grid, she first made sure View> Perspective Grid> Snap to Grid was enabled and then chose the Perspective Selection tool and clicked the Horizontal Grid plane portion of the Plane Switching Widget. Then she selected all of the tiles with the Perspective Selection tool and dragged them onto the grid.

Drew finished the room by creating the left wall. She drew a rectangle and filled it with a gradient. Then she selected the Perspective Selection tool, clicked the Left Grid plane portion of the Plane Switching Widget, and dragged the rectangle onto the grid.

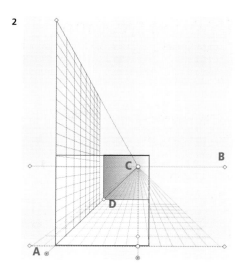

2

Perspective grid after all adjustments; **A** is the left Ground Level control, **B** is the Horizontal Level control, **C** is the Vanishing Point control, **D** is the Extent of Grid control

3

(Left) Turning off the perspective grid by clicking inside the circle of the Plane Switching Widget with the Perspective Grid or Perspective Selection tool; (right) selecting the Horizontal Grid plane

The original square tile and circular petal tile artwork created in Illustrator before being modified by the AI_Alpha_1 SVG filter

Out of controls?

While only four perspective grid controls were used here, 13 more await you. Find out about them by accessing Help> *Illustrator Help*. Click Drawing and then Perspective. The About Perspective Grid section shows and describes all 17 grid controls.

Amplified Angles

Creating Details with Two-Point Perspective

Overview: *Set up a two-point perspective grid; use drawing and editing tools to create the basic drawing in perspective; add basic shapes in perspective; add more details to achieve the final result.*

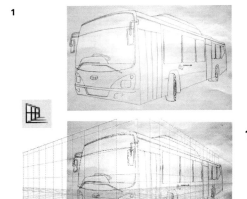

Using the Perspective Grid tool (at left) to set up and position the grid; the ground, right, and left plane controls visible on top of the sketch

(Top) Using the Perspective Grid tool to click a side in the widget to activate a plane (first 3 widgets from left) or outside the cube in the widget to deactivate all planes (far right widget); (bottom) creating the basic bus shapes in perspective using the Rectangle, Rounded Rectangle, and Ellipse tools

AHUJA

Anil Ahuja, a senior product specialist working for Adobe, created this bus for instructional materials that explain how to work with Illustrator's perspective tools.

1 **Setting up a perspective grid.** Ahuja sketched the bus from a photo reference, scanned it, and then placed it into Illustrator as a template layer. When you select the Perspective Grid tool, your artboard will, by default, display a two-point perspective grid. Ahuja then adjusted the grid to fit the scanned sketch by aligning the control points on the grid to match the sketch. Using the Perspective Grid tool, he then began by moving the ground level control point (the diamond on either extremity of the ground level), which allowed him to move all the planes together in any direction (this is indicated by the four-way arrow that appears next to the cursor when it is over this control point). Then he moved the left and right planes individually by using the tool to drag the right and left grid plane controls (the small circles beneath each visible grid). He then also adjusted the horizon (the diamond on either extremity of the horizon line) and vanishing points (circles on the horizon line where the planes converge).

2 **Drawing in perspective.** Clicking a widget side to activate the plane he wished to work in, Ahuja then drew the

basic shapes of the bus in perspective using tools such as the Rectangle, Rounded Rectangle, and Ellipse tools. After creating one side window, he held Option/Alt while dragging it to create the others. Duplicating objects this way automatically transformed them to their new perspective position as he dragged them.

3 Drawing complex elements. Ahuja created complex elements (such as the wheels) outside of the perspective grid and then attached them to the perspective grid by dragging them within the grid using the Perspective Selection tool. He converted the fills of some grid objects into gradients and others into gradient mesh by clicking them with the Gradient Mesh tool (meshes must be made by converting objects already in the grid; they can't be created first and then moved into a grid). He duplicated the outer rim of the tire to create the inner rim by holding Option/Alt (this makes the duplicate) and the 5 key (this makes the drag perpendicular to the original). To create the tire surface he used the curvature of the tire as a guide, used the Pen tool to draw a closed path within the space, and then filled it with a gradient.

Ahuja drew a few doors and windows using the Rounded Rectangle tool. After creating one door panel or side window, he duplicated it by holding Option-Shift/Alt-Shift while he dragged it to the desired location, using ⌘-D/Ctrl-D to transform again if needed. For each door or window he copied and used Paste in Front, converted this copy to a gradient mesh, and reduced the opacity of mesh points by clicking <u>Opacity</u> in the Control panel.

4 The finishing touches. Ahuja created the most complex elements (like the logo and text) separately and then attached them to the perspective grid using the Perspective Selection tool. For the bus shadow, Ahuja first selected the ground plane and drew a rectangle on the plane using the Rectangle tool, and choosing Effect> Blur> Gaussian Blur. He created the building side by drawing a series of filled and stroked rectangles in the perspective grid.

3

(Left) The wheels created outside the perspective grid; (middle) using the Perspective Grid tool to move the wheel into perspective and duplicating the outer rim (holding Option-5/Alt-5 while dragging); (right) after drawing a closed path to create the tire surface

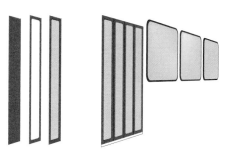

(Left) Building one door panel by layering versions (shown alongside one another for clarity); (right) after creating one of each door panel and window type, duplicating them within the Perspective Grid tool to create the others

4

Creating the bus logo separately before attaching it to the perspective grid

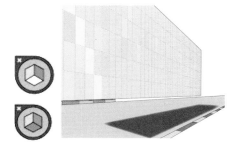

Selecting the right plane to draw the building side and the ground plane to create the bus shadow

Modifying a Photo

Inserting Photographs in Perspective

Overview: *Place a photograph and adjust the perspective grid to conform to the perspective of the image; add graphic elements in perspective; modify the photo to create a new product.*

Distant grid control points

If the lines you create as guides (to help you find a vanishing point) extend way beyond the artboard, try using two windows (Window> New Window). Zoom in on one window, and set the other to the full extent of the grid control points. You can make adjustments rapidly by switching between windows, even though the grid is only visible in the active window.

1

(Top) The original product; (directly above) shown after drawing two pink lines on the left side, extending back until they intersect to form the left vanishing point, and relocating the horizon line to this point using the Perspective Grid tool

Aaron McGarry, an illustrator working for the electronics industry in California, was able to use a photo of an existing product and the perspective grid to conceptualize the next generation of the device.

1 Working with an established perspective. To add new elements to this photo, McGarry needed to find a way to fit a two-point grid to this uneven perspective. Using the Perspective Grid tool, he first grabbed the Ground Level control point and moved the entire grid so that the three-plane intersection point rested at the foremost point on the device. McGarry then needed to adjust the grid to the photo perspective. He began by identifying two parallel edges on the left side of the device. To use these edges as a guide, he used the Line tool to draw two lines along these edges, extending the lines into the background until they intersected (see heavy pink lines in image at left). This gave him the left vanishing point. He then used the Perspective Grid tool to grab the Horizon Line control point and move the horizon line up to meet the intersection point of the two guide lines.

Since the right plane of the device is essentially rounded with no straight edges to reference for guide lines, McGarry took the foremost straight edge on the top surface (heavy blue line in image) and extended a line back to intersect the horizon line, which gave him the right vanishing point. Since the horizon line was already in position, only one guideline was needed for this side.

2 Creating the side buttons. McGarry began detailed items, like the icons and buttons, outside of the perspective grid. He sampled a light and dark color from the original buttons using the Eyedropper tool and then saved them as swatches. To make it appear that the button was recessed, he created a linear gradient using the sampled swatches and then adjusted the gradient stops so that the lighter color was pushed to a far edge. After rotating the icons 90° clockwise (you can't rotate objects within the perspective grid!), he activated the left plane, marquee-selected the buttons using the Perspective Selection tool, and then positioned them. After resizing the buttons using the bounding box, he completed the bottom ledge on the buttons by drawing a narrow rectangle in perspective mode, then added a gradient; since gradients do not transform when put into the grid, he adjusted the angle in the Gradient panel to match the plane angle. He held Option/Alt as he dragged this ledge to create the other.

3 Creating the LCD screen. Activating the floor plane, McGarry used the Rectangle tool to create a rectangle in perspective and filled it with a Sky gradient (from Swatch Libraries). Outside of the perspective grid, he next created the screen text and icon, rotated them, and then attached them to the perspective plane with the Perspective Selection tool. To create the illusion that the LCD screen was backlit, he layered an offset transparent copy of the LCD above the text. To do this he selected the LCD object and then used perpendicular movement by clicking the Floor Plane control point to open the Floor Plane dialog. Entering a 2-pt value in the Location field, he selected Copy Selected Objects and clicked OK. With this duplicate now selected, he created a new layer and moved the duplicate to this layer by dragging the selection square (in the Layers panel). Using the bounding box, McGarry then brought the two foremost edges of the top LCD screen out to match the edges of the bottom one. Finally, he reduced the opacity of the top LCD in the Control panel, giving depth to the glass while also fading the text and icon.

(Left) Two buttons that needed to be relocated from the top of the device to the side to make room for the new LCD and LED; (right) after being rotated and color matched to the originals on the image

With the left plane activated, McGarry used the Perspective Selection tool to attach the buttons to the perspective grid

(Left) Before adding the light bottom ledge; (right) after adding the ledge by duplicating the first one (by holding Option/Alt while moving it with the Perspective Selection tool)

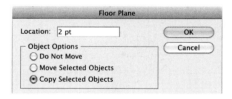

Selecting the LCD with the Perspective Selection tool and then clicking on the Floor Plane control point opens the Floor Plane dialog; moving a copy of the LCD up 2 points

Text and icon are on a separate layer between two LCD layers, with opacity of the top LCD reduced showing the text, icon, and bottom LCD below

Establishing Perspective

Aligning Grids & Planes to an Architectural Sketch

MARIC

Advanced Technique

Overview: *Import a sketch with a visible horizon line; set up and align a perspective grid; construct the rendering using the perspective grid.*

1

Horizon line shown in red

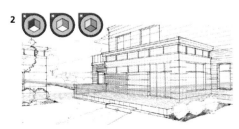

2

Detail of the original drawing on a template layer with a perspective grid placed accurately over the sketch

Creating architectural renderings in Illustrator got a whole lot easier with the addition of the Perspective Grid tool. For traditional illustrators like Pete Maric, who learned how to create architectural renderings by hand, this tool is similar to setting up vanishing points on a drafting board. Upon constructing the perspective grid, all lines and forms drawn snap to the grid for a faster workflow and provide perspective accuracy. The perspective grid can be repositioned for adjacent walls or turned off to create "out-of-perspective" elements.

1 Creating a reference image. Maric relied on a hand-drawn sketch as reference for the illustration, making certain that there is a strong visible horizon line to later help him establish the vanishing points. In Illustrator, using File> Place, he enabled the Template option to import the sketch into a locked template layer.

2 Constructing the perspective grid. Selecting the Perspective Grid tool in the Tools panel activated the default grid. Maric then began to align the grid to the sketch by moving the grid plane control handles until the grid matched the perspective of the sketch. Starting with the left (blue) plane, he click-dragged the control handle to align with the right front of the building. He aligned the right (orange) plane to the receding front wall and the bottom (green) plane to the porch. He then click-dragged each vanishing point control handle, moving them into position until both were aligned to the visible horizon line in his sketch.

3 Creating the architectural elements in perspective.
Leaving the perspective grid active and sketch template layer visible, Maric was able to easily focus on the current active drawing plane using the Plane Switching Widget. Maric primarily used the Rectangle tool to create the front entrance of the building and main architectural elements. He organized drawn elements (façade, windows, mullions) in the Layers panel in accordance with the way they appear in real life. This way, windows would be lower on the layer stack, mullions would be in front of windows, and the façade would be on top of the layer stack. By selecting the right plane in the Plane Switching Widget, he created the receding front wall, windows, and mullions to align with this plane.

4 Moving the perspective grid to create additional architectural geometry and adding detail. Once one portion of the building was complete, he could reposition the perspective grid to create walls in other areas of the illustration. However, before moving the grid to adjacent walls, Maric saved customized grids for each plane of the structure by using View> Perspective Grid> Save Grid as Preset. Then he could realign the perspective grid by clicking and dragging the grid plane control handles so he could use the grid to construct different walls. To create repeating linear details within the walls, Maric needed to draw only one line, he then duplicated it in perspective by holding Option/Alt while dragging it.

3

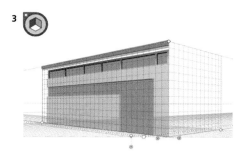

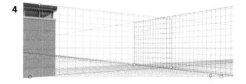

Creating architectural elements in perspective using the Perspective Grid tool and Plane Switching Widget

4

Aligning the perspective grid to adjacent walls and creating detail with the Line tool

DEL VECHIO

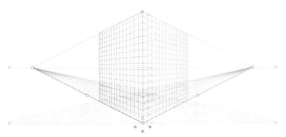

PHOTO BY JOHN MURPHY

Gustavo Del Vechio

Del Vechio placed a photo by John Murphy as a template reference for his Carrot Tree restaurant illustration. He chose the Perspective Grid tool (which enabled the visible grid) and then used the tool to set the horizon line and adjust each plane to match the perspective of the photo template. To create each portion of the building in proper perspective, he first would use the Perspective Selection tool to enable one plane and then use a variety of Illustrator's vector tools to create most of the objects for that plane directly on the perspective grid. He repeated this process for each plane until he had built most of the restaurant on each of the three planes. In a few cases he created objects with the grid disabled and then—enabling the grid—used the Perspective Selection tool to select the objects and dragged and dropped them onto a highlighted plane of the grid. To add variety and texture, he used custom bristle brushes to paint the sky and the foreground fade. To constrain his brush strokes to areas such as the lawn, he selected that object and enabled the Draw Inside mode (see "Draw Behind and Draw Inside" in the *Rethinking Construction* chapter for more about this). Finally, he resized the artboard using the Artboard tool to crop the image to his desired dimensions.

GAUSE

Monika Gause

Monika Gause, an artist and author, created "Cityscape" as a frontpiece illustration for the typography chapter in her encyclopedic hardcover book for German readers, *Adobe Illustrator CC*. Her artistic influences included films about Berlin nightlife from the 1920s, the film *Kapitaal* by a Dutch design studio, and photos of Asian "tiger cities" by night. The neon *Zierfische* (above "TAXI") is a quite famous Berlin sign. She began by creating an initial color sketch in Adobe Ideas and opened it into Illustrator (directly above, left). Moving this sketch off to the side, she then constructed another very loose sketch on her main artboard with the Bristle Brush tool to help her visualize the perspective. Next, using her loose sketch as a guide, Gause set up her two-point perspective grid. Because you can't extract undistorted

elements from the grid once attached, she created the type and graphic elements for her image outside of the grid and off the artboard (on either side of the color sketch). After creating a black rectangle the size of her horizontal artboard she began constructing her cityscape. For each of her elements she activated the desired plane and used the Perspective Selection tool to Option/Alt drag a copy of it into the grid and position it within the composition. With her base image complete, and after confirming that the Lock Station Point toggle was enabled, she shifted the perspective in her grid and moved the horizon line up, and her artwork within the grid automatically updated (directly above, right). (See Gause's files for details on how she created an outlined text version, which she then reattached to the grid.)

Perspective Shifts

Locking Station Point to Auto-Update Art

Advanced Technique

Overview: *Create the illusion of 3D space; attach a variety of objects to a box; use Lock Station Point so that objects in the grid automatically adjust with changes of perspective.*

MCGARRY

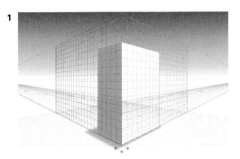

McGarry's basic prototype box placed in a two-point perspective grid, along with cast shadow and background gradient adding depth of field

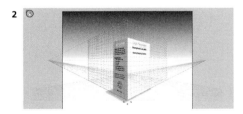

Attaching additional detailed objects to the box, already in the original grid

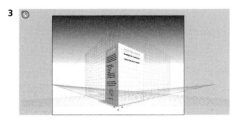

With Lock Station Point enabled, adjusting the grid means that the attached objects will follow along and conform to new perspective positions

Aaron McGarry, an illustrator working for the high-tech industry in California, is often called upon to create prototypes in simulated 3D perspective. Using the Lock Station Point feature he's now able to adjust his perspective grid after his prototypes are in place, and the objects within the grid will update automatically.

1 Creating the basic artwork. McGarry used the default Two-Point perspective grid to begin building his prototype box. Drawing directly on the grid, he used the Rectangle tool to draw both sides of a box; he applied a gradient to the strokes of both filled rectangles to give the box "weight." On a layer below he created the illusion of a cast shadow by drawing another rectangle and then softened the edges with a blur effect (Effect> Blur> Gaussian Blur). To increase the illusion of 3D space, he applied a gradient to another rectangle on the bottom layer.

2 Bringing details into the grid. He created the text and recycle symbol for the box in normal view. He then used the Perspective Selection tool to attach and then resize and position the graphics for each side to the box.

3 Shifting perspective. After his basic prototype was assembled, McGarry needed a more dramatic perspective. Before adjusting anything he enabled Lock Station Point (View> Perspective Grid> Lock Station Point). He was then able to move the Left Vanishing point to the right and lower his Horizon Line. With Lock Station Point enabled, the objects within the grid automatically update and conform to the new perspective positioning.

MCGARRY

Aaron McGarry

McGarry needed to add a photo of the product to the front of his box prototype (see his lesson opposite). However, because non-vector objects like raster photographs can't be added to the perspective grid, he needed to first convert his photo to a vector object using Image Trace. In case he'd need the same traced version again and because attaching art to the grid is permanent, he traced the photo in a separate file. McGarry selected the photo, clicked the Image Trace panel in the Control panel, and began adjusting parameters. For Mode he chose Color, and for the Palette he chose Full Tone. To optimize file size and image quality, he used the Color slider to reduce the number of colors and paths. Saving this file, he then copy-and-pasted the vectorized photo to the file with his perspective grid. To permanently vectorize

this tracing so he could attach it to the grid, he clicked Expand in the Control panel. Using the Perspective Selection tool he then attached the traced image to the grid. Once it was attached, he again used the Perspective Selection tool to resize and position the image. With this working process, McGarry was able to keep the entire product in place within the grid so he could easily update the product angle. As long as Lock Station Point was still enabled (it's saved with the document), he would be able to create alternate perspective angles and have the box automatically adjust and update.

Puppet Warping

Using Puppet Warp for Smooth Arcs

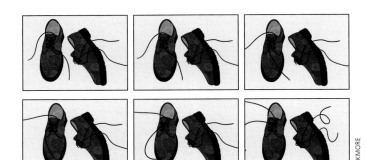

JACKMORE

Overview: *Apply the Puppet Warp tool to brushed paths and to adjust pins; Rotate a pin to flip a path arc; Continue to place and remove pins to achieve desired effects.*

1

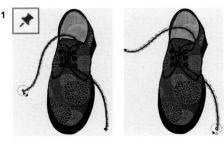

The Puppet Warp tool and selecting the lace objects (left); after clicking the Puppet Warp tool, placing pins at both ends of each shoelace (right)

2

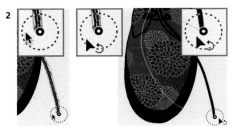

Bottom pin and cursor (left); enlarged Rotate cursor (center); swinging the pin by rotating counterclockwise (right)

3

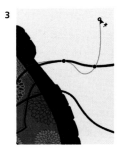 

Swinging up the top point (left); some shoelaces required more pins to properly bend (right)

When Lisa Jackmore began storyboarding her art animation of Dr. Martens shoes, she found it difficult to smoothly reposition the brushed-path shoelaces using selection tools. Switching to the Puppet Warp tool, she was easily able to fluidly reposition the laces.

1 Applying puppet warp to move objects; deleting and adding points as needed. Jackmore found that with four pins, one at each end of each shoelace, she could create most of the shoelace movements. With the Selection or Group Selection tool, select objects you want to adjust; then click the Puppet Warp tool. Click in the mesh to place new pins. To remove a pin, click it (Shift-click to select multiple pins) and Delete/Backspace. (See this chapter's **CC** intro for more on puppet warp controls.)

2 Rotating a pin. To flip the arc of the lowest shoelace, Jackmore selected its endpoint and moved her cursor toward the edge of the pin's circle until the rotate icon appeared and then click-dragged counterclockwise to rotate the pin and form the lace's sweeping arc she needed.

3 Continuing to add, delete, and move pins. Jackmore continued to add, delete, move, and rotate points as needed, being careful not to drop her selection or change tools, as this can remove or relocate pins. She was able to create the smooth tight bend needed for the loop by placing three pins in close proximity near the lace ends. By moving and rotating pins, she was able to create the flowing arc-shaped laces she needed for her animation.

WEINSTEIN

Ari M. Weinstein

Ari Weinstein was tasked to create a mascot in vector format for Three Rivers Manufacturing (TRM)'s precision manufacturing of premium pocket knives. The new vector logo would be printed and machine embroidered for packaging and promotional merchandise. His subject, "Ti the TiCOON," was a silky terrier inspired by the client's dogs, whose photos were used as reference for the project. After fully rendering Ti standing on his forelegs, Weinstein was asked to adjust Ti into a seated posture. Instead of entirely redrawing Ti's lower portion, he decided to see if he could use the powerful Puppet Warp tool to adjust the position of the already-drawn paws. With the Enable Content Aware Defaults preference disabled (see this chapter's **CC** intro for details about how disabling this preference starts you off without any pins), he fully selected all of the objects that formed Ti's legs. Clicking the Puppet Warp tool, the selected objects became grouped into the layer of the group's top object. After experimenting with pin placement (placing, warping, undoing, and placing again), Weinstein eventually found he needed five pins on Ti's leg joints to adjust and foreshorten his legs. To make Ti appear wider and more settled into this seated pose, he selected discrete paths and applied puppet warp to that area of the illustration. When the illustration and logo were complete, Weinstein worked with a custom patch manufacturer to produce the final embroidered patch from his vector artwork.

CHANA MESSER

Chana Messer

After download-
ing an Adobe
Stock photo of
a pair of bal-
let dancers, Chana
Messer masked the female
ballerina in Photoshop and
opened it in Illustrator. Using
a combination of Image Trace
(Properties or Control panel
buttons) and the Pen tool, she
created a stylized vector version
of the ballerina (top left). Messer
found that by carefully using the
Puppet Warp tool to place pins at critical points on joints and costume, she was able
to isolate selected areas for adjustment while
unselected pins kept areas stationary. Careful
selection of pins allowed the ballerina's pose
to be subtly adjusted and elongated. For maximum control of the Puppet Warp tool in articu-
lating figure movement, begin by disabling

Enable Content Aware
Defaults in Preferences>
General. Select your figure;
then use the Puppet Warp
tool to place pins where
you want movement
articulated, as well as at
nearby points to indi-
cate where you want
to anchor the figure.
For instance, with pins
placed on each leg, foot,
and hip joint, you'd also want
to pin the waist and skirt. To lift
the torso, select the torso pins;
to stretch the left leg, select those pins. Changing tools while you're working may results in
your having to re-place pins when you return to
the Puppet Warp tool. Figures above right show
original with pins (top), pins adjusted (middle),
and pins adjusted in black outline on top of
original shown in red outline (bottom).

7

Mastering Complexity

Mastering Complexity

<table>
<tr><td valign="top">

Permanent Pattern panel

To keep the Pattern Options panel in your workspace, dock it where you want it, and then *disable* Auto-Exit Pattern Editing Mode in the panel's pop-out menu. To ensure the panel stays permanently docked, save a custom workspace (see the chapter *Your Creative Workspace*). To start a new pattern, use one of the methods to enter Pattern Editing Mode (see "Entering Pattern Editing Mode (PEM)" at right).

Expanded pattern objects

Illustrator has to expand objects such as symbols and brushes before it can create a pattern swatch. To keep those features "live" for future edits, either design those portions of the artwork on the artboard first, bringing them into PEM, or after PEM warns you about expanding, cancel the save. Still within PEM, select and copy the objects to the clipboard, then save the pattern and exit PEM. Paste the objects to your artboard. They won't be part of the pattern, but you can still edit them as symbols, brushes, etc., rather than only having the option to edit them as discreet objects within the swatch itself.

</td><td valign="top">

The organized whole is more than the sum of its parts. Combining tools and techniques in Illustrator can yield **WOW!** results. In this chapter we'll look at such synergy.

Please keep in mind that this chapter will be quite daunting, if not overwhelming, if you're not comfortable with what has been covered in previous chapters.

In this chapter you'll find a variety of techniques, including making patterns; working with opacity and transparency; creating multiple-object, shaped blends; working with different kinds of masks; and combining features to solve complex problems.

PATTERN MAKING

Prior to CS6, creating a pattern was laboriously manual. You had to draw all of the elements in a pattern tile within a bounding box. With the new Pattern Options panel, you can draw a pattern, adjust the size of the tile, create a repeat offset, and edit the elements, all while previewing multiple repeats with live updating of your edits.

Entering Pattern Editing Mode (PEM)

You can still create a pattern by simply dragging a pattern tile to the Swatches panel, but to explore the power of designing patterns in Illustrator you must enter Pattern Editing Mode (PEM). PEM is a special kind of isolation mode that fades back objects you're not working on and inserts a gray control bar (the PEM isolation bar) between your document and the title bar (if you're not familiar with isolation mode, see "Using Isolation Mode" in the chapter *Your Creative Workspace*). If you have specific artwork that you want to use in your pattern, select it before entering PEM. If you have nothing selected, you'll begin with a blank tile 100 px by 100 px, or the equivalent size measured in whatever units you're currently using. There are two steps to being able to work in PEM: 1) you must open the Pattern Options panel, and 2) you must actually

</td></tr>
</table>

enter PEM. Following are a few ways to simultaneously open the Pattern Options panel and enter PEM:

- **Choose Object> Pattern> Make**—if you make patterns infrequently and you don't mind using menus.
- **Create a custom keyboard shortcut** (Edit menu) to quickly access the command if you make patterns often.
- **Double-click on an existing pattern swatch** in the Swatches panel. This places the swatch on the artboard in PEM and opens the Pattern Options panel.

Creating the pattern

While working in PEM you can always change the size of your pattern tile. To do this, either enter a new Width and Height for it in the Pattern Options panel or use the Pattern Tile tool (located at the top of the Pattern Options panel) to interactively adjust the tile's dimensions.

Within a PEM session, you can create your pattern using virtually any of Illustrator's drawing tools. Use symbols and brushes, add gradients and effects, or modify paths with the Width tool, and Illustrator will happily allow you to make use of all these features *within* a PEM work session. However, because pattern swatches can't retain brushes, symbols, and other complex features, Illustrator will expand these objects when you save your pattern as a swatch, and you won't be able to take advantage of these features if you later try to re-edit the pattern. But unlike with older methods for creating pattern swatches, if you try to save a swatch in PEM, you'll see a warning dialog that Illustrator needs to expand some objects in order to create the pattern swatch.

Upon entering PEM, you'll be able to experiment with different layouts—in addition to a basic Grid layout, there are Brick and Hex layouts, both of which offer row and column offset options. Because editing a pattern with complex effects and appearances can slow down the redraw of your computer screen, you can control the number of tile repeats included in your preview from the Copies drop-down list. Directly below Copies you can choose to dim the repeats by a certain percentage and

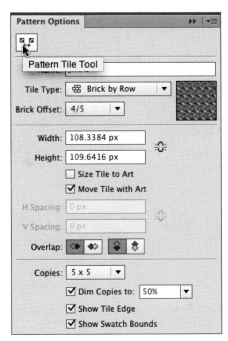

The Pattern Tile tool (not yet selected) for adjusting tiles, Swatch Bounds, and offsets interactively

The PEM isolation bar

Vanishing artwork?

Objects and guides that were on the artboard before you entered PEM remain on the artboard when you exit PEM. However, you can't select guides with objects to take with you into PEM. If you create artwork while in PEM, Illustrator clears the artboard of those objects when you exit. Objects that get saved to the Pattern Swatch itself (because it is partially or wholly within the Swatch Bounds) will be accessible as discrete objects later if you edit the swatch in PEM.

What you *can't* do in PEM

- You *can't* enter isolation mode to edit the individual objects.
- You *can't* use Draw Inside but can use Draw Behind.
- You *can't* duplicate layers, or add new layers or sublayers.

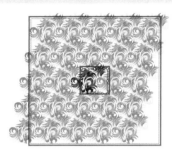

Using Brick or Hex offsets you may see differences between Swatch Bounds (the outside boundary) and Tile Bounds—shown in red for clarity

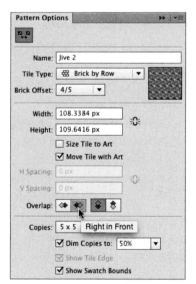

Changing the Overlap from Left In Front (left) to Right In Front (right), altering the appearance of the pattern

hide or show both the tile edge and the bounding box (called Swatch Bounds) of the full repeat. Your Swatch Bounds might be larger than your tile edge when you use an offset to create the pattern.

As you work on your pattern, you still have access to most Illustrator tools so you can edit paths and objects. Add and remove objects from the tile—even place objects straddling the tile edges. You'll be able to judge how your pattern will work while you edit and adjust the layout, offset, and tile repeats. The repeats effectively let you see the pattern as it wraps around to the other side. Objects can overlap, and you can interactively alter how they overlap using the graphical buttons in the Pattern Options panel—right over left, top over bottom, or vice versa.

Leaving Pattern Editing Mode (PEM)

Once you've designed your pattern tile, there are several ways to exit Pattern Editing Mode (to keep the panel in your workspace, see the Tip "Permanent Pattern panel" at the beginning of this introduction):

- Double-click with a Selection tool outside the artwork.
- Click the Done button on the PEM isolation bar (similar to the isolation mode bar).
- Click the Exit Pattern Editing Mode arrow beside the pattern's name on the PEM isolation bar.
- Press the Esc key.
- To simply exit Pattern Editing Mode *without* saving a swatch, click Cancel on the PEM isolation bar.

Creating variations on a pattern

If you intend to enter PEM by double-clicking a current pattern swatch, it's best to get in the habit of editing a duplicate of the original first, and then double-click the *duplicate* to begin editing. To do this, in the Swatches panel drag the pattern you want to duplicate over the New Swatch icon. When you then double-click the duplicate, you'll be editing the duplicate.

While inside Pattern Editing Mode, Illustrator lets you edit only one pattern swatch at a time. However, if as you work you create something that you want to save as a variation, you can save a copy of the pattern swatch in its current state, and then continue to work on your main pattern. To do this, click Save A Copy on the PEM isolation bar and name the copy, which is then placed in your Swatches panel. You'll then be returned to PEM and can resume editing your main pattern.

Editing pattern swatches without PEM

You can still edit your swatches conventionally outside of PEM; simply drag the pattern swatch onto the artboard and make whatever changes you like there. Edit the objects inside the main group, use Recolor Artwork, transform the scale of the pattern swatch, or add, remove, or reshape individual objects after selecting them with the Direct Selection tool. To make this tile back into a pattern, select the swatch with the Selection tool and drag it back into the Swatches panel. To replace a swatch, hold down the Option/Alt key as you drag a new swatch over an existing one.

TRANSPARENCY

Although the artboard may look white, Illustrator treats it as transparent. To visually distinguish the transparent areas from the non-transparent ones, choose View> Show Transparency Grid. Change the size and colors of the transparency grid in the File> Document Setup dialog. You can enable Simulate Colored Paper in the same dialog, if you'll be printing on a colored stock. Click the top swatch next to Grid Size to open the color picker and select a "paper" color. Both Transparency Grid and paper color are non-printing attributes that are only visible in on-screen preview once you click OK to exit the dialog.

The term *transparency* refers to any blending mode other than Normal and to any opacity setting that is less than 100%. Opacity masks and effects such as Feather or Drop Shadow use these settings as well. As a result, when you apply opacity masks or certain effects, you're using Illustrator's transparency features.

VON R. GLITSCHKA

Using the Pattern Tile tool to interactively change the Brick offset by dragging on the diamond widget

Recoloring your patterns?

You've made a lovely pattern, but now you want to create color variations. Rather than just selecting individual objects within a pattern and assigning new colors, enter Recolor Artwork and apply custom color groups, or try to randomly rearrange color assignments! See the "Recolor a Pattern" lesson in the *Color Transitions* chapter for details on how to work with Recolor Artwork while in PEM.

Exporting to Photoshop

When you export Illustrator artwork in Photoshop (PSD) format, you may end up with many sublayers if the artwork uses objects such as brushes, symbols, and blends. To simplify the exported document, target the sublayer that contains the problematic objects, enable the Knockout Group checkbox in the Transparency panel, and then export again.

(Top) The "People's Health Assembly" conference logo by Ellen Papciak-Rose is made up of many different kinds of objects and text; (middle group above) a radial gradient on top of the illustration that will be turned into an opacity mask by selecting the objects and clicking the Make Mask button in the Transparency panel; (directly above) after clicking the Make Mask button, the top object (the radial gradient) made into an opacity mask, creating a spotlight effect, shown with the Transparency and Layers panels

Objects being masked by an opacity mask are indicated by an underscore in the Layers panel

Opacity and blending modes

To reduce opacity, select or target an object, layer, or group in the Layers panel; then choose a blending mode or reduce the Opacity slider in the Transparency panel. You can also reveal Transparency panel controls for a selected object by clicking <u>Opacity</u> in the Appearance or Control panel. As it's called "Opacity" (and not "Transparency"), an object or group is completely opaque when Opacity is 100% and invisible when Opacity is 0%.

Blending modes control how the colors of objects, groups, or layers interact with one another. Blending modes will yield different results in RGB and CMYK. As in Photoshop, the blending modes show no effect when they're over the *transparent* artboard. To see the effect of blending modes, you need to add a color-filled or white-filled element behind your transparent object or group.

OPACITY MASKS

With an opacity mask, you can use the dark and light areas of one object (the mask) to mark transparent areas of other objects. Black areas of the mask will create transparent areas in the artwork it masks; white areas of the mask leave corresponding areas of the artwork opaque and visible; and gray values create a range of transparency. (This works exactly like Photoshop *layer masks*.)

To create an opacity mask, position one object or group you want to use as the mask in front of the artwork you want to mask. Select both the artwork and the masking object. (To mask a layer, first target the layer in the Layers panel.) Finally, click Make Mask in the Transparency panel. The topmost object or group automatically becomes the opacity mask.

You may want to start with an empty mask and draw into it—in effect, painting your objects into visibility. To create an empty mask, start by targeting a single object, group, or layer. Double-click the empty right-hand thumbnail to add an empty opacity mask and enter mask editing mode. Since the default behavior of new opacity masks is clipping (with a black background), you'll need to turn off the "New Opacity Masks Are Clipping" option in the Transparency panel menu. If you don't do this and your targeted artwork disappears when you first create the empty mask, simply disable the Clip checkbox in the Transparency panel.

Now use your drawing and editing tools to create your mask. (For instance, if you create an object filled with a gradient, you'll see your artwork through the dark areas of the gradient.) While the <Opacity Mask> thumbnail is selected, you won't be able to select or edit anything else in your document. You're in another type of isolation mode. To exit this mask-editing mode, you must click the artwork thumbnail on the right in the Transparency panel.

A few hints can help you with opacity masks. First, opacity masks are converted to grayscale, behind the scenes, when a mask is created (even though the opacity mask thumbnail still appears in color). The gray values between white and black simply determine how opaque or transparent the masked object is—light areas of the mask will be more opaque, and dark areas will be more transparent. In addition, if you select Invert Mask, you'll reverse the effect of dark and light values on the opacity—dark areas of the mask will be more opaque, and light areas will be more transparent. To identify which elements have been masked by an opacity mask, look for the dashed underline in the Layers panel.

The link icon in the Transparency panel indicates that the position of the opacity mask will remain associated with the position of the object, group, or layer it is masking. Unlinking allows you to move the artwork without moving the mask. The content of the mask can be selected and edited just like any other object. You can transform or apply a blending mode and/or an opacity percentage to each individual object within the mask.

Precisely targeting and editing transparency

You can apply transparency to so many levels of a document that it can be a challenge to keep track of where you've applied it. For example, you can apply a blending

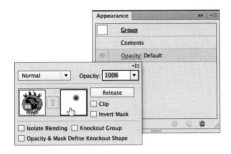

*Display the Transparency panel by clicking the underlined word Opacity for a selected object in the Appearance, Control, or Properties (**CC**) panel,here focused on the opacity mask for illustration on the opposite page*

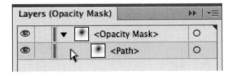

When you click the opacity mask thumbnail in the Transparency panel, the Layers panel displays only the objects within the opacity mask, and is indicated by the Layers panel tab name; try to keep the Layers, Transparency, and Appearance panels open when editing opacity masks

Editing opacity masks

- **Disable/Enable:** Shift-click the mask thumbnail to toggle the mask off (a red **X** will appear over the preview) and on.

- **Mask View:** Option-click/Alt-click the mask thumbnail to toggle the viewing and editing between the masking objects on the artboard, and the mask grayscale values.

- **Release (in the Transparency panel):** This releases the mask.

- **Working on artwork or opacity mask:** Click the appropriate icon to control what you are editing.

- **Link or unlink the opacity mask to artwork:** Click the space between the mask and artwork to toggle the link/unlink icon.

Why can't I draw now?

If you're having trouble seeing what you've just drawn, check the following:

- Are you still in mask-editing mode? When you have an opacity mask selected, the file title and Layers panel tab will display <Opacity Mask>.

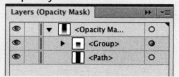

- Are you in Draw Behind or Draw Inside mode? Check the Draw Mode icons at the bottom of the Toolbar to make sure you're in Draw Normal mode.

The art of flattening

In Illustrator, transparency exists only within the program. In order to print or save in another format, Illustrator will "flatten" the objects where they overlap with transparency; in the case of printing, Illustrator flattens only temporarily, but if you save in formats such as EPS, or AI 9 or earlier, your image will be permanently flattened. When flattened, some objects may be split into many separate objects, while others may be rasterized. For more details, search adobe.com for "print production guide transparency" to access "Adobe Applications: A Print Production Guide."

mode to a path, then group it with several other objects and apply an opacity level to that group or to the layer that contains the group. To quickly and precisely locate and edit any transparent object, use the Layers, Appearance (or Properties in **CC**), and Transparency panels together. This is especially useful when you want to identify and edit the transparency of specific objects after using the Flattener Preview panel (covered in the next section) to see how current transparency settings will affect flattened output.

Remember that a gradient-filled circle in the Layers panel indicates that transparency is applied to an object, group, or layer, and an underlined name indicates that an opacity mask is applied. If the Appearance panel is open, it gives you access to the appearance details for the targeted object. Clicking the word Opacity in the Appearance panel (or the Control panel) displays detailed transparency settings for the targeted object. If you targeted an opacity mask, clicking the opacity mask thumbnail in the Transparency panel makes the Layers and Appearance panels provide information about the opacity mask.

BLENDS

Although gradients and mesh allow you to transition from one color to another, blends give you a way to "morph" one object's shape and/or color into another. You can create blends between multiple objects, and even blend gradients, symbols, compound paths such as letters, or even Point type objects. Because blends are *live*, you can edit the key objects' shape, color, size, location, or rotation, and the resulting *in-between* objects will automatically update. You can also distribute a blend along a custom path (see details later in this chapter).

The simplest way to create a blend is to double-click the Blend tool to choose a setting for it and then select the objects you wish to blend and choose Object> Blend> Make (⌘-Option-B/Ctrl-Alt-B). The setting you choose is persistent, so if you don't first double-click the tool, your setting for it becomes the last-used setting. To later adjust settings on an existing blend: select the blend then double-click the Blend tool (or choose Objects> Blend> Blend Options).

Another way to create blends between individual paths is to *point map* using the Blend tool. In the past, the Blend tool was used to achieve smooth transitions between blended objects. Now that it's been modified, however, it's probably best to use it for special morphing or twirling effects. To use the *point map* technique, begin by clicking an anchor point of one object, and then on an anchor point of another object. Continue clicking anchor points of any object you want to include in the blend. You can also click anywhere on the path of an object to achieve random blending effects.

To modify a key object before or after making a blend, Direct-Select the key object first and then use any editing tool (including the Pencil, Smooth, and Path Eraser tools) to make your changes.

Blend Options

To specify options as you blend, use the Blend tool (see the "point map" directions in the previous section) and press the Option/Alt key as you click the second point. In Blend Options you can change settings before making the blend. To adjust options on a completed blend, select it and double-click the Blend tool (or choose Object> Blend> Blend Options). Opening Blend Options without a blend selected sets the defaults for creating blends *in this work session—* these options reset each time you restart the program:

- **Specified Steps** specifies the number of steps between each pair of key objects (the limit is 1,000). Using fewer steps results in clearly distinguishable objects; a larger number of steps results in an almost airbrushed effect.
- **Specified Distance** places a specified distance between the objects of the blend.
- **Smooth Color** automatically calculates the ideal number of steps between key objects in a blend in order to achieve the smoothest color transition. If objects are the same color, or are gradients or patterns, this option equally distributes the objects within the blend, based on their size.

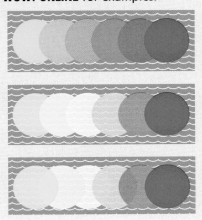

Group-Select a key object and Option-drag/Alt-drag to insert a new key object (the blend will reflow). You can also insert new objects by double-clicking it to enter isolation mode or by dragging them into the blend in the Layers panel.

Blend tool (W)

AARON McGARRY

*Aaron McGarry created this image of ripening tomatoes on a vine image using a variety of blends: the smooth color option for the vine, groups of objects blended into each other with Specified Steps, and a custom **S** curve "spine" (see Aaron McGarry's explanation on **WOW! ONLINE**)*

What can you do with blends?

Besides editing objects you can:

- Reverse the direction of a blend, with Object> Blend> Reverse Front to Back. Or reverse the order of objects on a spine by choosing Object> Blend> Reverse Spine.
- Release blends (Object> Blend> Release) to remove blends, leaving key objects and spines. *Hint:* Select> Select All releases multiple blends simultaneously.
- Choose Object> Blend> Expand to turn a blend into a group of separate, editable objects.

- **Orientation** determines how the individual blend objects rotate as they follow the path's curves. **Align to Page** (the default, first icon) prevents objects from rotating as they're distributed along the path's curve (objects stay "upright" as they blend along the curve). **Align to Path** allows blend objects to rotate as they follow along the path.

Blends along a path

There are two ways to make blends follow a curved path. The first way is to use the Direct Selection tool to select the *spine* of a blend (the path automatically created by the blend) and then use the Add/Delete Anchor Point tools, or any of the following tools, to curve or edit the path: the Direct Selection, Lasso, Convert Anchor Point, Pencil, Smooth, or even Path Eraser tool. As you edit the spine of the blend, Illustrator automatically redraws the blend objects to align to the edited spine.

In a second way, you can also replace the spine with a customized path. Select both the customized path and the blend, and choose Object> Blend> Replace Spine. This command moves the blend to its new spine.

You can also blend between pairs of grouped objects. If you're not getting the results you expect, try creating your first set of objects and grouping them (⌘-G/Ctrl-G). Now copy and paste a duplicate set (or Option/Alt and drag to create a copy of your group). Select the two sets of grouped objects and blend by choosing Specified Steps as the blend option. Once the objects are blended, you can rotate and scale them and use the Direct Selection tool to edit the objects or the spine. (To experiment with a pair of grouped blends in this way, find the figures you see opposite on **WOW! ONLINE** as "AaronMcGarry-blends.ai.")

CLIPPING MASKS

All of the objects involved in a mask are organized in one of two ways depending on how you choose to make your mask. One method collects all selected objects into a group. The other method allows you to keep your layer structure, by placing layers within a master "container" layer (see the Layers panel illustrations, next page). With any kind of clipping mask, the topmost object of that group is the *clipping path;* this clips (hides) portions of the other objects in the group that extend beyond the clipping mask boundaries, leaving only the parts within these boundaries visible. Regardless of the attributes assigned to this top object, once you create the mask, it becomes an unfilled and unstroked clipping path (but keep reading to see how you can apply a stroke and fill to the new clipping path!). In the Layers panel, an active clipping mask will appear as an underlined <u><Clipping Path></u> and will remain underlined even if you rename it.

To make a clipping mask from an object, you must first create that object. Only a single path can be used as a clipping mask, which means that complex shapes or multiple paths must be combined into a single "compound path" before being used as a mask (using Object> Compound Path> Make). Make sure your path or compound path is above the objects to be clipped and then create the clipping mask using one of two options—use either the Make/ Release Clipping Mask icon on the Layers panel, or the Object> Clipping Mask> Make command. Each has its inherent advantages and disadvantages. The Object menu command gathers all the objects into a new group as it masks, allowing you to have multiple masked objects within a layer. It also gives you the ability to freely move masked objects within a layer structure without breaking the mask. However, if you have a carefully planned layer structure, it will be lost when everything is grouped. In contrast, the Layers panel command maintains your layer structure as it masks, but you can't have separately masked objects within a layer without building sublayers or grouping them first. This makes it difficult to move masked objects as a unit.

After you've created a clipping mask, you can edit the masking object, and the objects within the mask, by selecting it using any selection tools, such as the Lasso or Direct Selection tools, and then editing it with your typical path-editing tools, including live effects. When

Draw Inside (fast masks)

See the *Rethinking Construction* chapter for details on the super quick way to make a clipping mask: using the Draw Inside mode.

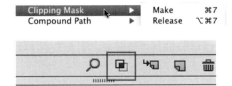

Choose *Clipping Mask> Make from the Object menu (top), or use the Make/Release Clipping Mask icon on the Layers panel (bottom)*

Pasting objects into a mask

To paste cut or copied objects into a clipping mask, make sure Paste Remembers Layers is off (in the Layers panel menu), then select an object within the mask and use Paste in Front or Back to place the copied object within the mask. You can also create or paste objects while in isolation mode.

Clipping Mask icon disabled

In the Layers panel, you must select the *container* (layer, sublayer, or group) that holds your intended clipping object before you can apply a clipping mask. Also, in order for the icon in the Layers panel to be enabled, the top item inside the highlighted container must be something that can be turned into a clipping path.

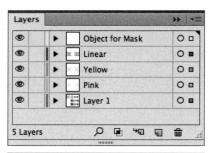

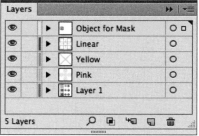

Choosing Object> Clipping Mask> Make puts all of the masked objects into a group with the clipping path at the top of the group

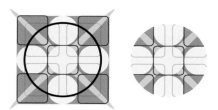

Before masking (left), the black-stroked circle is positioned as the topmost object in the stacking order, so it will become the clipping path when the clipping mask is created (right)

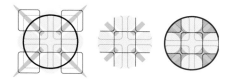

You can add a stroke and fill to a mask. The middle figure shows an unstroked mask; the right figure shows a dark blue stroke and a light blue fill added to the clipping mask

Selecting clipping masks

To select all of your currently unlocked clipping masks at once, choose Select> Object> Clipping Masks.

working with masks created using the Object menu, clipped objects are now hidden when clipped by a mask; when the mask contents aren't selected, you won't accidentally select clipped objects outside of the masked path.

To move your clipped object (path and contents) simply select it with the Selection tool and move it. If you wish to select, move, or edit the clipping path or the contents independently, then you have a few options. If neither is selected, you can simply click the clipping path or contents with the Direct Selection or Group Selection tool to edit or move that path or selection. If any portion of the mask or contents is already selected, you can click the Edit Clipping Path or Edit Contents buttons in the Control panel to focus on which portion will be selected and can be edited.

You also can edit your clipping group in isolation mode. To isolate the entire clipping <Group>, double-click any portion of it with the Selection tool; this dims all other objects on your artboard. If you prefer, enter isolation mode via the Layers panel. Highlight the <Clipping Path> or any of the paths within the <Group> and choose Enter Isolation Mode from the Layers panel pop-up menu. You can now use the Edit Clipping Path or Edit Contents buttons or use the Direct Selection and Group Selection tools.

Once in isolation mode you can freely edit or move the paths without affecting any other objects. If you are in isolation mode with one of the objects within the mask, you can even add additional objects within that grouping. To exit, double-click on the artboard (outside of the clipping group), press the Esc key, click on the gray isolation bar, or choose Exit Isolation Mode from the Layers panel pop-up menu.

Yet another way that you can determine which portion of your clipping group you wish to edit is by choosing Object> Clipping Mask> Edit Mask (or Object> Clipping Mask> Edit Content).

Once you have created a clipping group and mask, you can then add a stroke (it will appear as if it's in front of all masked objects) and/or a fill (it appears as if it's behind all masked objects). In addition, once the mask has been made, in the Layers panel you can even move the clipping path lower in the stacking order of the group or container (where it may no longer be the top path in the layer order) and still keep its masking effect.

Masking technique #1: The Object command

The simplest way to create masks for objects is using the Object menu command (⌘-7/Ctrl-7). Use this method when you want to confine the clipping mask to a specific object or group of objects that need to be easily duplicated or relocated or when you have more than one clipping mask per layer. Since this method modifies your layer structure, don't use it if you need to maintain objects on specific layers.

As before, start by creating an object or compound object that will become your clipping mask. Make sure that it's the topmost object and then select it and *all* the objects you want to be masked (this topmost object will become the mask). Now, choose Object> Clipping Mask> Make. When you use this method, all the objects, including the new clipping path, will move to the layer that contains your topmost object and will be collected into a new <Group>. This will restrict the masking effect to only those objects within the group; you can easily use the Selection tool to select the entire clipping group. If you expand the <Group> in the Layers panel (by clicking the expansion triangle), you'll be able to move objects into or out of the clipping group or move objects up or down within the group to change the stacking order. (Don't miss the Tip "Magical clipping path" at right.)

Masking technique #2: The Layers panel method

To mask unwanted areas of art within a *container* (meaning any group, sublayer, or layer), first create an object to use as your mask—make sure it's the topmost object in your container. Next, highlight that object's *container* and click the Make/Release Clipping Mask icon on the

At left the clipping mask (outlined in blue) above the floral illustration was created as 7 separate objects (6 petals and 1 center circle) and then united into a single compound path (using Object> Compound Path); at right after positioning this compound path on top of other objects, then using it as a clipping mask

Mask error message

If you get the message "Selection cannot contain objects within different groups unless the entire group is selected," cut or copy your selected objects (to remove them from the group) and then Paste in Front. Now you can apply Object> Clipping Mask> Make.

In the Control panel: when a placed image is selected, the Mask button (left) appears; when an object using a mask is selected, the Edit Clipping Path and Edit Contents buttons (left and right respectively in the right-hand figure)

Figuring out if it's a mask

- <Clipping Path> in the Layers panel will be underlined if it's a mask (even if you've renamed it), and the background color for the icon will be gray.
- The phrase "Clip Group" in your Control panel means your selection contains a clipping mask.
- An *opacity mask* appears in the Layers panel as < Path > with a dotted underline, but as <Opacity Mask> if it's active in the Transparency panel.
- Select> Object> Clipping Masks to help you find masks within a file (but not inside linked files).

Collect in New Layer

To collect selected layers into one "master layer," Shift-click or ⌘-click/Ctrl-click multiple layers and choose Collect in New Layer from the Layers menu.

Layers panel. The result: The topmost object, *within* the highlighted container, becomes the clipping path, and all elements within that container extending beyond the clipping path are hidden (for details on how to use complex objects as a mask, see the section "Using type, compound paths, or shapes as a mask" below).

Once you've created a clipping mask, you can move objects up or down within the container (layer, sublayer, or group) to change the stacking order. But if you move items outside of the clipping mask container, they'll no longer be masked. Moving the clipping path itself outside of its container releases the mask completely.

Mask button

If you use File> Place to place an image and the placed image is selected, you can instantly create a clipping path for the image by clicking the Mask button in the Control panel (or Properties in **CC**). However, masking is not immediately apparent as the clipping path has the same dimensions as the placed image's bounding box. Make sure the Edit Clipping Path button is enabled, then adjust the clipping path mask that's "cropping" your image.

Using type, compound paths, or shapes as a mask

You can use editable type as a mask to give the appearance that the type is filled with any image or group of objects. Select the type and the image or objects with which you want to fill the text. Make sure the type is on top, then choose Object> Clipping Mask> Make.

To use separate type characters as a single clipping mask, you have to first make them into a compound shape or compound path. You can make a compound shape from either outlined or live text. You can make a compound path only from outlined text (not live text). Once you've made a compound path or shape out of separate type elements, you can use it as a mask. Look for Chana Messer's typographic poster gallery at the end of the *Designing Type & Layout* chapter for an example of using Draw Inside mode to mask an image with type.

COMBINING COMPLEXITY WITH ILLUSTRATOR CC

With every new version of Illustrator, we all find our-selves counting how many brand-new, high-impact features the version includes and seldom pay much attention to those less dramatic features that will help us be more productive. With added complexity in our artwork, however, every enhancement saves us time and frustration. But some of the smaller new features might actually be game-changers in the way we interact with Illustrator, from the most basic drawing functions to the most complex artwork and layouts we can create.

The galleries in the **CC** section at the end of this chapter further explore integrating Photoshop with the creation of raster brushes, enlist Live Rectangles as clipping masks, use Live Corners for creating complex repeating patterns, and of course, provide you with amazing inspiration. If you're using CC, try using the CS6-compatible lessons and galleries as a fresh start-ing point for exploring CC features. Imagine creating the following examples with the latest Illustrator CC enhancements:

- **Stephen Klema's Guides for Arcs lesson,** in *Designing Type & Layout*—placing guides precisely by clicking the ruler instead of entering numeric positioning data.
- **Raymond Larrett's Pattern Brushes lesson,** in *Expressive Strokes*—creating the shapes for the robots using raster brushes and possibly auto-generated corners.
- **Dedree Drees' "The Dory,"** in *Reshaping Dimensions*—drawing undulating seagrass with the Pencil tool's new Fidelity smoothing algorithm.
- **Gustavo del Vechio's "Carrot Tree Restaurant,"** in *Reshaping Dimensions*—altering the perspective after creating the artwork on a Two Point Perspective Grid.
- **Chris Nielsen's motorcycles** in this chapter—creating photographic hyperrealism with the Pen tool's drawing enhancements.

Whether illustrating or designing, Illustrator CC's enhancements help remove complexity, freeing you to concentrate more than ever on being creative.

A Live Rectangle bonus

When you add additional strokes or fills to a Live Rect-angle via the Appearance panel, even if you add effects, all will maintain the same corner radii as the origi-nal rectangle when the object is edited using either widgets or the Transform panel. —*Gary Ferster*

Tracing with strokes

To trace line art (like that found in a children's coloring book), using the "centerline" model (so you have a single path defining a stroke, and not paths on either side of a stroke), make sure that your art is easily translated by stroked (not filled) paths, and choose Line Art as a preset. This can be great for tracing logos or hand lettering.

Artboards can mask artwork

Illustrator artboards can them-selves act as cropping masks for the artwork that extends beyond the artboard. Create as many artboards as you wish to define detail areas (overlapping is fine). On placing the .ai file into InDe-sign or Photoshop, enable "Show Import Options," choose your de-sired artboard (Page), and in Op-tions choose Crop To> Media.

Pattern Making
Navigating the Pattern Options Panel

Advanced Technique

Overview: *Create a pattern or edit an existing one; work in Pattern Editing Mode with the Pattern Options panel to adjust repeats, varying spacing, offset, and overlap; duplicate patterns and experiment with offsets and settings to create and save pattern variations to the Swatches panel.*

Using the Pattern Tile tool (top-left corner of Pattern Options) and experimenting with settings

Using the Pattern Tile tool to change the gap between repeats with a Grid layout

To create one "Garden Walk" tile, Von Glitschka used primarily the Polygon and Pen tools to create individual elements, expanded white strokes with Pathfinder filters, and filled objects with global colors. Bringing the grouped tile into Pattern Options, he chose Hex by Row with gaps set to half of the white "stroke" width; when gaps double in the pattern repeat, they equal the tile "stroke" width. Experiment with transforming your own graphic objects into patterns by exploring all Pattern Option parameters and by adjusting settings both numerically and manually.

1 **Creating the first pattern repeat.** To follow along using Glitchka's "Garden Walk" pattern, first protect the original by copying it (drag the pattern in the Swatches panel to the New Swatch icon) and then double-click the copy to automatically open the Pattern Options panel and enter Pattern Editing Mode (PEM). To use your own artwork instead, select it and choose Object> Pattern> Make. In PEM, changes to settings immediately update, so when you adjust settings for Copies, be aware that with complex artwork, increased repeats can slow down screen redraw. When you open an existing pattern in PEM, PEM loads the Tile Type saved with the pattern. If you create a new pattern, then the default Tile Type will be Grid. You control the space between repeats by adjusting the size of the tile's bounding box, either with Size Tile to Art enabled and numeric input for H and V Spacing or interactively by using the Pattern Tile tool. With the Pattern Tile tool

selected, use the square anchors to enlarge or reduce the gap between repeats. To create an overlap, make the tile bounding box smaller and choose the desired Overlap features. As your pattern progresses, you might want to evaluate it by zooming out, temporarily disabling both Dim Copies and Show Tile Edge and increasing the repeats. Undo/Redo is available while in PEM and can even back you out of PEM. At any time you can save the current version of the pattern as a swatch, but stay in PEM to create more variations by clicking Save a Copy and naming it. Now you can continue editing and experimenting with the pattern. To save this version as the final one and exit PEM, click Done. If you click Cancel, no changes are saved to your original pattern in the Swatches panel.

2 Experimenting with pattern offsets. To experiment with pattern offsets, you can stay in PEM or start over with a new copy. Make sure that both Show Tile Edge and Show Swatch Bounds are enabled. Any artwork that is within, overlaps, or touches the Swatch Bounds will be included in the pattern. To make your tile resize to the exact size of your art, enable Size Tile to Art (if it's enabled, you may have to disable and then re-enable it).

Glitschka offset "Garden Walk" using the Hex by Row tile type, which naturally fits this design with little manipulation, but you can also use Brick by Row with a Brick Offset of ½ to tuck the repeats close together. Brick Offset controls the position of each repeat relative to the others. With the Pattern Tile tool active, you can adjust the Brick Offset in fixed intervals by dragging the diamond widget on the Tile Edge to the right or left. Switch to Brick by Row as your Tile Type (shown at right), grab a corner anchor, and drag straight down until it "snaps." Your pattern should match the Hex by Row results.

When dragging a corner with the Pattern Tile tool, hold Option/Alt to symmetrically adjust spacing on opposite sides. Hold Shift to constrain spacing to a square. Disable the tool to scale your art within the tile-spacing box or to edit your art and objects with normal vector tools.

Viewing multiple repeats with both Dim Copies and Show Tile Edge disabled

The Pattern isolation bar showing the pattern name, controls for saving the current state to the Swatches panel, and ways to exit PEM

Using Hex by Row to start an offset repeat of the pattern, adjusted with the Pattern Tile tool to make the repeats fit with a slender gap between them

Resizing the Tile Edge by dragging a corner down until it "snaps" (before and after figures above); you can also slide the diamond widgets to change the pattern repeat offset at fixed intervals from $^1/_4$ up to $^4/_5$ the distance of a full repeat

Layered Patterns

Building Depth and Complexity in PEM

Advanced Technique

Overview: *Design basic elements for your pattern and enter PEM; establish a height and width for your tile; choose a Tile Type; position the pattern elements and experiment with Swatch Bounds; vary the level of detail to enhance depth.*

1

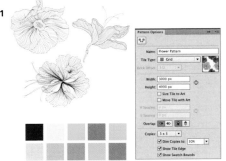

Planning ahead by drawing artwork, creating a color group, and setting the size of the pattern tile

Pattern elements shown in full color, with repeats dimmed to 50%, and the Swatch Bounds/Tile Edge outlined in red for clarity

Sabine Reinhart specializes in creating richly complex, layered patterns, constructed so all the elements involved enhance the illusion of depth. Illustrator's Pattern Editing Mode (PEM) makes it easier than ever to experiment with the placement of elements as Reinhart gradually builds up her pattern. Although her patterns are often large enough to slow most computers down to a crawl, the organic look she achieves rewards her patience.

1 Starting the pattern tile with its first elements. Reinhart had drawn her main elements, created a color group, and determined the size and tile type (Grid in this case) before she began her pattern. Selecting her artwork, she entered Pattern Editing Mode (Object> Pattern> Make) and manually entered the Width and Height in the Patterns panel. Using the Move tool, she adjusted the position of each flower so that it overlapped the Swatch Bounds (which in the Grid tile type is the same as the Tile size, and shown at left outlined in red for clarity), leaving room for adding subordinate artwork both above and below the first objects.

2 Designing patterns using Swatch Bounds. As long as you are within PEM, you can freely use the entire canvas to design new elements and plan your pattern. Because the Swatch Bounds define the parameters of the actual pattern, however, your pattern will only be made up of any objects that are at least partially touching the edge or the interior of the Swatch bounds. Objects contained by the Swatch Bounds, overlapping it, or touching an edge somewhere will automatically appear in the opposite quadrants of the pattern repeat. For instance, when Reinhart placed a dark green flower outside—but still touching—the Swatch bounds, it was included in the pattern, and as long as she set Copies to more than 1 x 1, she could preview where the object was repeated within the pattern.

Be aware that if you're using Brick or Hex layout (instead of Grid), changing the offset or offset type (by row or column) can cause the Swatch Bounds to grow or shrink in size. Artwork that was previously outside Swatch Bounds might now fall within the pattern, and vice versa. In addition, when you create art in PEM, any objects that aren't included in the pattern swatch will be deleted; if you wish to keep any objects that are not included in the pattern, copy the objects to the clipboard before exiting PEM, and paste them into a new file.

3 Adding new artwork. After getting the first flowers placed, Reinhart started adding more flowers, duplicating, transforming, and coloring them while inside PEM. She emphasized depth by overlapping some flowers in front and in back of others, by scaling, and by altering the artwork to show less detail as she moved it further to the back of the stack. She intermingled a few butterflies and, at the very bottom, added a light-colored rectangle with no stroke to conceal any gaps in the pattern and give it an airy, organic appearance. She named the pattern in the Patterns panel and clicked Done to save her pattern to the Swatches panel. Later, she would use Recolor Artwork to create variations (see her lesson in the *Color Transitions* chapter for details about how she did this).

2

Adding layers both above and below the initial artwork; elements transformed and recolored

3

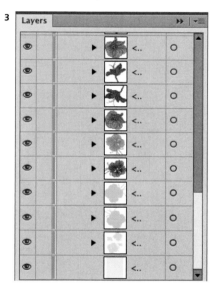

The bottom of the stack of layers showing how Reinhart created depth by incorporating more detail in upper layers, with diminishing detail as she moved further to the back of the stack

The final pattern tile with Swatch Bounds visible

Roping in Paths

Using Masks and Pathfinders for Shapes

Advanced Technique

Overview: *Create and organize layers, place a scanned sketch, and draw shapes; draw paths for the rope, outline their strokes, feather their fills, and draw masks; make a compound path, duplicate it, and reshape it.*

1

Hamann's scan of the pencil sketch he made from the photographs he took of himself

When *Angels on Earth* magazine needed an online illustration featuring a heroic angel saving a woman from drowning, illustrator Brad Hamann responded with layering, masks, and pathfinder tools in "Angel in the Rapids."

1 Scanning a sketch, organizing layers, and drawing shapes. Hamann began by drawing and scanning a pencil sketch and placing it in Illustrator on a template layer.

Hamann's design called for layering so that artwork like the tubes and rope appeared in front of or behind other artwork. He created layers in the Layers panel based on visual hierarchy. To outline the angel against the rest of the image, Hamann created a blue outline of the angel and then a white one. To do this he copied the head and body objects, then used Paste in Back, and then applied Pathfinder> Unite. Giving this new shape a blue stroke and fill, he copied it, used Paste in Back, and then gave this duplicate outline a white fill and a wider white stroke.

2 Making and masking the rope. Hamann created the rope in sections, drawing paths between objects for the

Hamann organizing his Layers panel

tubes and hands. He smoothed the curvature of the ropes by adjusting direction lines with the Direct Selection tool. To give the selected rope paths a dark blue edge with a light fill, he first changed the paths to a 4-pt, dark blue stroke. Next Hamann chose Object> Path> Outline Stroke and changed the stroke to 1 pt and the fill to orange. Finally, to add a subtle highlight to the rope, Hamann chose Effect> Stylize> Inner Glow and in the dialog entered 24 for Opacity and 0.03 inches for Blur and clicked OK.

Where each rope section was cut off by another object, Hamann masked the rope by the edge of the other objects' strokes. He decided that drawing the masks by hand would be precise enough for the resolution of a web graphic. To mask the rope where it joined the fist, for example, Hamann drew a shape with the Pen tool that loosely surrounded the rope except for where the rope was cut off by the fist. For that area, he drew the path of the masking shape by hand along the edge of the fist's blue stroke. Finally, he selected the masking shape and the rope and chose Object> Clipping Mask> Make.

3 Drawing the tube. For the tube draped over the angel's left arm, Hamann drew a yellow-filled path for the tube's outer edge and another path for the tube's center hole. He selected both objects and chose Object> Compound Path> Make. To form shadows, he copied the compound path and used Paste in Front and then filled this duplicate with a darker yellow. With the duplicate still selected, Hamann used the Scissors tool to make two cuts on the right side of the outer edge and then selected and deleted the outer left edge of the compound path. Next, he used the Pen tool to redraw the shadow path between the two open points. When he completed the path, he filled it with a darker yellow and then chose Effect> Stylize> Feather, changed the feather radius to 0.05, and clicked OK. Hamann finished by drawing highlight shapes and pasting another duplicate of the tube in front, changing its fill to None and stroke to dark blue.

2

On the left, the paths for two sections of rope; on the right, the paths after choosing Object> Path> Outline Stroke, filling them with orange, and then applying Inner Glow to the fills

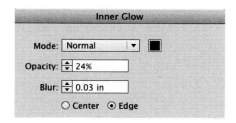

The mask drawn as a green-stroked path

The Inner Glow dialog

3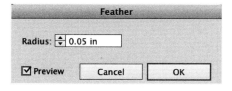

On the left, the drawn compound path; on the right, the compound path filled with yellow

On the left, a copy of the compound path pasted in front of the yellow tube; in the middle, the compound path cut on the right side; on the right, the finished shape filled with dark yellow

The Feather dialog

Adding Highlights

Using Transparency to Create Highlights

Advanced Technique

Overview: *Create highlights in objects for the interior of the cell using the Blend tool; stack them and lower opacity; create highlights with gradients for other objects and reduce opacity; create a bright lens flare.*

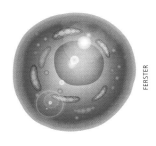

FERSTER

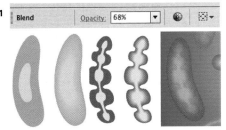

After creating an object by blending a light object with a darker, same-shaped object to represent a highlight, transparency further blends the "lit" object (mitochondrion) into its surroundings

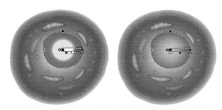

Adjusting the radial gradient adjusts the size and edge of the highlight, while transparency settings adjust the final blend into another object

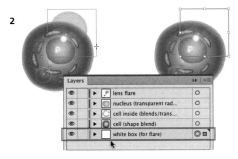

The Lens Flare tool needs a non-transparent background to reach maximum brightness

Adding transparency to blended or gradient-filled objects, or, conversely, eliminating transparency beneath a lens flare, gives you a great deal of versatility when constructing believable highlights.

1 Using multiple techniques for blending colors in order to simulate natural highlighting. When Gary Ferster wanted to illustrate a living cell, he chose various methods for constructing blended highlights. For the mitochondrion (pinkish objects), he used the Blend tool to create two initial shapes, one very light, and one the "local" color. When blended smoothly, this method created soft highlights. He then stacked one blended object over the other and reduced the opacity in each, in order to make them appear to be part of the cell. For the small bubbles (lysosomes) and nucleus in the cell, however, Ferster used simple radial gradients with a very light center gradating to the local color of the object. By adjusting the gradient stops, he could make highlights bigger or smaller, with sharper or more feathered edges, and then adjust opacity to blend these objects into the cell.

2 Using the Lens Flare tool for maximum highlighting. Nothing suggests a powerful light source quite like a lens flare, but Ferster had observed that using the Lens Flare tool over a transparent background creates a dulled, gray flare. A simple solution was to draw a solid white rectangle, at least as big as the flare, behind all the objects. The part of the lens flare that extended beyond the cell became white, disappearing into the background entirely.

GUSMAN JOLY

Annie Gusman Joly

Transparency can be created with Blending Modes that interact with the layers beneath, forming new colors based on the type of Blending Mode used. Artist Annie Gusman Joly uses them here to create a complex pattern of shadows. In this tropical forest, light filters through the leaves and flowers to fall on the ground beneath the white bird's feet. To create the random and overlapping patterns, Joly first fills a large object on one layer with a solid blue. After drawing the path for the shadows on the

layer above, she fills it with blue and sets Blending Mode to Multiply. If the shadow color is too dark, she reduces the layer Opacity to increase the shadow layer's transparency. She uses the same technique for the shadow beneath her three-toed sloth.

Moonlighting

Using Transparency for Glows & Highlights

Advanced Technique

Overview: *Create a Radial gradient with transparency for a circular object; use the Blend tool with a duplicate object to create a circular or oval blend with transparency; create a glow or highlight for a non-circular object.*

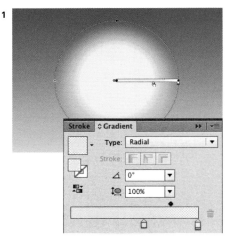

Using the Gradient tool with either the Gradient Annotator (top) or Gradient panel (bottom) to create a gradient with transparency

Drag the color stop for the inner object toward the transparent stop to make the object larger; drag the diamond to alter the size of the glow

Because the glowing moon is circular in Annie Gusman Joly's "Solo-Flight" illustration about growing up an identical twin, it could be created by using either a radial gradient or a shaped blend. The key to making a gradient or blend work against any background is to use transparency for the edge of the object that touches the background.

1 **Creating a glow from a Radial gradient.** With the object selected, click it once with the Gradient tool to fill with the last-used or default gradient, and, if necessary, change the type in the Gradient panel to Radial. Either in the Gradient panel or with the aid of the Gradient Annotator, double-click each color stop and choose the same color for them. Reduce the opacity for the stop that represents the outer edge to 0%; drag the opposite color stop inward to make the solid part of the object bigger and more solid, and adjust the Gradient slider between them (the diamond shape on the top of the gradient bar) to create a larger or smaller amount of feather (or "glow").

2 Creating a glow for a circular object from an object blend. With a pale yellow Fill color, choose a stroke of None, and draw a circle (Shift-drag with the Ellipse tool). With Smart Guides on (View menu), move your cursor over the circle until you see the word "center," hold down Option/Alt, and Shift-drag out a new, smaller circle. Set the Opacity of the larger circle to 0%. Select both circles and choose Object> Blend> Make (⌘-Option-B/Ctrl-Alt-B); then double-click the Blend tool in the toolbox to adjust the steps. For this example, somewhere between 20 and 30 steps makes a very glowing moon.

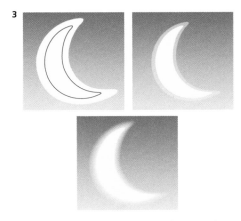

Creating a blend between two circles with one set to 0% Opacity

3 Shaping a glow with a blend made from non-circular objects. When you don't have a circle or oval path, only a blend can "shape" the glow evenly around the object. So that the glowing object can be placed over any background, we'll continue to create the glow with transparency. Create your first object—here, a crescent moon filled with pale yellow and no stroke. Many asymmetrical shapes don't scale easily relative to the original's boundaries, so with your object selected, choose Object> Path> Offset Path. Enable Preview and use a negative number for a smaller object. Select the larger object and, in the Transparency panel, set Opacity to 0%. Now select both paths and choose Object> Blend> Make. If you haven't already created a blend with the Specified Steps or Specified Distance Spacing option in your current working session, Illustrator might use Smooth Color. Smooth Color doesn't create a glow but rings the inner crescent moon with a lighter color. To get the glow, double-click the Blend tool to open the dialog and choose Specified Steps for the Spacing option. Around 25 steps should create a decent glow. If necessary, adjust the offset, miter, and path edges until the blend is smooth and glowing.

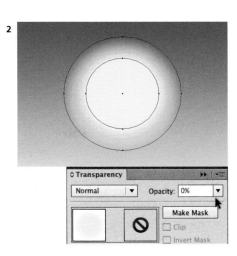

Creating the second object with Offset Path (top left) and using Object> Blend> Make; the default Smooth Color doesn't blend (top right), but switching to Specified Steps creates the glow

This shaped-blend method can also be used for making any shape or size of highlight for any object. By creating the highlight as a separate object, you gain the advantage of being able to change the object's color later without having to reconstruct the object and the blend.

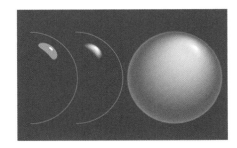

Creating a highlight using a shaped blend with one opaque and one transparent object

"CHINGON"

NIELSEN

Chris Nielsen

When Chris Nielsen came across this one-of-a-kind, custom chopper by Matt Hotch, he knew he had to illustrate it with his signature PhotoRealist technique. He knew his basic 8 MP digital point-and-shoot camera would capture enough detail, but with many other custom bikes parked in the same shop, getting the reference shot at all was a major undertaking. Once he brought it into Illustrator, he used the same methods described on the opposite page, relying on the Pen tool to draw progressively smaller details, and the Path-finder panel with the Divide command to create the areas representing every nuance of the bike and its reflections. He worked on a section at a time, starting with less detailed areas, and bringing each to near completion before moving to the next area. Nielsen would often zoom to a comfortable 300% or so to work on fine details, but rarely more than that. In this manner, he always managed to keep an eye on the way the area he was working on was affecting the image as a whole. Color started with the photo itself, but Nielsen didn't rely upon the photo to produce the most accurate and pleasing tones. He used his artist's eye to adjust colors until the right hues and values were represented. Since Nielsen's work is so photorealistic, he purposely leaves sections in an "outline view" appearance so the viewer will realize that it is still a drawing they're looking at and *not* a photograph. When completed, Nielsen's "Chingon" brought to life a rare, custom motorcycle for everyone to enjoy.

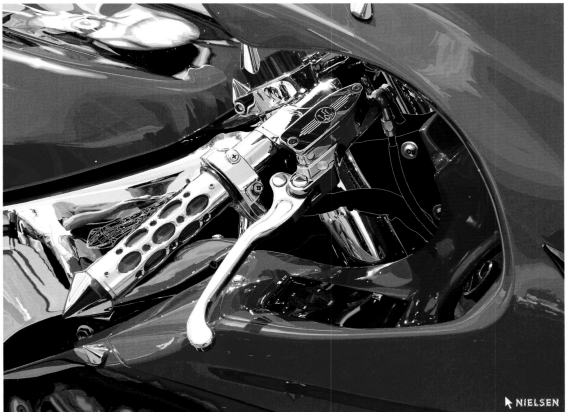

"Reflections In Red"

Chris Nielsen

Chris Nielsen created another stunning image using the same drawing technique described on the opposite page. Nielsen likes to begin drawing an area of the photograph that contains a large object, such as a gas tank or big pipe. Working over a template layer that contained his original photograph, he first drew the outline of a large object with the Pen tool. Then he drew paths for each area where the color value changed within that object. He selected the paths and clicked the Divide Pathfinder icon. He continued in this manner until there were enough shapes to define the object. This

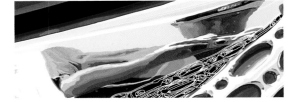

was a particularly challenging motorcycle to draw because there are only slight variations in one overall color. Nielsen filled each individual object with a custom color chosen from the Swatches panel. In all of his motorcycle illustrations, the reflection of Nielsen taking the photograph is visible—here it is shown in the magnified detail above.

Masking Images

Simple to Complex Clipping Masks

Advanced Technique

Overview: *Create a clipping mask; gather and order objects to clip; use the mask to clip objects; position masked objects; add finishing touches.*

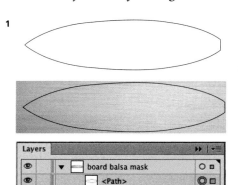

The surfboard path outline (top); with the balsa wood image placed and the path moved above it (middle); the stacking order of the two objects in the layers panel before making the clipping mask (directly above)

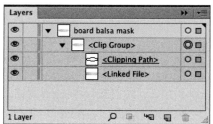

(Top and middle) Using Object> Clipping Mask> Make to turn the top path into a clipping path; (directly above) the Layers panel showing the surfboard <Clipping Path> masking the <Linked File> wood JPG

This custom surfboard design made of masks within masks was created by San Diego–based illustrator Aaron McGarry, who finds much of his work inspired by a life tailored to the beach communities and industries of southern California.

1 Inserting wood texture with a clipping mask. In a new document McGarry double-clicked the layer name to customize it. He used the Pen tool to draw the outline of a surfboard, which he would use as a clipping path for his new surfboard design. To add the wood texture for the board, McGarry used File> Place to place a JPG image of balsa wood into his document (making certain that the Template option was disabled). With his image selected, he used Object> Arrange> Send to Back to move the image to the back of the stacking order, making his surfboard outline the top-most object. Adjusting the alignment of the path and the wood, he then selected both objects and chose Object> Clipping Mask> Make (⌘-7/ Ctrl-7); this clipped the image into the path and thereby created the wooden surfboard.

2 Creating a complex (compound) clipping mask. With the surfboard itself prepared, and since his logo would be used for other purposes, McGarry created the logo in a separate document using the Pen tool, Pathfinder panel, and text. He would be "filling" this logo with a blue underwater image by using the logo itself as a clipping mask. His initial logo design consisted of two separate paths plus type, all styled initially with a black stroke and no fill so he could see his design as he worked. Only one path can be used as a clipping path for a mask, so if you have multiple elements (such as type and logo objects) you'll have to first combine the elements into a compound path or compound shape. McGarry had outlined his text so he could make some adjustments, so in order for all of the letters and the logo to behave as one mask, he needed to combine them into one compound path using Object> Compound Path> Make (⌘-7/Ctrl-7). Alternatively, if you're working with live type, you can combine logo design elements and type into a Compound Shape by choosing Make Compound Shape from the Pathfinder panel.

With this complex compound path prepared, McGarry placed his underwater JPG image. Using the Layers panel he positioned his logo path above his placed image. McGarry then selected both the logo and the image, then used ⌘-7/Ctrl-7 to make all of his logo objects into a clipping group. Then he renamed the layer "logo masked."

3 Assembling the objects and finishing touches. To add finishing details, McGarry created two more layers. On one layer ("speargun") he put additional type; into the "board edge" layer he moved a copy of board outline path (by holding Option/Alt while dragging the object proxy to the new layer); and then increased the stroke weight. He then created the light-to-dark edging around the board by applying a wood gradient to the stroke (from Swatch Libraries> Gradients) and in the Gradient panel. He enabled the first Stroke option (Apply gradient within stroke) and adjusted the angle in the field below to create the desired lighting effect. Finally, with the board edge outline still selected he chose the Draw Inside drawing mode to constrain his paint and used a charcoal art brush (Window> Brush Libraries> Artistic> Artistic_ChalkCharcoalPencil) to paint rough white streaks on the board surface (see the *Expressive Strokes* chapter for more about how to do this). Finally, McGarry made sure that Paste Remembers Layers was enabled (from the Layers panel pop-up menu), and with both documents open, McGarry used drag and drop to move his logo into his surfboard document, automatically adding the layer names as well. He positioned his logo on top of the surfboard and resized it to fit.

2

Selecting all parts of the logo and using Object> Compound Path> Make to create a single compound object that behaves as one path

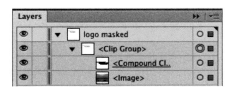

Selecting both compound logo and placed image before and after using Object> Clipping Mask> Make to create the mask

The Layers panel showing the objects <Clip Group> after applying the clipping mask, with the logo (<Compound Clipping Path>) above the underwater image (<Image>)

3

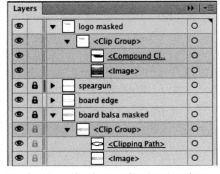

The surfboard outline after adding white streaks and applying a wood gradient to the edging path

The final layers for the completed project showing the mask layers expanded

MCKIBILLO
(AKA Josh McKible)

For years MCKIBILLO's NaniBird project was devoted to the art of papercraft. In addition to MCKIBILLO's own NaniBirds, the project inspired designs and papercraft characters by many other collaborators. MCKIBILLO spent a lot of time refining the original NaniBird silhouette, always mindful that, like a little sculpture, his papertoy, required consideration of all sides of the design. The blank NaniBird PDF template (on **WOW! ONLINE**) was created from a layered Illustrator file, with separate, simple, vector objects. To insert your art into the template, you can fill each object with a pattern, you can use Draw Inside mode to paint within a selected object (see the *Rethinking Construction* chapter for details about how to do this), or you can use each path as a separate clipping path to mask any objects (or images) within. It's tricky to visualize, so print proofs and assemble to ensure artwork within is correctly oriented. The photo above shows a NaniBird surrounded by NaniPeeps.

MCKIBILLO

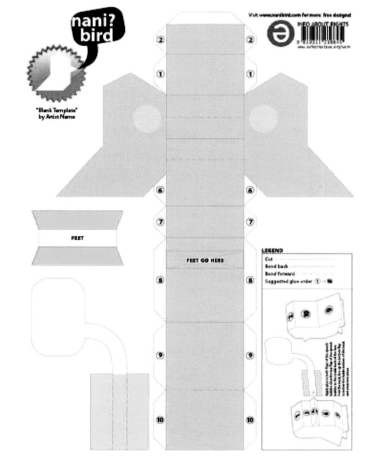

GAUSE

Monika Gause

Monika Gause, the artist behind the European Illustrator website Vektogarten (http://vektorgarten.de), made her papercraft zebra as an homage to NaniBirds and similar projects (see the previous Gallery). After working out how to physically construct her Paperzebra (paper-colored animal in the photo, above right), she then deconstructed it and designed the flat template. Gause draws into the template with the Pencil tool; then she uses Live Paint to add color to the blank spaces formed between the lines (see the *Rethinking Construction* chapter for help working with Live Paint). Once she figured out her first zebra, she set about making a number of variations, some with a tongue sticking out, others with a flat smiling row of teeth. Gause also allows anyone to use her templates, saying that her goal is "to get a zebra into every home on the planet."

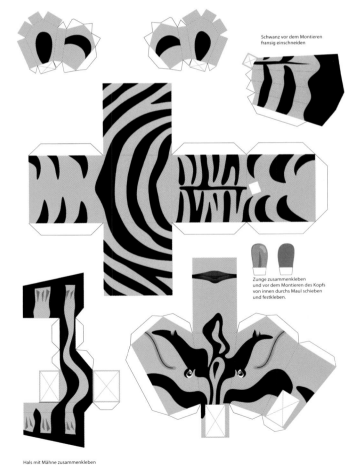

Schwanz vor dem Montieren fransig einschneiden

Zunge zusammenkleben und vor dem Montieren des Kopfs von innen durchs Maul schieben und festkleben.

Hals mit Mähne zusammenkleben

Opacity Masking

Smooth Transitions & Intertwining Objects

Advanced Technique

Overview: *Create soft transitions using single-object opacity masks; interweave objects using complex multi-object opacity masks.*

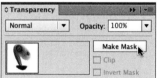

The head overlapping the hollow tendril (left); adding an oval with a Feather effect (middle); Shift-selecting the head <Clip Group> and oval; clicking on the Make Mask button (right/below)

The finished critter and tendrils (including feathered ovals blending the tendrils into the pot)

Chris Leavens' fantastic realms are made plausible by the way objects interact with each other, creating depth and disguising vector edges. He often uses opacity masks to overlap objects believably, as well as to soften transitions between shadow and full light or between transparent and opaque. Instead of cutting objects apart to create the illusion of objects intermingling, with opacity masks you can keep objects intact so you can continue to make adjustments. Whenever complex interactions or soft transitions are called for, Leavens finds it easier to construct and work with opacity masks than with clipping masks.

1 Masking with shadows for soft transitions. In order to create the illusion that a critter's head was inside the tendril's tube, Leavens attached a feathered oval for the area of the neck that would gradually disappear into the gradient that creates the hole in the tendril. To do this he drew a black oval on top of the neck and feathered it (Effect> Stylize> Feather). Because the head consisted of several objects contained within a <Clip Group>, to attach an opacity mask to the head, Leavens targeted the <Clip Group> in the Layers panel, held down Shift, and also selected the feathered oval. Opening the Transparency panel, he disabled "New opacity masks are clipping" from the panel menu so all new masks would be solid white (reveal all). Then he clicked the Make Mask button, turning the top object (the black feathered oval) into an opacity mask for the critter head clip group.

2 **Masking with multiple objects.** Leavens began by drawing the snake and palms individually. All the objects were complex, and each was contained within a clip group, with a single clipping path defining its contour. To create the illusion that the snake was weaving through the trees, Leavens created an opacity mask for the snake by modifying a copy of the contour paths for the trees. Using the Make Mask button would only turn the top tree into a mask, so he needed to manually create the mask. To do this he selected all three clipping paths used to define the outline of the trees by holding Shift and clicking each clipping path with the Group Selection tool (or Shift-click each <Clipping Path> in the Layers panel) and copied them to the clipboard. He selected the snake's <Clip Group> with the Selection tool (or targeted it in the Layers panel), opened the Transparency panel and then double-clicked the empty mask thumbnail to enter Opacity Mask Mode for the snake's clip group (you'll see a thick line around the mask thumbnail, and <Opacity Mask> in the Layers panel). Leavens then used Paste in Front (⌘-F/Ctrl-F) to paste the copied trees in perfect registration; then he clicked on a Black swatch to solidly fill the semi-transparent outlines. The snake now appeared completely behind the trees. Using the Eraser tool, he erased sections of the mask where he wanted the snake to appear in front of the tree. When the mask was finished, he clicked the image thumbnail to exit Opacity Mask Mode.

2
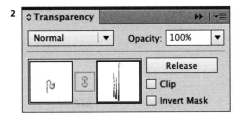

The default Transparency dialog with "New opacity masks are clipping" disabled in the panel menu in order to paste a concealing (black) object into the mask

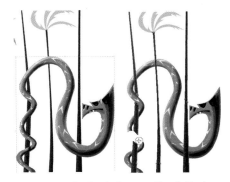

The snake and palms before masking (left); the snake with copies of the palms' clipping paths pasted into an opacity mask, and portions of the mask being erased (right)

After erasing the mask to reveal the snake slithering in front and behind the palm trunks, Leavens added the shadows cast by the palms to the snake's clip group

HUBIG

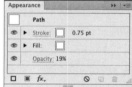

Dan Hubig

In this Illustration for *California Magazine*, Dan Hubig first combined blends, gradients, and transparency in Illustrator, and then enhanced his image in Photoshop with Blurs, Brushes, and Adjustment layers. Hubig used transparency to render the cloak and torso only partially opaque, which kept his options open for expressing invisibility in Photoshop. He created his "cloak of invisibility" in Illustrator with a white Fill and Stroke and an opacity of only 19%, then duplicated it with a Stroke and no Fill to a new layer on top. By planning ahead, he would be able to reduce the cloak's visibility to zero, if he chose, but maintain that important outline. For one version, Hubig also made the man's torso completely invisible, but for the final version, he retained a hint of opacity. To learn more about how Hubig creates his illustrations, see the "Planning Ahead" lesson in the *Creatively Combining Apps* chapter.

BURKE

Pariah Burke

Pariah Burke used Illustrator to construct the cover illustration for his book, *ePublishing with InDesign*. Because he knew that projects often change as they progress, he also chose to construct his Illustrator file to be flexible for future editing. He divided the project into three parts: the book cover, the iPad, and the joining blank pages. He first constructed a highly realistic iPad that he later altered to a more generic tablet. He created a front view of the iPad, complete with a placed JPG image of an actual eBook page, clipped to fit precisely within the tablet's screen area. To distort the image and position it along with the bevel onto the iPad body, Burke selected the bevel and page objects and chose Object> Envelope Distort> Make with Mesh. He chose one row and one column, turning the mesh into a transform bounding box that he could continue to modify, and even un-transform (rare in Illustrator!). To edit or replace elements within the envelope, in the Layers panel he could move an object above

"Envelope" to remove the effect (moving all at once deletes the mesh), or drag elements into the Envelope group to apply (or reapply) the effect. Using Isolation mode made it even easier for him to focus on just the envelope objects. He made the book cover with equal attention to detail and again selected all the objects that would be placed onto the book's cover, distorting them using Envelope Mesh with the same method. To make the pages, Burke made individual, gradient-filled polygons, and added thin, white-filled shapes to represent the page edges. With the book-to-iPad constructed, he made a custom drop shadow by drawing two paths (one white and one dark gray), choosing Object> Blend> Make, and then applying a Multiply blending mode to the blend. Before the project was finished, he had to make several alterations to accommodate his publisher, a relatively easy task thanks to envelope mesh.

Chapter 7 *Mastering Complexity*   **265**

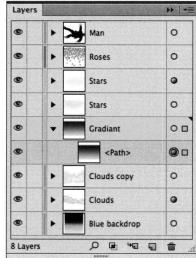

AUBÉ

Jean Aubé

Jean Aubé created "Falling" as a personal response to lingering discussions with a friend about the emotional impact of the 9/11 disaster. He used many different techniques throughout, including Image Trace, scatter brush (to distribute the stars), gradients, and many instances of reducing opacity and changing blending modes. The hard edges of the man and roses falling from above keep these narrative elements in full focus, while the soft layers of clouds create a rich depth of field. To create these clouds Aubé first used Image Trace on scans of his pastel-drawn clouds. He then placed and offset layer upon layer of clouds, adjusting opacity and blending modes, and finally overlaying a gradient (purple to white) set to multiply mode.

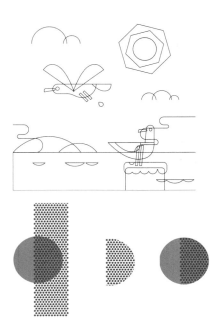

PEREZ

Richard Perez

To add warmth to his crisp vector objects, San Francisco–based illustrator Richard Perez often adds just a few touches of texture. Sometimes his textures are scans, while other times he creates textures out of repeating Illustrator objects. Depending on where and how he wants to add texture, he applies and constrains it using opacity masks or clipping masks. Perez often begins with a muted, restricted color palette and builds the basics of his image using mostly the Rectangle, Ellipse, and Polygon tools. He uses the Direct Selection tool to select points to delete or move, creating some open objects and elongating others, often constraining movement to 180°, 90°, and 45° axes. Though he sometimes combines objects using Pathfinder> Unite, often he keeps objects separate (such as the half-ovals that form the clouds) so he can make subtle adjustments to positioning.

With the main elements in place, he brings in the textural elements, which he collects and keeps in separate files for reuse. In the case of this lovely ode to the San Francisco Embarcadero waterfront, Perez brought in a field of repeating dots. Using a sequence of Option-dragging/Alt-dragging to duplicate, then ⌘-D/Ctrl-D to repeat the duplication, he transformed one dot into a line of dots, offsetting that line of dots into a pair, and then duplicating/repeating that pair into a field of dots. For the circle with dots (above left), he selected his masking object with the dot set beneath it and applied Object> Clipping Mask> Make. The masking object's fill disappeared, but by Direct Selecting (or targeting the <Clipping Path> in the Layers panel), he could reapply the fill. Keeping the dots related in color to the fill beneath helps to imply a halftone, overlay, or transparency.

Moses Tan

Moses Tan accurately rendered most of the details of this Kyoto Bus Station by carefully tracing over his own reference photograph using closed filled paths drawn with the Pen tool. In a few cases, how-

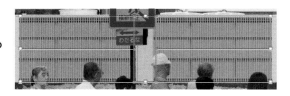

ever, he used Illustrator's more powerful features such as blends, gradients, and clipping masks. To draw the central grill unit (detail directly above), Tan drew one vertical column, copied it, and Shift-dragged it to the opposite side. With both objects selected he double-clicked the Blend tool to show Options, entered 50 for the Specified Steps, and set the orientation to Align to Page. Selecting the objects he choose Object> Blend> Make. Tan began the shadows beneath the passengers using linear gradients; then within the Appearance panel

he selected the fill, clicked the *fx* icon, and chose Blur> Gaussian Blur. For other shadows he filled objects with gradients, then reduced the opacity and changed the blending mode (such as Overlay or Multiply).

Chris Nielsen

Chris Nielsen has trained his artistic eye to recognize subtle shifts of color within a photograph and translate them into a striking image using layers of filled paths. Nielsen first placed an original photograph in a bottom layer to trace upon. He worked on one small section at a time, such as the eye in the detail to the right. With the Pen tool he made paths (no fill, with a black stroke) and traced the areas of primary color he saw in the photograph. He chose the darkest value first (dark blue or black); then on another layer, he drew the objects with progressively lighter values (a lighter blue, red, gray, etc.). He continued building layers of paths until the area was completely covered. He moved throughout the image this way until the portrait was finished. When all of the paths were drawn, he began to fill them with color. Nielsen chose the Eyedropper tool, pressed and held the ⌘/Ctrl key to switch to the Direct Selection tool, and selected an object to color. Then he toggled back to the Eyedropper tool by releasing the ⌘/Ctrl key and sampled a color from the photograph. He toggled between the Direct Selection tool and the Eyedropper tool until the paths were filled. Most of the time, Nielsen liked the sampled colors, but if not, he would tweak the color using the slid-

NIELSEN

ers in the Color panel. Once all of the paths were filled with color, Nielsen hid the template layer. He saw small gaps of white in his drawing where the paths didn't quite meet or overlap. To fill these gaps, he made a large object that covered the area, filled it with a dark color, and moved it to the bottom-most layer.

JACKSON

Lance Jackson

To create the cover illustration for *The Adobe Illustrator CS5 WOW! Book*, Lance Jackson generated atmosphere and depth with the Bristle Brush and constructed many of the details using the Blob Brush. He used various tools to block in the main components of his composition. He used the Pen tool to draw the basic cables and roadway for the Golden Gate Bridge, then modified the strokes with the Width tool. Next Jackson began brushing over the water and bridge with various brushes from the Bristle Brush library, especially Deerfoot, Cat's Tongue, Dome,

and Fan. To constrain the brushes to each main element, he often selected a base object and chose the Draw Inside mode. For added texture, he also used brushes from the Artistic and Grunge Brush Vector Pack libraries. Jackson drew a few cars and pedestrians using the Blob Brush, then duplicated and recolored several of them. Jackson toned down his palette, adding fog and more depth, by reducing the opacity of his brushstrokes, layering the strokes, and sometimes even changing the blending mode (by clicking Opacity in the Control panel).

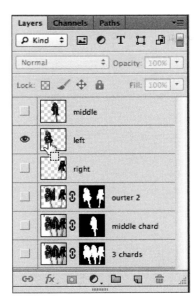

STEUER

Sharon Steuer

Sharon Steuer chose her photo of three rainbow chard leaves on a white background as source material for raster Illustrator brushes. In Photoshop Steuer used a combination of tools to isolate each chard leaf from the others and from the white background (her Photoshop Layers panel above). She saved each leaf in its own file in PNG format. In a new Illustrator file she chose File> Place, disabled the Link option (so the placed files would be embedded), then she selected all three chard leaf PNG files in the dialog (holding Shift), and clicked OK. Moving her loaded cursor into her artboard she clicked to place each of her images, one after the other. Dragging the first leaf into the Brushes panel, she chose Art Brush and clicked OK, but received a warning dialog that the artwork's resolution was too high. She cancelled, resized the three chard leaves, and then duplicated them. Selecting one of the duplicates, she chose Object> Rasterize, then enabled the Medium

(150 ppi) and Transparency settings, and clicked OK. Dragging this downsized image into the Brushes panel, she chose Art Brush and clicked OK. This time Art Brush Options opened, where she enabled Stretch to Fit Stroke Length and the up-pointing direction arrow before clicking OK. She then applied Rasterize to the other two duplicates and made brushes for each of them as well. With the three chard brushes prepared, Steuer switched to the Artboard tool and created a new artboard. She then drew a pair of colorful rectangles as a background. Locking this layer, she created another layer above for artwork. With the Paintbrush tool, she painted with this set of brushes, creating a simple chard forest. (See her other "chard forest" gallery in the *Creatively Combining Apps* chapter, and go to sharonsteuer.com/lynda for links to a 7-day free trial to view movies of this process.)

Chapter 7 *Mastering Complexity*   271

Von R. Glitschka

Von R. Glitschka (Glitschka Studios) created this "Scroll Work" pattern in Illustrator for his "Drawing Vector Graphics: Patterns" course on lynda.com. Glitschka began by tracing a scan of his hand-drawn sketch with the Pen tool. With the objects complete, he decided that the point of each curve should be slightly (and uniformly) rounded, instead of ending in sharp points. Although he could have used Live Corners to convert all corners to curves in selected objects, that would have rounded the creases between curves as well as the corner ends. Instead, he carefully applied a Live Corner radius value to just the end points of the outward curls, preserving the sharp creases between the curves. To do this he used the Direct Selection tool to marquee-select each of the points that he wanted to change (holding Shift to select many at once), and then clicked Corners in the Control panel. After entering .7 (pt) in the Radius field he pressed Return to gently round the end of each curlicue (above left shows the original sharp curves in magenta stroke, with the

rounded ends in filled turquoise). Selecting all the elements, he chose Object> Pattern> Make to enter the Pattern Editor (top right). Here he adjusted the placement of the pattern tile to form his desired repeat then clicked OK (final pattern directly above). See his gallery opposite on how he combined this pattern to create the complex pattern on the cover of this book.

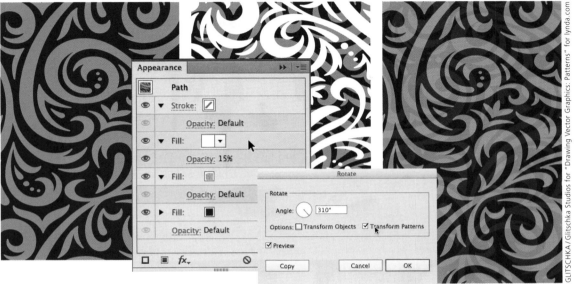

Von R. Glitschka

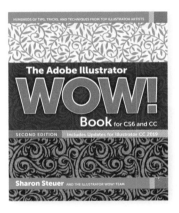

Using his Scroll Work pattern (shown in the previous gallery) as a starting point, Von R. Glitschka of Glitschka Studios created the variation used for the cover of this book by layering this pattern onto itself. After adding to his set of custom fill colors, he duplicated the first pattern by dragging its swatch to the New Swatch icon in the Swatches panel; he then double-clicked the duplicate to open it in Pattern Editing mode. To create a white variation, he selected all (⌘-A/Ctrl-A) and changed the fill to white (rendering the pattern temporarily invisible on the artboard). Exiting the editor, he drew a rectangle on his artboard and chose his original turquoise pattern as the fill. Opening the Appearance panel, he clicked the Add New Fill icon and chose one of his dark blue custom colors for the bottom Fill. With the blue showing behind the turquoise swirls, in the Appearance panel he duplicated his pattern fill (dragging it to the Duplicate Selected Item icon), then changed the duplicate fill to his new white pattern, and from Opacity reduced the slider to 15%. To offset the layered white pattern, he highlighted it in the Appearance panel; then back on his artboard he Option-clicked/Alt-clicked his filled rectangle with the Rotate tool. With Transform Objects disabled and Transform Patterns enabled he experimented with rotation angle values, updating the Preview by enabling/disabling it (to transform a pattern manually in en_US versions of CS6 and **CC**, hold the ~ key). For more on Glitschka pattern process, see his "Drawing Vector Graphics: Patterns" course on lynda.com.

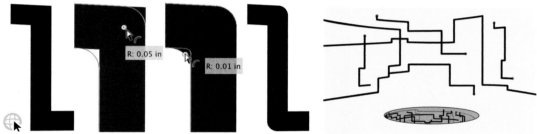

Lisa Poje

Illustrator and animator Lisa Poje worked on "Robot Bath Time" through two versions of Illustrator. She began in CS6, but Live Corners in Illustrator **CC** finally gave her a tool that allowed her to create corners both intuitively and non-destructively. She first used the Pen tool to draw the pipes seen in both the background and the floor. She employed a simple Shift-click routine to lay down pipe at right angles and then applied a fat 10–15 point stroke. Once all the pipe paths were laid down, she converted the stroked paths to filled objects with Object> Path> Outline Stroke. Keeping the paths selected, she switched to the Direct Selection tool, grabbed one Live Corner widget, and rounded all the corners at once by dragging on the widget; even the sharp pipe ends were perfectly rounded. Because all the corners are live and editable, she selected inner corners separately from the newly rounded outer corners and dragged those widgets back to once again form a sharp corner. Poje prefers working visually with the widgets to typing numbers in dialogs but appreciated that precision was always available to her when editing the pipes. For her, the significant advantage to using Live Corners for this piece was not having to slowly and individually add anchors with the Pen tool to create Bézier curves at the pipe junctions and then to individually remove original corner anchors.

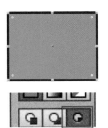

FERSTER

Gary Ferster

In the planning stages for a promotional email template for his reelwelldone.com website, Gary Ferster intended to create rectangles and apply uniform rounded corners to them using *fx*> Stylize> Round Corners from the Appearance panel. However, Ferster has since discovered that creating and modifying rounded corners using Live Rectangles provides him with superior control and flexibility. He began his design in a new document, choosing the Web profile (which sets pixels as the default units) and a width of 600 pixels. After setting an orange fill and increasing his black stroke to 3 (pixels) in the Control panel, he used the Rectangle tool to draw a rectangle on the artboard, which opened the Transform panel. While the rectangle was still selected, he entered 10 in one corner radius value box, and (with the default link enabled) all radii updated to 10 pixels. To place a photo "inside" the still-selected rectangle without losing its styling, Ferster switched to Draw Inside mode (Shift-D), pressed ⌘-Shift-P/Ctrl-Shift-P (File> Place), located the desired photo, and clicked OK. With the loaded cursor he click-dragged over the bottom portion of his rectangle, placing the image "inside" the rectangle, which then became a filled and stroked clipping mask. Still in Draw Inside mode, he typed "Drama" as point type on the artboard, moved it over the top portion of the rectangle, and changed its fill color to white. Returning to regular drawing mode (Shift-D), he duplicated this rectangle by selecting it, holding Option-Shift/Alt-Shift and dragging horizontally to create a second, then pressed ⌘-D/Ctrl-D twice to create two more. After typing the correct text label, he replaced each image by clicking it with the Direct Selection tool, pressing ⌘-Shift-P/Ctrl-Shift-P, choosing the new image, enabling Replace, and clicking OK. Finally, he used File> Save for Web, with the JPEG High and Type Optimized settings.

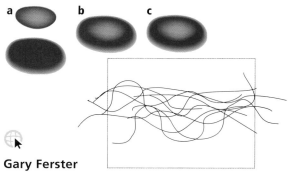

a   b   c

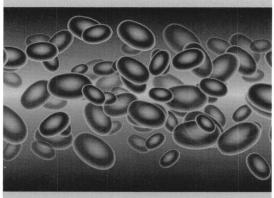

FERSTER

Gary Ferster

For the most part, Gary Ferster's Illustrator work has tended to be clean and linear. He prefers 3D applications such as Lightwave 3D for rendering complex illustrations, saying "It would take me forever to create a vector environment that equalled or matched the 3D artwork." Once rendered in 3D, replicating complex objects is simple, but in Illustrator replicating complex objects, such as gradient mesh or blended objects, has been much more labor and time intensive. Gradient mesh objects are too complex to make into an Illustrator brush, and although they can be made into symbols (as vectors or rasterized), the Symbolism tools aren't precise enough for medical illustration purposes. However, in **CC** he can rasterize versions of his complex elements, then create raster brushes from those element (this chapter's **CC** intro includes a similar form he created with the Freeform Gradient tool). Beginning with a larger gradient mesh oval and a smaller object blend (figure **a**, above left), he then stacked the blend on top of the mesh and grouped them together (figure **b**). After creating a duplicate of the group to preserve a vector version of his blood cell, he selected the duplicate and chose Object> Rasterize, set the Resolution to High (300 ppi), and clicked OK (figure **c**). Next,

dragging that rasterized cell into the Brushes panel, he chose Scatter brush, clicked OK, and accepted the default settings. Choosing the Paintbrush tool he drew a path with this new brush and then double-clicked the brush in the panel. He turned Preview on, set all the parameters to Random, and then adjusted each slider, watching his changes live. When he was satisfied with the settings, Ferster clicked OK and painted with his scatter brush. To create a sense of depth he selected each path individually and adjusted the Opacity in the Control panel, assigning paths at the back with low opacity (20%) and increasing opacity as the paths stacked toward the top, with the topmost path at 100% opacity. Because each brushed path was easily edited and adjusted with vector path tools (Direct Selection, Smooth tool, etc.), without any further adjustment to brush Options, Ferster was able to control the exact position of each cell. The gradient background is (in medical terms) a "lumen" (artery), with the lighter middle area implying a tube-like form, simulating the blood flow through a cross section of an artery. The final brushed paths appear simple when viewed in Outline mode (above left).

8

Creatively Combining Apps

Creatively Combining Apps

<div class="sidebar">

No Preview or Place option?

When you save in .ai, disabling the default PDF-Compatible file option allows you to create a smaller file, but you can only open the file in that version of Illustrator or later. Most applications—including Adobe InDesign and Photoshop—can only open or place files with "PDF Content." Unless you're sure you'll never need the file outside your current version, save with Create PDF Compatible File enabled. Otherwise only disable this option on duplicates of a file.

Recovering missing linked files

If you don't have the original linked files for an .ai file, you can get the images from the "PDF Content" side of the file—as long as Create PDF Compatible File was enabled when it was saved. If it was, drag and drop the .ai file onto the Photoshop icon, and in the Import PDF dialog choose Images. You can open any images from the PDF portion of the Illustrator file, save the images, and relink them in Illustrator.

—*Jean-Claude Tremblay*

Placing a file using the Link option

</div>

This chapter showcases some of the ways you can use Illustrator together with other programs. Moving artwork between Illustrator and other applications—such as Photoshop, After Effects, or Adobe Draw—is often straightforward. But there are always rules and limits to moving files between programs, and the following pages address some ways to make your life easier when working with Illustrator and other programs.

LINKING VS. EMBEDDING IN ILLUSTRATOR

The major choice you'll need to make when placing art in Illustrator is whether to *link* or *embed* the file. When you link a file, you don't actually include the artwork in the Illustrator file. Instead a copy of the artwork acts as a placeholder, while the image remains in a separate file. Linking leaves the file editable in the original program, making it easy to update when the original is changed. Not only are .ai files with linked images smaller than those with embedded images, but linking permits you to link the same file several times in your document without increasing the file size for each instance. The Links panel keeps track of all the raster images used in your document, regardless of whether they were created within Illustrator, opened, or introduced via the Place command. Just remember that you have to include the separate, linked files if you move the .ai file to another computer.

When you embed artwork, you're actually including it in the file, which can sometimes be helpful even though the file size increases. Although it's trickier to update an embedded file in the original program, embedding is the answer if you need to be positive an image is included in the document. Consider embedding the image if you need to edit it in Illustrator or it's the only way to retain its transparency. Also, if there's a danger the linked file won't travel with the document when sending it to a client or press, you'll want to embed the file.

ILLUSTRATOR TO NON-ADOBE PROGRAMS

When moving artwork from Illustrator to non-Adobe programs, you must decide which objects in your artwork you want to remain as vectors, if possible, and which you can allow to become rasterized. What you'll be able to do with your Illustrator artwork in that other program depends both on how you prepare your Illustrator files as well as the strengths and limitations of the program into which you'll be moving your artwork. Parameters that you might be able to control include moving only selected objects or the entire file; bringing Illustrator files in as paths, styled vectors, or rasters; and bringing in images flat or with layers.

Copy and paste/drag and drop

You may be able to preserve the vector format in programs outside the Creative Suite if they support PostScript drag and drop behavior. In order for this to work, enable AICB (Adobe Illustrator Clipboard) in Preferences> File Handling & Clipboard (disabled by default). When you copy/paste or drag and drop into a raster-based program without vector support, your artwork will be either automatically rasterized at the resolution set in that program or from Illustrator's Document Raster Effects Settings.

ILLUSTRATOR & ADOBE PHOTOSHOP

There are many options for moving artwork between Illustrator and Photoshop. In many cases you can control whether you want to maintain vector data, rasterize in part or whole, or whether to maintain layers, although those processes don't always work as you'd expect.

Illustrator to Photoshop: Smart Objects

Illustrator art brought in as a Smart Object can be scaled, rotated, duplicated, modified using Adjustment layers or Smart Filters, or even warped without loss of data. Smart Objects keep the original dimensions of your artwork, so further edits in Illustrator need to fit the original bounding box or the objects will be distorted in Photoshop.

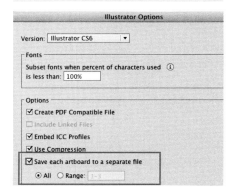

To save multiple artboards, with each artboard to its own file, in Save As under Options enable Save each artboard to a separate file

Smart Objects and CC Library

To place your Illustrator file into a Photoshop file and be able to continue to edit it as vectors in Illustrator, place it as a Smart Object (it can be either Linked or Embedded). If your file is in your **CC** Library, drag it into Photoshop to create a linked Smart Object (with a Cloud badge on its thumbnail). If you double-click to edit it in Illustrator, you'll update the Library file. To break the link to the Library, Option/Alt-drag the file into Photoshop instead (you'll see a regular Smart Object badge). Now if you double-click to edit it in Illustrator, you'll only update the file embedded in the document, and not the Library file.

Importing PS Layer Comps

If you know you'll be placing your Photoshop file in Illustrator, use Layer Comps in Photoshop to give you better control over which layers are visible once you place your PSD file in Illustrator.

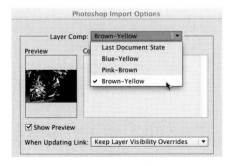

Choosing a Layer Comp in Illustrator's Photoshop Import Options

- **To create Photoshop Smart Objects from Illustrator data,** copy/paste to open the Paste dialog and choose Smart Object. Or create a Smart Object automatically by dragging and dropping or choosing File> Place.
- **To edit an Illustrator Smart Object,** double-click on its thumbnail in Photoshop's Layers panel to automatically launch Illustrator and open a working copy of your artwork. To update your Photoshop file, save your edits in Illustrator before returning to Photoshop.
- **To replace a Smart Object file with a different file on disk,** choose Layer> Smart Objects> Replace Content. This means you can use Smart Objects as placeholders for content you place in Photoshop later.

Illustrator to Photoshop: pixels, paths, and layers

- **To create a pixel image, path, or Shape layer,** copy and paste an object, selecting from among these options in the Paste dialog that opens.
- **To preserve layers and keep text editable,** place the text on a top-level layer, not a sublayer, and choose Export to save the file in "Photoshop (psd)" format. The other vector objects are rasterized, but text stays editable. You can even use Illustrator's anti-aliasing options—None, Sharp, Crisp, Strong—which are comparable to and supported by Photoshop's text options.
- **To reliably export compound shapes to Photoshop,** place your compound shape on a top-level layer. To keep both the shape and any strokes you've added on separate layers so each is editable, remove strokes before exporting, or Photoshop might treat your shape and its stroke as a single object. Apply your strokes in Photoshop.

Photoshop to Illustrator

- **To keep text live,** in Photoshop save the file in PSD format. In Illustrator, choose File> Open (or File> Place with the Link checkbox disabled), and in the Photoshop Import Options dialog, enable Convert to Layers.
- **To link a file, rather than embed it,** choose File> Place and enable the Link. You can always embed the file later.

- **When linking a file,** you will be able to relink or edit the original and have the link update reflect your modifications, but you can't import layers from PSD or TIFF files.
- **For access to layers in a PSD or TIFF file,** you must embed it (don't enable link). With an embedded file, you can import text layers, keeping them live, and you can enable options to either flatten image layers or import image layers (even hidden layers). But remember, if you embed a file, it won't update if you edit the original.
- **When importing Photoshop Adjustment layers,** Illustrator doesn't understand them and will flatten all the non-text layers in a file if it encounters an Adjustment layer. To prevent that, merge an Adjustment layer with the layer it's modifying before saving the PSD or TIFF file. Then, when using Place or Open, enable the Convert to Layers option.
- **To preserve the appearance** of Density or Feather options applied to a layer mask, apply the mask to the layer in Photoshop before you embed the file. Illustrator ignores Feather and Mask Density options.
- **To see the Import Options Dialog,** Show Import Option must be enabled in the Place dialog (unless changed, the settings will remain from the last time you placed a file)

ILLUSTRATOR & ADOBE INDESIGN

- **To be able to edit Illustrator objects copy/pasted into InDesign,** first enable AICB in Illustrator Preferences> File Handling & Clipboard> Copy As (On Copy for **CC**). To maximize path editability enable Preserve Paths; complex appearances such as brushes, effects, or gradients will be lost. To maintain the visual look of complex appearances, enable Preserve Appearance and Overprints (complex objects will be flattened and expanded). Then in InDesign, before pasting make sure Prefer PDF when Pasting is disabled in Preferences> Clipboard Handling.
- **To place Illustrator artwork (linking it rather than embedding),** you'll need a PDF compatible file, as In Design can only read the PDF portion of an Illustrator file. In **CC** files saved in Libraries are automatically

Pasting text into InDesign

Before taking text into InDesign, choose from these options:
- To keep text editable, in Illustrator, choose Preferences> File Handling & Clipboard> Clipboard> enable AICB and Preserve Path, and in InDesign Preferences> Clipboard Handling, and select Text Only (in **CC** you can use a Library)
- To preserve the graphic appearance, you'll turn it into an image. If using the Clipboard with copy/paste, choose All Information in InDesign's Preferences> Clipboard Handling (in **CC** hold ⌘/Ctrl as you drag the text into a library)

Illustrator layers in InDesign

To control the layer visibility of an Illustrator file in InDesign, when you choose Place, enable "Show Import Options," or select a file you've already placed in InDesign and choose Object> Object Layer Options. In the Object Layer Options dialog, click an Eye icon to hide or show any layer. At the bottom of the dialog you can choose whether to update layer visibility settings for a linked Illustrator file when the link is updated.

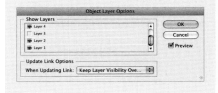

Illustrator & 3D Programs

In addition to Illustrator's 3D effects (see the *Reshaping Dimensions* chapter), you can also import Illustrator paths into 3D programs to use as outlines and extrusion paths. Once you import a path, you can transform it into a 3D object. Photoshop's 3D features can work with any closed path whether pasted as pixels, path, or Shape layer. (Most CAD/3D modeling apps import Illustrator paths.)

Opening multiple PDF pages

Before CC 2018, you could only open one PDF page at a time in Illustrator. In current versions of **CC**, when you choose a multiple-page PDF, you can select which page or ranges of pages to import, and each page will appear on its own artboard.

Anti-alias & Save for Web

If you use Save for Web, choose Type Optimized in the Image Size options to preserve character-level anti-aliasing choices.

Animate with Graphic Symbols

If you use Illustrator layers to create an animation that doesn't need to be tweened in Animate CC, try importing the layers as keyframes in a Graphic Symbol. The animation is complete when you insert a frame on the Timeline for every keyframe you made.

saved in the Creative Cloud with PDF compatibility ,and then by default placed as linked in other programs when dragged into them. If you don't want to use Libraries, first save your file in Illustrator with the Create PDF Compatible File option enabled (it's on by default). Then you can place it in InDesign.

- **To control how an Illustrator file imports,** enable Show Import Options in the Place dialog. If you're placing an Illustrator file containing multiple artboards, InDesign allows you to select which artboard to import; the Layers tab in the Import dialog lets you control visibility of top-level Illustrator layers.

ILLUSTRATOR, PDF, AND ADOBE ACROBAT

Acrobat's Portable Document Format (PDF) lets you transfer files between different operating systems and applications. By default, all Illustrator files created now are also PDF-compatible files. And when you open an Illustrator document newer than the version of the program that you have, you're actually opening the PDF portion of the .ai file. When you choose File> Save As, keep the "Create PDF Compatible File" option enabled so Acrobat (and earlier versions of Illustrator) can open an .ai file.

- **To access the complete set of PDF options,** choose "Adobe PDF (pdf)" from the Save As format pop-up and click Save, which opens the Adobe PDF Options dialog; then choose from among the full range of PDF options, such as Optimize for Fast Web View.
- **To save layered Illustrator files as layered Acrobat files,** enable the "Create Acrobat Layers From Top-Level Layers" option in the Adobe PDF Options dialog.
- In **CC** 2018 and up, you can open multipage PDFs, as well as a selection of pages, which can be embedded or linked.

WEB GRAPHICS

This section looks at some of the complexities of creating web graphics for modern displays. Adobe has worked to eliminate obstacles between Illustrator and web programs, but some of its features can produce large files that result in long load times, or objects that don't scale to large and small displays.

Document profiles and templates were designed to optimize your design for the web from the start. If you choose the Web or Devices profiles (Web or Mobile in **CC**) when creating a new document, most of the settings—including artboards, resolution, RGB color mode, pixels for ruler units, and enabling Align to Pixel Grid—are geared for screen display.

Use multiple artboards; these are a great aid for sharing resources when you need to maintain a look or prep a number of files for quick export. Use Export to choose a format and output selected artboards. Save for Web keeps the assets, but only exports the active artboard. (See "Exporting Graphics to Web and Mobile Devices" in the **CC** section at the end of this chapter to learn about enhancements to exporting assets.

- **To prevent colors from being altered when working for print and display,** work in CMYK (the more limited color space), and then convert a copy of your file to RGB.
- **To assist in creating bold graphics,** turn on Pixel Preview to see how the anti-aliasing is affecting each object.
- **To keep sharp-edged objects crisp and reduce anti-aliasing** wherever Illustrator paths line up with the pixel grid, enable Align to Pixel Grid in the Transform panel (it will be enabled by default if you chose a Web or Devices (Mobile in **CC**) document profile). In **CC**, also find Align to Pixel Grid in the Properties and Control panels, and via the Object menu as "Make Pixel Perfect."

CREATING ANIMATION WITH LAYERS

You can use Illustrator layers to design a sequence for an animation, or export it to another program for further manipulation. You can also place the parts of objects you want to animate on top-level layers, instead of a sequence. For best results, export in .ai format when possible.

- **To create layers so each object (or layer) can be manipulated/animated separately** in another program, such as After Effects, choose Release to Layers (Sequence).

Flash Morphed into Animate

With the deprecation of the Flash player and the SWF file format, Flash turned into HTML friendly Animate. Illustrator users can find most of the same features and functions for producing their animations in Animate, including exporting files in SWF format, but the program is now geared toward publishing to modern websites and mobile devices.

Crop Image Tips

- In Preferences> General, if "Enable Content Aware Defaults" is active, Crop Image will automatically guess the most likely subject and sets the bounding box accordingly. Be aware that Puppet Warp and Freeform Gradients are also affected by this preference.
- To avoid surprises, work on a duplicate of your image.

Import into After Effects

To create a composition to import into After Effects, use the Video & Film Document Profile (Film & Video in **CC**). This creates two artboards—one large artboard that serves as a "scratch" area for objects used later in AE, and one sized for your chosen video format. To retain each artboard and the layers, create a multi-layered file and save with Create PDF Compatible File enabled.

- **To create the animation in Illustrator before exporting it** (similar to onion-skinning), choose the Build option; the bottom layer's object gets placed on every layer, with the next object placed on every layer except the first layer, and so on, until all objects are placed on the top layer to complete the animation sequence.

CC FEATURES FOR CREATIVELY COMBINING APPS
Raster Image Crop

When you select a raster image in Illustrator, a Crop Image button will now appear in the Control and Properties panels. If the selected image is linked, you'll first get a warning saying that in order to crop you'll embed the image (and it will no longer be linked to the original file). Next you can set numeric dimensions and resolution, and/or drag the bounding box to interactively set the crop boundaries. To apply Crop Image to vector images or multiple raster images, first apply Object> Rasterize. (Also see the Warning Tip "Crop Image Tips" at left, and a **CC** example of Crop Image at the end of this chapter.)

Illustrator to Others—Creative Cloud Libraries

Whether you work alone or collaborate with colleagues all over the world, Adobe's Creative Cloud Libraries can help you share your Illustrator assets with other programs and other people. Through the Creative Cloud, apps for mobile devices, such as Capture and Draw, can send files directly to Illustrator, and many other types of assets can be placed in an Illustrator library. Because the Creative Cloud is the intermediary, you and any users you collaborate with need to have a Creative Cloud account and an internet connection when you add to a library or sync files from one.

However, if you "own" the library (you created it) or you have been invited to share someone else's library and you've synced your Illustrator assets, you can use the library without an internet connection. Illustrator libraries can store swatches and color themes, text, character and paragraph styles, and graphics. Dragging an Illustrator object into another program (or onto another computer), links the object to the library as a Creative Cloud Smart Object (with a Cloud badge), allowing for updating in Illustrator. Holding Option/Alt while dragging from the Library into any program, including Illustrator, breaks the link, embedding it. Assets get automatically converted to the right format when brought into either desktop or mobile apps. You can also embed a file to ensure it travels with the document even when the library isn't available.

Place Multiple Files

Before Illustrator CC, placing multiple files into a document was a time-consuming process of choosing one file at a time. Illustrator **CC** has now added the option to place multiple files using a feature that operates similarly to InDesign's "place gun." Choose File> Place (⌘-Shift-P/Ctrl-Shift-P), and in the Place dialog, Shift-click contiguous files, or ⌘-click/Ctrl-click discontiguous files to select several files at the same time. Choose whether to link the files or embed them, and whether or not to show Import Options when placing them. The options that you'll be presented with if you enable the Show Import Options checkbox will vary depending upon factors such as the selected file's format, whether it's one or multiple files, and whether you've enabled the Link option or are embedding the file. See the Tip nearby "Using Place with Area Type" before attempting to place text. Templates and Replace are unavailable when more than one file has been selected.

Once you've clicked OK, Illustrator's cursor will display the thumbnail of the file you're about to place, along with its number in the sequence of files you've selected—for instance, **2/7** means you've selected the second of seven files. To place a file that isn't displayed, use the left and right arrows on your keyboard to cycle through to the one you do want. If you decide now you don't want a file, press the Esc key to drop that file from the queue.

Place the image in your document by dragging out a marquee (which is constrained proportionally to the image) or by clicking once in the document to place

Illustrator is *not* InDesign

Although Illustrator and InDesign have many similar features, such as the new multi-file Place feature, Illustrator's Place is not identical to InDesign's. InDesign lets you undo when placing files, reloading the "place gun" with each undo, even after you've placed the last file. Illustrator lets you undo and reload the cursor only until you have placed the last file. Once the place gun is empty, choosing Undo doesn't reload. InDesign also allows you to select multiple files in Bridge and drag them onto your document, loading the "place gun" cursor with all those files at the same time. As of this writing, Illustrator only lets you drag and drop one file from Bridge, although using Place from the context menu does allow for multiple files. And finally, you won't be able to create a grid while placing files as you can with InDesign.

Using Place with Area type

When placing Area type, Illustrator doesn't recognize a pre-drawn container. After selecting the text file, drag with your cursor to draw a frame the size you want, and the text will pour into that frame. To place text in a vector object, use the Type tool to copy it to the clipboard, convert the object to an area type container, and then paste the text into it.

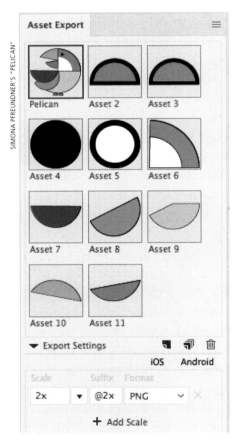

SIMONA PFREUNDNER'S "PELICAN"

The top portion of the Asset Export panel with the first thumbnail showing a multi-object group asset (made by dragging it over the panel, hovering until a + appears, and then holding Option/ Alt and releasing); other thumbnails show that same group's components, dragged into the panel without holding the Option/Alt modifier

the file at full size. If you didn't choose to show Import Options in the Place dialog, and depending upon both whether the file type supports options and whether or not you have Link enabled, you can still sometimes choose Import Options on the fly; press Shift and click once to bring up that file's Import Options, select an option, click OK, and you're back to the Place cursor ready to place the file. If you choose Show Import Options in the Place dialog, Illustrator will first page through the files, bringing up any import options for each one, before you place any.

Improved SVG features

When saving web assets in SVG format you'll be able to make them Responsive—that is, they'll be scalable on websites that adapt to different devices, such as cellphones and tablets. By default, type is now saved in standard SVG format, which is visually faithful but lacks hinting at small sizes, while precision for vectors is set to the lowest quality to produce the smallest possible file. If you use the SVG format frequently, enable the option in Preferences> File Handling & Clipboard to include the SVG code whenever you copy an object to the clipboard. Opening an Illustrator SVG file aligns it to the pixel grid by default.

You can also use Open Type SVG fonts, which is the format for type with multiple colors and gradients in a single glyph, as well as the format for emojis. Both the Asset Export panel and File> Export for Screens allow you to save your objects and files in SVG at the same time as you save them in other formats.

EXPORTING GRAPHICS TO WEB AND MOBILE DEVICES

This section focuses on two recent ways to export images (and artboards) created for the web and mobile devices: Export for Screens and the Asset Export panel.

The Asset Export panel

This panel is especially useful for prepping several objects/ groups at a time for use in other applications, and it's essential for doing so if all of your artwork isn't organized within separate artboards. To define assets, select individual or grouped objects and drag them separately into the upper half of the panel. To combine multiple selected objects or groups into a single asset, hold down the Option/Alt key when you drag them together.

To determine how assets will be exported, adjust Export Settings in the bottom half of the panel (these apply to all the assets, not individually). Here you can set the desired levels of scaling and then select the format—PNG, JPEG, SVG, or PDF—choosing the level of quality you want for PNG and JPEG. Click the +Add Scale button to add another option, even if you're adding SVG or PDF, which don't scale. If you choose to add iOS presets by clicking the iOS button, the Suffix column will update to reflect iOS options for scaling, while Android will do the same, but adding suffixes that pertain to the Android platform. The icon next to the Export button (at the bottom of the panel) opens the Export for Screens dialog, where you can export either artboards or assets.

Export for Screens

Choose the Export for Screens option from File> Export. The major benefit to this dialog, apart from it providing you with the control to be able to export artboards or assets in one place, is that it provides a visual guide to your artboards. When you want to export only a range of artboards, and not all at once, you can deselect all the artboards you don't want to export while looking at the contents of each artboard. You don't have to remember what's on Artboard 27 to decide whether or not you want to export that particular one. If you don't need the visual aid, you can view more at a time using the list view rather than the thumbnail view. You're able to include Bleed, choose your destination, and create subfolders at the same time. Much like Asset Export, you can add scaling, change formats, and choose compatibility with iOS or Android devices; clicking a gear icon lets you select options for a format, such as the Background Color for a PNG file. You also have the option to add a Prefix of your own choosing.

Export Selection

Export Selection, found on its own in the File menu, is just another way to open the Export for Screens dialog with the Assets section active. If you have the Asset Export panel in your workspace, the selected artwork will also be placed in that panel.

Quickest way to export

The quickest way to export your artwork (when you don't need to scale it or export it to multiple formats) is with File> Export As. You can choose to export Artboards (set a range or export all). Pick your export format (including Photoshop, Windows Metafile, and the standard SVG format), and then choose from any options that format provides.

Save for Web (Legacy)

Finally under the Export section of the File menu you'll find Save for Web (Legacy) that is still available whenever you need all of the options you have used in the past to optimize, resize, export slices, or use a Color Table. Save for Web (Legacy) also offers full support for the GIF format. Most of what web designers need is included in the Export for Screens dialog, but to cover it all, there's still the Save for Web (Legacy) option.

Ready to Export

Exporting Options for Layers to Photoshop

Illustrator & Photoshop

Overview: *Organize objects on layers that Photoshop can understand; use Export to Photoshop (PSD) or Copy/ Paste as Smart Object for editing layers in Photoshop; add texture or run other filters as Smart Filters.*

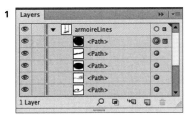

Each brush object is listed in the Layers panel as a <Path> with a filled target icon (see the chapter Your Creative Workspace for help with targeting)

Upon Export to Photoshop, each object stroked with a brush in Illustrator becomes a layer within a Layer Group in Photoshop

If Knockout Group is enabled in Illustrator's Transparency panel (see the Mastering Complexity chapter intro for more about the Transparency panel), sublayers become one layer in Photoshop

ATTEBERRY

When Kevan Atteberry wants to add finishing touches to his illustrations in Photoshop, he has several options for preparing and exporting his artwork from Illustrator. Shown above is a detail from his "Frankie Stein" series, where Atteberry uses Illustrator's ability to write Photoshop layers when exporting to the PSD format, as well as Photoshop's ability to paste selected and copied objects directly as Smart Objects. Exporting layers as PSD layers is the quickest method for adding texture or other raster effects in Photoshop. To use Transform on the object (scale, rotate, etc.), Atteberry copies and pastes it from Illustrator as a Smart Object, which preserves the underlying vector for Photoshop to work with. (For the full illustration, see the "Frankie Stein" gallery following this.)

1 Organizing and rasterizing the layers in Illustrator for export as Photoshop PSD. When Illustrator writes layers for a Photoshop file, it attempts to maintain the layer structure, including all the sublayers. But some types of objects, such as those created with brushes, blends, symbols, or envelopes, generate an unmanageable number of extra sublayers. Two important steps in Illustrator can prevent this from becoming a nuisance in Photoshop. First, Atteberry collects all paths that make up a given object into a named layer. This might be a sublayer of a layer that contains more of a subject, such as the "MUM-layers" containing a "mumsDress" layer. This is just like organizing your hard drive in miniature, making it easy to quickly identify what objects the layers contain. Next, he targets the sublayers, opens the Transparency panel, and enables Knockout Group (you may need to expand panel options). To extend our example, "mumsDress" now becomes a single, rasterized layer in Photoshop, but is still separate from "mumsHair," and both are contained in a Layer Group called "MUMlayers." Photoshop now can preserve Illustrator's file structure and layer names, without creating too many nested groups.

Well-named layers and enabling Knockout Group keeps layers manageable in Photoshop

2 **Using Smart Objects and Smart Filters.** Although any layer or Layer Group can be converted to a Smart Object inside Photoshop, Atteberry copies and pastes Smart Objects directly from Illustrator when he wants to Transform or Warp them. After importing and merging layers as described above, he goes back to Illustrator, selects and copies an object—such as Mum's hand—that he wants to fine-tune in the final version in Photoshop. With the object copied to the clipboard, he returns to Photoshop and chooses Paste. A dialog pops up with options, and he chooses Smart Object. Once the Smart Object is in the right position both in the image and in the stack of layers, he hits Return/Enter to accept it. He then can delete the rasterized layer he had exported earlier, if it doesn't contain other paths. The new layer will always link to the vector file for transforming (so the art won't degrade the way pixel-based artwork would) and for editing in Illustrator.

If he doesn't need to transform an object but wants to add texture inside Photoshop using a filter, instead of copying and pasting from Illustrator again, Atteberry converts the layer to a Smart Object from within Photoshop. Now he can run a Smart Filter on the Smart Object layer (in our example, mumsDress). This allows him to reopen the filter dialog at any time, change settings, delete or add filters, etc., all without altering the original object.

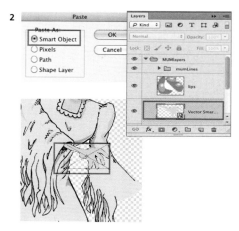

Pasting an object into Photoshop as a Smart Object in order to Transform the object without pixel degradation (blurring)

The dress before adding texture in Photoshop—and after, running Texturizer as a Smart Filter

After choosing Filter> Convert for Smart Filters, a Smart Object layer protects the original pixels and any filter becomes editable

ATTEBERRY

Kevan Atteberry

Illustrator & Photoshop

For his "Frankie Stein" series of illustrated children's books, Atteberry uses Illustrator to create the basic illustration and then moves into Photoshop to add textures and special effects. He carefully constructs his layers in Illustrator to make sure that he can work freely and easily in Photoshop, taking advantage of Photoshop's unique way of creating original artwork. In this illustration (spread over two pages), he prepared his Illustrator layers to use filters, Layer Styles, and Photoshop's soft, feathered brushes. He did this by ensuring the elements that would receive the same treatment in Photoshop were kept on different layers from other elements. See the "Ready to Export" lesson earlier in this chapter for more about layer organization.

ATTEBERRY

Kevan Atteberry
Illustrator & Photoshop

Once Atteberry has imported his descriptively named Illustrator layers to become rasterized Photoshop layers, he depends upon Photoshop's ability to add texture with filters and images, blending it seamlessly into the objects he drew in Illustrator. He makes extensive use of Photoshop's natural soft, feathery brushes to add shadows and highlights to his characters and their environment. He even paints entirely new characters, such as the ghost (opposite page), using soft brushes and building it up gradually with multiple layers set to varying opacities, giving it its ethereal, ghostly quality. Adjustment layers are added to tweak color. The final results of his multi-layered approach achieve his unique blend of the real and the imaginary.

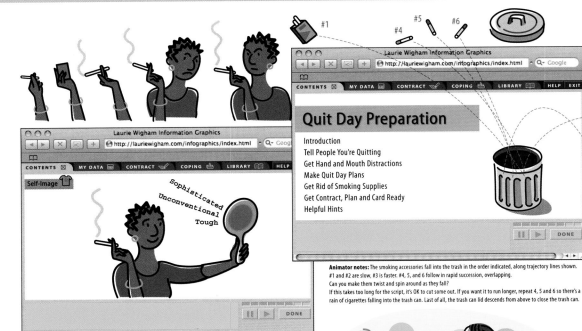

Animator notes: The smoking accessories fall into the trash in the order indicated, along trajectory lines shown. #1 and #2 are slow, #3 is faster. #4, 5, and 6 follow in rapid succession, overlapping. Can you make them twist and spin around as they fall? If this takes too long for the script, it's OK to cut some out. If you want it to run longer, repeat 4, 5 and 6 so there's a rain of cigarettes falling into the trash can. Last of all, the trash can lid descends from above to close the trash can.

Laurie Wigham

Illustrator & Animation

Using Illustrator, Laurie Wigham created the art for the Flash animation, "The Last Draw," a web-based application designed to help people stop smoking (produced by Health Promotion Services, Inc., funded by the National Heart, Lung, and Blood Institute). To make the lines simple and expressive, Wigham drew the characters and other objects with the Pen tool. To create a relaxed and casual look, she drew open-ended unfilled paths, using a thick black stroke with a rounded end cap and corners (Window> Stroke). Beneath the outlines she created unstroked solid-colored objects, deliberately misaligned with the strokes to produce a loose, cut-paper look. Wigham created a collection of drawings that would provide a library of symbols for the animator to later assemble in Flash. She drew each character with differ-

ent positions and facial expressions, including a collection of separate body parts and props that could move independently. She assembled all the drawings needed for each tutorial unit in a single file, positioned on a "stage," framed by the navigation and play controls of the website and browser. Each master layer in the file contained all the elements for a key frame within the animation, as well as motion paths and detailed instructions for the animator.

WIGHAM / Health Promotion Services, Inc.

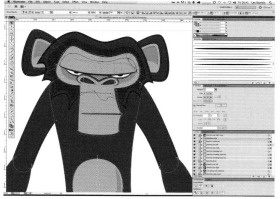

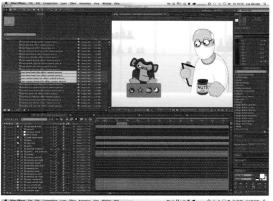

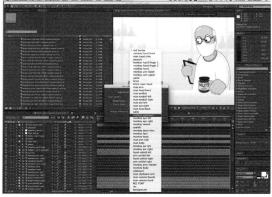

LeeDanielsART
Illustrator & After Effects

Lee Daniels is a UK-based artist and animator who moves fluidly between Illustrator, Photoshop, and After Effects (AE). Daniels's memorable animated shorts add cinematic production values to his classic vector art characters. Although his animations end up in AE, they all begin with his meticulous organization in Illustrator. It's in Illustrator that he creates every possible animated component of each character, separated into vector object groups and organized within a clear and well-labeled layer structure in Illustrator. Once everything is clearly organized, Daniels can move into AE to pull in layers and choose specific objects (such as "monkey eyebrows") to move into position in the AE timeline. As long as his Illustrator files are logical and orderly, once he's in AE he can find what he needs to keep production flowing (the two screenshots directly above). You can see this and many others Daniels animations at www.LeeDanielsART.com.

STIKALICIOUS™

Stikalicious™ Artists

Illustrator & iPad App Development

Mark "Atomos" Pilon, Podgy Panda, Frazer, Dacosta!, Charuca, Tokyo-go-go, Jared Nickerson, Steve Talkowski; Killamari, kaNO, MAD, Abe Lincoln Jr., Gabriel Mourelle, Shawnimals, EdWarner, Junichi Tsuneoka
(top to bottom; left column then right)
Using Illustrator, artists from all over the world create the Stikalicious™ characters that Dacosta! of Chocolate Soop® then prepares

for his wallpaper app for the iPad (see their lesson in the *Your Creative Workspace* chapter for more). Users purchase character sets, and then drag a background and characters into the screen area. Overlay controls allow you to move, scale, rotate, and change the characters stacking order. Wallpaper designs are automatically saved to your workspace (WIP), where you can edit, copy, delete, or even share a design.

RIDDLE & JOLY

Mic Riddle & Dave Joly
Illustrator, Cinema 4D, & After Effects

Still working on their "Trick or Treat" movie, Mic Riddle and Dave Joly created the 3D scenes for the animation. Again, they often began inside Illustrator. Most 3D programs are able to import Illustrator paths and use them as the start for creating an extruded or lathed object, such as the doorway and clock shown here, both of which have dimension. It's these surfaces that, once lit in Cinema 4D or another 3D application, cast and receive shadows that convince us the objects are no longer flat illustrations. And just as they created a layer for each 2D part they intended to animate in Flash, they drew each "object" on its own layer that would be extruded in Cinema 4D, making extensive use of compound paths to represent both a solid dimensional surface and a hole for windows, or the cavity for a clock's pendulum. They added more animation and camera movements, color, texture, and pattern, and then they rendered their movie "scenes" to be imported into After Effects. They used After Effects both for features that were easier to produce there and to save some time tweaking a scene by not jumping back and forth between programs. Finally, files were collected in Final Cut Pro, where they added sound and performed final edits, and saved as a .mov file (find a low-res version of the animation on **WOW! ONLINE**).

Finishing Touches

Adding Scenic Entourage Elements & Using Photoshop for Lighting Effects

MARIC

Illustrator, Painter, Go Media, & Photoshop

Overview: *Place a photo sky as the background; add entourage elements; create lighting effects in Photoshop.*

Sky background image created in Corel Painter

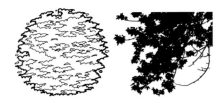

Go Media's bush and "foreground" tree vector entourage elements

To complete his architectural rendering created with Illustrator's perspective grid, Pete Maric inserted a photo background, added scenic "entourage" elements, and manually created lighting effects in Photoshop.

1 Replacing the sky background image and importing entourage elements. Maric decided to change the mood of the illustration by replacing the background sky image to reflect a dusk setting. In Illustrator, Maric created a new bottom layer and chose File> Place to choose a JPG of a sunset that he photographed and transformed with Corel Painter. Maric relies heavily on a library of entourage elements (cars, people, trees, bushes, etc.) to add interest to his illustrations. After importing a couple of his own trees, Maric opened Go Media's Architectural Elements Vector Pack and chose a bush and a foreground tree detail to copy and paste into his rendering. He sampled the grass color with the Eyedropper tool and then filled each bush with that color by holding Option/Alt and clicking. To populate the scene he duplicated each bush individually by holding Option/Alt while dragging it into place, using the bounding box to scale when needed.

2 Creating lighting effects in Photoshop. In Photoshop, he rasterized the Illustrator file using File> Open, enabled the Constrain Proportions setting, and set the Resolution to 300 pixels/inch. To help focus the image on the architecture, he darkened the corners by adding a blue solid rectangle layer, set the transparency to Multiply, created a layer mask, and applied a radial gradient to the center of the mask. Maric then manually created mood lighting effects by overlaying another series of gradient-filled layers on top of the image. He created the gradients by sampling color from his image using Photoshop's Eyedropper tool. He created the gradients on separate layers, and then he painted on one layer, added layer masks as necessary to each of them, adjusted the layer opacity, and applied different blending modes.

3 Adding realistic reflections to the windows and simulating interior artificial lighting. To create a reflection in the windows, Maric used Photoshop's Pen tool to create an accurate selection inside the windows. He then opened a photo, selected and copied it to the clipboard, and pasted it into the window selection using Edit> Paste Special> Paste Into. To integrate the reflection photograph into the overall look of the illustration, he applied Gaussian Blur and Watercolor effects to it. To create an interior light glow effect, Maric added an additional 50px feather to the window selection using Select> Modify> Feather, created a new layer, filled it with a light yellow color, and reduced the layer opacity. For added interest and to mimic hotspots from interior lights, he created a new layer, used the Elliptical Marquee tool to select a small circular area within the windows, feathered the selection by 10px, and filled the selection with the same color used for the glow layer. To duplicate the highlight, he held Option/Alt and click-dragged it into place. He continued to duplicate the highlights for most of the front windows.

The illustration with all entourage added

2

The light effect layers created in Photoshop

3

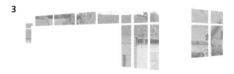

The window reflections photograph shown after being pasted inside the window selection

Window glow and highlights in Photoshop

Rick Johnson

Illustrator, CADtools, & Photoshop

Rick Johnson illustrated this GG1 electric locomotive, most of which were built in the late 1930s for the Pennsylvania Railroad by General Electric, for *Classic Trains* magazine using blueprints, photographs, and field notes. One might be tempted to draw this using Illustrator's perspective tools, but Johnson needed this drawing to be as technically accurate as possible. He began by drawing everything precisely to scale in "flat" orthographic top, front, and side views in Illustrator using HotDoor's CADtools plug-in (download the latest demo versions from www.hotdoor.com/cadtools). Then, also using CADtools, Johnson projected those surfaces to their respective trimetric angles. With the help of custom-angle Smart Guides (set to 39°, –12°, 90° in Preferences> Smart Guides),

he aligned the pieces to their appropriate X, Y, and Z axis. He divided the art into 76 layers based on logical groups (e.g., tracks and power trucks, underframe, interior components, skeleton, and shell). He then exported the art to a layered Photoshop (psd) file, and in Photoshop he adjusted the coloring, contouring, and shading. He used layer masks to reveal the most (and most interesting) interior detail while still showing the outside form of this classic locomotive, which meant sometimes ghosting several layers at once. Since he had already drawn the entire locomotive from the inside out, the ctr.trains.com website was able to repurpose the art, so visitors could disassemble the locomotive, peeling away a layer at a time.

Von Glitschka
Illustrator & InkScribe/VectorScribe

For its part in the 2011 London International Technology Show, Astute Graphics commissioned Von Glitschka to create a poster with a British theme to showcase their Illustrator plug-in InkScribe. Glitschka researched heraldry, then combined a rampant lion with the recently-popularized 1939 WW II "Keep Calm and Carry On" posters, and came up with this poster concept. Glitschka made the initial sketch on paper and then scanned and opened it in Illustrator. To begin manually tracing over it, he selected the InkScribe tool. InkScribe consists of a tool (added to the Tools) and a panel with a new set of functions (accessed from the Window menu), so using it is completely seamless with using any other Illustrator features. The InkScribe tool replaces not only the Pen tool but also its editing tools (Add, Convert,

Direct Selection, etc.). The InkScribe tool requires minimal use of modifier keys to perform most functions and also includes a customizable Annotations overlay (see middle, above), making for a very efficient workflow. Glitschka used the InkScribe tool to both draw and edit his paths. The user-customizable functions and onscreen annotations made it easier for him to precisely adjust Bézier handles, change anchor point type, and minimize the number of anchor points as he drew, making clean-up and editing much easier. He occasionally also used Illustrator's geometric shapes and Pathfinder operations, such as when he created the lion's claws, and used Astute Graphics' Dynamic Corners plug-in, part of Astute's VectorScribe set, to round off some of the very sharp corners, adding a more organic flow to the vector art.

GLITSCHKA / GlitschkaStudios.com

Planning Ahead

Working Between Illustrator & Photoshop

**Illustrator & Photoshop
Advanced Technique**

Overview: *Plan ahead for export to Photoshop with layer organization; group or separate some objects on layers based on the Photoshop technique you will use; make a registration rectangle for precise placement.*

HUBIG

The Illustrator file before export to Photoshop

Keeping overlapping objects on separate layers, making it easier in Photoshop to add texture and effects to objects without making selections

When Dan Hubig creates an illustration like "Soothing Nervous Patients," above, he relies upon both Illustrator and Photoshop to get the job done efficiently and quickly. Consequently, he constructs his files in Illustrator with Photoshop's strengths and weaknesses in mind. Because the two programs have very different features, even when those features share the same name (such as brushes), Hubig organizes his objects so their Photoshop layers will allow him complete flexibility and ease in creating the finishing touches. And by setting his layers to flatten sublayers on export, he reduces the RAM requirements of his large files and shortens the time it takes Illustrator to create the Photoshop file.

1 Planning ahead. The main rule Hubig has when organizing his layers is that overlapping objects he will work on in Photoshop *do not* reside on the same layer. As long as they are on separate layers when exported to Photoshop, he'll be able to lock transparency (which acts like a mask limiting a tool to actual pixels), clip an Adjustment layer so it affects only that object, etc.—all without having to make tedious selections inside Photoshop. By constructing his layer organization this way, rather than grouping by subject (such as the dentist on one main layer, with its parts as sublayers), he can rasterize all the sublayers, so Photoshop doesn't import them as nested Groups when he uses Knockout Group to export the blends he likes to use (see the lesson "Ready to Export" for a full description of this method). The trade-off, however, is that if Hubig doesn't pay careful attention to naming the layers, once they're in Photoshop, his layer organization may not always be as "intuitive" as it would be if grouped according to subject matter.

In Photoshop, creating a Smart Object to apply a Smart Filter on two Illustrator objects placed on one layer, and reducing opacity for both at the same time

2 **Preparing artwork for finishing in Photoshop.** Aware of the Photoshop techniques he plans to use, Hubig is also able to save time by putting objects that will receive the same treatment in Photoshop on the same layer. If you look at the two floor shadows in the illustration, you can see they both have Gaussian Blurs and reduced opacity. By creating them on a single Illustrator layer, Hubig is able to apply the blur and change the layer opacity in Photoshop just once for both objects. On the other hand, by keeping the blue cloud on a separate layer, Hubig is able to make changes even though it overlaps other objects visually. He can adjust the cloud's opacity, and by locking the layer's transparency he can loosely apply a brush with a broad "Scattering" (set in the Brushes panel), knowing his paint won't spill onto other objects.

Locking just the transparency in a layer to limit the effect of a tool or command to just the pixels—essentially, "auto-masking" the object

3 **Bringing new objects into Photoshop with a registration rectangle.** Although Hubig typically eyeballs the placement of objects in Photoshop, you might have a need for precision when moving objects into Photoshop. Make sure your artboard and image sizes in Photoshop are the same. Then, to achieve precise registration, create an unstroked, unfilled rectangle on the top layer (to select easily) that is the same size as the artboard. Select both the object(s) and the registration rectangle, and copy and paste them as pixels in Photoshop. This positions your new art precisely where it belongs with respect to earlier artwork, and on its own layer. Finally, drag the artwork layer into position among the other layers, if necessary.

Creating a registration rectangle with no stroke, no fill, and selecting both it and an object to paste as pixels in Photoshop for precise alignment with existing artwork

DEL VECHIO

Gustavo Del Vechio
Illustrator & Photoshop

When Gustavo Del Vechio wanted an illustration to go along with his humanistic interpretation of an urban development project, he decided to make it appear as if the designer could make a real city rise up from his pencil-and-paper drawing. He contrasted the flat paper with the dimensional illustration, and the illustration with the full three-dimensionality of a photograph; then he lit the whole to place the designer under a drafting lamp. He made the background from a simple rectangle filled with a white to black radial gradient. He filled another rectangle with white and used Effect> Stylize> Scribble on black-filled objects to create very flat-looking hatch marks representing the urban area. Del Vechio then linked the photos of each hand to a separate layer,

adding Effect> Drop Shadow to one with a positive X value, and to the other with a negative X value, maintaining the illusion of radial light from above. Finally he added the completed illustration from his project for the urban development proposal. He had used 3D Studio Max for the initial structures, hand-traced the rendering, and later turned it into a Live Paint group to complete the colorful illustration (see his lesson in the *Rethinking Construction* chapter). Having placed his buildings in a designer's environment, his final illustration demonstrated what goes into creating a city, from the artist's initial concept to a three-dimensional reality.

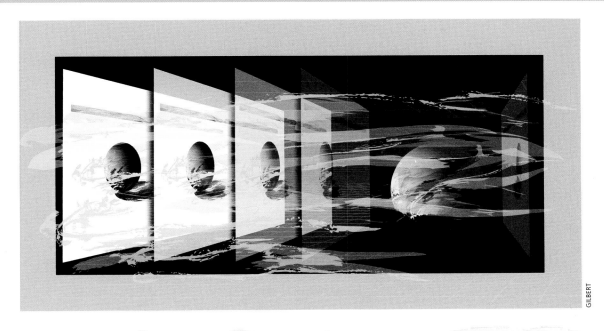

GILBERT

Katharine Gilbert

Illustrator & Photoshop

Katharine Gilbert moves freely between Illustrator and Photoshop, mixing vector, raster, and 3D to express her vision.

For "Wind," Gilbert began in Illustrator with an abstract painting that she created with art brushes (loaded from Window> Brush Libraries> Artistic> Artistic_Paintbrush and Artistic_Water-color). She then moved to Photoshop Extended where she applied the painting as a surface to a 3D sphere. After applying the texture image to her "world," she placed a rasterized version of it in a new Illustrator file to act as a guide for painting the "wind" layers. She used the same art brushes as before, tweaking them slightly as needed. She turned off the image layers and exported only the vector artwork, which she saved with PDF compatibility. Back in Photoshop, Gilbert opened the .ai file as a Photoshop

PDF, and then experimented with the sphere, her Illustrator art, and some Photoshop brush-work to add shadows and more depth to the sphere. She duplicated the elements, merging them into a 3D Postcard, rendered several copies at different angles, and added more image elements for added depth and contrast. She placed the sphere above and then tied her universe together by placing her Illustrator painting of the wind over all.

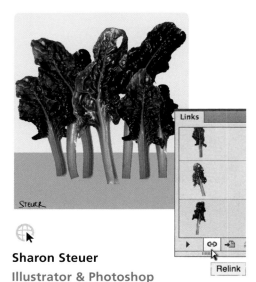

Sharon Steuer
Illustrator & Photoshop

After creating a chard leaf forest from raster art brushes (see her "chard forest" gallery in the *Mastering Complexity* chapter), Sharon Steuer was able to quickly correct an error and then make a new variation on her composition. When a friend spotted a mistake in the mask of a leaf, she opened the original leaf in Photoshop, repaired the mask, and saved the new file. Back in Illustrator, she selected the problem leaf, opened the Links panel, clicked the Relink button, and selected the new image, which then automatically resized to match the original dimensions. After applying Rasterize to this version at 150 ppi, she held Option/Alt as she dragged the repaired leaf over the original. After making sure her Options settings were correct, she clicked OK and then enabled Apply to Strokes to automatically update all instances of that brush. To create a variation on the composition, Steuer first duplicated her chard forest artboard. She opened the Brushes panel, then selected each leaf, and clicked a different brush to apply that brush to the selected path. By nudging a few paths with the cursor keys, using the Bounding Box to scale or slightly rotate a leaf, or using the Layers panel to move a leaf up and down in the stacking order, so in just a few minutes she was able to create a variation on the chard forest arrangement. In the image directly above she also used the Pencil and Smooth tools to create hills; applied gradients to copies of the background rectangles (Fading Sky for the blue, a customized Foliage gradient from the Swatch Libraries menu for the greens); and adjusted the angle and range of each gradient using the Gradient tool. Finally, locking the background layer, Steuer selected all the leaves and enlarged the leaves as a unit using the Bounding Box. (Find links to movies demonstrating this process with a free lynda.com trial via sharonsteuer.com/lynda.)

Lance Jackson
Illustrator & SVG

Artist Lance Jackson created this dystopian illustration for the opinion special report "Climate Change: A Rising Tide," in the *Orange County Register*. When creating illustrations for use on the web, Jackson often prefers to save the art in the vector-based SVG format rather than PNG, GIF, or JPEG files, which are pixel-based. Used properly, SVG files are faster-loading and scalable, with no loss of resolution. While drawing, Jackson was careful to use the fewest number of points possible, as these make the SVG bulkier (though the Object> Path> Simplify controls can help). Once the art was finished, he selected the Artboard panel, chose Artboard Options and then Fit To Artwork Bounds in the Preset drop-down menu, and clicked OK. This sizes the artboard to the exact dimension of the art. To export the art as SVG, Jackson selected File> Save As (⌘-Shift-S/Ctrl-Shift-S), named the file, and clicked Save. In the SVG Options panel, Jackson set the SVG Profiles drop-down menu to SVG 1.1 (the optimal setting for most situations). In the Fonts section he set Format to SVG and Subsetting (which controls how fonts are handled in SVG files) at None (use system fonts), as there was no text in his image. In the Options section he enabled Embed, since he planned to insert the SVG code directly into his HTML document, rather than link to an external file. The Preserve Illustrator Editing Capabilities option increases the file size, so he made sure it was disabled. Jackson then clicked the More Options button at the bottom of the panel, made sure Responsive was enabled, and

JACKSON (for The Orange County Register)

clicked OK. Jackson then opened the SVG file in a text editor, copied the code to the clipboard, and pasted it directly into the HTML file. The responsive SVG image automatically gets larger or smaller, adapting to the size of the browser window with no loss of resolution (above left). This is important for responsive websites, which are designed to rescale their content on mobile devices. When an SVG image is not responsive, it will get cut off when the browser window changes size (above right).

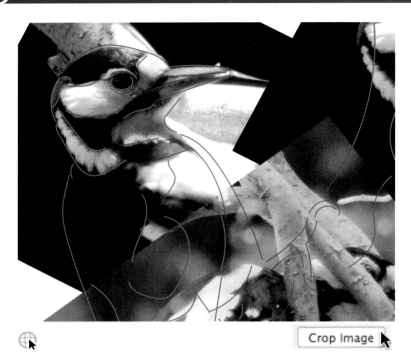

Crop Image

GAUSE

Monika Gause (Vektorgarten)

Illustrator & Photographs

To prepare for a digital rendering of the Great Spotted Woodpecker, Monika Gause looked through photos she'd recently taken. Though none of the photos met all her requirements, she was able to assemble the needed level of detail and overall pose information using a portions of a half-dozen photos. To use these photos as references in Illustrator before **CC** added Crop Image, Gause would have had to first save out separate cropped and enlarged portions of photos she thought she might need from Photoshop. Instead, she was able to place all the photos she might need off to the side of her artboard. Then, as she identified a detail she needed, she'd hold Option/Alt to duplicate that photo into her main work area; reduce, enlarge, and/or flip it as needed; and then click the Crop Image button in the Properties (or Control) panel. Adjusting the crop to fit the desired detail, she clicked Apply. She can continue to flip, rotate, and further enlarge the cropped version. As she worked, she sometimes overlapped photos, rotating them into relative position to help her visualize the assembled reference. Locking the reference layers, she created the vector illustration on layers above. Above left shows some of the photos in position as she constructed the vector outlines (the photo she used for the head is flipped and cropped); directly above right shows the final bird in place (flipped and cropped).

Production Notes for

The Adobe Illustrator WOW! Book for CS6 and CC *(1st & 2nd Editions)*

Interior Book Design and Production

This book was primarily produced in Illustrator CC, Photoshop CC, and InDesign CC, using Adobe's Minion Pro and Frutiger LT Std OpenType fonts. Barbara Sudick is the artist behind the original **Illustrator WOW!** design and typography, using Jill Davis's layout of **The Photoshop WOW! Book** as a starting point. Cary Norsworthy and Mimi Heft (who also designed our book cover) contributed to additional page-design specs. Victor Von Salza led the porting of our templates from QuarkXpress to InDesign CS and modernized our style sheets. In addition to being principal writers, **Cristen Gillespie** wears many hats including updating our style guides, and **Steven H. Gordon** is a curatorial co-conspirator. The amazing **Jean-Claude Tremblay** is not only the **WOW!** technical editor, but his company Proficiografik produces (and troubleshoots) all the commercial and press-ready PDFs for the book. We tested pages with Adobe Acrobat DC. Premedia Systems wrote custom scripts for lessons in the book and helped us to update and sync the many InDesign files. Many of us use Wacom tablets and Art Pens.

Our fabulous WOW! Testers

Monika Gause is a graphic designer, illustrator, teacher, and author of books on Adobe Illustrator published in Germany and is a featured artist in this book; **Federico Platón** likes to re-create urban scenes and common objects using the wide variety of Illustrator tools, using a close realism approach. **Victor van Dijk** is a web and multimedia enthusiast, and you can find him at viavictorvandijk.nl, on social media @vfvandijk, and at vfvandijk@gmail.com. **Nini Tjäder** is a Mac nerd (since 1984) with a love for photography and a lot of other things, and is a former educator in most Adobe applications since the end of the 80s. **Chana Messer** is an artist, designer, and manager of the LA Adobe Illustrator User Group and is an Adobe Certified Expert in Illustrator, InDesign, Photoshop, and Lightroom. Additional testers for this edition: **Destery Hildenbrand**, **Brad Hamann**, **Greg Geisler**, **Ari Weinstein**, **Kat Gilbert**, **Stéphane Nahmani**, and **Simona Pfreundner**. Please see **The Adobe Illustrator WOW! Team** and **Acknowledgments** sections for full details on **WOW!** contributors.

How to Contact the Author

To find out about the latest **WOW!** articles or publications, report a change you've discovered due to updated CC content, or submit artwork for consideration in future **Illustrator WOW!** books, please send Sharon a link to a web page containing samples of your work (please do not send files!) via **sharonsteuer.com/contact**. You can also keep in touch with Sharon via social media **@SharonSteuer**.

Artists Appendix

Ray Acosta
ray_acosta@yahoo.com
rayacosta.com
@rayacosta

Anil Ahuja
Adobe Systems
I-1A, Sec-25A
Noida UP-201301 INDIA
+91-9810566779
ahuja@adobe.com

Kenneth Albert
kennethalbert.com
kennethalbert@carbonmade.com

Kevan Atteberry
P.O. Box 40188
Bellevue, WA 98015-4188
206-550-6353
kevan@oddisgood.com
oddisgood.com

Jean Aubé
785 Versailles #301
Montréal Québec
CANADA H3C 1Z5
jeanaube01@videotron.ca

Janaína Cesar de Oliveira Baldacci
São Paulo City, São Paulo
Brasil
(011) 37910918, (011)
73687068
janacesar@gmail.com
jana@janabaldacci.com
janabaldacci.com

Billie Bryan
717-363-8500
888-455-3384
billie@beethedesigner.com
beethedesigner.com

Pariah Burke
503-422-7499
me@iampariah.com
iampariah.com
@iamPariah

Cinthia A. Burnett
cinabur@yahoo.com

James Cassidy
860-223-8441
alliancewebdesign.com
@alliancewebdsgn

Charuca
charuca.eu

George Coghill
george@coghillcartooning.com
coghillcartooning.com
@gcoghill

Sandee Cohen
33 Fifth Avenue, #10B
New York, NY 10003
212-677-7763
sandee@vectorbabe.com
vectorbabe.com

Sally Cox
408-628-2780
sally@kreatable.com
kreatable.com
@kreatable

Laura Coyle
illustratoring.com
coyleart.com
@illustratoring

Mike Cressy
mikecressy.com

Dacosta!
info@chocolatesoop.com
chocolatesoop.com
@chocolatesoop

Lee Daniels
+44 7909 583226
inbox@LeeDanielsART.com

Gustavo Del Vechio
Brazil
gustavodelvechio@gmail.com
nucleodoilustrator.com
@gudelvechio

Victor van Dijk
vfvandijk@gmail.com
victorvandijk.nl
IG/FB: @vfvandijk

Suzanne Drapeau
sdrapeau@sbcglobal.net

Dedree Drees
5307 Wayne Ave.
Baltimore, MD 21207
410-448-3317
443-840-4423
dedreedrees@cavtel.net
ddreesart.wordpress.com

Elaine Drew
elaine-drew@comcast.net
elainedrew.com

Nicole Dzienis

EdWarner
edwarner.wordpress.com

Gary Ferster
1250 Route 34 Bldg. 2 #14
Tinton Falls, NJ 07753
732-757-1937
gferster@verizon.net
garyferster.com
TW: @garyillustrator

Frazer
frazercreative.com

Monika Gause
Archenholzstr. 56, 22117
Hamburg, Germany
+4940-78071100
m.gause@mediawerk.de
vektorgarten.de
IG/FB/TW: @vektorgarten

Greg Geisler
512-619-3635
greg@raytracer.com
raytracer.com

Katharine Gilbert
550 Hazelwood Road
Aylett, VA 23009
804-994-2929
mail@truschgilbertdesign.com
inthewoodonline.com
@katgilbert

Von R. Glitschka
Glitschka Studios
1976 Fitzpatrick Ave SE
Salem, OR 97306
971-223-6143
von@glitschka.com
GlitschkaStudios.com
IG: @vglitschka
FB: @glitschkastudios
TW: @vonster

Mordy Golding
rwillustrator.blogspot.com
mordy@mordy.com

Steven H. Gordon
Cartagram, LLC
136 Mill Creek Crossing
Madison, AL 35758
cartagram@outlook.com
cartagram.com

Laurie Grace
laurie.grace@gmail.com
lauriegrace.com

Cheryl Graham
cherylgraham.net
@FreeTransform

Gusman, *see* Joly

Brad Hamann
Brad Hamann Illustration
& Design
brad@bradhamann.com
bradhamann.com

Dan Hubig
209 Mississippi St.
San Francisco, CA 94107
415-824-0838
dan@danhubig.com
danhubig.com

Lisa Jackmore
ljackmore@comcast.net
IG: @lisajackmore

Lance Jackson
Lance Jackson Design
noirture.com
lancejackson.net

Mahalia Johnson
mahaliaclarke85@yahoo.com

Rick Johnson
Graffix plug-ins
rj-graffix.com

Donal Jolley
10505 Wren Ridge Road
Johns Creek, GA 30022
770-751-0553
don@donaljolley.com
donaljolley.com
@donaljolley

Annie Gusman Joly
860-928-1042
annie@picturedance.com
anniejoly.com

Dave Joly
860-928-1042
dave@picturedance.com
picturedance.com

kaNO
kanokid.com

Killamari
killamari.com

Mike Kimball
PO Box 77492
San Francisco, CA 94107
mkimballsf@aim.com
MKSF-Gallery.com

Steve King
Senior Illustrator/Designer
U-Haul International, Inc.
9010 S Priest Drive #1216
Tempe, AZ 85284
480-252-0720
stevekingartist@gmail.com
kingillustration.com
IG: @ kingillustration
TW: @art_kingsteve
FB: @ kingbookartist

Stephen Klema
69 Walnut St.
Winsted, CT 06098
860-379-1579
stephen@stephenklema.com
sklema@txcc.comnet.edu
stephenklema.com
SnotArt.org

Raymond Larrett
715 Frederick Street
San Francisco, CA 94117
415-595-8240
rlarrett@puzzledsquirrel.com
puzzledsquirrel.com
@PSquirreleBooks

Chris Leavens
chris@unloosen.com
chrisleavens.com

Adam Z Lein
530-330-5346
adamz@adamlein.com
adamlein.com

Jean-Benoit Levy
Studio AND
2278 15th Street #4
San Francisco, CA 94114
415-252-0506
jbl@and.ch
and.ch

Abe Lincoln Jr.
girlsbike.com

Amber Loukoumis

MAD
madtoydesign.com

Pete Maric
440-487-4205
contact@petemaric.com
petemaric.com

Danuta Markiewicz (Danka)
pazourek@gmail.com

Jeffrey Martin
jmartin584@gmail.com

Greg Maxson
116 W. Florida Ave
Urbana, IL 61801
217-898-6560
gregdraws@gmail.com
gregmaxson.com
@gregdraws

Aaron McGarry
amcgarry.com
aaronmcgarry.com

MCKIBILLO
josh@mckibillo.com
mckibillo.com
@mckibillo

Chana Messer
5535 Westlawn Ave #334
Los Angeles CA 90066
310 980-1583
chana.messer@gmail.com
chanamesser.myportfolio.com/
IG: @chana53
FB: @chana.messer

Nobuko Miyamoto
Matubacho 3-8
Tokorozawasi
Saitama Prefecture/
359-0044
+81-42-998-6631
venus@gol.com
venus.oracchi.com/

Yukio Miyamoto
Matubacho 3-8
Tokorozawasi
Saitama Prefec-
ture/359-0044
+81-42-998-6631
yukio-m@ppp.bekkoame.ne.jp
bekkoame.ne.jp/
~yukio-m/intro

Tamara Morrison
524 Torringford East Street
Torrington, CT 06790
860-806-2951
tamaramorrisongraphics@
gmail.com
tamaramorrisongraphics.com

Gabriel Mourelle
gabrielmourelle.com.ar

Sebastian Murra Ramirez
(mu!)
info@mu-illustration.com
mu-illustration.com
@muillustration

Stéphane Nahmani
sholby@sholby.net
sholby.net

Jared Nickerson
jthreeconcepts.com

Chris D. Nielsen
6662 Timaru Circle
Cypress, CA 90630
714-323-1602
carartwork@ca.rr.com
chris@pentoolart.com
pentoolart.com

Ann Paidrick
ann.paidrick@ebypaidrick.com
ebypaidrick.com

Ellen Papciak-Rose
info@ellenpapciakrose.com
ellenpapciakrose.com

Franck Payen
fr32c.free.fr
thekandinskycomplex.
bandcamp.com/
@fr32c

Richard Perez
119 Haight St, Apt 28
San Francisco, CA 94102
415-656-6576
info@skinnyships.com
skinnyships.com
@skinnyships

Stephanie Pernal

Simona Pfreundner
Montreal, Canada
info@vectortwist.com
vectortwist.com
IG: @vectortwist
FB: @simona.vectortwist

Mark 'Atomos' Pilon
markpilon.com

Federico Platon
José Martinez Velasco 8, 5i.
Madrid 28007 Spain
34-1-5732467
grafintek@gmail.com

Podgy Panda
podgypanda.com

Lisa Poje
pojemotion.com
lisa@pojemotion.com
@pojemotion

Ryan Putnam
ryan@rypearts.com
rypearts.com
@rypearts

Sabine Reinhart
Jakob Hoogen Straße 61
41844 Wegberg, Germany
sabine@sabinereinhart.de
sabinereinhart.de
@SabineReinhart

Michael (Mic) Riddle
micrid3d@mac.com

Andrew Roberts
01223 571538
ar@andyrobertsdesign.com
andyrobertsillustration.com
@arillustrate

Jolynne Roorda
folktheory.com

Andrew Rudmann
Design Lead at Tinder
Los Angeles, CA
Arudmann@gmail.com

Rachel Sellers
256-282-9333
rachel@rsdirectionaldesign.com

Shawnimals
shawnimals.com

Sharon Steuer
(Illustrator **WOW!** author)
San Francisco CA
sharonsteuer.com
sharonsteuer.com/contact
IG/FB/TW: @SharonSteuer

Kevin Stohlmeyer
222 E. Erie Street, Suite 330
Milwaukee, WI 53202
kevinstohlmeyer.com
@kstohl

Brian & Janet Stoppee
M2 Media Studios, Inc.
m2media.com/
light@m2media.com
@BrianStoppee
FB: @brian.stoppee
FB: @janet.stoppee

Ilene Strizver
The Type Studio
Westport, CT
203-227-5929
ilene@thetypestudio.com
thetypestudio.com

Shawn Sullivan
Artist, Illustrator
22482 Alma Aldea #250
Rancho Santa Margarita,
CA 92688
714-390-8553
sullycreative@gmail.com
customgraffiti.com
IG/FB/TW: @CustomGraffiti

Brenda Sutherland
345 Park Avenue
San Jose, CA 95124

Steve Talkowski
sketchbot.tv

Moses Tan
37 Kingloch Parade
Wantirna, Victoria
Australia 3152
03 97291120
mosestan@optusnet.com.au

Nini Tjäder
ninisworld.com
ninisworld.com/wordpress
ninisworld-blog.blogspot.com
@ninitj
FB: @nini.tjader
Pinterest: @nini_tjader

Tokyo-go-go
tokyo-go-go.com

Jack Tom
1042 Broad Street
Bridgeport, CT 06604
203-579-0889
art2go2006@yahoo.com
jacktom.com

Jean-Claude Tremblay
Proficiografik
191 Chemin Haendel
Candiac, Québec J5R 1S6
CANADA
514-629-0949
info@proficiografik.com
proficiografik.com

Junichi Tsuneoka
stubbornsideburn.com

David Turton
thegraphiclibrary.com

Ed Warner
edwarner.wordpress.com

Ari M. Weinstein
24 Vascello Rd
New Windsor NY 12553
845-475-8704
ari@ariw.com
ariw.com
IG/FB/TW: @AriDublyu

Laurie Wigham
laurie@lauriewigham.com
lauriewigham.com

Darren Winder
daw design
darren@dawdesign.net
dawdesign.com

Jillian Winkel

Jamal Wynn
56 White Oak Avenue
Plainville, CT 06062
860-631-7767
MrJrWynn@gmail.com
FB: @JamalWynn

Brian Yap
briankyap@gmail.com

General Index

> arrow symbol, 22
• • • (more options, three dots symbol), 14, 15, 227, 228
> key, 165
< key, 165
V arrow symbol, 22
+ (plus) sign
　cursor using, 16
　overflow text indicator, 16

A

Abe Lincoln, Jr., 294, 310
Abutting option (Image Trace panel), 69
acknowledgments, xxii
Acosta, Ray, 101, 308
Adjust Adjoining Width Points option (Width Point Edit dialog), 111
adjustment layers (Photoshop), 281, 300
Adobe Acrobat, 282
Adobe Color Themes panel, 171–172
Adobe Creative Suite, xviii
Adobe Fonts, 12, 44
Adobe Ideas, 225
Adobe Illustrator Clipboard (AICB), 279
Adobe Illustrator **WOW!** Book, The
　CS5 cover photo, 270
　CS6 and CC cover photo, 273
　how to use, xiv-xvi
　organization of, xvi-xvii
　tip boxes in, xvi
Adobe Kuler. See Adobe Color Themes panel
Advanced Toolbar, 13, 15
After Effects, 293, 295
Ahuja, Anil, 129, 215, 218–219, 308
.ai files
　Bevels.ai file, 199
　compatibility with InDesign and Photoshop, 278
　opening as Photoshop PDF, 303
　preserving layers and **CC** features with, 279
　recovering missing linked files for, 278

AICB (Adobe Illustrator Clipboard), 279
Albert, Kenneth, 133, 308
Alias Sketchbook Pro, 124
Align panel, 69–70
Align to Page option (Blend Option dialog), 240
Align to Path option (Blend Option dialog), 240
aligning
　grids and planes in sketches, 222–223
　objects, 69–70
　symbols, 283
　type to path, 51–52
Anchor Point tool, 77
anchor points
　adding to gradient mesh, 183
　altering with Live Corners, 74–75
　converting to line in freeform gradient, 173
　removing excess, 70
　reshaping paths via, 77
　width points vs., 111
"And Then I Swam" (Rudmann), 20
"Angels in the Rapids" illustration, 250–251
Animate, 117, 284, 292
animating
　Graphic Symbols, 282
　Illustrator vector objects, 293
　layers, 283–284
　preparing art for Flash, 292
　symbols in, 117
　3D scenes with layers and objects, 295
anti-aliasing, 282, 283
appearance attributes
　adding to logos, 58
　finding, 81
　Frosty cones graphic design, 59
　making and applying, 24–25
　preserving exported Photoshop, 281
　sampling and applying text, 37
　visibility of, 8
Appearance panel
　accessing pop-up instances from, 162
　adding graphic styles via, 9
　adjusting type on, 58, 59
　attributes on, 24, 25
　basic appearance settings for, 9
　decreasing opacity in, 185

editing type characters and type objects, 37–38
locating *fx* icon on, 24, 25, 29
managing objects in, 5–6
New Art Has Basic Appearance setting, xv-xvi, 9, 200
styling text with, 61
targeting path's Stroke attribute, 181
using, 8–9
viewing Layers and, 8
Application Frame (Mac), 2
Arc Segment Tool Options dialog, 27
architectural sketches
　aligning grids and planes in, 222–223
　scaling, 28–29
arcs
　arcing labels, 51
　drawing with Pen tool, 26, 27
　guides for, 245
　placing type on, 54–55
area type
　converting to point type, 42
　features of, 33
　placing, 285
　refining type elements with, 47
　using Touch Type tool with, 60
Area Type Options dialog, 47
arrowheads, 112–113
art brushes
　applying to Pen and pencil paths, 133
　creating, 115
　customizing, 145
　stroke for, 113–114
Art Pens. See Wacom Art pens
Artboard Options dialog, 10, 48
Artboard panel, 10, 40
Artboard ruler, 4–5
　X,Y changing ruler origin, 47
artboards
　acting as cropping masks, 245
　copying art to, 11, 40
　creating company identity with multiple, 48–49
　duplicating, 96
　exporting, 11, 41
　finishing for permits, 29
　multiple, 9–11, 39–41
　overlapping, 11, 41, 134
　perspective limits for, 205
　printing, 41
　renaming, 40, 46
　resizing, 11, 16, 40, 46, 97, 224

saving as file, 41, 279
sharing, 49
showing rulers, Smart Guides, and grids, 4–5
Trim View and Presentation Mode displays for, 16
vanishing point extended beyond, 220
artichoke sketch, 136–137
"Artistic Painting with Illustrator" courses, 120, 121, 158, 159
artists appendix, 308–311
artwork. See also artboards; freehand drawing; painterly style
adding in PEM, 249
Auto-Corners in, 153
auto-scaling, 28–29
coloring line art with Live Paint, 84–85
completing as fine art piece, 135
converting to symbols, 11, 40, 116
corner tile adjustments for, 156
creative brushstrokes for, 128
designing to edge of artboard, 10
detail added with scatter brushes, 145
downsampling images, 120
effect of PEM on, 233
exporting in PSD format, 235
exporting to web/mobile devices, 286–287
finding symbol instances in, 117
finishing in Photoshop, 301
hand-drawn styles for, 124, 130–131
inserting in NaniBird template, 260
linking vs. embedding, 278
linking/unlinking opacity mask to, 237
maintaining quality of raster, 120
mapping onto objects, 202–203
modifying photo in perspective, 220–221
moving from Illustrator to non-Adobe apps, 279
painterly and calligraphic marks in, 130–131
preparing Photoshop photos for, 135
saving projects in stages, 96

saving unapplied color groups, 169
switching between brushes, colors, and layers, 134
symmetrical, 26–27
web previews of, 283
Asset Export panel, 286–287
Assign tab (Edit Color/Recolor Artwork dialog), 169, 170–171
Astute Graphics, 299
Atteberry, Kevan, 288–289, 290, 291, 308
Aubé, Jean, 266, 308
Auto Collapse Icon Panels option (Preferences dialog), 3
Auto Rotate option (Print dialog), 41
Auto-Exit Pattern Editing Mode option (Pattern Options panel), 232
auto-generated corners, 148, 149–151
Auto-Between, 150, 153
Auto-Centered Tiles, 148, 150, 153
Auto-Overlap, 151, 153
Auto-Sliced, 151, 153, 156
creating pattern brush with, 121, 149–151, 156
auto-scaling artwork, 28–29
Automatic Plane Positioning feature, 205, 215
averaging endpoints, 70

B

Baldacci, Janaina Cesar de Oliveira, 141, 308
ballerina, 230
banners, 50–51
Basic toolbar, 13
beaded necklaces, 146, 154, 155
"Beautiful" (Glitschka), 211
bevels. See also 3D Extrude & Bevel Options dialog
error messages applying to objects, 201
3D, 199
Bevels.ai file, 199
Bézier curves
creating and adjusting with Pen tool, 77, 104, 274
drawing fish image with, 104, 105
editing outlined type as, 39
revealing with Direct Selection tool, 78

bleed, 46–47
Blend Options dialog, 239
Blend tool, 238–239, 252
blending modes
about, 236
creating transparency with, 253
shaping non-circular glow, 255
blends
adding highlights to, 252
adjusting 3D, 199
creating and modifying, 238–239
exporting with Knockout Group enabled, 239, 301
extruding, 210
options for creating, 239–240
reversing, releasing, or expanding, 240
setting defaults for work session, 239
Blind Men and the Elephant illustration, 124
Blob Brush tool
accessing Smooth tool from, 65
adding fast shading, 99
Cheetah/Rabbit sketch with, 89
combining objects with, 64
converting objects to Live Paint Groups, 87
editing paths with, 66
Fidelity options for, 86–87, 88, 93, 99
Golden Gate Bridge details with, 270
painting with, 65–66, 110
stroke becoming filled shape, 110
working with paths with, 64
blood cell illustrations, 172, 252, 276
"Blue Mirror" (Geisler), 138–139
book covers
applying drop shadows to ebook, 265
designing for novel, 46–47
Golden Gate Bridge cover photo, 270
Scroll Work pattern for, 273
Boquete, Panama travel guide, 42, 60–61
bounding box, 135
Brick layout
Brick by Row option for, 247
changing offset for, 235
offset's effect on Swatch Bounds size, 249
working in PEM, 233–234

bristle brushes
  about, 113
  atmosphere and depth with, 270
  features of, 115
  illustrating animal fur with, 141
  interesting brushstrokes with, 128
  opacity options for, 115
  using Draw Inside with, 136–137
broomstick illustration, 209
Brush panel, 116
brushes. See also stroke; and types of brushes
  adjusting stroke fidelity, 93, 99, 131, 132
  application-level preferences for, 115–116
  atmosphere and depth created with, 270
  developing brush-and-ink style lines, 108
  editing art that makes up, 115
  expressive illustrations using, 132–133
  fidelity options for blob, 86–87, 88, 93, 99
  Go Media's, 296
  Illustrator's types of, 113–115
  Jolley's sampler of, 144
  learning characteristics of, 125
  making and duplicating raster image, 271
  modifying stroke of, 116
  painting with chard forest, 271, 304
  pattern, 120–121
  Photoshop's, 290, 291
  recoloring, 168
  Steuer's courses on, 120, 121
  unable to colorize raster, 121
Brushes library, 133, 138, 141
Brushes panel
  adding custom brushes to, 134
  editing automatic corner tiles, 121
Bryan, Billie, 58, 308
bulldog illustration, 141
Burke, Pariah, 265, 308
Burnett, Cinthia A., 133, 308
bus sketch, 218–219

C
CADtools, 298
calligraphic brushes
  applying to Pen and Pencil paths, 133
  Blob Brush creating effect of, 66
  customizing stroke of, 131
  features of, 113
  interesting brushstrokes with, 128
  pressure sensitive settings for, 140
  shell and starfish made with, 157
  stroke opacity of, 129
  Width tool unavailable for, 126
caps, line
  choosing styles of, 124
  dashes with end, 112–113
  designing spirals with round, 127
caps, small, 40
Carrot Tree restaurant illustration, 224, 245
cartoon logos and art, 30, 108
Cassidy, James, 133, 308
"Castle Brush" gallery, 121
CC (Creative Cloud) features. See also CC libraries
  about your Creative Cloud account, 12
  accessing Appearance via Properties panel, 8
  Adobe Color Themes panel, 171–172
  alternate glyphs, 45
  in and out port indicators, 35
  animating Graphic Symbols, 282
  appearance of stroked text, 38
  auto-generated corners, 148, 149–151
  basing pattern brush on photo, 148
  bending mesh, 182–183
  bitmap image used as pattern brush, 152
  Blob Brush Fidelity settings, 86–87, 88, 93, 99
  bristle brushes and Draw Inside mode, 115
  cartoon logos created with, 30
  CC icon indicating, xiv-xv
  CC panels and workspace, 12–16
  choosing stylistic sets, 45

coloring pattern brush's vector elements, 157
converting point and area type, 42
corner tiles for pattern brushes, 121
cropping images with content aware defaults, 173, 284
cropping raster images, 284
Curvature tool, 78
degree symbol automatically inserted in, 199
displaying Transparency panel by clicking on object Opacity, 237
Dynamic Symbols, 116, 119, 160
editing Illustrator objects in InDesign, 281
editing transparent objects, 238
embedded PNG files for pattern brush, 158
enabling/disabling basic Appearance panel options, 9
examples of complex CC enhancements, 245
exporting graphics to web/ mobile devices, 286–287
exporting Illustrator SVG files, 286
finding fonts, 39, 43–45
formats preserving layers with, 279
formatting text, 35–36
Free Transform touch interface, 74
freeform gradients, 172–173, 192, 193
freeform paths, 104
hiding selection edges, 5
highlighting substituted fonts, 44
introductions to, xvi
learning about, 2
Live Corners, 74–75, 102–103
Live Rectangles, 101, 102–103, 159, 245, 275
Live Shapes, 74, 75–76
Lock Station Point, 206, 225, 226, 227
merging objects with Blob Brush, 65
multiple file placement in CC, 285–286

New Window dialog features, 10

number of artboards available, 9

opening multiple PDF pages in Illustrator, 282

overview of new, xviii–xxi

Paintbrush Fidelity options, 131, 132

pasting text into InDesign, 281

Path Segment Reshape feature, 77, 104, 108

pattern brushes created using, 143, 154, 155

Pen tool Reshape Segment cursor, 77

Pencil tool Fidelity slider changes, 19, 77–78, 136

photographic hyperrealism with Pen tool in, 245, 256, 257

Pixel Preview option, 283

preserving vector format of imported files, 279

proxy icons, 171

Puppet Warp, 173, 206–207, 228–230

raster image brushes, 119–121, 276

relocating Gradient Annotator in **CC**, 165–166

resizing artboards, 40

scaling text frames only, 33

Select Similar vs. Global Edit options, 79–80

Shape Builder object construction, 66–67, 95, 96–97

Shaper tool for drawing, 106, 107

starting/stopping paths with Pen tool, 19

swatches added to Creative Cloud library, 162, 171

tip boxes for, xvi

Touch Type tool, 36, 42, 60–61

tracing sketch with Blob Brush, 86–87

trouble seeing what was just drawn, 239

two New Document dialogs, 4

Type cursor appearance in **CC**, 33

updated Swatches panel, 171

useful in combining apps, 284–286

using Web-compatible profiles, 283

working with Crop Image, 306

CC icon explaining, xiv-xv

CC libraries
adding swatches to, 162, 171

PDF compatibility of files in, 281–282

placing Illustrator Smart Object files in, 280

preventing addition of swatches to, 162

sharing and managing, 284–285

Character panel
about, 35

showing Touch Type Tool in, 42

Small Caps option, 40

character styles, 36

Character Styles panel, 35–36

characters. See also type
modifying with Touch Type tool, 43, 60–61

type object vs., 37, 38

"Chard Forest" gallery (Steuer), 271, 304

Charuca, 294, 308

Cheetah/Rabbit sketch, 89

"Chingon" motorcycle, 256, 257

Cinema 4D, 295

circles
setting Path type on, 34

using pattern brush in, 159

"Cityscape" (Gause), 225

Classic Trains magazine, 298

Clipboard, 279

clipping groups
creating, 258–259, 263

editing in isolation mode, 242

clipping masks
active, 241

creating from Object menu, 243

Draw Inside for making, 71, 98, 136, 241

fitting envelope mesh object to shape with, 186

identifying, 244

opacity masks vs., 262

path for rope, 251

preparing objects for, 259

releasing, 241, 243

stroke and fill added to, 242

texturizing objects with, 267

using Layers panel to create, 243–244

working with, 240–243

clipping path
appearance in Layers panel, 244

function of, 241

"cloak of invisibility" illustration, 264

Clone Stamp tool (Photoshop), 148

closed paths, 33, 78

CMYK color space
Adobe Color Themes used in, 172

color outside gamut of, 163

using for web and print art, 162, 283

Coghill, George, xiii, xviii, 30, 100, 108, 308

Cohen, Sandee, 35, 308

collapsing columns and panels, 2, 3

color. See also color transitions; Edit Color/Recolor Artwork dialog; global color
adding inside line art, 100

adding to gradient, 165

adjusting for time of day, 209

applying and editing easily, 85

applying custom gradient to text, 55

applying to vector elements of pattern brush, 157

assigning layers unique, 23

blocking out planes of, 140

bristle brush, tablet, and Art Pen to add, 134

Colorizer script for adding, 96–97

customizing color swatches, 174–175

default for new text objects, 32

deleting in Swatch panel, 162

determining composition's, 20–21

experimenting with different colorways, 188–189

filling Zebra template with, 261

freeform gradient, 173, 192

global process, 163

gradient mesh objects, 166–168

harmony rules for, 163–164, 169

Live Color, 168

Live Paint for adding, 84–85, 87

process, 162

recognizing subtle shifts of, 269

recoloring patterns, 188–189, 235

color, *continued*
  reducing number in project, 170–171
  resetting gradient to default, 164
  sampling with Eyedropper, 167
  selecting for Image Trace objects, 69
  shading with Blob Brush and Draw Inside, 98–99
  smoothing blend, 239
  spot, 162, 163, 201
  tinting self-portrait, 93
  using washes below strokes, 131
  warming objects with, 267
  working with in Shape Builder, 67, 100
  working with template photo, 256, 257
color groups
  creating, 175
  deleting, 169
  naming and renaming, 169, 189
  saving custom, 163–164, 169, 175
  saving in Recolor Artwork, 189
Color Guide panel
  features of, 163–164
  illustrated, 164
  working with color, 162
color mode, 174–175
Color panel
  accessing pop-up instances with, 162, 165
  working with, 162–164
Color Picker, 171
Color Reduction Options dialog, 170–171
Color Rule icon (Adobe Color Themes panel), 172
color spaces. See also CMYK color space; RGB color space
  compatible with web document formats, 162, 283
  selecting from Color panel pop-up menu, 174-175
color stops
  adding, 187
  adjusting on Gradient panel, 254

color transitions, 162–194
  applying gradient to stroke, 180
  bending mesh to art's contours, 182–183
  changing object colors easily, 191
  Color and Swatches panel options for, 162–163
  color groups and Color Guide, 163–164
  contouring with freeform gradients, 192–193
  controlling gradient fills with Gradient Annotator, 187
  creating custom coloring, 174–175
  creating transparent gradient mesh objects, 184–185
  creating variations in Recolor Artwork, 189
  deleting colors in Swatch panel, 162, 169
  Edit Color/Recolor Artwork dialogs, 168–171
  experimenting with different colorways, 188–189
  feature overview, xx
  gradient mesh objects, 166–168
  gradients for, 164–166
  pairing swatches with characters, 194
  role of, 162
  swirling color, 190
  updated **CC** color features, 171–173
  workflow using gradients, 178–179
columns, 3
combining apps, 278–306. See also embedding; Illustrator and Photoshop combinations
  about, 278
  animating Illustrator symbols, 292
  Corel Painter, 296
  creating **CC** raster brushes from Lightwave 3D art, 276
  developing iPad wallpaper app with Illustrator, 294

dimensions illustrated with 3D Studio Max, 84, 302
  drawing using CADtools, Photoshop, and Illustrator, 298
  exporting Illustrator layers to Photoshop, 288–289
  feature overview, xxi
  Final Cut Pro, 295
  Flash (now Animate), 117, 284, 292
  Go Media brushes in Illustrator, 296
  InkScribe with Illustrator, 299
  linking vs. embedding artwork, 278
  moving between Illustrator, Photoshop, and After Effects, 293
  moving Illustrator art to non-Adobe apps, 279
  Photoshop lighting effects, 296–297
  preparing 3D scenes for animation, 295
  preserving exported Photoshop appearance attributes, 281
  3D effects in Illustrator and Photoshop, 303
  tracing with Alias Sketchbook Pro pen, 124
  using InDesign with Illustrator, 245, 278, 281–282, 285
  working in Illustrator and Photoshop, 279–281, 288–291, 300–301
complex objects
  building doors for bus sketch, 219
  drawing, 219
  organizing with layers, 20, 21, 250
  working with, 71
compound paths
  combining elements into, 258–259
  creating objects with, 71, 72
  used in drawing tube, 251
  using as mask, 241, 244
compound shapes
  creating objects with, 72, 73
  exporting to Photoshop, 280
  using as mask, 244

Constrain Angle option
(Preferences dialog), 4
constructing objects, 64–108
adding interior colors to line
art, 100
aligning and distributing
objects, 69–70
Blob Brush features for, 65–66
CC Live Corners for, 74–75
CC Live Shapes for, 74, 75–76
CC Pencil tool for, 77–78
CC Shaper tool for, 78–79
coloring line art, 84–85
combining paths to create
objects, 82–83
compound shapes and paths
for, 72–73
connecting overlapping open
paths, 78
converting drawings to objects,
101
creating Cheetah/Rabbit
sketch, 89
creating Tiger with pen-and-
ink style, 88
Draw Inside mode for, 98–99
drawing freeform paths, 104
drawing modes and, 71–72
Eraser tools for, 64–65
feature overview, xix-xx
Fidelity options for self-
portrait, 93
foil-stamped card design, 105
Image Trace for, 68–69
joining endpoints, 70–71
Live Paint features for, 67–68
map symbols, 102–103
multidimensional images, 92
overview, 64
reshaping paths when, 77
sculpture template, 94
seed packet illustration design,
90
Shape Builder for, 66–67, 95,
96–97
tracing and coloring sketches,
91
working with Shaper tool, 106,
107
Content-Aware defaults option
(Preferences dialog), 206,
207, 229, 284
Context-Aware defaults option
(Preferences dialog), 173,
192, 193
continuous curves, 110

Control panel
accessing pop-up instances
in, 162
adjusting stroke from, 127
buttons for envelopes, 196
Crop Image button, 284
decreasing opacity in, 185
enabling Move/Copy Artwork,
49
Global Edit icon, 81
identifying clipping masks
from, 244
quick access to Symbol features
on, 116
reducing stroke weight from,
153
rounding corners with,
102–103
selecting similar objects in, 80
using Variable Width Profile
in, 154
copying
art between artboards, 11
artwork with artboards, 49
current artboards, 96
elements to artboards, 40
master layers, 23
objects, 7
objects before applying Puppet
Warp, 207
patterns, 232
preserving imported vector
images when, 279
selected width points, 111
Smart Objects for Photoshop
editing, 289
styling and appearance with
Eyedropper, 36–37
Corel Painter, 296
corner joins, 112–113
corners. See also auto-generated
corners; Live Corners
brush, 152–153
Dynamic Corners plug-in, 299
joining points of, 70
methods for inner/outer
pattern brush, 151
rounded rectangle, 82–83, 103
rounding, 102–103
scaling with Live Shapes, 75
simulating, 159
Cox, Sally, 112, 308
Coyle, Laura, 105, 194, 308
Create tab (Adobe Color Themes
panel), 171–172
Creative Cloud. See also CC
features; CC libraries

Creative Cloud account, 12
Creative Suite, xviii
CreativePro.com, xviii, 138
Cressy, Michael, 197, 208–209,
308
cropping images
with content aware defaults,
173, 206, 207, 229,
284
cropping images in CC, 284,
306
in Photoshop, 153
to tile size, 153
cursors
Layers panel + (plus), 16
Reshape Segment cursor, 77,
104, 108
Select Behind, 5, 7
Type tool, 32
Curvature tool, 78
curved paths
tracing, 19
type on, 33–34, 51
curves
bending shape to arch, 208
developing for "Scroll Work"
pattern, 272
discontinuous and continuous,
110
orientation of blends along,
240
Custom Tools panel, 30
customizing
arrowheads, 113
art and scatter brushes, 145
bevels, 199
Blob Brush tool, 65–66
bristle brush, 137, 138
brushes and adding to Brushes
panel, 134
calligraphic brush stroke, 131
color swatches, 174–175
graphic styles, 59
perspective grid, 216–217
spirals with Width tool, 127
stroke width, 122–123, 124,
125
toolbars, 14, 15, 30

D

Dacosta!, 294, 308
Daniels, Lee, 293, 308
Darren (Winder), 181
dashes with end caps, 112–113
Define Grid dialog, 204
Define Perspective Grid dialog, 216
degree symbol, 199
Del Vechio, Gustavo, xiii, 68, 84, 149–151, 224, 245, 302, 308
deleting
    arrowhead presets, 113
    color groups, 169
    colors on Swatch panel, 162, 169
    drawn inside clipping mask, 136
    excess anchor points, 70
    intersecting edges, 85
    mesh points, 197
    Puppet Warp pins, 228
    swatches, 175
    tools from toolbar, 14
designing type and layout, 32–62
    Appearance panel options for type, 37–38
    arcing type with envelopes, 54–55
    converting point and area type, 42
    converting type to outlines, 38–39
    copying type styling and appearance, 36–37
    creating materials for company identity, 48–49
    curving and warping type, 50–51, 52
    customizing type for map labels, 53
    designing book covers, 46–47
    feature overview, xix
    finding right fonts, 43–45
    formatting text, 35–36
    glyphs, 39, 45
    Illustrator for, 46–47, 62
    picking apart type styles, 56
    smartphone case design, 190
    stylizing logos, 58
    threaded text, 34–35
    Touch Type tool, 36, 42, 60–61
    types of type objects, 32–34
    working with multiple artboards, 9–11, 39–41
    wrapping text, 35

"Diadem" pattern, 246–247
dialogs. See also Edit Color/Recolor Artwork dialog; and specific dialogs
    choosing default or legacy New Document, 4
    New Window CC features, 10
Diffused Shading option, 201
Dijk, Victor van, 308
Dim Copies option (Pattern Options panel), 246, 247
Direct Selection tool
    accessing Reshape Segment cursor in, 77
    converting corner points with, 102
    emphasizing translucency with, 129
    modifying objects with, 190
    repairing holes in tracing edges, 90
    selecting points of curves with, 272
disabling. See enabling/disabling
disclosure triangle, 43
disco ntinuous curves, 110
Distort & Transform live effects, 208, 209
Distort tools, 167
distorting. See also envelopes; warps
    artwork with envelopes, 197
    effect on raster image brush work, 120
    gradient mesh shape, 167
    objects with Puppet Warp, 206–207
    text, 54–55
    type, 39, 60–61
Divide Pathfinder icon, 255, 256
Doc Martin shoes, 228
docking panels
    about, 3
    permanently, 14, 232
documents
    accessing legacy, 4
    adding symbol instance to, 117
    choosing color space for web, 162
    packaging with Adobe Fonts for, 44
    page setup for, 46–47
    previewing, 23
    saving list of fonts used, 45
    tabbed, 2
    using Web-compatible profiles for, 283

Dogney Dangerfield logo, 30
"Dory, The" (Drees), 210, 245
dots symbol(...), 14, 15, 227, 228
double-arrow
    indicating tabbed documents, 2
    using, 3
Double-click to Isolate option (Preferences dialog), 6
downsampling images, 120
downsizing image resolution, 271
dragging/dropping
    gradient swatch to Gradient slider, 165
    preserving imported vector images when, 279
    with Reshape Segment cursor, 77
    width points, 123
dragonfly, 129
Drapeau, Suzanne, 133, 308
Draw Behind mode
    about, 71
    unable to draw in, 238
    viewing, 97
Draw Inside mode
    about, 71–72
    adding image and text inside rectangles with, 275
    bristle brushes with, 115
    constraining brush strokes with, 224, 270
    making clipping mask with, 71, 98, 136, 241
    painterly styles with bristle brush and, 136–137
    PEM disabled in, 234
    trouble seeing art drawn in, 238
    unable to draw in, 238
    viewing, 97
Draw Normal mode
    about, 71
    drawing only from, 238
    viewing in, 97
drawing. See also freehand drawing; Pen tool; Pencil tool
    adding interior colors to line art, 100
    arcs, 26, 27
    effect of Appearance panel on, 9
    Fidelity slider for precision, 19, 77–78, 86–87, 136
    freeform, 84–85
    freeform paths, 104

open paths with Live Paint, 21
in perspective, 218–219
with rubber band, 76
scaling architectural, 28–29
sketch for Illustrator template,
86, 122–123, 138–139,
250
Tiger with pen-and-ink style,
88
tracing and coloring sketches,
91
using strokes with reusable
profiles, 124
drawing mode icons, 71–72
"Drawing Vector Graphics:
Patterns" course (Glitschka),
272, 273
Drees, Dedree, 210, 245, 308
Drew, Elaine, 216–217, 308
drop shadows
adding to icons, 7
adjusting for 3D objects, 214
applying to ebook cover
design, 265
stylizing, 25, 157
duplicating. See also copying
art with Transform effect, 29
artboards, 96
artwork with artboards, 49
brush from Bristle Brush
library, 138
fill, stroke, and effects, 8
raster image brushes, 271
Dynamic Corners plug-in, 299
Dynamic symbols, 116, 119, 160
dystopian Disneyland illustration,
305
Dzienis, Nicole, 132, 308

E
ebook cover design, 265
edges
creating converging
perspective with,
203–205
designing artboard to, 10
hiding/showing path, 5
refining Blob Brush
brushstroke, 66
removing unwanted
intersecting, 85
repairing holes in tracing, 90
showing tile, 247
Edit Clipping Path button, 244
Edit Color/Recolor Artwork
dialog
about, 168–169

altering or introducing color
with, 190
Assign tab, 169, 170–171
changing object colors easily,
191
Color Reduction Options for,
170–171
creating color variations in,
189
Edit tab, 170
editing pattern swatch with,
188–189
icons of, 169, 170, 188
illustrated, 168
options of, 169–171
recoloring brushes and
symbols, 168
Edit Contents button, 244
Edit tab (Edit Color/Recolor
Artwork dialog), 170
editing. See also Edit Color/
Recolor Artwork dialog
automatic corner tiles, 156
envelopes, 196
gradient mesh objects, 183
gradients with Gradient
Annotator, 165–166,
176–177, 178, 179
Illustrator objects in InDesign,
281
master layer, 28, 29
opacity masks, 236–237
paths with Blob Brush, 66
ruler's unit of measure, 4
selecting similar objects for,
79–80
Shaper objects, 79
Smart Objects, 280
symbol without modifying
original, 117
type characters and objects,
37–38
using Global Edit, 81
width point numerically, 111
EdWarner, 294, 308, 311
effects. See also drop shadows;
Live Effect; 3D effects
duplicating, 8
Ellipse tool, 214
embedding
and distorting photo in
envelope warp, 186
flattened linked images, 279
graphs, 116
Illustrator artwork, 278
images for raster brush art, 120
Photoshop files, 156, 281

PNG files for pattern brush,
158
Enable Context Aware Defaults
option (Preference dialog),
173, 192, 193
enabling/disabling
Auto-Exit Pattern Editing
Mode, 232
Context-Aware preferences,
173, 192, 193
drawing with rubber band, 76
Live Paint strokes, 85
Move/Copy Artwork, 49
New Art Has Basic Appearance
setting, xv–xvi, 9, 200
opacity masks, 237
PDF-Compatible file option,
278
Perspective Grid, 203, 204, 217
endpoints, 70–71
envelope distort
developing ebook cover with,
265
using, 208
envelope mesh
developing ebook cover with,
265
fitting to object with clipping
mask, 186
envelope warp, 197–198
envelopes
applying, 197–198
arcing type with, 54
Control panel buttons for, 196
prospective grid unavailable
in, 205
warps vs., 196
EPS files, 279
ePublishing with InDesign
(Burke), 265
Eraser tool
Cheetah/Rabbit sketch with, 89
cutting objects into parts,
64–65
enhancing Tiger's whiskers
with, 88
erasing parts of objects, 106
pressure-sensitive preferences
for, 87
Esc key, 76
Essentials workspace, 13
Every-line Composer, 37
exiting
isolation mode, 6
PEM, 232, 234
Expand dialog, 183
Expand panel, 167

expanding
    blends, 240
    columns and panels, 3
    linear gradient to gradient
        mesh, 182–183
    Live Paint objects, 68
    pattern objects, 232
**Explore tab (Adobe Color Themes
    panel), 172**
**Export for Screens option (File
    menu), 287**
**Export Selection option (File
    menu), 287**
exporting
    artboards, 11, 41
    artwork in PSD format, 235,
        280
    artwork in SVG format, 305
    blends to Photoshop with
        Knockout Group
        enabled, 301
    compound Illustrator shapes to
        Photoshop, 280
    graphics for web/mobile
        devices, 283
    Illustrator layers to Photoshop,
        288–289
    layer animation, 284
    objects using Asset Export
        panel, 286–287
    Photoshop Density or Feather
        options, 281
    PS Layer Comps to Illustrator,
        280
    type with custom spacing, 39
    using Export Selection option,
        287
**extruding. See also 3D Extrude &
    Bevel Options dialog**
    artwork for 3D key and fob,
        213, 214
    objects with spot color
        preserved, 201
    2D objects, 198–199
Eye icon
    displaying layers, 23
    showing/hiding attributes, 8
Eyedropper tool
    adding color to mesh point,
        183, 185
    copying styling and appearance
        with, 36–37
    filling paths with color with,
        269
    sampling mesh object color,
        167

F

"Falling" (Aubé), 266
**Ferster, Gary, xiii, 104, 153, 172,
    192, 252, 275, 276, 308**
fidelity
    adjusting Blob Brush for,
        86–87, 88, 93, 99
    adjusting Pencil tool, 19,
        77–78, 136
    setting brush stroke, 93, 99,
        131, 132
File menu
    Export for Screens option, 287
    Export Selection option, 287
    Save for Web (Legacy) option,
        287
**files. See also .ai files; exporting;
    importing; PDF files; PSD
    files**
    accessing Photoshop layers in
        PSD or TIFF, 281
    EPS, 279
    exporting artboards as, 11
    finding **WOW! ONLINE**, xiv
    formats preserving layers and
        CC features, 279
    overlapping objects flattened
        for printing, 238
    placing with keyboard or
        mouse, 16
    planning for projects in
        Illustrator and
        Photoshop, 300–301
    PNG, 156, 158
    recovering missing linked, 278
    saved with PDF compatibility
        in CC library, 281–
        282
    saving artboards as, 41
    showing import options when
        artboard is cropping
        mask, 245
    SVG, 286, 305
    TIFF, 281
fill. See also gradient
    adding to clipping mask, 242
    adding to Live Rectangles, 245
    applying to type objects, 38
    converting stroke to filled
        shape, 65, 110
    duplicating, 8
    feathering for paths, 251
    Gradient Annotator and
        gradient, 165–166
    gradient strokes vs. gradient,
        164–165

    radial, 166, 252
    using in Dynamic symbols, 119
Final Cut Pro, 295
Find Font dialog, 45
finding
    all symbol instances, 117
    appearance attributes, 81
    fonts, 39, 43–45
    hidden Bevels.ai file, 199
    list of modifier keys, 64
    masks in Layers panel, 244
    similar shapes, 81
    swatches, 171
    tools with dots symbol (...), 14,
        15, 227, 228
fish with gradient fill, 176–177
Flare tool, 205
Flash
    becomes Animate, 284
    Illustrator symbols affecting,
        117
    preparing art for animations,
        292
Flat Fan bristle brush, 139
flattening
    and embedding linked images,
        279
    overlapping objects for
        printing, 238
Floor Plane dialog, 215, 221
foil-stamped card design, 105
fonts
    Adobe Fonts, 12, 44
    avoiding formatting overrides
        for, 36
    distributing to service bureaus,
        39
    finding, 39, 43–45
    glyphs for, 39, 45
    highlighting substituted, 44
    listing document's, 45
    packaging with document, 44
formatting
    avoiding formatting overrides,
        36
    text, 35–36
**four-color-process separations,
    creating, 163**
**"Frankie Stein" series (Atteberry),
    288–289, 290, 291**
Frazer, 294, 308
**Free Transform touch interface,
    74**

freeform gradients
applying to filled object, 192
gradient mesh and, 172–173
underwater scenes using, 193, 236
using lines vs. points with, 172, 173
freehand drawing
converting to Illustrator, 101
creating pen-and-ink style Tiger, 88
with Pen tool, 84–85
Frosty cones graphic design, 38, 59
fx icon
locating on Appearance panel, 24, 25, 29
selecting 3D effects via, 199
fx pop-up menu. See also Live Effect
accessing, 337, 338
applying effects from, 61

G

galleries, xvii
gaps
adjusting between patterns, 246
coloring after hiding template, 269
setting for Shape Builder tool, 66
"Gardener, The" (Leavens), 98–99
gastric bypass illustration, 192
Gause, Monika, xxi, 164, 225, 261, 286, 306, 308
Gaussian Blur effect
adjusting object shadows with, 268
capturing bulldog's fur and folds with, 141
Geisler, Greg, 138–139, 140, 308
GG1 electric locomotive, 298
Gilbert, Katharine, 92, 303, 309
Gillespie, Cristen, xii, 36
Glitschka, Von R., 211, 235, 246–247, 272, 273, 299, 309
global color
adding tints of, 93
deleting in Swatches panel, 162
identifying, 164
Global Edit option
adding Live Effect via, 72
editing groups with, 81
Select Similar vs., 79–80
global process colors, 163

Global rulers, 4–5
Global swatches, 85
glossary, xv, xvii, 337–338
glows
adding soft shadow within object, 211
creating from Radial gradient, 254–255
glyphs
accessing, 39
applying alternate, 45
Golden Gate Bridge
cover artwork, 270
poster, 17
Golding, Mordy, 196, 197, 309
"Good Food in the Microhood" (Steuer), 134, 135
Gordon, Steven H., xiii, xx, 7, 22–23, 24–25, 33, 42, 52–53, 60–61, 102, 160, 309
Grace, Laurie, 309
gradient. See also freeform gradients; Gradient Annotator; gradient mesh objects
across stroke, 59
adding custom gradient to text, 55
adjusting sky color with, 160
applying to fills and strokes, 164–165
changing length of, 187
color added to, 165
controlling with Gradient Annotator, 187
expanding linear gradient to gradient mesh, 182–183
freeform gradients, 172–173
gradient fills vs. strokes, 164–165
overlaying in multiply mode, 266
rasterized when mapped as symbols, 202
resetting to defaults, 164
reusing, 179
stroke options on Gradient panel, 164
techniques using, 178
unifying across multiple objects, 176–177
using on path, 180
wood-toned, 181
Gradient Annotator
adding color stops to, 187

adding transparency to radial gradient, 254
editing with, 165–166, 176–177, 178, 179
using with Gradient tool, 176–177, 254
gradient mesh objects
about, 166–168
changing colors easily, 191
converting gradient-filled objects to, 183
expanding linear gradient to, 182–183
transparency in, 184–185
unable to transform to perspective grid, 205
Gradient panel
enlarging size of slider, 164
options for stroke gradients, 166
selecting Radial gradients on, 165
working with color, 162
gradient swatch
dragging to Gradient slider, 165
resetting, 164
saving aspect ratio and angle for, 166
Gradient tool, 176–177, 254
Graham, Cheryl, 93, 309
graphic novel cover design, 46–47
graphic styles
about, 9
applying and saving, 55
developing new, 59
saving with gradient swatch, 166
width profiles saved as, 110, 111
Graphic Styles panel, 9
graphic symbols
animating, 282
preserving artwork as, 160
graphics. See artwork
graphs, embedding, 116
Greater Bridgeport Transit artwork, 50–51
grids
perspective, 5, 196, 204, 206
Pixel Preview, 5, 283
showing, 5
unable to create while placing files, 285

groups. *See also* color groups
  adding layers above, 118
  blending between pairs of, 240
  clipping, 242, 258–259, 263
  Global Edit option with, 81
guides. *See also* Smart Guides
  achieving perspective with, 17
  for arcs, 245
  cancelling with keyboard or mouse, 16
  creating, 16
  customizing document, 47
  locking/unlocking, 5, 26
  outlining with Pen tool, 186
  perspective, 17
  snapping objects to, 64
  templates for arc construction, 26–27
  working with, 5
guitar image, 181
Gusman. *See* Joly, Annie Gusman

H

Halloween video game scene, 208–209
Hamann, Brad, 250–251, 309
harmony rules, 163–164, 169
heart pattern, 121
Help
  customizing arrowheads, 113
  finding list of modifier keys in, 64
  getting, xvii
  locating Illustrator, 12
  perspective grid controls, 217
Hex layout
  offset's effect on Swatch Bounds size, 249
  using Hex by Row tile type, 247
  working in PEM, 233–234
Hide/Show Edges option, 5
hiding. *See* showing/hiding
highlighting substituted fonts, 44
H.L. Hunley image, 179
holes
  compound paths for cutting, 71, 72
  repairing in tracing edges, 90
Home button, 13
Home Screen features, 12–13
Honfleur, France, 130–131
horizon line, 222
Hubig, Dan, 264, 300–301, 309
hyphenation, 37

I

icons. *See also* Eye icon
  adding drop shadow to, 7
  CC, xiv–xv
  collapsing panels to, 2
  creating illustration of, 174
  developing with Dynamic Symbol, 160
  Divide Pathfinder, 255, 256
  drawing mode, 71–72
  Edit Color/Recolor Artwork dialog, 169, 170
  fx, 24, 25, 29, 199
  Live Corner, 102
  Locate Object, 23
  Make/Release Clipping Mask, 241, 243
  New Color Group, 163
  Recolor Artwork, 188
  Swatch proxy, 171
  Trash, 162
  WOW! ONLINE, about, xiv, 337–338
Ignore White option (Image Trace panel), 69, 91
Illustrator. *See also* **CC** features; combining apps; **Illustrator and Photoshop combinations**
  .ai file compatibility with InDesign and Photoshop, 278
  collaborating with InDesign, 281–282
  completing image as fine art piece, 135
  creating **CC** raster brushes from Lightwave 3D artwork, 276
  CS6 features in, xviii
  differences between CS6 and CC, xiv–xv
  drawing using CADtools, Photoshop, and, 298
  exporting art into Cinema 4D and After Effects, 295
  legacy options, 4, 76, 205, 287
  linking vs. embedding in, 278
  moving artwork to non-Adobe apps, 279
  moving between Photoshop, After Effects and, 293
  new **CC** features in, xviii–xxi
  painterly and calligraphic marks in artwork, 130–131

  PDF options and compatibility in, 41, 278, 279, 281–282
  Place feature in InDesign and, 285
  planning projects in Photoshop and, 300–301
  preventing fake small caps in, 40
  Puppet Warp in **CC**, 206–207
  shortcuts and keystrokes, xv, 337, 338
  tracing with InkScribe in, 299
  using bitmap image as brush, 152
  varying brush stroke with Wacom Art pens, 144
  versatility in designing type, 62
Illustrator and Photoshop combinations
  Adjustment layers imported to Illustrator, 281
  .ai file compatibility with InDesign and Photoshop, 278
  drawing Photoshop sketch for Illustrator template, 86, 122–123, 138
  drawing using CADtools, Illustrator and Photoshop, 298
  embedding photo in Illustrator envelope, 186
  embedding Photoshop file in Illustrator, 156, 158
  enhancing Illustrator transparency in, 264
  exporting artwork in PSD format, 235
  finding hidden Photoshop Bevels.ai file, 199
  Illustrator artboards as Photoshop cropping masks, 245
  Illustrator layers in Photoshop, 288–289
  importing/exporting PS Layer Comps, 280
  moving between After Effects, Illustrator and Photoshop, 293
  moving "Frankie Stein" art to Photoshop, 288–289, 290, 291

PDF options and compatibility in Illustrator, 41, 278, 279, 281–282
Photoshop lighting effects in Illustrator, 296–297
planning projects for, 300–301
preparing Photoshop image for Illustrator, 90, 152, 156
sharing text in, 280
Smart Objects in, 279–280
working on, 279–281
Illustrator Appearance Book (Miyamoto), 56
Illustrator CC, O que ha de novo? (Del Vechio), 149
Illustrator Options dialog, 279
Illustrator Support Center, xvii
Image Crop
Enable Content Aware Defaults option and, 173, 284
reducing size of raster images with, 120, 152, 284
Image Trace panel
adding clouds using, 266
converting photo to vector object, 68–69, 227
creating multidimensional image with Photoshop and, 92
features of, 68, 69
simplifying reference photo with, 93
tracing Photoshop images using, 90
turning off Preview for, 68
images. See also cropping images; embedding; Image Trace panel
adding layers to, 135
adding to product packaging, 227
developing template from, 222, 224
Illustrator art as pixel, 280
JPG used as background, 186, 258, 259
masking and cropping to tile size, 153
masking scanned stone, 154
multidimensional, 92
PhotoRealistic art developed from, 245, 256, 257, 269
providing realistic look for 3D surfaces, 212

scanning and tracing template, 18, 250
using as brush, 152
using masked photo as pattern brush, 157
visibility of template, 130
working with chard leaves in Photoshop, 271, 304
working with established perspective of, 220–221
importing
Illustrator files to InDesign, 282
Illustrator layers as keyframes in Graphic Symbol, 282
Illustrator paths to 3D programs, 282
Photoshop Adjustment layers, 281
SVG files to Illustrator, 286
in port, 33, 35
InDesign
file compatibility with, 278
importing Illustrator artboards, 282
Place feature in Illustrator and, 285
using Illustrator artboard as cropping mask, 245
working with Illustrator artwork, 281–282
InkScribe plug-in poster, 299
Inner Glow effect, 211
instances of symbols, 117
Intersect Pathfinder command, 83
inverting opacity masks, 237
iPad wallpaper app, 294
isolation mode. See also Pattern Edit Mode
editing clipping group in, 242
entering/exiting, 6
envelope editing in, 196
finishing painting details in, 137
Live Paint Groups in, 67
PEM disabled in, 234
preventing object merging with, 65
symbol editing in, 117
working in, 6–7
Italian "push puppet", 158

J
Jackmore, Lisa, xiii, xxi, 64, 69, 72, 118, 121, 126, 128, 136, 148, 152–153, 154, 155, 182–183, 228, 309
Jackson, Lance, 89, 270, 305, 309
Johnson, Mahalia, 133, 309
Johnson, Rick, 298, 309
Join tool, 78
joining
endpoints, 70–71
and intersecting objects, 82–83
path joins and caps, 112–113
Jolley, Donal, 33, 35, 37, 125, 144, 309
Joly, Annie Gusman, 253, 254–255, 309
Joly, Dave, 176–177, 295, 309
JPG background image, 186, 258, 259
justification, 37

K
kaNO, 294, 309
kerning, 51
key and fob illustration, 198, 212–213, 214
key objects in blends, 239, 240
keyboard functions, 16
keyboard shortcuts. See shortcuts and keystrokes
Killamari, 294, 309
Kimball, Mike, 17, 309
King, Steve, 178, 179, 309
Klema, Stephen, 26–27, 94, 95, 132–133, 245, 309
Knockout Group checkbox (Transparency panel)
effect on sublayers, 288
isolating opacity and blending with, 239, 301
simplifying art for exporting with, 235, 301
Kyoto Bus Station illustration, 268

L
labels
aligning type to path on, 52
curving, 51
customizing type for, 53
landscape orientation, 41
Larrett, Raymond, xiii, 46, 142–143, 245, 309
"Last Draw, The" (Wigham), 292
layer comps, exporting to Illustrator, 280

layered patterns, 248–249
layers. See also master layers; sublayers
  accessing in PSD or TIFF files, 281
  adding time-of-day tint with, 209
  adding to photo image, 135
  animating, 283–284
  appearance attributes assigned to, 25
  assigning color to, 23
  in chard forest gallery, 271
  color wash added to, 131
  creating for guide sets, 5
  exporting as .ai files, 283
  exporting in PSD format, 288–289
  exporting layer animation, 284
  exporting to Photoshop, 288–289
  hiding unwanted lines on, 134
  image definition using, 141
  importing as keyframes in Graphic Symbol, 282
  locking/unlocking, 21, 88
  manually tracing template, 18–19
  naming, 5–6
  navigating, 22–23
  organizing, 5–6, 20, 21, 137, 250
  painting with bristle brushes in, 138–139
  Paste Remembers Layers option, 7
  PEM effects on, 234
  Photoshop Adjustment, 281
  planning for Illustrator/ Photoshop projects, 300–301
  preserving with .ai, PSD, or PDF formats, 279
  preventing strokes from merging on, 88
  remain expanded/collapsed when saved, 16
  running Smart Filters on Smart Object, 289
  separating color areas on different, 140
  showing/hiding, 21, 23
  sublayers, 22–23, 117, 118, 288
  template visibility on, 130
  transform effects applied to, 29
  visibility of Illustrator layers in InDesign, 281

Layers panel (Illustrator)
  active clipping masks on, 241
  adding new layer at level of path sublayer, 118
  changing display, 23
  editing envelope elements with, 265
  finding masks in, 244
  identifying transparency and opacity masks on, 238
  isolation mode's effect on, 6
  managing objects in, 5–6
  + (plus) cursor for, 16
  selection and targeting indicators on, 7–8
  showing clipping groups and masks in, 258, 259
  viewing Appearance and, 8
  working with clipping masks, 241, 243–244
Layers panel (Photoshop), 280
LCD screen illustration, 221
leaders for text, 37
Learn Screen features, 12
Leavens, Chris, 98–99, 262–263, 309
legacy options
  choosing legacy documents, 4
  converting static to Live Shapes, 76
  Legacy "File New" Interface, 4
  legacy text on perspective grids, 205
  opening New Document legacy dialog, 4
  Save for Web, 287
Lein, Adam Z., 309
Lens Flare tool, 252
Levy, Jean-Benoit, 57, 310
"Libertad" (Freedom) (Acosta), 101
libraries. See also CC libraries
  adding swatches to CC, 162, 171
  applying Metals, 180
  Brushes, 133, 138, 141
  combining Go Media's entourage elements in Illustrator, 296
  creating swatch, 175
  Metals, 180, 214
  preparing symbols for animation, 292
  saving symbols to, 116
  sharing artboards via, 49
  Swatch, 175, 246
  Symbols, 147

light source sphere (More Options dialog), 201–202
lighting
  Photoshop effects used for, 296–297
  simulating with Lens Flare tool, 252
  3D artwork, 213, 214
Lightwave 3D, 276
limiting number of colors, 170–171
Lincoln, Jr., Abe, 294, 310
line art
  adding interior colors to, 100
  using placed image as reference for, 136
lines. See also caps, line
  brush-and-ink style, 108
  contouring freeform gradients to, 192, 193
  customizing width of, 122–123, 124, 125
  freeform gradient points vs., 172, 173
  hiding unwanted, 134
  resizing weight and stroke, 70
  tracing, 18–19
Lines option (Freeform Gradients), 172, 173
linked files
  flattening and embedding linked images, 279
  recovering missing, 278
linking/unlinking
  Illustrator art in InDesign, 281
  opacity mask to artwork, 237
  Photoshop files to Illustrator, 280–281
Links panel, 278
Liquify tools, 190
Live Color, 168
Live Corners
  applying to end points of curls, 272
  converting freehand lines to, 101
  creating corners in, 274
  features of, 74–75
  icons for, 102
  map symbols using, 102–103
Live Effect
  adding Gaussian Blur, 141, 268
  adding with global edit, 72
  choosing 3D effects, 199, 210
  Distort & Transform effect, 208, 209

editing dynamic symbol objects having, 119
modifying Drop Shadow attribute, 20

Live Paint
adding color to Zebra template, 261
coloring line art with, 84–85, 87
designing template for sculpture with, 94
drawing open paths with, 21
expanding/releasing, 68
filling segments with color, 106, 107
working with, 67–68

Live Paint Bucket tool
adding fill with, 87, 106, 107
adjusting stroke with, 85

Live Paint Groups
adding new members to, 67
applying to 3D model, 84, 85
coloring objects without drawing separately, 21
converting Blob Brush objects to, 87

Live Rectangles
adding strokes and fills to, 245
advantages using, 275
rounding manually, 101
simulating corners, 159
toll road symbols created with, 102–103

Live Shapes, 74, 75–76
Live Trace. See Image Trace panel
Locate Object icon, 23
locating artboards visually, 11
Lock Station Point, 206, 225, 226, 227

locking/unlocking
effect on Global Edit and Select Similar, 81
guides, 5, 26
layers, 21, 88
Perspective Grid, 206

logos
adding in perspective grid, 219
appearance attributes added to, 58
bus, 219
cartoon, 30
product art, 258–259
saving as a symbol, 49

Loukoumis, Amber, 132, 310
Louveaux, Pierre, 167
lynda.com courses

"Artistic Painting with Illustrator", 120, 121, 158, 159
Glitschka's, 272
Steuer's, xii, 120, 121, 271, 304

M

Mac computers
Application Frame, 2
shortcuts and keystrokes for, xv, 338

MAD (madtodesign.com), 294, 310
Madison, Alabama web app, 22–23, 52
madtodesign.com (MAD), 294, 310
magazine headline type, 54–55
Make/Release Clipping Mask icon, 241, 243
Map Art dialog, 201, 202, 203, 213

mapping
gradients saved as symbols, 202
sizing artwork for, 212
3D surfaces, 202–203, 213, 214

maps, graphic
adding labels to, 52–53
appearance attributes on, 24–25
creating symbols for, 102–103

Maric, Pete, 222, 296–297, 310
Markiewicz, Danuta (Danka), 91, 310
Martin, Jeffrey, 132, 310
Mask button (Control panel), 244
mask-editing mode, 238

master layers
copying and moving, 23
creating, 244
editing, 28, 29
illustrated, 22

mastering complex features, 232–276
about, 232
adding object highlights, 252
blends, 238–240
brushes developing atmosphere and depth, 270
CC enhancements for, 245
clipping masks, 240–244, 258–259
complex shadow patterns, 253
conveying emotional impact via art, 266

creating raster brush from Lightwave 3D art, 276
designing cover for future editing, 265
developing PhotoRealistic art, 245, 256, 257, 269
drawing rope and tube, 250–251
enhancing transparency in Photoshop, 264
feature overview, xxi
filling NaniBird template with art, 260
layered patterns, 248–249
Live Corners, 274
making patterns, 246–247, 272, 273
opacity masks, 262–263
placing photo inside rounded rectangles, 275
texturizing objects with masks, 267
transparency, 235–238
working in Pattern Editing Mode, 232–235

Maxson, Greg, 310
McGarry, Aaron, xiii, 147, 180, 198, 200, 203, 206, 212–213, 214, 220–221, 226, 227, 240, 258–259, 310
MCKIBILLO (AKA Josh McKible), 124, 260, 310
Measure tool, 11
megapixel size, 120
menu design, 104

merging
objects with Blob Brush tool, 65
preventing objects from, 65

mesh. See also gradient mesh objects; mesh points
assigning transparency to objects of, 168
bending to art's contours, 182–183
envelope, 186, 265
extracting path from, 167
showing/hiding Puppet Warp, 207

mesh points
adding, 186
adjusting, 184, 185
applying transparency to, 185
color and, 166–167
coloring with Eyedropper, 183, 185
deleting, 197

Mesh tool, 167, 183
Messer, Chana, xix, 62, 230, 244, 310
Metals library, 180, 214
Minus Front Pathfinder command, 83
Missing Fonts dialog, 44–45
missing linked files, 278
miter join, 112
Miyamoto, Nobuko, 146, 310
Miyamoto, Yukio, 56, 146, 187, 310
modifier keys
    adjusting brush size with [ ], 137
    applying gradients with < >, 165
    finding list of, 64
Mont Belvieu map, 102–103
More Options dialog, 199, 201–202
Morrison, Tamara, 132, 310
mosaic grid for packaging, 106, 107
Mourelle, Gabriel, 294, 310
mouse functions, 16
moving
    clipped objects, 242
    "Frankie Stein" art to Photoshop, 288–289, 290, 291
    Illustrator artwork to non-Adobe apps, 279
    between Illustrator, Photoshop, and After Effects, 293
    master layers, 23
    Perspective Grid, 223
    Puppet Warp pins, 228
multidimensional truck image, 92
multiple artboards
    applying masks for, 243
    creating company identity with, 48–49
    exporting graphics for web/mobile devices from, 283
    organizing, 48–49
    saving each as separate file, 279
    working with, 9–11, 39–41
Murphy, John, 224
Murra (Mu!), Sebastian, 190, 310
My Themes tab (Adobe Color Themes panel), 172

N
Nahmani, Stéphane, 7, 310
naming
    active artboard, 10, 40, 46
    convention used for Live Shape names, 76
    custom toolbars, 15
    layers, 5–6
    pattern brush objects, 142–143
    pattern brushes, 142
    saved color groups, 189
    swatches of characters, 194
NaniBird project, 260
navigating
    Artboard panel layers, 11
    layers, 22–23
Navigator panel tips, 93
New Art Has Basic Appearance option (Appearance panel)
    effects of, xv-xvi, 9
    3D effects and, 200
New Brush dialog
    creating calligraphic brush from, 131
    making pattern brush from, 143
New Color Group dialog, 163
New Document dialog
    default vs. legacy, 4
    Home Screen opening panel, 12
    setting up document in, 46
New Document Profile preset folder, 4
New Swatch dialog, 163
New Window dialog, 10
Nickerson, Jared, 294, 310
Nielsen, Chris, 245, 256, 257, 269, 310
9-slice scaling, 117, 283
Noise filter (Photoshop), 92
Norman Rockwell Museum garden gate, 26–27

O
Object Layer Options dialog, 281
Object menu, 243
objects. See also complex objects; constructing objects; isolation mode
    adjusting Constrain Angle for, 4
    aligning and distributing, 69–70
    appearance attributes for, 24–25
    applying gradient to, 165–166

    Blob Brush objects converted to Live Paint Groups, 87
    changing colors easily, 191
    changing perspective of, 200, 203
    characters vs. type, 37, 38
    color of new text, 32
    compressing in bounding box, 135
    constructing oval, 66, 71, 96–97
    converting to artboard, 11
    converting to symbols, 116
    copying before applying Puppet Warp, 207
    copying/pasting, 7
    creating freeform gradient, 173
    creating with **CC** Shaper tool, 78–79
    depth and overlap added to, 262–263
    editing Illustrator objects in InDesign (**CC**), 281
    erasing portions of, 106
    error message when masking, 244
    expanding pattern, 232
    extruding 2D, 198–199
    filling with linear gradients, 182
    glows for circular, 255
    gradient mesh, 166–168, 183
    highlights added to, 252
    inserting into blend, 240
    isolating, 6–7
    joining and intersecting, 82–83
    lifting from background, 211
    Locate Object icon, 23
    making brush from rasterized, 271
    mapping art onto, 202–203
    merging with Blob Brush, 65
    modifying and combining multiple, 66
    pasting into clipping mask, 241
    preventing merging of, 65
    reattaching to plane, 205
    recognizing names for Live Shape, 76
    saving stroke profiles as Graphic Style, 110
    selecting buried, 5
    Shape Builder's effect on, 67
    snapping to guide, 64
    soft shadow added within, 211
    stacking order of, 5–6

threading text between, 33, 34–35
3D effects applied to, 199
tools for building, 19
turning blend into editable objects, 240
unifying gradient across multiple, 176–177
warping, 91
offset paths
moving stroke inward, 105
selecting path from mesh object, 167
shaping glow with, 255
offsets. See offset paths; pattern offsets
One Point Perspective, 203, 216
"100 days" project (Klema), 95
opacity
adjusting object glow, 255
assigning to mesh object, 168
bristle brush options for, 115
changing with keyboard or mouse, 16
decreasing, 185
enhancing transparency in Photoshop, 264
reducing, 236
setting for time-of-day tint, 209
shadow patterns and, 253
opacity masks
appearance of
creating and editing, 236–238, 262–263
soft transitions with, 262–263
texturizing objects with, 267
transparency features of, 235
open paths
applying Path type to, 33
coloring objects with, 21
connecting overlapping, 78
drawing with Live Paint, 21
ending, 76
joining endpoints of, 70–71
Open Type fonts, 43
orientation
of blends along curves, 240
creating art oriented to path, 120–121
landscape and portrait, 41
out port, 33, 34–35
Outer Glow effect, 211
outline type, 38–39
oval object construction, 66, 71, 96–97
overflow text
adding object for, 34, 35

indicator for, 16
Overlap options (Pattern Options panel), 234
overlapping artboards
printing, 41
sizing differently, 134
working with, 11
overlapping objects
adjusting stacking order for, 97
constructing bowl from, 96–97
flattening for printing, 238
keeping on separate layers, 300–301
overlapping paths, 78, 88

P
packaging Adobe Fonts, 44
pages
opening multiple PDF, 282
setting up document, 46–47
Paidrick, Ann, 127, 167, 184–185, 186, 191, 310
Paint Bucket tool, 67
Paintbrush tool
accessing Reshape Segment from, 108
accessing Smooth tool from, 65
adjusting brush size with [ ] keys, 137
creating brushstrokes with, 113
Fidelity options, 131, 132
painting with chard brushes, 271
setting brush preferences with, 115
switching to Selection from, 137
Paintbrush Tool Options dialog, 131
painterly style
bristle brush and Draw Inside for, 136–137
calligraphic brush for, 140
customizing bristle brushes for, 138–139
in Illustrator, 130–131
painting
"Artistic Painting with Illustrator" courses, 120, 121, 158, 159
Blob Brush tool for, 65, 110
with bristle brushes in layers, 138–139
with chard forest brushes, 271, 304
finishing details in isolation mode, 137

with raster images, 158
panels. See also specific panels by name
accessing pop-up instances with, 162
docking, 3, 14, 232
hiding/showing, 2
open in Essentials workspace, 13
opening from Appearance panel, 8–9
opening multiple, 3
organizing, 2–3, 14
Properties, 13–14
units and math in, 4
used for coloring art, 162
Papciak-Rose, Ellen, 236, 310
"Paper Dolls" (Steuer), 121, 159
papercraft templates, 260, 261
Paragraph panel, 35
Paragraph Styles panel, 35–36
Paste in Back option, 7
Paste in Front option, 7
Paste in Place option, 7
Paste on All Artboards option, 7
Paste Remembers Layers option (Layers panel), 7
pasting
on all artboards, 11
objects, 7
objects into clipping mask, 241
preserving imported vector images when, 279
Smart Objects for Photoshop editing, 289
text into InDesign, 281
Path Eraser tool, 65
Path Segment Reshape feature, 77, 104, 108
Path type, 33–34
Pathfinder panel
combining paths with options, 82–83
creating compound shapes with Shape Mode, 73
creating new objects with, 72, 73
illustrated, 72
paths. See also offset paths; open paths
applying pattern brush to, 154
arching with Puppet Warp, 228
blending along, 240
CC reshaping features for, 77
choosing brush for, 133
closing with **CC** Pencil tool, 78

paths, *continued*
  combining with Pathfinder options, 82–83
  copying/pasting Illustrator paths in Photoshop, 280
  creating compound, 72
  curving and aligning type on, 51–52
  dashes as, 112–113
  dividing, 256
  drawing for pattern brush elements, 143
  drawing inside with bristle brush, 137
  drawing tools to edit, 104
  editing with Blob Brush, 66
  envelope applied as, 197
  erasing parts of, 64–65
  extracting from mesh, 167
  feathering fill of, 251
  flipping type on, 34
  freehand drawings converted to, 101
  gradients on a, 180, 181
  hiding/showing edges of, 5
  importing to 3D programs, 282
  joins and caps for, 112
  masking compound, 241
  overlapping, 78, 88
  protecting, 64, 65
  scattering copies of artwork along, 114
  Shape Builder for generating compound, 66
  shaping glow with offset, 255
  simplifying, 70, 93, 167
  starting/stopping, 15, 19
  stroked paths converted to filled objects, 274
  3D Bevel, 199
  tracing curved, 19
  type on, 33–34
Pattern Brush Options dialog
  adjusting pattern brush from, 142
  enabling Show Auto Generated Corner Tiles, 151
  order of tiles in, 121
  using Auto-Centered Corner Tile option, 148
pattern brushes
  applying color with, 157
  beaded necklace design with, 146, 154, 155
  building characters with, 142–143

corner tiles for, 121
creating, 115
features of, 114–115
inner/outer corner methods for, 151
making variations to, 155
orienting art to path, 120–121
photo as basis for, 148
using in circle and rounded rectangles, 159
Pattern Edit Mode (PEM)
  creating patterns in, 233–234, 246–247
  creating spiral patterns in, 127
  entering pattern width/height in, 248
  entering Recolor Artwork in, 188–189
  functions disallowed in, 234
  layouts for, 233–234
  leaving, 234
  methods of entering, 232–233
  working in, 233
pattern offsets
  about, 247
  changing Brick, 235
  effect on Swatch Bounds size, 249
Pattern Options panel, 246–247
pattern swatches
  editing outside PEM, 235
  entering PEM via, 233
  recoloring pattern in, 188–189
Pattern Tile tool, 233, 235
patterns. See also tiles
  complex shadow, 253
  creating in PEM, 233–234, 246–247
  designing, copying, and saving, 232
  designing floor tiles for perspective grid, 217
  expanding pattern objects, 232
  experimenting with offsets, 246, 247
  layered, 248–249
  recoloring, 188–189, 235
  saving, 232, 249
  starting new, 232
  variations on, 234–235
  varying color, opacity, and rotation of, 273
Payen, Franck, 310
PDF files
  opening multiple pages in Illustrator, 282

  preserving layers and **CC** features with, 279
  saving .ai files with PDF-Compatible option, 278
  saving artboards as, 41
  using with Illustrator, 279
PEM. See Pattern Edit Mode
pen illustration, 187
Pen tool
  applying brushes to paths of, 133
  CC Reshape Segment cursor for, 77
  curves drawn and reshaped with, 104
  designing sculpture template with, 94
  developing PhotoRealistic art with, 269
  drawing arcs with, 26, 27
  ending path when drawing with, 76
  freeform drawing with, 84–85
  Golden Gate Bridge drawing with, 270
  outlining dragonfly wings with, 129
  photographic hyperrealism with **CC**, 245
  replacing with InkScribe, 299
  rope and masking shape drawn with, 251
  sketching basic elements with, 20–22
  sketching outlines for guides, 186
  starting/stopping paths with, 19
  stroke used for power cord image, 180
  tracing sketch with, 122, 125, 268
  white outlines against black background with, 141
Pencil tool
  accessing Smooth tool from, 65
  applying brushes to paths of, 133
  blocking out color planes with, 140
  freeform paths with, 104
Pencil Tool Options dialog
  adjusting Fidelity slider on, 19, 77–78, 136
  CC changes to, 77–78

"People's Health Assembly" conference logo, 236
Perez, Richard, 267, 310
Pernal, Stephanie, 132, 310
perspective
adjusting photo template to, 224
CC Lock Station Point for, 206, 225, 226, 227
changing for objects, 200
changing on copied objects, 203
choosing and positioning active planes, 204–205
constructing Taj Mahal in, 215
guides for, 17
limits for artboards, 205
new **CC** features for, 206
simulating one-point perspective, 216–217
working with photo's, 220–221
Perspective Grid
about, 5, 203–205
adding vector image to, 227
aligning to architectural sketch, 222–223
controls of, 217
creating distant control points on, 220
customizing, 216–217
legacy text on, 205
locking, 206
moving, 223
setting up two-point perspective, 218–219, 225
uses for, 196
Perspective Grid Options dialog, 205
perspective guides, 17
"Perspective" illustration, 128
Perspective Selection tool, 205
Pfreundner, Simona, xix, 79, 106, 107, 310
PhotoRealist techniques, 245, 256, 257, 269
photos. See images
Photoshop. See also Illustrator and Photoshop combinations
collage photo created in, 134
creating pattern brush from photo, 148
file compatibility with, 278
lighting effects from, 296–297
masking and cropping image in, 153

pasting compound shapes into, 73
photos prepared for artwork in, 135
placing art in registration rectangle, 301
separating rainbow chard leaves in, 271, 304
soft brushes in, 290, 291
textures from, 91
using Smart Objects as content placeholders, 280
Photoshop Import Options dialog, 280
pie-wedge from circles with the Shaper tool, 79, 106
Pilon, Mark "Atomos", 294, 310
pins, Puppet Warp
adjusting, 228, 229, 230
preventing automatic placing of, 207
selecting, 207, 230
Pixel Grid, 5, 283
Pixel Preview option, 283
Place dialog
enabling Show Import Option in, 281, 282
features in Illustrator vs. InDesign, 285
multiple file placement in **CC**, 285–286
placed art
creating template of, 130
embedding, 116
placing with Photoshop registration rectangle, 301
placeholders
Photoshop content, 280
placeholder text, 44
Plane Switching Widget
activating planes with, 218, 219
deactivating all planes with, 204, 205
selecting active plane, 204–205
turning off perspective grid with, 217
planes. See also Plane Switching Widget
aligning grids and, 222–223
attaching objects to, 205
automatic positioning of, 205, 215
selecting active, 204–205
Plastic Shading option, 201
Platon, Federico, 310

plug-ins, InkScribe and Dynamic Corners, 299
plus (+) sign
Layers panel + cursor, 16
overflow text indicator, 16
PNG file format
saving push puppet elements in, 158
saving raster image detail in, 156
Podgy Panda, 294, 310
point map, 239
Point option (Freeform Gradients), 172, 173
point type
converting to area type, 42
features of, 32–33
using Touch Type tool with, 60
Poje, Lisa, 274, 310
Polygon tool, 19
portrait orientation, 41
posters
customizing type and graphic styles, 57
Golden Gate Bridge, 17
illustrating with Touch Type tool, 62
Powell's 1869 expedition, 178
power cord, 180
precision drawing adjustments for Fidelity slider, 19, 77–78, 86–87, 136
preferences
Constrain Angle option for, 4
Content-Aware defaults option, 206, 207, 229, 284
Context-Aware defaults option, 173, 192, 193
Double-click to Isolate option, 6
enabling Clipboard in, 279
including SVG code for File Handling & Clipboard option, 286
saving changes to default toolbar, 15
Use Legacy "File New" Interface option, 4
Premedia Systems **WOW!** Artboard Resizer script, 97
Premedia Systems **WOW!** Artwork Colorizer script, 66, 96
Presentation Mode, 16
Preserve Illustrator Editing Capabilities option, 305

presets
arrowhead, 113
perspective grid, 204
saving New Document Profile, 4
pressure-sensitive preferences
for Eraser tools, 87
interesting brushstrokes with, 128
using calligraphic brushes, 140
previewing
disabling Image Trace, 68
documents, 23
stylistic sets, 45
Print dialog, 41, 163
printing
compound shapes, 71
flattening overlapping objects for, 238
to PDF, 41
selected artboards, 41
templates for construction, 27
process color, 162, 163
product packaging prototypes, 226–227
production process. See also printing
creating four-color-process separations, 163
distributing fonts in art to service bureau, 39
profile objects, 3D, 201
profiles
presets for New Document Profile, 4
saving stroke, 110
using strokes with reusable, 124
Web-compatible, 283
width, 110, 111, 122–123, 154
Properties panel
accessing **CC** Appearance panel via, 8
accessing options in, 13–14
Crop Image button, 284
locating type panels from, 32
proxy icons, 171
PSD files
accessing Photoshop layers in, 281
exporting Illustrator artwork to, 235
exporting Illustrator layers in PSD format, 288–289
preserving layers and **CC** features with, 279

puckering gradient mesh objects, 167
Puppet Warp. See also pins, Puppet Warp
adjusting position of dog's paws, 207, 229
Enable Content Aware Defaults option and, 173, 206, 207
placing and selecting pins for, 207, 228, 229, 230
preventing automatic pin placement, 207
using in **CC**, 206–207
Putnam, Ryan, 38, 48, 54–55, 59, 82–83, 86–87, 122–123, 174–175, 310

R
RA (Recolor Artwork dialog). See Edit Color/Recolor Artwork dialog
radial fill, 166, 252
radial gradient, 254
radius values (Transform panel), 103
rainbow chard leaves, 271, 304
raster image brushes
CC features for, 119–121
courses on, 271
creating from Lightwave 3D art, 276
making and duplicating, 271
raster images
converting to vector art, 68–69, 227
Crop Image **CC** feature for, 284
downsizing resolution of, 271
keeping track of, 278
painting with, 158
saving mapped gradients as rasterized symbols, 202
tracing and using as template, 306
using as pattern brush, 152–153
rearranging artboards, 10
Recolor Artwork dialog. See Edit Color/Recolor Artwork dialog
Recolor Artwork icon, 188
recoloring. See also Edit Color/Recolor Artwork dialog
brushes and symbols, 168
freeform gradients, 173
patterns, 188–189, 235

recovering missing linked files, 278
Rectangle Properties section (Transform panel), 102, 103
rectangles. See also Live Rectangles
bending into tree branches, 208
converting to artboard, 41
converting to Live Shape, 76
rounded corners of, 82–83, 103, 275
red tip boxes, xvi
reelwelldone.com email template, 275
reference point, 11
Reflect tool dialog, 27
reflections in windows, 297
Registration point, 117
Reinhart, Sabine, 188–189, 248–249, 311
releasing
blends, 240
compound shapes and paths, 71
guides, 5
Live Paint objects, 68
objects from isolation mode, 6
objects from text thread, 35
opacity masks, 237
Shape Mode, 73
single clipping mask on layer, 243
removing. See deleting
renaming
artboards, 40, 46
color groups, 169, 189
renumbering artboards, 40
reordering
artboards, 10–11
master layers and sublayers, 23
tools, 15
repairing holes in tracing edges, 90
repeating fields of dots, 267
replacing
content of Smart Objects, 280
Pen tool with InkScribe, 299
symbols, 117
resetting
gradients to default color, 164
symbols, 117
toolbar, 15
workspace configuration, 13
Reshape Segment cursor
adjusting Bézier curves with, 104, 106
dragging with, 77

reshaping dimensions, 196–230.
    See also Puppet Warp; 3D
    effects
    about, 196
    aligning grids and planes in
        sketches, 222–223
    bending shapes into curves,
        208
    feature overview, xx-xxi
    lifting text and image from
        background, 211
    mapping art onto objects,
        202–203, 213, 214
    mimicking seagrass blades,
        210, 245
    modifying photo in
        perspective, 220–221
    package design with
        perspective, 226–227
    perspective features for, 203–
        206, 215–221, 224
    setting up two-point
        perspective, 218–219,
        225
    texturizing with Roughen,
        208–209
    3D effects for, 198–203, 212–
        213, 214
    warps and envelopes for,
        196–198
resizing
    artboards, 11, 16, 40, 46, 97,
        224
    artwork to scale, 28–29
    line weight and stroke, 70
    panels, 3
    tiles to art, 247
    type with Touch Type tool, 60
restoring Dynamic symbol color,
    119
Revolve 3D effect, 197, 200
RGB color space
    default mode for Adobe Color
        Themes, 172
    working with web document
        formats in, 162
ribbon images, 191
Riddle, Michael (Mic), 295, 311
Riffe surfboard art, 258–259
Roberts, Andrew, 311
"Robot Bath Time" (Poje), 274
robot pattern brushes, 142–143
rolling hills illustration, 182–183
Roorda, Jolyanne, 311
Rotate dialog, 273

rotating
    blended groups, 240
    patterns, 273
Roughen dialog, 208
Round bristle brush, 139
round join, 112
rounded rectangle corners, 82–83,
    103, 275
Rounded Rectangles dialog, 82
rubber band feature, 76
"Rubber Ducky" (Jolley), 125
Rudmann, Andrew, 20, 311
rulers, 4–5
    changing X,Y origin, 47

S

Save for Web (Legacy) option
    (File menu), 287
saving
    .ai files without PDF-
        Compatible option,
        278
    artboards, 41, 279
    closed layers, 16
    color groups, 163–164, 169,
        175, 189
    gradient aspect ratio and angle,
        166
    graphic styles, 55
    layered files in Acrobat, 282
    list of document's fonts, 45
    patterns, 232, 249
    PDF files in Illustrator, 282
    perspective grid, 204, 206
    projects in stages, 96
    Recolor Artwork variations,
        191
    Shape Builder strokes, 66
    SVG files from Illustrator, 305
    swatch colors, 162
    toolbars with workspace, 15
    tracing for Photoshop
        compatibility, 92
    width profiles, 110, 111, 123
    workspaces, 232
Scale tool, 33, 70
scaling
    architectural drawings, 28–29
    art brush marks, 114
    blended groups, 240
    corners with Live Shapes, 75
    line weight and stroke, 70
    9-slice symbol, 117, 283
    pattern brush patterns, 114–
        115
    pattern brushes on path, 142
    type and text, 32–33

scanning and tracing template
    images, 18, 250
Scatter Brush dialog, 114
scatter brushes
    adding stars with, 266
    creating, 115
    customizing, 145
    features of, 114
    symbols vs., 116
Schumacher-Rasmussen, Eric, xiii
scripts, 66, 96–97
"Scroll Work" pattern, 272
sculpture template design, 94
seagulls illustration, 267
searching. See finding
seed packet illustration, 90
Select Behind cursor, 5, 7
Select Similar Objects option
    finding shapes, 81
    Global Edit option vs., 79–80
selecting
    active plan, 204–205
    artboards for printing, 41
    buried objects, 5
    clipping masks, 242
    path from mesh object, 167
    positioning guide from
        Transform panel, 47
    Puppet Warp pins, 207, 230
    Radial gradients on Gradient
        panel, 165
    similar objects for editing
        (CC), 79–80
selection indicators (Layers
    panel), 7
self-portraits
    Cheryl Graham, 93
    Greg Geisler, 140
    Kevin Stohlmeyer, 77
Sellers, Rachel, 18–19, 311
service bureaus, 39
Shade Artwork option (Map Art
    dialog), 203
shadows. See also drop shadows
    adjusting with Gaussian Blur,
        268
    complex patterns of, 253
    creating with Inner/Outer
        Glow effects, 211
Shape Builder tool. See also the
    Shaper tool
    constructing objects in, 96–97
    filling objects with color with,
        100
    preparing objects for Draw
        Inside mode, 98–99
    saving time with, 95

Shape Builder tool, *continued*
setting gaps in, 66
using, 66–67
Shape Mode icon (Pathfinder panel), 73
Shaper tool. See also the Shape Builder tool
creating and editing with, 106, 107
features of, 78–79
shapes. See also specific shapes, Shaper tool, and Shape Builder tool
bending to curved arch, 208
building images with basic, 19
CC Shaper tool with geometric, 106, 107
Live Shapes features, 74, 75–76
modifying gradient mesh, 167
Shape Builder time-saving tips for, 95
Unite mode for creating compound, 105
working with compound, 71
sharonsteuer.com videos, xii, 120, 158, 271, 304
Shawnimals, 294, 311
shell frame, 157
shortcuts and keystrokes. See also modifier keys
about, xv
applying gradients with < > keys, 165
creating to access Pattern Editing Mode, 233
Global Edit option, 81
hiding panels with Tab or Shift-Tab, 2
Mac, 338
non-English, xv
toggling between drawing modes, 71
using while dragging width points, 123
Windows, 337
Show Auto Generated Corner Tiles option (Pattern Brush Options dialog), 151
Show Import Options
enabling in Place dialog, 281, 282
when using artboards as cropping masks, 245
Show pop-up menu (Glyphs panel), 39
Show Tile Edge option (Pattern Options panel), 247

showing/hiding
attributes, 8
effect on Global Edit and Select Similar, 81
with Eye icon, 8, 23
grids, 5
layers, 21, 23
Live Shape widgets, 75, 76
panels, 2
path edges, 5
Puppet Warp mesh, 207
template layer, 269
side buttons illustration, 221
Simplify command, 70, 93
Single-line Composer, 37
sizing image maps, 212
skyline template, 18–19
small caps, 40
Smart Filters, 289
Smart Guides
aligning symbols using, 283
turning on/off, 5, 84–85
using Shaper tool with, 106
Smart Objects
copying/pasting for editing in Photoshop, 289
placing Illustrator files in **CC** library, 280
replacing content of, 280
using Photoshop objects in Illustrator, 279
smartphone case, 190
Smooth tool, 65
Smoothness slider (Blob Brush tool), 88
Snap to Point option, 64
"Solo-Flight" (Joly), 254
"Soothing Nervous Patients" (Hubig), 300–301
spiral pattern design, 127
spot color
converting to process color, 163
deleting, 162
preserving on extruded objects, 201
stacking order
adjusting for overlapping objects, 97
effect on attribute appearance, 8
selecting objects buried in, 5
stacking panels, 3
Stairstep option (Type on a Path), 61
Static vs. Dynamic symbols, 116
steel-beam pattern brush, 156

step-by-step lessons, xvi–xvii
steps between key objects, 239
Steuer, Sharon
about, xii, 311
articles on Creative Pro website, xviii
galleries by, 96–97, 120, 121, 130–131, 134, 135, 157, 158, 271, 304
lynda.com courses by, xii, 120, 121, 271, 304
sharonsteuer.com videos, xii, 120, 158, 271, 304
Stikalicious™ characters, 294
Stingray City logo, 58
Stohlmeyer, Kevin, 77, 311
stone heart pattern brush, 154
Stoppee, Brian, 311
Stoppee, Janet, 90, 311
stops, color, 187, 254
storing symbols, 116, 117
Strizver, Ilene, 40, 311
stroke, see *Chapter 4: Expressive Strokes* **110–160**
adding to clipping mask, 242
adding to Live Rectangles, 245
adjusting one side of, 111
applying gradient to, 180
applying to type objects, 38
art brush, 113
auto-generated corners, 148, 149–151
basing pattern brush on photo, 148
bitmap image as pattern brush, 152
bristle brush, 138–139
calligraphic brush, 66, 113, 126, 131, 140
cap styles and joins, 112–113
color applied with pattern brush, 157
constraining with Draw Inside, 115
covering with opaque brushes, 139
custom art and scatter brush, 145
custom width of, 122–123, 124, 125
customizing with 6D Art Pen, 144
designing necklaces with pattern brush, 146, 154, 155
disabling Live Paint, 85
duplicating, 8

expressive uses of, 110, 132–133

feature overview, xx

fidelity of brush, 93, 99, 131, 132

gradient applied across, 59

gradient fills vs. gradient, 164–165

making type width and weight adjustments, 53

moving inward with Offset Path effect, 105

obscuring mapped art, 202

opacity adjustments to, 129

painterly styles using Draw Inside, 136–137

pressure-sensitive preferences for, 128

preventing from merging, 88

reducing scale of pattern by adjusting, 153

resizing line weight and, 70

rotating and transforming, 137

saving Shape Builder, 66

setting for spiral design, 127

steel-beam pattern brush, 156

symbols in urban portrait, 147

tracing with, 245

turning into filled shape, 65, 110

using in Dynamic symbols, 119

varying with pattern brushes, 142–143

width profiles for, 122–123

working with brush, 113–116

Stroke panel. See also stroke

Arrowheads section of, 113

custom Width Profiles in, 112

Reset icon, 110

settings controlled via, 111–112

student group illustration, 194

styles

assigning to groups and layers, 25

formatting text, 35–36

stylistic sets, 45

sublayers

adding layers above group or path, 118

adding to symbol's artwork, 117

creating, 22–23

Knockout Group's effect on, 288

Sullivan, Shawn, xx, 193, 311

surface shading for 3D objects, 201–202

surfboard design, 259

"SUSTAINA3LC" poster (Levy), 57

Sutherland, Brenda, 197, 202, 311

SVG files, 286, 305

SVG fonts, Open Type, 43

swatch. See also gradient swatch; Swatch library; Swatches panel

creating groups, 85

customizing color, 174–175

dragging to Gradient slider, 165

finding, 171

pairing with characters and names, 194

preventing addition to **CC** library, 162

resetting gradient, 164

Swatch library

creating, 175

Diadem pattern, 246

Swatch proxy icons, 171

Swatches panel

accessing pop-up instances with, 162, 165

adding and naming pattern brush objects in, 142–143

deleting color in, 162, 169

identifying global colors in, 164

updated **CC** features of, 171

working with, 162–164

switching rulers, 4

symbol instances

adding to documents, 117

edits of Dynamic symbols unreflected in, 119

Symbol Sprayer tool, 118

Symbolism tools, 118–119

Symbolism Tools Option dialog, 116

symbols

aligning, 283

attaching to active plane, 205

camera icon as dynamic, 160

changing perspective on object, 203

creating map, 102–103

degree symbol automatically inserted in **CC**, 199

designing urban portrait with, 147

gradients saved as, 202

instances of, 117, 119

making artwork into, 11, 40

9-slice scaling of, 117, 283

recoloring, 168

saving artwork for maps as, 212

scatter brushes vs., 116

Static and Dynamic, 116, 119

3D Bevel paths as, 199

transforming, 117

using Symbolism tools, 118–119

working with, 116–118

Symbols libraries, 147

Symbols panel

accessing Symbols libraries from, 147

converting Static to Dynamic symbols, 116, 119

dragging logo to, 49

illustrated, 117

T

T-shirt designs, 50–51

tablets. See also pressure-sensitive preferences

calligraphic Blob Brush strokes on, 66

creating overlapping paths on, 88

developing brushstrokes on, 113–114, 128

"Rubber Ducky" painted with, 125

Wacom Touch Ring settings, 136, 137

tabs and leaders for text, 37

Tabs panel, 37

Taj Mahal artwork, 215

Talkowski, Steve, 294, 311

Tan, Moses, 145, 268, 311

target indicators (Layers panel), 7

template layer, 18

templates

adjusting to perspective grid, 224

construction design using, 26–27

creating from placed art, 130

designing sculptures from sketch, 94

drawing sketch in Photoshop for, 86, 122–123, 138

NaniBird PDF, 260

Photoshop collage for, 134

templates, *continued*
    scanning and tracing images
        for, 18, 250
    using scanned image as
        template layer, 18
    Zebra, 261
text. See also type
    adding gradient with Draw
        Inside mode, 72
    appearance of stroked **CC**, 38
    applying glyphs, 39, 45
    attaching to active plane, 205
    changing offset for, 47
    copying styling and appearance
        for, 36–37
    custom gradient for, 55
    distorting, 54–55
    formatting, 35–36
    importing/exporting between
        Illustrator and
        Photoshop, 280
    integrating with traced
        sketches, 91
    legacy, 205
    lifting from background, 211
    line breaks for, 37
    outlining and reattaching to
        grid, 225
    overflow objects for, 34, 35
    pasting into InDesign, 281
    placeholder, 44
    placing in vector object, 285
    preserving anti-aliasing for
        web documents, 282
    repositioning letters within
        word, 60–61
    small caps in, 40
    tabs and leaders for, 37
    threading, 33, 34–35
    wrapping, 32, 33, 35
texture
    adding with clipping masks,
        267
    adding with Roughen, 208–209
    brushes adding, 270
    Photoshop, 91
    using in "Frankie Stein" art,
        288–289, 290, 291
threaded text, 33, 34–35
Three Point Perspective, 203, 206
3D effects. See also 3D Extrude &
    Bevel Options dialog
    animating 3D scenes with
        layers and objects, 295
    combining apps for, 303
    dimensions illustrated with 3D
        Studio Max, 84, 302

    enabling New Art Has Basic
        Appearance setting
        for, 200
    extruding objects with, 198
    extruding 3D key and fob art,
        213, 214
    fx icon to apply, 199
    illustrating packaging
        prototypes using, 226
    importing Illustrator paths to
        3D apps, 282
    light source and surface
        shading for, 201–202
    mapping and lighting surfaces,
        202–203, 213, 214
    rendering 2D objects with, 198,
        212
    rotating objects in 3D space,
        200
    transforming shapes with,
        198–199
    using, 197
    X, Y, and Z axes in, 199, 200
3D Extrude & Bevel Options
    dialog
    applying surface shading with,
        201
    blending seagrass color and
        thickness with, 210
    effects using, 197, 198
    exploding view created with,
        214
    illustrated, 213
3D Revolve Options dialog, 201
3D Rotate dialog, 201
3D Studio Max, 84, 302
Threshold filter (Photoshop), 92
"TI the TICOON Mascot", 207,
    229
TIFF files, 281
tiger's head illustration, 88
tile roof, 147
tiles
    designing for perspective grid,
        217
    designing patterns with Swatch
        Bounds, 248, 249
    height and width of, 248
    pattern brush corner, 121
    placing swatches in, 143
    resizing, 247
    showing edges of, 247
time of day, color adjustments
    for, 209
tinting layers, 209
tip boxes, xvi
titles, 55

Tjader, Nini, 311
Tokyo-go-go, 294, 311
Tom, Jack, 50–51, 311
tomatoes on vine image, 240
Tool Options button, 14
toolbar drawer, 14–15
toolbars
    Advanced, 13, 15
    Basic, 13
    customizing, 14, 15, 30
    saving with workspace, 15
tools. See also toolbars; and
    specific tools
    accessing options of, 14
    building objects with
        Illustrator, 19
    customizing sets of, 30
    editing paths with drawing,
        104
    modifier keys for, 64
    modifying gradient mesh
        shape with Distort,
        167
    removing from toolbar, 14
    reordering, 15
    used for cartoon logos, 30
Tools panel, 15, 71–72
toucan, 79
Touch Type tool
    features of, 36, 42
    illustrating posters by, 62
    modifying characters with, 43,
        60–61
    showing, 42
tracing. See also Image Trace
    panel
    Alias Sketchbook Pro pen for,
        124
    and coloring sketches, 91
    creating template from, 18–19,
        250, 306
    curved paths, 19
    with InkScribe, 299
    Pen tool for, 122, 125, 268
    Photoshop photo in Illustrator,
        90
    repairing holes in edges of, 90
    saving for Photoshop
        compatibility, 92
    sketch with Blob Brush, 86–87
    with stroke, 245
tracking, 51
trade show menu, 104
Transform effects
    applying, 28, 29
    copying artwork to another
        artboard with, 11, 40

offsetting stroke with, 58
Transform panel
    customizing positioning guide
        from, 47
    disabling opening when using
        Shape tool, 76
    moving and copying artwork
        with, 11
    setting rectangle properties,
        102, 103
transforming/distorting type,
    39, 42
transparency. See also
    Transparency panel
    adding to seagrass blades, 210
    adjusting for highlights, 252
    applying to mesh points, 185
    assigning to mesh object, 168
    Direct Selection tool to
        emphasize, 129
    enhancing in Photoshop, 264
    glows and highlights with,
        254–255
    gradient mesh objects with,
        184–185
    targeting and editing, 237–238
    working with, 235–236
Transparency panel. See also
    Knockout Group checkbox
    (Transparency panel)
    appearance of active opacity
        masks on, 244
    decreasing opacity in, 185
    isolating blending and
        knockout groups
        from, 239
    masking objects from, 262
    working with opacity masks
        in, 237
Trash icon, 162, 169
Tremblay, Jean-Claude, xii, 33,
    196, 199, 201, 243, 311
"Trick or Treat" movie, 295
Trim View, 16
True Love tattoo, 86–87
Tsuneoka, Junichi, 294, 311
Tunxis Community College, 132
Turton, David, 88, 311
Two Point Perspective
    as default perspective, 203
    designing package prototype
        with, 226
    relocating vanishing point in,
        206
    setting up, 218–219, 225, 245
2D objects
    extruding, 198–199, 212

revolving around Y axis, 199
type. See also Touch Type tool
    adding to map labels, 52–53
    applying glyphs, 39, 45
    arcing, 54–55
    converting to outline, 38–39
    copying styling and appearance
        with Eyedropper,
        36–37
    customizing graphic styles for
        posters, 57
    feature overview for, xix
    finding missing fonts, 39,
        44–45
    formatting text, 35–36
    kinds of, 32
    Miyamoto's mastery of, 56
    moving, 50–51
    new CC features for, 42–45
    protecting custom spacing
        when exporting, 39
    scaling, 32–33
    small caps, 40
    tabs and leaders, 37
    threading text, 34–35
    transforming/distorting, 39
    type object vs., 37, 38
    using as clipping mask, 244
    warping, 51
Type on a Path
    dialog for, 51, 52
    using Touch Type tool with, 60
Type tool
    applying Path type to open/
        closed paths, 33
    cursors for, 32
    formatting text, 35–36
Typekit, 44

U

U-Haul "Super-Graphics", 178,
    179
underwater freeform gradients,
    193
Undo option, 206
Unite Pathfinder command
    creating compound shape, 105
    melding brushstrokes into
        frame object, 139
    option on Pathfinder panel,
        82-83
units of measure
    auto-scaling artwork from,
        28–29
    using or changing, 4
unlocking. See locking/unlocking

UntappedCities.com, 134, 135
Urban Development proposal
    (Del Vechio), 84, 302
urban portrait, 147

V

vanishing point
    adjusting, 204
    customizing, 217
    extending beyond artboard,
        220
    multiple, 203
    relocating with CC Lock
        Station Point, 206,
        225, 226, 227
variable fonts, 43
Variable Width Profile, 154
vase illustration, 184–186
vector images
    adding to Perspective Grid, 227
    animating Illustrator vector
        objects, 293
    applying color with pattern
        brush, 157
    converting photo to, 68–69,
        227
    creating embroidered patch
        from, 229
    "Drawing Vector Graphics:
        Patterns" course, 272,
        273
    preserving format of imported,
        279
"Vegan phở" (Steuer), 135
Vektogarten website, 261, 306
"Vintage" (Gilbert), 92

W

Wacom Art pens. See also Wacom
    tablets
    adjusting settings for, 128
    rotating brush to vary stroke
        diameter, 131
    simulating bristle brushes with,
        113
    using Illustrator brushes with,
        144
Wacom tablets. See also tablets
    modifying Touch Ring settings,
        136, 137
    Touch Ring for, 136, 137
    Wacom Cintiq21UX tablet
        computer, 88
    Wacom Intuos4 tablet, 128
Warner, Ed, 294, 308, 311

Warp Options dialog
    bending shapes to curved arch, 208
    illustrated, 51
warps. See also Puppet Warp
    applying, 196–197
    distorting embedded photo in envelope, 186
    envelopes vs. warps, 196
    gradient mesh objects, 167
    objects, 91
    type, 51
washes, color, 131
web banner art, 160
web-compatible documents
    anti-aliasing preserved for, 282
    CMYK color space for, 162, 283
    color space compatibility with, 162, 283
    exporting graphics to web/ mobile devices, 286–287
    using Web-compatible profiles for, 283
Weinstein, Ari, 207, 229, 311
widgets
    adjusting Live Rectangles with, 101
    hollow and solid, 41
    Live Corner, 74, 274
    Plane Switching, 204, 205, 217, 218, 219
    showing/hiding Live Shape, 75, 76
Width Point Edit dialog, 111
width points
    using modifier keys while dragging, 123
    working with, 111
width profiles
    adjusting stroke width for, 122–123
    saving, 110, 111
Width tool
    adjusting strokes, 122–123
    customizing spirals with, 127
    uses for, 110–111
Wigham, Laurie, 28–29, 292, 311
"Wind" (Gilbert), 303
Winder, Darren, 181, 311
Windows computers, shortcuts and keystrokes, xv, 337
Winkel, Jillian, 132, 311
woodpecker image, 306
"Wood's Revenge" (Klema), 94

workflow. See also combining apps
    adding transparency in art, 235–236, 237–238
    assembling Taj Mahal image, 215
    basic to complex compositions, 20–21
    changing object colors easily, 191
    collecting textural elements, 267
    drawing GG1 electric locomotive, 298
    editing unified gradients, 176–177
    modifying artwork created by others, 8
    moving Illustrator art to Photoshop, 288–289, 290, 291
    organizing complex objects with layers, 20, 21, 250
    planning projects in Illustrator and Photoshop, 300–301
    reducing number of project's colors, 170–171
    repairing masks, 304
    saving special color sets, 169
    screen redraw time for pattern repeats, 246
    techniques using gradients, 178–179
    working with Crop Image, 306
    working with Live Corners, 274
workspace
    accessing pop-panels, 162
    CC Home Screen, 12–13
    CC panels and, 12–16
    Essentials, 13
    feature overview for, xviii-xix
    managing objects, 5–11
    organizing, 2–5
    resetting configuration, 13
    saving custom, 232
    saving toolbars with, 15
    switching, 3
    uncluttering, 2, 14

WOW! Artboard Resizer, 97
WOW! Artwork Colorizer script, 66, 96
WOW! Glossary, xv, xvii, 337–338
WOW! ONLINE
    AaronMcGarry-blends.ai ReadMe file, 240
    about, xiv, 337–338
    "Blue Mirror" PDF ReadMe file, 138
    finding files for, xiv, xvii, 337, 338
    icon for, xiv, xvii, 337, 338
    NaniBird PDF template, 260
    Opacity&Blending.ai PDF ReadMe file, 215, 239
    scripts, 66, 96–97
    "Taj Mahal" PDF ReadMe file, 215
    Trick or Treat animation, 295
wrapping text, 32, 33, 35
Wynn, Jamal, 133, 311

X
X axis, 199, 200
X,Y ruler origin, 47

Y
Y axis, 199, 200
Y ruler origin, 47
Yap, Brian, 311

Z
Z axis, 199, 200
Zebra template, 261
zooming
    size of artboard, 11

Windows WOW! Glossary

and essential Adobe Illustrator shortcuts

Ctrl	Ctrl always refers to the Ctrl (Control) key
Alt	Alt always refers to the Alt key
Marquee	With any Selection tool, click-drag over object(s) to select
Toggle	Menu selection acts as a switch; choose once turns it on, choosing again turns it off
Contextual menu	Right-click to access contextual menus
Group	Ctrl-G to group objects together onto one layer
Copy, Cut, Paste, Undo	Ctrl-C, Ctrl-X, Ctrl-V, Ctrl-Z
Select All, Deselect	Ctrl-A, Ctrl-Shift-A
Paste Remembers Layers	With Paste Remembers Layers on (from the Layers panel menu), pasting from the clipboard places objects on the same layers that they were on originally; if you don't have the layers, Paste Remembers Layers will make the layers for you
Paste in Front	Use Ctrl-F to paste objects on the clipboard directly in front of selected objects, and in exact registration from where it was cut (if nothing is selected, it pastes in front of current layer with Paste Remembers Layers off)
Paste in Back	Use Ctrl-B to paste objects on the clipboard directly in back of selected objects, and in exact registration from where it was cut (if nothing is selected, it pastes in back of current layer with Paste Remembers Layers off)
Toggle rulers on/off	Ctrl-R
***fx* menu**	From the Appearance panel, click the *fx* icon to access effects
Select contiguous	Hold Shift while selecting to select contiguous layers, swatches, etc.
Select non-contiguous	Hold Ctrl while selecting to select non-contiguous layers, swatches, etc.
Toggle Smart Guides on/off	Ctrl-U
Turn objects into guides	Ctrl-5
Turn guides back into objects	Ctrl-Alt-5 (you must select the guide first; if guides are locked, you must unlock them first from the contextual menu or from the View> Guides submenu)
...	Indicates you can find "more" options if you click the three dots within a panel
⊕	Find related files or artwork in that chapter's folder on **WOW! ONLINE**

Mac WOW! Glossary

and essential Adobe Illustrator shortcuts

⌘ **Option**	The Command key (this key may have a ⌘ or a ⌘ on it) The Option key
Marquee	With any Selection tool, click-drag over object(s) to select
Toggle	Menu selection acts as a switch; choose once turns it on, choosing again turns it off
Control key/Contextual menu	Right-click or hold the Mac Control key to access contextual menus
Group	⌘-G to group objects together onto one layer
Copy, Cut, Paste, Undo	⌘-C, ⌘-X, ⌘-V, ⌘-Z
Select All, Deselect	⌘-A, ⌘-Shift-A
Paste Remembers Layers	With Paste Remembers Layers on (from the Layers panel menu), pasting from the clipboard places objects on the same layers that they were on originally; if you don't have the layers, Paste Remembers Layers will make the layers for you
Paste in Front	Use ⌘-F to paste objects on the clipboard directly in front of selected objects, and in exact registration from where it was cut (if nothing is selected, it pastes in front of current layer with Paste Remembers Layers off)
Paste in Back	Use ⌘-B to paste objects on the clipboard directly in back of selected objects, and in exact registration from where it was cut (if nothing is selected, it pastes in back of current layer with Paste Remembers Layers off)
Toggle rulers on/off	⌘-R
fx **menu**	From the Appearance panel, click the *fx* icon to access effects
Select contiguous	Hold Shift while selecting to select contiguous layers, swatches, etc.
Select non-contiguous	Hold ⌘ while selecting to select non-contiguous layers, swatches, etc.
Toggle Smart Guides on/off	⌘-U
Turn objects into guides	⌘-5
Turn guides back into objects	⌘-Option-5 (you must select the guide first; if guides are locked, you must unlock them first from the contextual menu or from the View> Guides submenu)
...	Indicates you can find "more" options if you click the three dots within a panel
⊕	Find related files or artwork in that chapter's folder on **WOW! ONLINE**